CHILD SERVICES
On Behalf of Children

CHILD SERVICES
On Behalf of Children

Francine Deutsch
San Diego State University

Brooks/Cole Publishing Company
Monterey, California

Brooks/Cole Publishing Company
A Division of Wadsworth, Inc.

Printed in the United States of America

10 9 8 7 6 5 4 3 2 1

Library of Congress Cataloging in Publication Data

Deutsch, Francine, [date]
    Child services.

    Bibliography: p.
    Includes index.
    1. Children—Services for—United States.
I. Title.
HU741.D48   1982   362.7'042   82-14570
ISBN 0-534-01221-3

Photo credits: Pages 8, 23, 105, 125, 134, 176, 189, 216, 235, and 249 Marjorie M. Lozoff. Pages 13, 32, 40, 50, 65, 79, 82, 93, 114, 155, 162, 211, 227, and 246 Kira Godbe. Pages 57, 197, and 205 Carole A. Leland. Page 148 Francine Deutsch.

Subject Editor: *C. Deborah Laughton*
Production Editor: *Patricia E. Cain*
Manuscript Editor: *Linda Chase*
Interior and Cover Design: *Victoria A. Van Deventer*
Cover Illustration: *Chelsea Haga*
Typesetting: *Instant Type, Monterey, California*

To Carole for her efficacious perspective and persistent patience

Preface

At the age of 76, John Dewey, a philosopher and educator, admitted his confusion about children. Was the issue "what we are going to do with and for youth" or "what youth is going to do with us, later"? "In all probability," he concluded, "what we do in the next few years for and with our youth will determine in later years what they do with and to the institutions in which they find themselves" (1935, p. 9). Dewey's prediction introduces this book because, in dealing with major issues, policies, and services affecting children and youth, we will recount constantly his "we" and "they"—the adults and youths of our society. Here, we examine child services from an ecological perspective by focusing on the direct (family, school, and community) and indirect (economics, law, and politics) contexts of care.

The book is divided into three sections. Section 1, "The Context of Care," contains four chapters that form the historical, philosophical, and ideological framework for understanding child services and illustrates the utility of an ecological framework. Section 2, "Working with Children," looks in depth at specific child services for various types of children who confront different problems in different settings. Section 3, "Working for Children," concludes the book with commentaries on critical areas related to child services (child/family advocacy, professional roles, and program evaluation) and with speculations about the future.

Child services is a dynamic, diverse, and complex area with developmental, political, economic, and moral implications. The objective here is to present the major controversies and contradictions in this field. Individuals involved in child services are trained in a variety of disciplines (for example, biology, economics, education, political science, psychology, and sociology), and they assume myriad professional roles (for example, counselor, child-care worker, child developmentalist, lawyer, lobbyist, nurse, nutritionist, physician, policy maker, social worker, teacher, and therapist). The text therefore addresses a wide audience of educators, health-care providers, and social workers. The special interests of present and future child-service professionals are considered by examining processes associated with service delivery; by presenting programs designed to serve children in varied family situations, institutions, and community settings; and by profiling different professional experiences. Child-service providers often have mutual values, interests, and goals for a variety of reasons, such as to enhance intervention effectiveness by coordinating efforts between providers and to increase the likelihood of government funding by organizing community-action groups or lobbying groups.

For our purposes the meaning of "we" and "they" is broadly conceived because it has relevance for each citizen in our society. Today's children are, after all, tomorrow's adults.

The highway of ideas to published text is pitted with treacherous turns and seductive stopping places. Many people helped along the way, and I want to express my most grateful appreciation to them all.

To my colleagues and students at The Pennsylvania State University, San Diego State University, and other institutions and agencies around the country who shared ideas, contributed chapters, and reviewed various drafts of the manuscript: Jean D. Dickerscheid (Ohio State University, Columbus), Happy Craven Fernandez (Temple University), James Garbarino (The Pennsylvania State University), Diane Henschel (California State University, Dominguez Hills), J. Ronald Hershberger (Thoits, Lehman and Love, Palo Alto), Sally A. Koblinsky (San Diego State University), Ronald A. Madle (The Pennsylvania State University), William C. Morse (University of Michigan, Ann Arbor), Ellen A. Skinner (Max Planck Institute, Germany), Megan Spencer Flynn (The Pennsylvania State University), Karen VanderVen (University of Pittsburgh), and Mary Weir (Long Beach City College).

To my secretarial staff: Sally Barber, Joy Barger, Kathy Hooven, and Sally Saxion, who typed many drafts of the first stages of the manuscript, and especially to Teddy J. Ralph for her technical accuracy during the final phases.

To all the anonymous individuals who have shared their thoughts and feelings with me over the years so that some of the ideas in the book could be made alive by life experiences.

To Kira Godbe, Carole A. Leland, and Marjorie M. Lozoff, who contributed their photographic talents.

To C. Deborah Laughton and Trisha Cain, my editors, and Vicki Van Deventer, the designer, and all the staff at Brooks/Cole who transformed raw materials into a finished product. A big hug to Chelsea Haga for drawing the cover.

And, finally, to my family and friends and especially to Carole, Shakes, Dante, David, Joe, Hedy, Lena, Sandy, Rosemary, and Milton, who provided their love and support.

Francine Deutsch

Contents

ix

8

Substitute Child-Care Services   130

9

Services for Developmentally Dysfunctional Children   152

10

Parent/Child Interaction and Intervention   172

SECTION **3**

Working for Children   193

11

Child and Family Advocacy: Toward Social Policy   194

CHILD SERVICES
On Behalf of Children

The Context
of Child Care

Now more than at any other time, the United States has relatively few children compared to its adult population, and the number of elderly people continues to grow. In just the decade of the 1970s, for example, the number of children under age 15 dropped by 6.4 million, or 4.5%; however, the young-adult group (aged 25 to 35) grew by 7.9 million, or 32%; and the number of adults 65 years of age and older increased by 3.4 million, or 17%. By the close of the decade, only 38% of U.S. households included one or more children (U.S. Department of Health, Education, and Welfare, 1978).

Our ecology—the way we deal with our environment and how we distribute resources—produces social patterns and demographic trends. For example, today people tend to marry and have children at later ages. More individuals are remaining single, and couples are increasingly deciding not to have children. And many families are experiencing severe economic pressure as a result of the current recession and the inflation of the late 1970s. The increased number of women in the labor force means that in many homes both husbands and wives—fathers and mothers—work. As a society, we have experienced a sharp rise in the cost of supporting a child. By the end of the 1970s, middle-class parents reported that it took more than $50,000 to raise a child to the age of 18, without saving any money for higher education or technical training (Pifer, 1978). That's just middle-class parents (defined in economic terms). What about other parents? What problems do they experience? What are the ecological constraints on the lower class, for example? How does society respond to their concerns?

In his presidential report to the Carnegie Corporation, Pifer (1978) expresses concern with the steady decline in birthrate and with the increased cost of child rearing. He suggests that we, individually and collectively, should "do our best by those [children] we have" (p. 7). But an irony exists: as the child population declines, public opinion has not become more favorable toward children—it has become dramatically more negative and indifferent. For instance, in some places families with children are excluded from housing; public education is experiencing dramatic cutbacks, especially in arenas that extend options to children (such as the arts, experiential learning, and summer-recreation programs); and many taxpayers openly oppose aid to low-income families. Pifer (1978) contends that, for these and other reasons,

> young people will probably continue to be seen as economic burdens rather than assets; their problems will go unrecognized or be subordinated to the claims of older groups; they will be given little chance to play a constructive role in the nation; and they will be regarded essentially as a threat to the comfort and security of adults [p. 10].

The concept of children as liabilities, as objects owned by parents, or as investments of the state does not represent some new or distorted view. These economic attitudes have historical roots and help form a sense of urgency in our contemporary climate. Although 1979 was designated the International Year of the Child and a great deal of discussion and literature on children has been generated, this does not mean that children's needs have been provided for. As Pifer (1978) cautions:

> No nation, and especially not this one at this stage in its history, can afford to neglect its children. . . . Not only are they our future security, but their dreams and ideals can provide the much-needed renaissance of spirit in what is becoming an aging, tired, and disillusioned society. In the end the "only" thing we have is our young people. If we fail them, all else is in vain [p. 11].

Thus, the first major assumption of this book is that "shaping children into healthy, productive individuals is the task of each of us in responsible positions of influencing other people. . . . It hinges upon our ability and our willingness to love, to care, and to do" (Porter, 1979, p. 15).

How have children been viewed, and what attitude is held now? Chapter 1 examines the role of children in society and offers the dynamic interaction model as a way to interpret the position of children. Then a definition of child services is offered, followed by an examination of the ways societal structures, which are key intervention vehicles, have shifted over time. The theme of change within a total context is illustrated by alterations in family and societal patterns over time. Thus, two critical concepts—children and services—are explored from past and present perspectives to arrive at definitions for use throughout this book. These concepts are also used to explore the concept of an ecological framework.

A second major assumption of this book is that parents should not be blamed for their circumstances. According to Urie Bronfenbrenner (1979a), who is an advocate of an ecological framework for studying individuals and families, "Most families are doing the best they can under difficult circumstances; what we should try to do is to change the circumstances, not the families" (p. 849). Chapter 2 argues that we should not scape-goat parents, and it addresses one basic question: "How have we arrived at our current social policy for child services?" The evolution of child services is firmly rooted in society's values and history, and changes are reflected in legislation concerning children. Many child-service issues persist and affect the ways we deal with children and our attitudes toward them.

The third major assumption of this book is that we all want quality care for our children, whatever the type of care. Chapter 3 argues for enhancing the quality of child care. The argument suggests an ecological perspective, offers a variety of evidence, and emphasizes particular ideals. This chapter challenges current values and practices and suggests ways to change the status quo.

Section One concludes by discussing intervention. What are the professional and client choices for services? What ethical and moral issues surface when we intervene in the lives of children? What are some current attitudes and issues related to intervention? And what resources are or should be available? The example of juvenile misbehavior shows how complex the answers to such questions may be. The challenge remains: *what* to change for *whom*.

Mahoney (1976), a former student of Bronfenbrenner, argues that we need to change our ecology in order to address the needs of families. Resources could support alternative ways for mothers and fathers to fulfill their parent roles. Parents should not be forced to have less and less time with their children; instead, the environment should provide opportunities for them to share more and more time. Television, teachers, and peers have become surreptitious surrogates for parents, in transmitting our culture. Mahoney (1976) suggests that

> Highest in priority should be guaranteed minimum income so that parents, especially single parents, may make a choice as to whether or not they work. The creation of part-time job opportunities is crucial for families in all income levels. Day care centers near work settings would also afford more time for parents to be with their children. A reintegration of children with the world of work might be achieved through programs which involve children in responsible activities along with adults. Until such social policies help to reunite generations in daily activities, children may remain first in American sentimentality, but their needs will not be met in American reality [p. 12].

1

Perspective:
The World of Child Services

Chapter overview

Children assume certain roles in our society, and those roles influence what care they need, whether they receive it, and who provides it. This chapter focuses on the societal role of children. It addresses the impact of environmental change on children and considers how families and societies create the needs and wants children have.

Issues to consider

What are child services?
Why and how have child services shifted since their inception?
Can we categorize and classify child services?
What roles do mother, father, and significant others play in child care?
How can we conceptualize the interactions of child, family, and society today?
How do children acquire culture, and why should they?
Do children have a role in the social aging process?
What changes in family functions and societal patterns make a difference?

Introduction

On 15 February 1909 Theodore Roosevelt urged favorable action toward a bill pending in both Houses of Congress for the establishment of a Children's Bureau (Senate Bill No. 8323 and House Bill No. 24148),which

> shall investigate and report upon all matters pertaining to the welfare of children and child life, and shall especially investigate the question of infant mortality, the birth rate, physical degeneracy, orphanage, juvenile delinquency and juvenile courts, desertion and illegitimacy, dangerous occupations, accidents and diseases of children of the working classes, employment, legislation affecting children in the several States and Territories, and such other facts as have a bearing upon the health, efficiency, character, and training of children [Roosevelt, 1909, pp. 6–7].

Some individuals opposed the bill on the grounds that it was not constitutional. In essence, it allowed the federal government jurisdiction over state and local agencies concerned with child welfare and deprived the U.S. family of some of its valued privacy and self-determination. Despite these concerns, the agency was established in 1912. The government thus gave notice that it supported an old axiom: just as "cheap" money will debase a sound currency, so too will incompetent citizens reduce the strength of the country (Bremner, 1974). This logic promoted the application of economic principles to child and family intervention that we will examine in Chapter 2.

The government endorsed a pyramid structure, a bureaucracy for promoting and protecting its young. The federal government itself occupied the top of the pyramid, using research, advice, and propaganda to stimulate and support the states and municipalities to achieve effective child care. Against this backdrop, this chapter explores the current status of child services. It asks the following questions: (1) "How are child services now defined?" (2) "How have child services changed over the years?" (3) "How are child services categorized?" and (4) the major question "Who is responsible for care?" The remaining portion of this chapter offers various portrayals of the child's world—from the conceptual to the controversial—to show what we

5

need to reckon with if we want to enhance the future of children. The specific historic and legislative evolution of child care in our country enters the scene in Chapter 2.

The contemporary status of child services

Society most often supports families through various forms of child services. What are child services? How have these services changed over time? What types of child services are available?

Child services defined

The term *services* connotes many images for different people. On the one hand, you may envision a variety of helping situations. A counselor empathically listens to a child, a teacher demonstrates how to make paste to a wide-eyed group of preschoolers, a physician administers immunizations, a nurse provides nutritional information to a family or to children in an orphanage or foster-home setting. On the other hand, you may visualize people standing in welfare lines, tax dollars evaporating, juveniles returned to parents only to misbehave again, housing projects in inner cities, a judge issuing a deposition to parents for the removal of their child, or a senator arguing for the passage of a bill. Any one of these images can be correct. The term *services* refers to all types of help people receive. This help can come from individuals, groups, or institutions. It can be legislated or not. It can serve some and not others. It can be sought or imposed. It can be effective or ineffective.

Activities are labeled *child services* when they affect children directly or indirectly. Direct services can include day care, food supplements, and immunizations. They are extended specifically to children, but often are only available when parents qualify or meet eligibility requirements or actually seek out services for their children. Because of the role parents or other caregivers play—that of intermediary—many direct services never reach children. Other services (such as parent education, income supports, and housing environments) affect children only peripherally and are called *indirect* services.

This broad definition of service underscores many dilemmas: bureaucratic red tape, coordination problems, problems of support, conflicts with religious beliefs, conflicts with societal values, and difficulty in determining types of professional training and retraining. Child services constitute an enormous enterprise influenced by historical ideologies, beliefs, and values as well as economics, politics, and the law. These multiple influences account for the dilemmas embedded in child services and for its broad definition—services delivered directly or indirectly at multiple levels (individual, group, institutional) to children in order to protect and nurture development by correcting, maintaining, preventing, or optimizing an aspect of their development or context. Table 1–1 summarizes and illustrates the concepts that define child services.

Concerns and caring for children may be no more intense today than they were when Theodore Roosevelt formalized our society's commitment to child care. Our intervention goals and processes, however, have shifted from correction to prevention and optimization. And we can anticipate continuous change in child services as we accumulate more experience and research evidence, and deeper insights into human development.

Current trends underscore the lessons of the past: First, the importance of keeping a family together has taken precedence as social-service workers have

TABLE 1-1 Concepts that define child services

Concept	Definition	Examples
Protect	To value the child's right to a decent environment and experiences at some minimal level or standard	Foster care for dependent or abused children
Nurture	To promote biological, cognitive, affective, and social development at some minimal level or standard	Immunization for childhood diseases or income supports in the case of parental job loss
Maintain	To sustain an individual in "normal" status	Free lunch programs or subsidized day care
Prevent	To avoid developmental problems (dysfunctions) by counteracting harmful circumstances before they can have an effect	Early screening for hearing, vision, and metabolic disorders; health-care programs
Correct	To make remedial or rehabilitative efforts to help a child regain or approximate "normal" functioning; rehabilitation entails a longer period of time	Programs for children with dysfunctional conditions or for juvenile delinquents
Optimize	To maximize potential or produce the best possible results	Community-based prenatal-care programs; mainstreaming for children with dysfunctions; or increasing parent participation in child programs

recognized the stress on all family members that separation can produce. Second, just as it has become desirable to keep families together, it has become necessary to design services that can include the needs of all family members. For instance, a child-centered program for abused children might only involve removal of the child to foster placement and prosecution of the parent. A family-centered approach to child abuse might incorporate some or all of the following: a day-care nursery to relieve the parent temporarily of child-care responsibility and to provide parent-education programs; a crisis hotline that potentially abusive parents could call for help when under stress; and referral to other agencies that offer other services required by the family, such as job training or housing support. (Protective services are examined in Chapter 7.)

With the recognition that the child should be served in the context of the family, services have changed in focus from the individual child to the child within the family. Unfortunately, all the services required by a family often are scattered among several agencies. For instance, nutrition programs, job-training programs, and health care may be provided by separate agencies. Even within a particular domain such as health, different family members may be served by different agencies. This organizational structure is not only disconcerting to the client but costly in bureaucratic inefficiency. The move toward family-centered services requires scrutiny of administrative structures in order to incorporate more comprehensive programs within single agencies. And change continues.

Types of child services

Child services are not alike, nor do their funds come consistently or predictably from the same sources. In fact, the type of agency determines how and why resources are allocated.

Agency categories. Four different agency categories describe social services in general or child services in particular: (1) private for profit, (2) private nonprofit, (3)

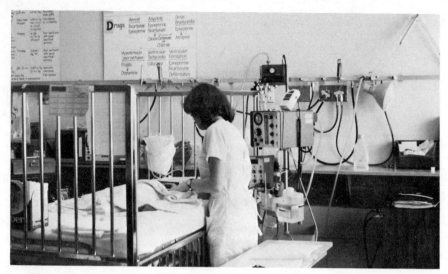

Neonatal intensive-care units are one of many biproducts of our technology that help to shift the focus of our service delivery from correction to prevention and optimization.

public, and (4) industrial. A private proprietary agency offers a service while making a profit. It usually requires inspection and licensure by some regulatory body (state or local community), and typically it receives income from fees (for example, from parents who pay to enroll children in day care) that are established by the competitive open market. The recipients of such service tend to be middle class.

Private nonprofit agencies are organized by individuals (professionals or nonprofessionals) who adhere to the nonprofit corporation laws of a governing unit, usually the state. Many are affiliated with organizations (such as the March of Dimes or Easter Seals) or with institutions (for example, schools or churches). Both private contributions and state or federal monies provide their funding. These agencies may have a single purpose, such as providing day care, or may serve multiple purposes (such as health services, parent training, and welfare and housing). Governed and administered by a voluntary board of directors, these agencies often must meet special requirements to receive federal financial support (for example, the Federal Interagency Day Care Requirements).

Public agencies are under the direct auspices of a governmental body (county, state, and so on). They are supported almost totally with public funds. The individuals who qualify to receive services are determined by specific eligibility requirements that produce a particularly homogeneous clientele. What these agencies provide and what their clients require are monitored closely.

Private-industry agencies usually are financed by unions or company management. Because the clientele are the company's employees or union's members and their families, their programs provide a fringe benefit to workers. Paid professionals run such programs and typically are accountable to a committee that the union or management has formed.

Depending on the agency, qualitatively different services are provided to children, varying opportunities for program participation are extended to parents, and homogeneous or heterogeneous groups are served. An awareness of agency differences can assist program selection. Agencies, along with other organizations and institutions (such as PTA's, schools, and churches and synagogues), can provide information and increase the effectiveness of a referral and delivery system.

Child-care programs. Child-care programs in the United States are categorized according to four basic settings: (1) in home, (2) other home, (3) center, and (4) institution. Any of these program types can function within the framework of the four agency categories already discussed. For instance, in-home care could be provided by a relative or friend, a paid housekeeper, a licensed nurse affiliated with a private for profit or nonprofit agency, or a professionally trained person employed by the company where one works.

Home care, whether in one's own home or someone else's, has the longest history. In the early 1970s, for example, 50% of children under age 6 and almost 80% of school-aged children received care in their own homes, according to a Westinghouse survey. In most cases, the care was provided by a relative. Over the years, this type of care has shifted toward family day care, and about 10% of family day-care programs are now licensed and regulated. Those that are not are monitored by public for profit or nonprofit agencies. Their programs often are referred to as "group day care" because 6 to 12 children are served in a familylike setting. Frequently, this care is informal (parent and provider make their own arrangements), with the provider deciding how many children can be integrated into the physical setting and their own family's pattern of living (Kamerman & Kahn, 1976).

Center care varies greatly in types of programs provided, the number of children served, staff–child ratios, physical facilities, and extent of parental involvement. Usually 12 or more children between the ages of 3 and 5 are served (see Chapters 5 and 6).

In institutional care, children are usually age segregated, housed in large numbers, and isolated from the community. Institutionalized children tend to be those suffering multiple dysfunctions such as being mentally retarded and cerebral palsied or difficult for parents to manage (such as children who repeat delinquent acts). Still others are institutionalized because family members cannot provide care due to unfortunate circumstances such as death, personal problems, unemployment, and so forth. These children are prime candidates for foster-care placements (see Chapter 7).

Table 1–2 summarizes some of the advantages and disadvantages of in-home, other-home, center, and institutional settings. It is impossible to indicate which setting is best for a particular child. Rather, the preferred setting should reflect a decision that takes into account the child's needs, not just parental convenience or community expedience.

We can also separate programs according to provided services (for example, custodial, protective, educational, parent education, and nutrition). The label *custodial*, however, has received the most serious criticism. It connotes the "impersonal 'warehousing' of children, insensitive supervision, and developmental 'dangers'" (Kamerman & Kahn, 1976, p. 49), serving the family's needs, not the child's.

Although the content of programs and the settings vary, two main goals are to protect and to nurture children. The actual implementation of this protection and nurturance can take the form of maintenance, prevention, correction, or optimization intervention. However, the delivery of services often cuts across intervention categories. For instance, among its efforts a day-care facility may provide lunch, health-care screening, an educational program for children, and a parenting program.

TABLE 1-2 Advantages and disadvantages of various child-care settings

Settings	Advantages	Disadvantages
In home	Inexpensive, flexible, individually oriented, familiar surrounds, familiar caregiver, leaves siblings together	Does not provide group socialization experiences, usually custodial, may be unreliable
Other home	Flexible but regular, individualized care, family setting, socialization (peers) experiences, leaves siblings together	Sometimes provides less emphasis on development, difficulty in monitoring health and safety
Center	Hours meet working parents' needs, enrichment emphasis, socialization experiences, regulated for quality	Less individualized care, transportation often difficult, cost a potential problem
Institutional	Offers only means of caring for certain types of children	Expensive, may stigmatize children, may isolate children from family and community experiences

Based on *Social Services in the United States*, by S. B. Kamerman and A. J. Kahn. Copyright © 1976 by Temple University Press. Reprinted by permission.

Separating out concepts of child services in our definition and examination of types of child-care programs does heighten clarity but should not be viewed as reality.

The children/family/society interface

From the previous definitions and descriptions, one might be tempted to view child services as (1) agencies excessively monitored by state and federal bodies, (2) programs aimed at children of adults who fail at parenting, and (3) supports primarily constructed for the poor. Furthermore, one might conclude that our society fosters a "Big Brother" attitude toward helping unfortunate children and families. Although many people may fear government intrusion into private matters—in this case, family life—and may resent bureaucratic intervention (given the tenets of our democratic society), such reactions have not surfaced suddenly in the 1980s. Over the years, diverse groups (political, educational, religious, and so forth) have debated who is responsible for child care. Should the government legislate care and protection of children, because children are a national and societal resource? Or should child care and protection rest with parents and other direct caregivers? Powerful lobbies, citizens' groups, and individuals continue to polarize views on how we as a society should ensure the care of our young.

Deciding who is responsible for child care is not like deciding to buy a pair of shoes on some Saturday in November. The decision requires far more than a mere statement of preference, because many complex influences affect the issue. A more analogous decision-making situation, perhaps, concerns abortion. All (and conflicting) positions reflect attitudes and values about individual rights, religious views, familial practices, personal behavior, and so forth. Researchers who represent different disciplines have long shown that our behaviors and our judgments interact in complex ways. So, if a woman has had an abortion, her attitudes about abortion will alter to accommodate her actions. Some theorists refer to this dynamic as *reducing dissonance or discrepancy*. Others feel that a variety of defenses are mobilized to handle any discrepancies between thoughts and actions. For example, individuals may rationalize, repress, or deny their conflict or even their behavior. Other individuals may move to a diametrically opposite position in their thinking or behavior; this dynamic is called *reaction formation*. Similarly, we all have been socialized to believe that there are certain roles the government and parents should play in child care. If we have had positive childhood experiences in which government assistance kept the family together and benefited members, no doubt our viewpoint will be quite different from those who have not experienced such intervention or from those who have experienced intervention and found the experience uncomfortable, and even more different from those who received assistance but have repressed or denied it.

Although the complexity associated with deciding the issue of responsibility for child care has been portrayed only briefly, let me stress one major point: the decision requires an understanding of the historical perspective, because we all are socialized in certain ways that determine our responses. It is apparent that children depend on adults to transmit culture, and society depends on the same adults to instruct and serve as appropriate models for the next generation. It also is obvious that human beings learn diverse patterns of behavior that are not as predictable as with other species, such as salmon, which always return from the sea to spawn in fresh water.

Accepting a developmental perspective supports the idea that the potential for change—in this case, the potential for learning—persists throughout the life span. It enables one to learn to perform new roles, such as friend, student, or parent, and to acquire ways to maximize rewards and minimize punishment. A developmental perspective permits one to adjust to new demands, and function in the social context, which constantly changes over time. Showing how differing age groups are treated in society and examining the dynamics of child/family/society interactions in the past and present helps demonstrate the usefulness of this developmental perspective and helps determine who is responsible for child care in our society.

The social aging process

For most of us, birthdays mark a variety of celebrations throughout our lives. Some of us, however, wish to forget that we are entering a new decade or that we have fewer years left than we have lived. The term *social aging process* refers to this use of age and its interpretation by a society. Depending on a society's degree of technological sophistication, age is used and interpreted differently. In technologically advanced societies such as ours, age divisions are more narrow and become the justification to slow the progression of one's active contribution to society. In nonindustrial societies, age is divided into broad categories to enable individuals to move quickly into society's mainstream. How age is used, therefore, represents a society's social organization. This organization is greatly influenced by many factors, including the number of individuals, the work positions available, and mortality rates. For instance, it makes good sense for a society to push adult responsibilities onto its young people early when infant and adult mortality rates are high. Likewise, when such rates are low and the population swells, it is logical to curtail and retard access to adulthood.

Age grades and age status. The terms *age grades* or *age classes* refer to the way a society categorizes age. It should be of no surprise that nonindustrial societies support two age grades—children and adults—and clearly mark the passage to adulthood, at the onset of sexual maturity, by celebrations. Residuals still occur in the form of religious rituals such as the Bar Mitzvah of 13-year-old Jewish males. Our society supports many age grades: infancy, early childhood, middle childhood, puberty, adolescence, young adulthood, middle age, and old age. In fact, we have reached a time when controversies occur as to the precise number of age grades we have. For example, some scientists (such as Hultsch & Deutsch, 1981) show the advantage of referring to the "young-old" and "old-old," because 60-year-olds are very different from 80-year-olds. The majority of our practices, however, lengthen the time to adulthood while allowing for some adult status. To illustrate, an individual must be 18 to vote, enlist in the armed forces, or marry without parental permission, but adult prices to attend a movie are paid at age 12, and in many states liquor cannot be purchased until age 21.

To move from one age grade to the next means to learn a society's norms and laws so members can expect when behaviors should occur. Opportunities for learning are afforded as a result of age-grade interactions, many of which occur in families. As movement to the next age grade occurs, old roles are shed and new roles are assumed. Roles may be inherited or achieved; for example, a child inherits the role of son or daughter and achieves the role of Boy Scout or juvenile delinquent. With development, multiple roles are assumed in an age grade. To illustrate, an adult often occupies the roles of son or daughter, parent, spouse, worker, and student. Each role occupied has its own status or associated importance sanctioned by society and interpreted by families. Adulthood usually is longingly eyed by children, who want to exercise what they believe to be independence and freedom. How age grades are interpreted and the subsequent ways society treats them depend greatly on the numbers of people we are dealing with.

Cohort flow and succession. Just as birthdays influence individuals, so do they influence society's social organization. The number of people born at one point in time is called a *cohort*. We can speak of a cohort very narrowly as people born on, for example, 25 December 1982 at 11:00 A.M. Or, we can refer to a cohort according to year of birth. More broadly, cohort is defined as those people sharing a common experience (for example, first-year undergraduates, Depression babies, or Flower Children).

Cohorts have their own developmental life cycles. Over time, they are modified and reduced through the death of members. These changes typically result from nonsocial events such as poor nutrition, illness, or disease.

Labeling a group as a cohort is arbitrary and is done for specific purposes. People 70 years of age or older represent the cohort of retired persons. Programs and services are designed with them in mind. Likewise, the cohort of infants and young children is targeted to receive health-care screening and immunizations. Children of certain ages participate in day care, and federal monies support children of low-income families to attend programs. Thus, cohort labeling defines who receives services and permits comparisons, especially during times of a stressed economy when less must go farther.

As each cohort ages, it is followed and preceded by other cohorts. Just as the birth-order position of a child influences family dynamics, so too cohort positions in historical time influence the dynamics of society. If a large child cohort is followed by a small one, obviously the needed services already in place in society will be more than adequate, at least in number, to assist fewer children. This pattern of small following large generally is perceived as most advantageous for the reduced cohort. However, it often is disadvantageous for service providers, whose positions are no longer

According to the dynamic interaction model, cultural values are transmitted to children through their relationships with members of different age grades.

necessary and who have no alternatives for economic or occupational support. On the contrary, when a large cohort follows a small one, we are in for a different kind of imbalance. When the baby-boom cohort born after World War II entered schools, we experienced a teacher and classroom shortage. Society accommodated by encouraging professional growth and supporting school construction. Monies were rerouted from other areas of need. When this cohort developed into adults, once again we experienced a variety of societal changes in services and functioning (such as forced retirements, incentives for higher education, and job-training programs).

It certainly would be easier to address the original issue of who is responsible for child care by excluding the concept of the social aging process of individuals and cohorts, but to do so would be to deny reality. It also is easy to become trapped into the simplicity of dichotomous thinking—governmental versus family responsibility for child care. Perhaps the concept of governmental versus family responsibility, when related to the social aging process, is too abstract to have meaning for grappling with the responsibility issue. A developmental interaction model may have more relevance because it concretely stresses (1) interaction, (2) development over time, and (3) role relationships.

The dynamic interaction model ✕ ⤵ p.15

Lerner and Spanier (1978) comment that

> the dynamic-interaction model proposed views . . . that individual development may only be adequately understood in the context of the constant reciprocal interaction between a changing person and his or her changing environment. This environment is necessarily composed of other people, themselves developing within a dynamic environmental setting. The setting, too, is shaped and textured by the evolving cultural and historical contexts within which all of the actions are embedded [p. 4].

The model enables us to see how three components we address in this book—child, family, and society—are constantly changing and to see that a change in one effects change in the others (Overton, 1977). The results can be unidirectional, almost like a line of dominos falling. For example, the Great Depression forced unemployment on many people, who were then unable to provide proper food and shelter for their families. Or the effects can be multidirectional. During the 1940s and 1950s, for example, the number of children suffering from polio peaked. Parents struggled to find protection from the crippling disease and killer. Was swimming a cause? Should liquids to be drunk be at room temperature? The government funded research and supported scientific inquiry finally to produce the successful polio vaccine, and children were immunized. The interaction had gone full circle—societal problem, child victims, family crises, societal mobilization, and eventual resolution.

Individuals in our democratic society can accept or reject services. Therefore, the model forces us to face some negative consequences of these integrated relationships as well. In 1977, for instance, 10 million children under the age of 15 were not immunized against polio (U.S. Department of Health and Human Services, 1980). Often those hurt the most are children, not parents, when societal concerns and subsequent solutions go unheeded.

Conceptually, the dynamic interaction model is useful because it views change as development, which transcends time. By supporting such a notion, we can attempt to explain the past and present and can plan for a future. This position also allows us to examine multiple-role relationships (such as working mother/wife, or parent/child) at any point along the time continuum and at any level of analysis (such as family/society, child/society, and child/family). And the model leads naturally to significant, researchable questions: What child-care arrangements were supported at which historical time? What societal values influenced these arrangements? What values are transmitted to children in different contexts (such as home and school)? Historically, how have different factors influenced the development of children? How has society served as a barometer for expected behaviors and as a watchdog to determine whether these behaviors are performed properly by families?

Changing family and societal patterns

Changes in norms and laws do not occur easily. Prior to modern times, the extended American family (parents, children, and relatives) represented normative behavior and performed seven major functions: affectional, economic, educational, protective, recreational, religious, and status giving. Families were essentially self-sufficient and offered children care and nurturance from many adults. If parents died, orphaned children were cared for by other relatives. If both parents worked, siblings, grandparents, or others kept children in the family setting. Today, the major function of the family is to provide emotional support to its members.

Here, we only highlight major alterations in families. Our goal is to underscore the interplay between family and society and to further illustrate the dynamic interaction model as an important tool for our perspective on child services. Bremner (1971, 1974) and Ariès (1962) offer extensive historical reviews of family changes.

After the American Revolution, colonial families exemplified the ideal of maintaining self-sufficiency. Freed from British rule, perhaps Americans wanted to establish their independence in every possible way. They freely contracted with each other to form communities, and they ignored the feudal ideas of lords or bonding people as serfs. Moral, political, and economic ideals became intertwined with the ideal of self-sufficiency. First, the virtue attributed to independence cast dependence as a misfortune and a sin. Personal industry, enterprise, and self-control characterized the virtuous person. Second, colonial politics spawned a federal government that was to assume a noninterfering role in individual and family lives except when interference was necessary to protect basic rights. Third, economic doctrine encouraged farmers and entrepreneurs to be self-sustaining. People would raise their own food, barter for goods, and labor only for what they could not produce for themselves. Work became glorified—good for the spirit and for the soul.

The colonial family required that each family member play a critical, productive role. Children were so much valued as economic assets that families that did not have children were considered unfortunate. Boys assumed farm work and girls assisted with domestic chores (such as housekeeping, spinning, weaving). As the children grew older, their parents benefited in other ways. Often children were the only sources of financial assistance in a time when no government aid or social security was available. It was not unusual for older adults to live with their children's families, and responsibility for parents was often assumed by married daughters.

The United States moved vigorously into the 19th century and all the complexities of industrialization. The family became a special unit in which mothers were supposed to protect children's innocence and care for them as dependents. The outside world of big business and mechanized productivity threatened to exert possibly negative, corruptive influences on children. Fathers became associated with and frequently subservient to this materialistic, demanding world, but they were not to let it touch their families. Hence, the concept of the self-sufficient person transferred to the family, which set new goals for a higher standard of living in a growing and exuberant new society but also sought to retain values that sustained home and family life.

Could all families offer the protection and isolation of the home and still prepare children to be productive societal members? The burgeoning number of immigrant families in 19th-century America suggested that perhaps the home could no longer be the only support system for children. In the opinion of several U.S. leaders, schools rather than families might do a better job of education and acculturation—teaching societal values and ideals (deLone & Carnegie Council, 1979). Public schooling had a major impact on families beyond these basic functions. The government held parents accountable for school attendance, and the concept of truancy evolved. Legally, children had to attend school; if they did not attend, courts labeled them truant and fined their parents. Thus, U.S. society passed laws to ensure needed supervision of juveniles. For the first time, parents could have their children removed from their custody by law, and no longer did decisions to rear or not rear their children, nor of what methods to use, rest solely or ultimately with them.

In less than a century, the dynamics of child, parental, and societal interaction had shifted, changing individual and institutional roles perceptibly and dramatically. With due regard for the wisdom of historical perspective, we now look at our own generation and societal context to further underscore our model's utility and the need to examine carefully the complex factors that instigate and define child services.

The responsibility of child care

In these last decades of the 20th century, parents still carry and confront substantial responsibilities and choices for their children. Their decisions are complicated not only by the pace and unpredictability of modern society but also, and more specifically, by the array of technological advances and professional expertise available for intervention.

The lack of sufficient evidence to determine which adults are better parents or which situation is better for different children exacerbates the problem. Many children from atypical family situations (such as a single-parent home with a once-married or never-married mother) are well adjusted and healthy, particularly when the family, whatever its composition, is supported. Other children suffer intense difficulties during times of family reorganization (such as death of a parent, divorce, or severe illness of a family member). With an increasing number of children living with a single parent—male or female, biological or foster—and more single adults adopting children, Bane (1976) estimates that between 34 and 46% of all children under 18 years of age will spend a lengthy portion of their childhood in a single-parent home. In short, our capacity to differentiate child and family problems has produced more alternatives for alleviating difficulties and, thus has extended parental responsibilities.

Given the fact that child care no longer must be a life long career for mothers, who then is the responsible caregiver? Changes in family function—for example, schooling and occupational training coupled with other societal factors, such as alternative child-care arrangements and education for handicapped children—mean a woman's total attention for child care requires fewer years. Parental roles for fathers (provider and protector) have changed, too, and extend beyond biology and economics. Researchers argue persuasively that fathers are parents with the same degree of empathy and ability in childcare as mothers (for example, Rossi, 1977; Woodward & Malamud, 1975).

As parents assume a less total obligation for their children's upbringing, they enter into responsible partnerships with teachers, physicians, and other professionals who provide child services (deLong & Carnegie Council, 1979). Keniston (Keniston & Carnegie Council, 1977) maintains that with this role change parents feel a loss of power in dealing with their children that causes them to blame themselves when things go wrong. Those who believe the contemporary American family is floundering feel strongly that, unless the government assumes responsibility for children, we will not be able to ensure our society's future. These advocates believe that support for families is warranted in order for parents to perform more ably in their roles. However, others believe in the right of family primacy and privacy. They view any federal legislation that intrudes into family life as a giant step toward parenting by the government, which threatens the very fabric of a democratic society.

The government has been and probably always will be involved in the lives of families and children, because not all adults perform adequately as parents, live in adequate environs, or find opportunities for adequate employment. When we filter such elusive, complex factors through the interaction analysis, it becomes clear that responsibility for children in a democratic, pluralistic, and increasingly dynamic society inevitably involves change. This change is often dramatic and overwhelming when war, depression, or disease invade personal and societal routines.

Currently, few people question the importance of the parent to the child. For instance, regardless of their focus or expertise, child-care programs take seriously the necessity and right of parents to share in the responsibility of child care. Many child-service programs have responded to recent research that substantiates the idea that the home has an overriding influence on a child's future academic success by including parents in program development and policies (Clarke & Clarke, 1976; Clarke-Stewart, 1977; Thomas & Chess, 1977; White, Kaban, Attanucci, & Shapiro, 1978). (See Chapters 5, 6, and 10 for discussions of parent involvement.)

This involvement of parents may reflect society's hope for and support of their prerogatives and roles in child care. We witness this attitude on many levels and diverse dimensions of modern life. Through television, magazines, and popular parenting books, public access to information on child development and child-rearing practices has become widespread (McCall, 1977). Changes in medical practices that permit mothers and fathers to have more joint involvement and control over the birth process, as well as changes in hospital policies toward family-centered childbirth, also reflect this shift (Garbarino, 1980a). Recent concern over welfare policies, which often require that fathers be absent before public assistance is granted, has spurred debate because eligibility requirements may reduce parental contact, may favor full-time maternal employment, and hence may detract from rather than enhance parental child rearing (Fraiberg, 1977).

In the field of clinical psychology, emphases have progressed from treatment of the child alone, to treatment of the parent/child dyad and family. Child-abuse cases often are handled in ways that are aimed at rehabilitating the parent while maintaining the intactness of the family. Community psychologists go still further, to treat the social network.

Conclusion

We do not yet know whether these shifts in social and professional concerns and practices reflect a general trend of support for the well-being of families, or only document temporary responses to crises. Perhaps we should not force a decision but rather be reflective about professional concerns and practices toward families, within the framework of freedom of choice—a longstanding societal value. The anthropologist Mead (1976) contends that

> there is no social need to press an individual into parenthood. We can free men and women alike to live as persons—to elect single blessedness, to choose companionship with a member of their own or the opposite sex, to decide to live a fully communal life, to bring up children on their own or to be actively solicitous of other people's children and children of the future. In the process, those who elect marriage and parenthood as their own fullest expression of love and concern for human life also will be freed. For they will know that they have been free to choose, and have chosen each other and a way of life together [p. 249].

Mead's sense of choice about parenthood and the associated positive effects reminds us that we can derive pleasure from caring for children. Watching a child learn to use a spoon, read a book, or ride a bicycle serves as an arena for personal joy and reminds us that being a parent or adult who has interaction opportunities with children is a privilege.

It is easy to forget the advantages of parenthood because more and more decisions about child care are problematic and force resolutions to persistent moral and ethical questions. For instance, it is one thing to give birth to an infant with serious health problems; we now have neonatal intensive-care systems that can save those who have special difficulties or deformities. But it is another issue to allow hospitals the authority to save these infants, assigning the medical right to life a higher priority than parental wishes. Still another issue is "Who should rear such children, and should they be institutionalized?" Finally, who bears the financial brunt, which increases as our technology expands our potentials for care.

Our commitment to the nurturance and protection of children must demand reason and reality. Although no cost may seem too great, our services must reflect balance between what needs to be done and what resources we have available.

Summary

With the establishment of the Child Service Bureau in 1912, the federal government assumed the responsibility for protecting and nurturing its youth. Since that time, child services have grown and now constitute an enormous enterprise influenced by historical ideologies, beliefs, and values as well as current economics, politics, and the law. These multiple influences account for the dilemmas embedded in child services and for its broad definition. As we accumulate experience and research evidence and deepen insights into human development, we can continue to expect shifting emphases in intervention goals and processes. We presently stress (1) prevention and optimization over correction and maintenance efforts, (2) design and implementation of family-centered services, and (3) keeping families together. Not all child services are alike, and their funds come neither consistently nor predictably from the same sources. The type of agency—that is, private for profit, private nonprofit, public, or industrial—determines how and why resources are allocated. Also, the types of programs often differentiated by setting (that is, in home, other home, center, and institution) and services (such as custodial, educational, and nutritional) provide help in dictating funding patterns.

Since the time when Theodore Roosevelt formalized this society's commitment to child care, controversy has surrounded implementation efforts. Should the government legislate care and protection of children because children are a national and societal resource? Or should child care and protection rest with parents and other direct caregivers?

A developmental perspective is proposed to show that the potential for change persists throughout time. The ways in which different age groups are treated in society and the dynamics of child/family/society interactions are examined to demonstrate the potential usefulness of this developmental perspective. Any society has a social organization; and the more technologically advanced a society is, the more complicated are its dynamics. Just as individuals age, so do cohorts, with accompanying changes in age grade, age status, and roles. A person's changing position in the family and society influences interaction dynamics, as does the development of cohorts. These factors produce different imbalances that directly determine the allocation of services.

If the social aging process is not considered, efforts are spent trying to distribute resources equitably across age grades rather than allocating monies and supports based on needs that often result from the denial of access to the next age grade. To emphasize and extend the relevance of the developmental perspective we have advanced, we examined a concrete model that may help us out of our entrapped thinking, and may promote useful researchable questions. This model also illuminates the ways in which society has served as a barometer for expected behaviors and as a watchdog to determine the adequacy of parental performance. Within this discussion, we highlighted specific changes in family and societal patterns and stressed that our contemporary capacity to distinguish child/family/societal problems has produced more alternatives for alleviating difficulties and, thus, has extended parental responsibility.

Our commitment to the nurturance and protection of children demands balance:

reason and reality, pleasure and pain, and questions and resolutions. What resources do we possess now, and what resources are we likely to possess in the near future? Which services are most effective—under what circumstances and at what times? How can our delivery systems be streamlined to enhance our efficiency? In essense, can we create responsible partnerships at multiple levels that mobilize our thoughts and actions and help us act on behalf of children?

2

Philosophy:
The Evolution of Child Services

Chapter overview

History and legislation have shaped child services in the United States today. This chapter examines the relationship between values and the law in U.S. history. Any understanding of our present ideology and direction requires a historical perspective.

Issues to consider

What role does and should government intervention play in people's lives?

What social values and philosophical assumptions underlie government interference with parental child rearing?

What factors can limit individual opportunity?

What major controversies surround the issue of government intervention with child rearing?

How have values and legislation interacted to produce child services as they are today?

What key laws on child services were enacted in the Jacksonian era, the era of the Roosevelts, and the Great Society?

How do current social services differ from those offered in earlier periods?

What philosophy guides our present child-care policy?

Introduction

The Fourteenth Amendment to the U.S. Constitution, adopted in 1868, states that "all persons born or naturalized in the United States and subject to the jurisdiction thereof, are citizens of the United States and the state wherein they reside." The Fourteenth Amendment states that, because they live in the United States, all citizens are subject to and must obey its laws. But the dynamics of citizens' interaction with the government—the rights and duties of the ruled and the ruler—are not specified because each level of government is established to serve the needs of the people by making, interpreting, and enforcing laws. This opinion implies that citizens and their government must work together, each receiving benefits and giving service within a mutually understood legal framework. Citizens have the right to ensure changes in the law by choosing officials who enact and uphold the law. Exercising the right to vote guarantees that citizens can respond to government and, when necessary, effect changes.

Voting rights are fundamental to our political system. We exercise those rights only when we reach a specified age—the age of majority (attained not on the person's birthday, but on the day before the birthdate). Today, child citizens are classified legally as having minority status as long as they are under 18 or 21, depending on state law and regardless of their specific situation. This age classification restricts children's rights (for example, the right to make a will, to sue or be sued, and to dispose of property) and is justified by the physical and intellectual differences apparent between most children and adults that make children dependent on adults. In the history of our country, as this dependent characteristic of children became a concern of society, children were given minority status.

As they grow older, children are granted some additional rights because it is assumed that increased competence accompanies physical maturity. For instance, the rights to drive a motor vehicle, to drop out of school, and to work take effect at specified ages depending on the state in which the child resides. A child is emancipated from parents or the control of guardians after marrying, entering the military, achieving economic independence, or meeting a specific statutory definition of maturity (such as reaching a given age). More recently, in several cases the U.S. Supreme Court has affirmed additional children's rights, which are discussed in Chapter 11.

Although the needs and capacities of children of different ages vary substantially, laws tend to obscure those differences. Child citizens have fewer rights than adult citizens and have in turn fewer responsibilities and duties. However, their needs historically exceed those of adults (Kleinfeld, 1970). For example, in the early 1900s 300,000 children under age 16 were state dependent or neglected; 300,000 to 500,000 were physically handicapped; 200,000 were judged delinquent by the courts; and 75,000 were illegitimate. These figures combined, representing about one-third of the population, are not precise because the U.S. Census Bureau was first established in 1902 and did not complete a census until the close of the decade (Bremner, 1971).

The United States is no longer a predominantly rural, agricultural society, and the status of children has been complicated by population growth, technological advancement, and economic development. The issues and complex factors that surround children's rights and society's responsibilities force one to confront not only the larger context of modern society but also the way personal and collective values promote major legislative actions. This chapter explores the relationship between values and the law.

Values and the law

Government intervention

For centuries, adult restrictions on children were legitimized or fostered by religious beliefs and practices. Children who had emotional outbursts were whipped to drive out evil spirits, and the dictum "Spare the rod and spoil the child" was supported by the Bible. Whipping continued well into the 1800s and is still practiced by some parents today (Radbill, 1974).

Whether or not people believed that children were occasionally possessed by the devil, they used physical restraints to protect children from themselves and from others in society. And parents played a primary role in assessing what was best for children and in administering discipline. The authority of a parent overshadowed that of a child. "Natural" parents had power. In fact, for centuries a child's position in the average family was in this order (from first to last): father, cattle, mother, and child (Despert, 1965).

American society has subscribed to the subordination of children to adults and has only slowly promoted children's rights and attempted to place limitations on parental controls. The major turnaround occurred during the early 1900s because many immigrants were unable to find work and care for their children. Children needed protection from unjustifiable punishment and required nurturance to develop into good citizens. Government intrusion into families resulted as social norms were developed that defined or prescribed the relationship between parent and child. Thus, most Americans currently favor parental control over a child, but they also support the doctrine of *parens patriae,* or government interference with parental prerogatives, even to the extent of terminating all parental rights when parents abuse their power. Legislation dealing with services for children promotes both parental dominance and government intervention in parent/child relationships.

In sum, certain philosophical assumptions about proper parent/child

Despite the most difficult of circumstances, children do adapt.

relationships prevail today: (1) the United States is a family- and child-centered society in which parents should maintain primary responsibility and control over children; (2) when parents are unable to or refuse to assume responsibility for a child, or when a child breaks the law, the government may intervene; (3) adults who represent the government must function in the "best interests" of the child; and (4) children should not be permitted to participate with parents and the government in decision making that affects their lives. Although state and federal laws codify these assumptions, adults—especially parents—often challenge these ideals in the name of a child's best interests and in the name of family privacy.

Intervention issues

Americans' beliefs about child rearing, while consistent with the pluralistic national character, result in laws that do not uniformly interpret the meaning of *best interests* for a given child. Laws against child abuse and neglect, for instance, allow the government to intervene in parent/child relationships, but it proves difficult to reach consensus about the exact conditions that justify such intervention. (See Chapter 12 for a discussion of court dispositions in child-mistreatment cases.) In a legal system that serves a diverse citizenry, certain societal members (such as members of the poor, minorities, and aliens) are the targets of majority prejudices and beliefs that can result in aberrant behavior (Katz, 1971). Existing social controls (for example, status offenses, such as incorrigibility, truancy, and running away) really are an attempt to make individuals (parents and children) comply with the norms of the majority. Unfortunately, thousands of children become labeled early as delinquent and experience a variety of types of confinement only because they have trouble growing up. (The juvenile justice system is examined in Chapter 4.)

Parents experience powerlessness in family relationships for many reasons, frequently economic ones. For example, being poor often results in inadequate care and increases the likelihood of government intrusion in the form of removing a child from his or her home. As Gross and Gross (1977) observe,

The children of the poor have the least protection of the laws, the poorest services, the most vulnerability to bad treatment. We permit our economic system—the "market"—to determine life and death. The infant mortality rates among the poor are more than one and one half times those for middle-income Americans. Money, in this case, can buy things that should not be for sale. This is capitalism gone berserk, the market become tyrant over the most inviolable human values [p. 6].

Other aspects of the human condition, beyond strictly economic factors, determine whether a person's future will be lush with freedom of choice or limited by minimal opportunities:

In the United States, as elsewhere, it is a penalty to be born poor. It is a compounding penalty to be born to parents with little education. It is a further penalty to be born to parents who are frequently unemployed and whose employment opportunities are limited to relatively uninteresting, dead-end jobs. All these penalties are increased still more for children in racial minorities. They are further increased for girls. Some of the penalties are immediate—the physical deprivations of poor nutrition, poor health, poor housing, inadequate medical care; some accumulate slowly, influencing the development of adult skills, aspirations and opportunities [deLone & Carnegie Council, 1979, p. 4].*

Should we be concerned about these limitations? What is the minimal standard or quality of life to which people are entitled? How should *essentials for a normal lifestyle* be defined? Do these essentials include education? health care? day care? free school lunches? Should all people be entitled to such services, or only those people whose lifestyles need to be brought up to a minimal standard? On what norm should this standard be based? Should it be based on our ideal of liberty—justice, freedom, and equality?

There is not always sufficient time for societal debate and consensus to answer these difficult questions before services are designed and delivered. Interpretations of the Fourteenth Amendment raise two specific questions to direct service-delivery efforts: (1) What minimal services should be provided (those services required for the client to overcome a crisis or to become self-sufficient)? and (2) What services should be provided to optimize development of all citizens (those services required to produce the best possible end result, given prevailing values, theories, and empirical evidence)? The first question reflects a belief in differential treatment, while the second one promotes the ideal of equality. Because resources are not plentiful, the guideline of differential treatment often must be used to deliver services. However, strong public opinion usually results in similar services being made available for everyone. These two attitudes toward the delivery of services are strongly rooted in our society and influence the services children and families receive today.

A historical perspective on laws concerning children

Various books discuss in detail the evolution of U.S. legislation on child care (for example, Kamerman & Kahn, 1976), day care (for example, Steiner, 1976), and social reform (for example, Bremner, 1974; deLone & Carnegie Council, 1979). The interested reader should refer to these sources for more definitive accounts. Because the central purpose of this text is to consider the issues surrounding child care in this country, the following sections highlight only major legislation and social reforms,

*From *Small Futures: Children, Inequality, and the Limits of Liberal Reform,* by R. H. deLone and The Carnegie Council on Children. Copyright © 1979 by Harcourt Brace Jovanovich. This and all other quotes from the same source are reprinted by permission of the publisher.

including an analysis of how child care has changed within certain political contexts.

The Jacksonian era

The United States moved into the 1800s with the hopes and dreams of a new, independent nation ready to grow and expand. Frontiers moved westward, the Puritan work ethic stimulated a vital, productive labor force, and the potential of science and industrialization encouraged people's aspirations for safer, more comfortable, richer lives. Social changes evolved naturally in the context of rapid political and economic developments. Women, for example, gained acceptance as employees, especially if they had no other means of support. Immigrants flocked to our shores in search of freedoms and opportunities. These converging political, economic, and social trends fostered the development of a number of child services, including day care, orphanages, and foster-care facilities. Long-term custodial care in the form of institutions was established. Public education flourished because it was thought to assist children in becoming productive citizens. Day supervision of children also was provided to free adults for economic productivity.

By the 1800s, Andrew Jackson was espousing notions of equal opportunity and the concepts fundamental to the Progressive era. In the words of Remini, a well-known historian writing about the Jacksonian era:

> Equality of talents, of education, or of wealth cannot be produced by human institutions. In the full enjoyment of the gifts of Heaven and the fruits of superior industry, economy, and virtue, every man is entitled to protection by law; but when the laws undertake to add to these natural and just advantages artificial distinctions, to grant titles, gratuities and exclusive privileges to make the rich richer and the potent more powerful, the humble members of society—the farmers, mechanics, and laborers—who have neither the time nor the means of securing like favors to themselves, have a right to complain of the injustice of their Government [Remini, 1972, pp. 81–82].

Jackson's populist ideology accepted the existence of social classes and did not embody an intent to overhaul the social order. Greater democracy simply meant a classic free-market position that endorsed the distribution of rewards through individual competition in the market. The Democrats had actually committed themselves to the inevitable—inequality. "The Jacksonians were singularly unresponsive towards women's rights, prison reform, educational improvements, protection of minors, and other forms of social betterment" (Remini, 1972, p. xix).

Demands for social harmony and social-reform movements stimulated by democratic and progressive ideas persisted throughout the 1800s. For example, Roger Taney, President Jackson's Secretary of the Treasury, told the House of Representatives in 1834: "It is a fixed principle of our political institutions to guard against the unnecessary accumulation of power over persons and property in any hands. And, no hands are less worthy to be trusted with it than those of a moneyed corporation" (cited in Schlesinger, 1909/1945, p. 105).

The Whigs supported a strong educational system to counter the corruptive effects of industrialization. Horace Mann, a Whig politician and first secretary of the Massachusetts Board of Education, feared that increasing industrial developments as a result of the steam engine would turn America's cities into areas like England's Manchester, which had filthy streets and whose parents raised children "dedicated to ignorance and vice" (Mann, 1868, p. 271). He urged stronger support for systematic schooling, with each child having the opportunity to attend.

The Roosevelts: Theodore, Eleanor, Franklin

Inflation and recession cycles caused great economic upheaval in the 1880s and 1890s. The rate of immigration rose to the highest levels in the nation's history. The rich seemed to get richer, and the poor got poorer—and children got caught in the middle. By the turn of the century, the wave of immigrants had peaked, and social conditions were not improving for most of the people. Some theorists reasoned that a chief cause of this situation was inherited imperfection or genetic inferiority—in other words, "poor stock." And class differences were more apparent than ever before.

Some of America's most illustrious social reformers became extremely concerned about the care of neglected and dependent children and reasoned that the public should take responsibility for them. (Table 2–1 chronologically details specific legislation, but it is by no means exhaustive.) In 1909 Theodore Roosevelt focused national concern by calling for the first White House Conference on Children. Conferees concluded that a solid home life is the basis of character development and recommended that income supports be given to "parents of worthy character, suffering from temporary misfortune, and children of reasonably efficient and deserving mothers who are without the support of the normal breadwinner, . . . such aid being given as may be necessary to maintain *suitable homes (Proceedings of the Conference on the Care of Dependent Children,* 1909, pp. 17-18).

Roosevelt's moral fervor and social activism found various outlets. Reformers labeled industrialists as greedy capitalists and tycoons who lacked concern for the poor and less fortunate. Scientists investigated the reasons that certain people prospered. The public demanded explanations to account for individual differences. Spearheaded by William James, individualistic psychology flourished. Individualism began to connote "being different."

Theories of child development focused on biology in the belief that perhaps heredity could account for individual differences. On the intelligence tests that were developed, poor people scored lower than rich people. Social reformers explored what differential treatments would be required to help poor people and what institutional changes would help identify and optimize people's varying abilities, enabling them to fit appropriately into the hierarchy of the workplace.

The theme of individual differences emerged with increased industrialization and work specialization. The concept of *inherent inequality* was used to explain the Horatio Algers of society, differential training of people in the labor force, and individual differences in situations, experiences, and abilities. The ideology of equality and equal opportunity was qualified to accommodate the emerging ideology of inequality inherent in individual differences.

It no longer seemed possible to keep society's functions separate and discrete. Families, schools, the labor market, industry, and government organizations were all becoming increasingly interdependent, in spite of—or perhaps because of—increasing specialization. For example, John Dewey, an educator/philosopher, coined the term *whole child* to express the expectation that the school should perform numerous functions hitherto reserved for the family. Schools hired nurses, nutritionists, social worker/counselors, and other specialists who took responsibility for a part of the "whole child." Paradoxically, the complex, bureaucratic, public education system was reducing parental responsibility in child rearing in the name of individualism and preservation of the family.

Efforts were launched to promote efficient interdependence among these

TABLE 2-1 Summary of important events affecting child care in the United States, in this century

1902	A permanent U.S. Census Bureau is established to provide descriptive, quantitative information about the lives of children and adults.
1908	The first Bureau of Child Hygiene is established by New York City. This move from private charity to public responsibility for the health care of children is a major step toward the assumption of a broad national responsibility by the federal government.
1909	President Theodore Roosevelt convenes the first White House Conference on Children, focusing on the care of the dependent and neglected. The smallest of such conferences, which have taken place every ten years since then, it is credited with having made the greatest impact on the health and welfare of children. One of its major recommendations calls for a federal children's bureau.
1912	The U.S. Children's Bureau is established by a law signed by President William Howard Taft. Housed in the Department of Commerce and Law, the bureau is credited with major work in fields of care of dependent children, child labor, juvenile delinquency, and child health over the next two decades.
1916	The Keating–Owen Act prohibits the shipment in interstate commerce of products manufactured by children under the age of 14; represents the first step in establishing child labor laws.
1920	Philanthropic foundations, largely funded by the Laura Spelman Rockefeller Memorial, the Rockefeller Foundation, the General Education Board, the Carnegie Corporation, the Russell Sage Foundation, and the Rosenwald Fund, are established to advance child care and development.
1930	The American Academy of Pediatrics is founded and promotes standards of children's health care, continuing education in pediatrics, education material for parents, and sponsorship of special studies.
1935	The Social Security Act is signed into law by President Franklin D. Roosevelt. Title IV provides for the general welfare by a system of old-age benefits and provision for the blind and for dependent and crippled children; maternal and child welfare; public health; and provides for the administration of unemployment-compensation laws.
1939	The Social Security Act amendments extend the program for the protection of families, the first use of federal funds for special-project grants.
1939	The Children's Bureau provides for state services to children with rheumatic fever and heart disease.
1939	Food Stamp Plan to dispose of agricultural commodities begins in Rochester, New York.
1940	The White House Conference on Children in a Democracy calls attention to inequalities in opportunities available to children and youth in rural areas, among the unemployed, and in low-income, migrant, and minority groups.
1941	The Lanham Act authorizes federal support for school construction in "impact areas" (those areas most in need of such construction).
1941	The Children's Bureau approves a project to provide medical care for wives and children of servicemen and sponsors a conference on day care for children of working mothers.
1942	Congress authorizes emergency grants to states for day care of children of working mothers.
1943	Congress appropriates initial funds for the Children's Bureau Emergency Maternal and Infant Care (EMIC) Program.
1946	The National School Lunch Act provides for grants to states and territories to establish school lunch programs.
1946	National Mental Health Act provides for research on psychiatric disorders and methods of prevention, diagnosis, and treatment, and authorizes the establishment of the National Institute of Mental Health, which later broadened their programs with amendments in 1956.
1949	The Housing Act is passed, establishing the goal of a "decent home and suitable living environment" for every person.
1950	The White House Conference on Children and Youth adopts the theme "How to provide each child with a fair chance to achieve a healthy personality"; at the conference, Kenneth B. Clark presents a paper on the effect of prejudice and discrimination on personality development.
1952	The Children's Bureau grants funds for special projects to develop and coordinate statewide programs for medical and social services for unwed mothers.
1954	In *Brown* v. *Board of Education* (347 U.S. 483), the U.S. Supreme Court unanimously reverses the doctrine of "separate but equal" and rules that legal separation on the basis of race violates the Fourteenth Amendment; in a separate ruling, lower courts are ordered to use "all deliberate speed" to admit Black children to public schools.
1954	A division of juvenile delinquency is established in the Children's Bureau.
1957	The second study of education for Blacks is commissioned by the Public Education Association.

TABLE 2-1 (continued)

1961	President Kennedy appoints a panel to study mental retardation. Its report of findings and recommendations in 1962 is the basis for Kennedy's special message to Congress on mental illness and mental retardation.
1961	The Fleming Ruling expands eligibility requirements for dependent children to receive monies.
1963	Congress amends the Social Security Act to assist states and communities in preventing and combating mental retardation.
1963	Following President Kennedy's proposal in 1961 and congressional legislation in 1962, the Surgeon General establishes the National Institute of Child Health and Human Development as part of the National Institute of Health to conduct research and training in maternal and child health, special health requirements of mothers, and human development.
1963	Following the report of the President's Panel on Mental Retardation, President Kennedy proposes programs to prevent retardation and improve mental health.
1963	Congress passes the Maternal and Child Health and Mental Retardation Planning Amendments to the Social Security Act to establish projects dealing with premature birth, infant mortality, retardation, neurological disease, and other problems of mothers and infants.
1963	The Mental Retardation Facilities and Community Health Centers Construction Act provides facilities for research and for expansion of services and training for the mentally retarded.
1965	Head Start programs are launched by the Office of Economic Opportunity to improve conditions of learning, social development, and health care of children of preschool age.
1966	The Child Nutrition Act is passed, which retains the school lunch and milk programs and provides financial aid for new breakfast programs for schools in poor areas. (Food programs for children in economically depressed areas are expanded in 1969.)
1967	The Children's Bureau is assigned to the Social and Rehabilitation Service of the U.S. Department of Health, Education, and Welfare (HEW).
1967	The Child Health Act adds three new types of medical-care project grants (infant care, family planning, and dental care) to the Social Security Act; 366,000 expectant mothers receive maternity services, and school children are screened to determine health conditions and needs.
1968	Congress further amends the Elementary and Secondary Education Act to authorize federal support to regional centers for education of handicapped children and to special centers for providing services to deaf and blind children; amendments also provide for recruiting personnel, distributing information on the handicapped, giving technical assistance to education in rural areas, providing bilingual education, and preventing dropouts.
1968	Congress passes the Juvenile Delinquency Prevention and Control Act to help courts, correctional systems, schools, and community agencies in research and training to prevent, treat, and control juvenile delinquency.
1969	The Office of Child Development, under the auspices of HEW, is created by President Nixon.
1969	Secretary Finch of HEW orders the reorganization of child health and welfare programs and functions and establishes the Board of Advisors on Child Development.
1969	Children's Bureau and the Bureau of Head Start and Early Childhood are transferred to the Office of Child Development.
1972	The Education for All Handicapped Children Act (Pub. L. 94-142) passes (in practice at the federal level in 1974 and at the state level in 1975).
1973	The U.S. Supreme Court decides that abortion is constitutional.
1974	The Child Abuse Act passes.
1974	The National Health Planning and Resources Development Act (Pub. L. 93-641) includes disease prevention and public education about health care.
1976	The National Consumer Health Information and Health Promotion Act (Pub. L. 94-317) passes.
1977	The Youth Employment Demonstration Projects Act (YEDPA) authorizes expenditures for a variety of "innovative demonstration projects" to explore effective ways of helping adolescents complete high school, enter the workforce, and attain job stability and achievement. Target groups include in-school and out-of-school adolescents, summer-school students, and young people under the jurisdiction of the juvenile-justice system.
1979	HEW is officially split into the Department of Education and the Department of Health and Human Services.

institutions. Efficiency studies were undertaken to determine what was needed to boost assembly-line productivity. The ability to memorize became a learning virtue both in school and at work. People were thought to achieve by being compliant and cooperative. Conformity and efficiency were rewarded. And specialists, of course, knew what was best for people and institutions.

As World War I approached, specialists diagnosed adults' and children's abilities to contribute to the society and the war effort. Children were carefully tracked in school, primarily according to IQ tests. Social Darwinism, the notion that "natural selection" and "survival of the fittest" apply to social as well as biological evolution, often was used to explain individual differences. As more was learned about biology and heredity, the eugenics movement grew. Many scientific contributions were made to our understanding of selective breeding. Socially, however, the impact of this movement presented problems. Many social reformers stepped over the delicate line to racism. Rather than simply accepting that genetics may account for some individual differences, some individuals relied exclusively on the concept of selective breeding in order to diagnose and train people for specialized productive, efficient societal roles. Individuals identified as mentally defective and criminals judged to be confirmed recidivists were sterilized by state agencies (Levine & Levine, 1970). Worldwide, racist attitudes took hold at governmental levels, resulting in "Jim Crow" policies in the United States and the extermination of Jews in Nazi Germany.

The prosperity enjoyed by Americans in the 1920s proved to be a transitory phenomenon. The country fell into the worst economic depression it had ever known. Under the leadership of Franklin Roosevelt, the government launched a wide array of programs to provide employment and social services. Eleanor Roosevelt, who crusaded for the rights of humanity, especially children, was largely (some people feel, solely) responsible for keeping the 1924 League of Nations document on children alive until the U.N. General Assembly adopted a Universal Declaration of Human Rights in 1946, following the conclusion of World War II (see U.N. General Assembly Resolution, 1959). A summary of the declaration is presented in Table 2–2. The world had waited almost a quarter of a century for this Declaration of Human Rights.

In the meantime, other major legislation affected children and families as part of the social reforms enacted under Franklin Roosevelt's administration. For example, Title IV of the Social Security Act of 1935 (Aid to Needy Families, 42 U.S.C.A. §§601–644) provided specific guidelines for delivering welfare services. The Act states its purpose as follows:

> To provide for the general welfare by establishing a system of Federal old-age benefits, and by enabling the general states to make more adequate provisions for aged persons, blind persons, dependent and crippled children, maternal and child welfare, public health, and the administration of the unemployment compensation laws [42 U.S.C.A. §603(1)].

Sponsors argued that the Social Security Act was an appropriate vehicle for addressing the care of children, because family security forms the foundation for their care. This security varies from provisions for regular employment, adequate medical care, and prevention of accidents to adequate educational opportunities, crime correction, and vocational guidance. Even old-age security applies, because, by removing the burden of support of the elderly from middle-aged adults, more resources can be shared with children.

Legislation specifically defined a dependent child as a person under the age of 16 who is deprived of parental support or care by reason of death or continued absence from home, or physical or mental incapacity. Such an individual may be living with a father, mother, grandfather, grandmother, brother, sister, stepfather, stepmother, stepbrother, stepsister, uncle, or aunt in a residence maintained by one or more of these people (Bremner, 1974).

The federal government also was to provide one-third of each state's program-administration costs, a maximum of one-third of no more than $18 ($6) per month

TABLE 2-2 Summary of the Universal Declaration of Human Rights

The Preamble states that the child, because of his [or her] physical and mental immaturity, needs special safeguards and care, both before and after birth, and that individuals and groups should strive to achieve children's rights by legislative and other means. [Humanity], it says, owes the child the best it has to give. In ten carefully worded principles, the declaration affirms that all children are entitled to

1. the enjoyment of the rights mentioned, without any exception whatsoever, regardless of race, color, sex, religion, or nationality;
2. special protection, opportunities, and facilities to enable them to develop in a healthy and normal manner, in freedom and dignity;
3. a name and nationality;
4. social security, including adequate nutrition, housing, recreation, and medical services;
5. special treatment, education, and care if handicapped;
6. love and understanding and an atmosphere of affection and security, in the care and under the responsibility of their parents whenever possible;
7. free education and recreation and equal opportunity to develop their individual abilities;
8. prompt protection and relief in times of disaster;
9. protection against all forms of neglect, cruelty, and exploitation;
10. protection from any form of racial, religious, or other discrimination, and an upbringing in a spirit of peace and universal brotherhood.

Finally, the General Assembly resolved that governments, nongovernmental organizations, and individuals should give this declaration the widest possible publicity as a means of encouraging its observance everywhere.

United Nations Declaration of the Rights of the Child
A five-point Declaration of the Rights of the Child was stated in 1923 by the International Union for Child Welfare, with 1948 revisions in a seven-point document. The League of Nations adopted the IUCW declaration in 1924. The Declaration of the Rights of the Child was adopted by the United Nations General Assembly in 1959.

From THE CHILDREN'S RIGHTS MOVEMENT. Copyright © 1977 by Ronald and Beatrice Gross. Reprinted by permission of Doubleday & Company, Inc. (Based on the United Nations, General Assembly Resolution 1386 (XIV), November 20, 1959, published in the *Official Records of the General Assembly, Fourteenth Session, Supplement No. 16, 1960.*)

for the first dependent child, and a maximum of one-third of $12 for each additional child. All states, regardless of means, received the same matching funds. This law is referred to as Title V of the Social Security Act and sets the precedent for the later Aid to Dependent Children (ADC) programs (Aid to Needy Families, 42 U.S.C.A. §603(a)(1)(A)).

However, the Social Security Act was not yet serving all those in need. In 1937–1938 a study by the U.S. Advisory Council on Social Security (1939) showed that sometimes fathers could not provide for their children, because of prolonged illness or serious injury. Hence, a separate insurance program was implemented to take care of children in this time period, before they become eligible to receive social security benefits.

By the end of 1938, over 600,000 children from more than 250,000 families were cared for with cash allowances from federal, state, and local funds. At the end of World War II, the rolls were well over 800,000, and by June 1950 they exceeded 2 million (Bremner, 1974, p. 545).

Roosevelt established the Work Projects Administration (WPA) to provide jobs during the Great Depression. One of the WPA programs offered day-care centers to provide employment for elementary school teachers. World War II increased the demand by working mothers for child care, and the Lanham Act, passed in 1942, established centers for that purpose. Employment of mothers was viewed as necessary for the U.S. war effort; almost all such programs were terminated after

World War II, when public attitudes again urged mothers to stay at home with their children. Programs that did continue served welfare mothers but encouraged them to work in order to reduce welfare rolls. In the Roosevelt years, the impetus for child care continued, as in the 1800s, to be focused on economic goals rather than on child-development goals.

The Great Society

From World War II through the 1950s, advances in preventive health care and nutrition had a tremendous impact on the lives of children. Research led to breakthroughs in immunizations for major childhood diseases. Methods used in developing the Salk polio vaccine, approved in 1955, led to effective breakthroughs in combating other illnesses, such as measles. Medical researchers also began to investigate causes of birth defects, which up to that time had been a major health problem. Among significant discoveries were the cause of and remedy for phenylketonuria (PKU), a metabolic disorder that can produce severe mental retardation if not controlled through dietary restrictions. This research also led to the general realization that proper prenatal care is an important prerequisite for children's health.

As more information was gathered confirming the importance of good nutrition for development in general, and school performance in particular, federal subsidies for school lunch programs increased, encompassing large populations of lower-class children. Programs funded by other kinds of federal grants-in-aid also broadened in scope. The public believed that children need a permanent home, preferably with their own parents. Programs such as homemaker services worked with parents and special groups of children—for example, the abused and retarded (U.S. Congress, 1960).

Not until the 1960s did many individual programs reach their culmination, resulting ultimately in the 1962 Public Law 87-543 (Pub. L. 87-543, 76 Stat. 174). This law stated that child welfare services were to have the following purposes:

> (1) preventing or remedying or assisting in the solution of problems which may result in the neglect, abuse, exploitation, or delinquency of children; (2) protecting and caring for homeless, dependent or neglected children; (3) protecting and promoting the welfare of children of working mothers; and (4) otherwise protecting and promoting the welfare of children, including strengthening of their own homes where possible or, where needed, the provision of adequate care of children away from their homes in foster family homes or day care or other child-care facilities [Aid to Needy Families, cited in Bremner, 1974, p. 630].

With these changes, the major legislation begun under the Kennedy administration was formalized and labeled as the "Great Society" under the Johnson administration. For example, the "suitable-home" requirement, which was often used to deny assistance to children who would otherwise be eligible, now was altered. Previously, monies were not received when a parent or caregiver lived with a member of the opposite sex without a valid marriage or without the establishment of paternity. The Fleming Ruling now finally removed these stigmas of immorality and illegitimacy, which had been hampering the delivery of child care.

The Social Security Act of 1962 changed the name of Title IV to Grants to States for Aid and Services to Needy Families with Dependent Children (thus the acronym

More Federal legislation relating to child welfare and public assistance was enacted in the 1960s than in any other decade in our history.

changed from ADC to AFDC). Major additional amendments were passed under Public Law 87-543 (42 U.S.C.A. §603) that

1. increased federal matching funds to 75% of state funds
2. extended federal monies to the second parent when unemployed or incapacitated and living at home with needy children
3. extended the aid for dependent children of unemployed parents to five years
4. provided permanent aid to children receiving foster care
5. authorized protective payments in behalf of dependent children
6. authorized monies for demonstration projects and training of personnel

These amendments represent the most comprehensive overhaul of federal legislation relating to child welfare and public assistance that Congress has ever enacted.

Legislation and social advances on behalf of children were also affected by racial issues and poverty. Some people credit Michael Harrington's *The Other America* (1971) with inspiring the national "War on Poverty." "Black" programs and urban ethnic communities had been ignored in the general shift toward social reform (Levine & Levine, 1970), perpetuating racial clashes within low-income groups. The persistent divisive issue of race kept the poor and powerless divided. The concept of inherent social inequality, which still had public support, was thought by some to be caused by genetic inferiority.

> There is always far more inequality between individuals than between groups. It follows then, when we compare the degree of inequality between groups to the degree of inequality between individuals, inequality between groups seems relatively unimportant. It seems quite shocking, for example, that white workers earn 50 percent more than black workers. But we are even more disturbed by the fact that the best-paid fifth of all white workers earns 600 percent more than the worst-paid fifth [Jencks, 1972, p. 14].

However, to thus obscure racial inequality by stressing that inequality exists within groups certainly does not help social reform to increase equality among all people.

Researchers have attempted to identify contributing environmental factors in order to offset such attitudes about racial inequality, inferiority, and poverty. Hunt

(1961) documented the impact of the environment on intelligence, and Bloom (1964) reported on the rapid growth of intelligence during the early years of childhood. It seemed that racial and poverty gaps could be closed. Possibly services could counter the injuries of inequality. Youth were targeted, and enrichment programs such as Head Start flourished. Extensive new jargon was coined. For example, the poor were now to be called "culturally deprived" rather than "genetically unfit" and other disparaging terms (Deutsch, 1966). The Social Security Act, amended in 1967, recognized environmental influences on cognitive development by providing developmental day-care services for past, present, and potential welfare recipients. This amendment subsumed Title V (Maternal and Child Health Services) into Title IVA (Aid to Families with Dependent Children), which was later subsumed under Title XX. Title IVB (Child Welfare Services) increased provision for foster care of dependent and neglected children based on comprehensive, coordinated social services.

Head Start did produce some cognitive gains for children, but critics questioned why increases did not continue over time. Some critics (for example, Caldwell, 1968) thought the effort started too late in a child's life. Two major consequences of assessments of Head Start were: (1) children were placed in programs at younger ages, and (2) parents were included in program efforts. (Chapters 5, 6, and 10 examine these effects.)

By the close of the decade of the Great Society, some legislators urged legislation to create comprehensive developmental services for all children. A bill sponsored in the Senate by W. Mondale, and in the House by J. Brademas, emphasized the following goals:

1. comprehensive services (educational, health, custodial, enriching)
2. high-quality supervisory care
3. focus on stimulating cognitive development
4. improvement of the self-image of (lower-income) parents through their participation in community-action programs
5. funding direct from the federal government to local programs, to allow community control

Both houses passed the legislation, but President Nixon vetoed the bill. He felt that the bill blocked the states' rights to implement and oversee funding, that program administration supporting direct federal-to-local funding would be costly, and that communal patterns of care would undermine the institution of the family (Nixon, 1971).

Then, in July 1975, HEW Secretary Weinberger spoke for the Ford administration at legislative hearings designed to consider a new family/child services bill. He stressed that a new system for child services would likely not incorporate existing programs. For this reason and because of the idea of saddling the government with sole delivery responsibility, he felt that opposition to the bill must mount.

Senator Mondale (1975) countered this argument in his opening statement at the joint Senate–House hearings on the Child and Family Services Act of 1975 (a new version of the original Mondale/Brademas bill). He believed the bill would

> assure that parents will have the opportunity to choose among the greatest possible variety of child and family services—including prenatal care, nutrition assistance, part-time programs like Head Start, after-school or full-day developmental day care for children of working mothers, in-the-home tutoring, early medical screening and

treatment to detect and remedy handicapped conditions, and classes for parents and prospective parents [p. 1].

During the Ford years, disagreement in both houses about the bill continued, and nothing was enacted. "Day care fell victim to infighting among its very supporters who failed to make a case for its need. This was so much so that a Democratic administration testified before Congress this year against a child care bill" (*Day Care and Child Development Reports,* 1979, p. 1).

Advances in a social policy toward children also were not made during Carter's term as president, and until prevailing values and ideologies are altered such steps seem unlikely. Perhaps differences of opinion will be put aside as societal factors continue to place families under stress that could be alleviated by alternative child-care arrangements.

Kiesler (1979) suggests that the government, preoccupied with social and political problems, applies a "problem-oriented" model to child-service programs and policies. She contends that a proclivity toward corrective intervention is not in the best interests of children because it avoids questions of how to *prevent* problems. Will we continue to support a de facto policy of care for our children? Will we continue to correct and restrain problems rather than seek to prevent problems? Will we ever try to realize our ideal of optimal development for all our children?

In the name of equality and individualization, corrective efforts have become extreme. The extensive use of medical explanations for why certain children fail to perform in school reflects continued interest in determining the causes of individual differences. Often moralism creeps in, as indicated by the following passage from a study of learning disabilities in children (Huessey & Cohen, 1975):

> Children who are identified early as having behavioral and learning problems are at risk for developing academic as well as social adjustment problems in adolescence. In comparison to our control group, our "hyperkinetic" children had lower mean grade point averages, achievement scores and I.Q. scores. . . . Our "hyperkinetic" adolescents were described [by school officials] as being immature, stubborn, unattentive, distractable, sneaky, lazy, easily discouraged, defiant, annoying, etc. [p. 12].

Of course, a social problem of inequality, with its existing stigmas of "being on welfare," "being poor," "being fatherless," and so forth cannot be corrected by further labeling. Some children do have learning disabilities, for which a medical diagnosis is helpful, but the associated moralism historically has been and still is questionable. In *Small Futures,* Richard deLone (deLone and Carnegie Council, 1979) expresses his fear of a continued use of labels:

> The ultimate danger is not simply that individual children—mostly from nonwhite or low-income families—will be stigmatized. It is that medical explanations of poverty, explanations that again locate the causes of inequality in individual pathology, will lead to yet another round of efforts to reduce inequality by reforming individuals [p. 73].

Conclusion

In five social welfare services—education, health care, housing, income security, and employment—the intervention thrust historically has been limited. The value placed on employment as a basic right in our society stems from an ideology of individualism and productivity. Each person is expected to be self-sufficient—but without guaranteed employment this goal may not become a reality. Hence, housing and income security are provided for those "deserving but unfortunate." Education has become not only a right of all citizens but also a necessity for optimal functioning in society. Some people argue that education serves other functions, such as needs for day care, socialization, and removal of children from the labor force. Health care has been improved by increased knowledge. As the costs of preventive measures such as immunization or public sanitation have begun to outweigh the expense of remedial measures, minimal health standards have been legislated. As the positive effects of improved standards become known, people have begun to demand health care and good sanitation as a right contributing to the quality of life.

Today's complex technological society creates very diverse environments for living. Close to 3 million children under the age of 6 live in families headed by mothers alone. But only about a million children from all types of families are enrolled in day-care centers. Millions of school-aged children could benefit from after-school supervised care, but only 100,000 are being served now by day-care programs. To be economically and socially viable, many families need government intervention (Fleming, 1976).

Kamerman and Kahn (1976, p. 505) suggest that the social-service system be more personalized—that is, tailored to individual and specific types of family needs. This direction could assist all families in their varied environments and communities because it emphasizes (1) community-support networks, (2) access to information and services, and (3) corrective and preventive efforts. They specify the exact goals of a "personal" social-service system:

1. to increase the dissemination of information and the access to services
2. to maintain a minimal level of social care for individuals with dysfunctions
3. to provide help, counseling, and guidance for individuals and families to overcome crises
4. to encourage mutual aid, self-help, and participation activities targeted at prevention within community contexts rather than institutions
5. to integrate different programs and services through networking efforts to maximize effectiveness.

A more personalized, decentralized system of diverse services might gain public support and in turn produce legislative action.

The axiom "The child is father of the man" represents the foundation for beliefs about the significance of individual development. Experiences in childhood greatly determine how adults will contribute to society. The social reforms we have enacted demonstrate our attempt to nurture and protect children directly or indirectly, primarily to further economic goals. But institutions designed to correct inequalities have often perpetuated inequalities instead. Thus, our efforts to provide equality and equal opportunity have generated unequal reforms, and failures have been attributed to individual pathologies and to genetic inferiority rather than to the ideas that generated the failures.

To observe that the social-service system is less than perfect is not to imply that a classless society resembling a socialistic political structure is desirable. Such a conclusion would be based on the false dichotomy that either the concept of *class distinctiveness* or the concept of *classlessness* must be supported. This dichotomy demonstrates the implicit difficulties our society has had in implementing a service-delivery system. To support opportunities for equality does not mean each citizen is treated similarly; and to recognize the impact of genetics does not mean to discount the impact of varying aspects of the environment.

By supporting dichotomies, we may have hampered our abilities to implement child services. Perhaps one reason why we do not enact comprehensive legislation for children is that we don't know what we want from or for our citizens of tomorrow. Meanwhile we try to both serve a large population and maintain individualism. Supporting diverse, pluralistic programs that encourage self-sufficiency and local community-support networks could be a solution that would let people answer their own questions about their own children. For example, should their children be obedient? happy? healthy? adaptive? militant? Should children support parental values? Maybe we have used our emphasis on individuality as our license to avoid responsibility in the care of the next generation. Any false dichotomy such as class distinction versus classlessness may only further perpetuate difficulties and hamper efforts. (We confront this issue again in Chapter 14.)

As the United States inches slowly but inexorably toward a comprehensive national policy on children, youth, and families similar to that in many other countries, it will need psychological data for planning, implementing, monitoring, and evaluating such a policy. . . . It is only then that the rhetoric of caring for the young as our most important resource, which has been touted in the United States for many decades, will have been translated into reality [Shore, 1979, p. 1019].

Summary

The Fourteenth Amendment, written in 1868, defines the relationship between citizens and government as one of cooperation. Historically, our society has subscribed to the concept that children should be subordinate to adults and has only slowly recognized separate rights for children by limiting parental control. Over time, we have formulated assumptions about what constitutes the proper parent/child relationship. Social conditions influence the likelihood that government will intrude into the family or will provide adequate services to support children when families do not. A social stigma is associated with the receipt of services.

Economic reasons have dominated our social reform efforts; for example, women with no other means of support entered the labor force, and day facilities were established for the care of their children. It was thought that economic growth meant people could have an equal chance for benefits and services. Thus, achievement was once considered to be the equalizer of class differences. When immigrants flocked to our shores, neglected and dependent children multiplied. But attempts at restoring social harmony (such as providing education) failed. Alleged genetic inferiority became the scapegoat for program failures.

In 1909, at the first White House Conference on Children, income supports were suggested for those "suffering temporary misfortune." People wanted to know why individual differences existed; "individualism" began to mean "being different." Industrialization with all its specialization perpetuated inequality, because people with different abilities needed to be identified early, because the marketplace fostered efficient productivity. Children were tracked in school. The theory of genetic inequality gained support from Social Darwinism and the eugenics movement as the reason some inequalities, especially those of wealth, could not be bridged. This tendency toward racism continued.

Finally, in 1924 the U.N. General Assembly adopted a Universal Declaration of Human Rights, which came to fruition in 1948 under the leadership of Eleanor Roosevelt. Major social reforms such as the Social Security Act were launched during the administration of Franklin D. Roosevelt. General welfare was provided to individuals and expanded in scope over these years. During the Great Depression, the WPA was formed to create jobs such as day-care supervision. And child care flourished again for an economic reason—to win World War II—because mothers were needed in the workforce.

The 1950s witnessed advances in health care and nutrition for children. Efforts went to produce resources for special parents and children. Finally, in 1961 "illegitimate" children were allowed to receive welfare. By 1962 child-care services had one major goal—to promote and protect the welfare of children by solving family child-care problems, by helping care for children of working women, and by caring for dependent and neglected children. Then, under the leadership of John F. Kennedy, Congress enacted a comprehensive overhaul of federal legislation relating to child welfare and public assistance. The "War on Poverty" began. Racial clashes occurred, especially within low-income groups, and some researchers once again resorted to genetics to explain social inequality.

Other researchers reported on the impact of the environment on intelligence and on the rapid changes in intelligence during the early years of childhood. Many believed that services could counter the injuries of inequality. Reflecting this new moralism, the poor were to be called "culturally deprived" or "disadvantaged." Head Start programs sprang up throughout the country. Children were enrolled in Head Start at younger ages, and parent-education and -training programs were developed. Legislation toward comprehensive developmental services for *all* children seemed imminent but was vetoed by President Nixon in 1971.

Many people believe that our policy of care for children is de facto, corrective, and problem oriented. They suggest that our efforts should be directed toward preventing injury, optimizing potential, and guarding against the use of labels. Although the social problem of inequality persists today, with its associated stigmas, we do have social services (employment, housing, income security, education, and health care) and we are trying to implement them at a more personal level. To enhance the delivery of child services, we must readdress our philosophy of child care: what qualities of care do we want, for whom, and under what human conditions?

3

Contemporary Climate:
The Issue Is Human Quality

This chapter, which was written in collaboration with JAMES GARBARINO as the senior author, is based on his original essay, "The Issue Is Human Quality: In Praise of Children," written in commemoration of the International Year of the Child while the author was at the Boys' Town Center for the Study of Youth Development; 1979 Mitchell Prize Winner, Permission from the Woodlands Conference on Growth Policy. Garbarino is currently at the Pennsylvania State University.

Chapter overview

Persistent social attitudes and values form Americans' philosophy toward children. As these attitudes and values change with the passage of time, so too do child-rearing practices. This chapter examines the philosophy about children subscribed to and promoted today, advancing the position that promoting human quality is an essential investment in the lives of America's children.

Issues to consider

Why should a society care about children?

What is the "good life"?

How should investments be made for children?

What are support systems, and how should they function for families and children?

What attitudes prevail about the psychosocial investment in children?

How is the quality of life for children determined by the institutional life of the community?

What are the implications of supporting the goal of improving the quality of children's lives?

Introduction

The following case history raises some vital questions about child care in the United States today:

> Jody was four years old when her parents brought her to Colorado General Hospital. She had suffered from severe child abuse all of her life and demonstrated one of the most severe cases of malnutrition that we have seen. She weighed only seventeen pounds and was covered with bruises and abrasions. Radiological studies revealed a fracture of the skull and arm and two fractures of her hands. She also presented a high intestinal obstruction due to a hematoma in the lumen of the duodenum.
>
> For years Jody's mother had expressed to her husband and other members of the family and community her concern about this child and the manner in which she was able to care for her. No one had been willing to accept the responsibility, and no help was offered the mother.
>
> Shortly after Jody was admitted to the hospital, the mother was told that we would not recommend that she be sent home because of our concern for her welfare. Without hesitation the mother in a very relieved tone stated, "I would be more frightened than you if she were sent home."
>
> Jody's progress in the hospital was dramatic. During the six months following discharge, she grew six inches and showed considerable developmental improvement. She has been permanently removed from her home and is now awaiting adoption [Kempe & Helfer, 1974, pp. xv–xvi].*

Where was the support system for Jody's parents? Why did it take so long for people to care about Jody's welfare?

This chapter explores the meaning of caring and the good life, critically considers children's needs, and examines the implications of making investments to fill those needs. Is it necessary that the inequalities mentioned in the previous chapter be perpetuated, or can they be changed? The issue, indeed, is the quality of human life.

*From *The Battered Child* (2nd ed.), by C. H. Kempe and R. E. Helfer (Eds.). Copyright © 1974 by the University of Chicago Press. Reprinted by permission. (Third edition, 1980.)

In modern society, it is not uncommon to find "latch-key children" returning home after school to care for themselves and younger siblings while their parents work.

Caring and the good life

Who cares?

In their manifesto for the future, *Human Growth: An Essay on Growth Values and the Quality of Life,* Cleveland and Wilson (1978) argue that the Good Society is visible on the horizon:

> Such a society is bound to move away from "growth" defined as quantitative product irrespective of what and whom it is for. Such a society is bound to consider basic human needs a first charge on available resources. Such a society is bound to bestow its highest priority upon the development of human resources—on enhancement of the human environment [p. 24].

When it comes to human resources, the bottom line is the welfare of children. A society that does not do well by its children forsakes the quality of its future.

In sharp contrast to the optimistic and glowing vision of Cleveland and Wilson stands a rather more pessimistic observation, based on public-opinion surveys, offered by Mary Ellen Burris at a recent marketing institute:

> A happy marriage, an interesting job, and a job that contributes to the welfare of society— each of these factors *decreased* in the percentage of people naming them as ingredients of the good life. In contrast, these things *increased* in importance: a color T.V., a lot of money, really nice clothes, a second color T.V. And consider this: in late 1975, more people named children as an ingredient in the good life than a car; now it's just the reverse [May 7, 1979].

Is this the beginning of an ugly future in which adults turn their backs on children in favor of material aggrandizement? Or is this simply a transitory dark hour before a new dawn? With the recent celebration of the International Year of the Child (1979), it is only fitting that efforts in designing a sustainable society (that is, one in which quality rather than quantitative concerns predominates) should focus on the role that children will play in that world to come. Realistically speaking, color televisions, cars, and nice clothes are a losing proposition in the long run when contrasted with children on both practical and moral grounds.

Why *should* society care for children? At the heart of any discussion of a sustainable society lies the development of human resources and the issue of where children fit into a modern social and technological environment. The issue of human quality is inseparable from the well-being of children: children *are* the future. The well-being of children is both the principal challenge faced by a modern society and the principal focal point for a society that can fulfill Cleveland and Wilson's mandate to "move away from 'growth' defined as quantitative product irrespective of what and whom it is for." Children must have first claim on such a society if it is to be both physically and socially sustainable. And if children are to have first claim, then parents and the conditions of parenthood must also be in the forefront of the nation's consciousness.

Any discussion of the welfare of children must begin with families because children and families have no meaning without each other. Although 1979 was proclaimed the International Year of the Child, it is foolhardy to think of children apart from their parents' conditions of life—1979 could easily have been called the Year of the Family. This theme emerged clearly when a panel of child-development experts was interviewed on their views concerning the status of children (American Psychological Association, 1979). Although they all began from different theoretical perspectives and research interests, all returned inexorably to families when asked about the status of children.

Children provide the focal point for assessing the quality of life for adults. By looking at children—and at the people who care for them—we gain a finer appreciation of what matters and what doesn't, what is genuine and what is ephemeral, what is qualitative and what is simply quantitative. The condition of children tells the story, for better or for worse. Child abuse is the "worse."

Commenting on domestic violence in the animal world, Morris (1970, p. 6) makes the following observation: "The viciousness with which children . . . are subjected to persecution is a measure of the weight of dominant pressures imposed on their persecutor." Complementing this observation is Rock's report (1978) that, when gorilla mothers are socially impoverished by being isolated from their peers, they have a striking propensity to mistreat their infants. However, when restored to the simian community, these mothers perform adequately.

Although comparisons between primates and humans are open to question, social impoverishment is clearly detrimental to child rearing, and domestic violence among humans reflects oppressive stresses and strains (Straus, Gelles, & Steinmetz, 1979). Both abuse and neglect are associated with isolation of the parent/child relationship from the nurturance and feedback provided by "potent pro-social support systems" (Garbarino, 1977, p. 726). On the negative side, the evidence is clear that, when the quality of life for adults suffers, children suffer. The lives of children mirror the lives of those adults whose job it is to care for them.

Any discussion of children, parents, and families is of necessity dialectical. For Burris's thesis that valuing things is taking the place of valuing children, there is the antithesis presented by public-opinion polls that continue to show family life at the top of people's lists of what is important. Based on a recent nationwide survey, Harris (1978, p. 1) concludes that "clearly, the most satisfying part of life to many Americans today is family life. A substantial 92% of the public say this is very important to them. And 67% say they are very satisfied with the way their family life is going." Despite flirtations with materialism, most people recognize that color televisions and the like are simply, as one Eastern philosopher puts it, "the unreal objects of this world." The challenge in designing a sustainable society is to bolster and clarify that recognition, not to obscure it by exploiting and falsifying people's basic material needs.

The things of real value that can be offered to children are time, interest, and attention. The conditions of life—the very structure of the society—determine how physically rewarding it will be to invest in social rather than material projects, in children and community life. To understand the dynamics of this process of investment, we must understand the sources of meaning in adult life.

What is the good life?

Searching for the meaning of the "good life" has been the traditional philosophical issue. The search, while largely abandoned by contemporary philosophy, has been taken up by psychology. Under the guidance of the gentle theorists Abraham Maslow and Carl Rogers, modern psychology has sought to answer the eternal question "What is the good life?" The meaning of personal fulfillment comes from within the individual and is situationally determined. There is a growing appreciation for the centrality of this most qualitative of issues. Quality of life is an important and growing research issue in its own right. To ask "What is the good life?" is to pose the fundamental issue of psychological quality. The question asks, "What brings meaning to human experience? What makes reality a positive experience?"

The issue of quality in a psychological context has new implications in the 20th century. In the past, considerations of quality were intrinsically elitist. The material conditions of life did not permit a wide-spread demand for quality. Families were busy producing in order to survive and did not have the luxury of indulging in consumption and leisure. But the Industrial Revolution raised the tantalizing prospect of improving conditions enough to permit quality of life to become a concern for the masses. Indeed, utopian writing since the 18th century is built on the premise that technological improvements permit the distribution of human quality to all people (Garbarino & Garbarino, 1978).

As is often the case, the fullest picture of reality comes not from social science but from fiction, where the rough edges of incomplete factual information can be smoothed by the visionary imagination. Wright's utopian novel *Islandia* (1942) presents a totally sustainable society in which the pursuit of human quality is totally preeminent over concerns with quantity. On the one hand, *Islandia* presents an alternative to all the superficial trappings of modern society. On the other hand, it incorporates the fundamental thesis of the modern society, namely that universal distribution of quality through a social organization and material technology permits the dignity of economic adequacy to all. The two characters—John, the contemporary American, and Dorn, the Islandian—are discussing how Islandia would change were it to become "modern."

John: "With us, progress means giving pleasures to those who haven't got them."
Dorn: "But doesn't progress create the very situation it seeks to cure—always changing the social adjustment so that someone is squeezed out. Decide on an indispensible minimum. See that everyone gets that, and until everyone has it, don't let anyone have any more. Don't let anyone ever have any more until they have cultivated fully what they have."
John: "To be unhappy is a sign we aren't stagnating."
Dorn: "Nor are we. 'Happy' wasn't the right word. We are quite as unhappy as you are. Things are too beautiful; those we love die; it hurts to grow old or be sick. Progress

won't change any of these things, except that medicine will mitigate the last. We cultivate medicine, and we are quite as far along as you are there"[Wright, 1942, pp. 84-85].

The essential issues of human experience presented in *Islandia* are direct, simple, universal, and unchanging: mating, childbearing, child rearing, puberty, adulthood, and, once again, mating. Wright envisioned a society in which technology is *selected* to permit a lifestyle in which those fundamental human concerns are the agenda for the human community, unencumbered by false issues of social change and social development. Wright's vision of what matters for quality in human life is paralleled in the scientific study of human experience. Psychology thus merges with ethics.

Campbell (1976) noted the fundamental falseness of modern objective measures of human society because they exclude the subjective experience of reality, which is the ultimate criterion for judging meaning. Campbell builds on the findings from national surveys, showing that during the period between 1957 and 1972, when most of the economic and social indicators were rising rapidly, the proportion of the American population that described itself as "very happy" had declined steadily. This decline was most apparent among the most affluent part of the population. Moreover, when people living in those states (primarily in the Southeast) that have the lowest objective quality of life were asked about the subjective quality of their life, they reported more positive experiences than did their counterparts in the more affluent "developed" states. Campbell concluded that indicators of personal well-being are needed to complement conventional social indicators.

These subjective measures indicate how things stand between children and their parents. Rather than being a simple collection of characteristics, human development is the process by which an individual constructs a picture of the world and acquires the tools to live in and with that picture. Child psychologist Urie Bronfenbrenner defines *development* as "the person's evolving conception of the ecological environment, and his [or her] relation to it, as well as the person's growing capacity to discover, sustain, or alter its properties" (1979b, p. 9).

This concept of development figures prominently in efforts to understand how the future of a sustainable society depends on the quality of life it offers to children. Although children develop abstractions, they do *not* develop in response to abstractions. Children are a genuine reflection of the actual quality of life as it is directly experienced. The "problem" of adults is that they are much more susceptible than children to delusion, to being drawn away from "the basics." But just what are the basics that bring about the experience of quality for the subjective human organism? Campbell concludes that they are "the presence or absence of those various forms of interpersonal exchange that provides psychological support to people" (1976, p. 122). Those interpersonal supports both enlarge the capacity of the developing human to use the environment and provide the raw material that humans need to fashion a satisfying existence. The need for interpersonal support is the fundamental human need, the satisfaction of which is the foundation of social quality. Campbell's concern with this fundamental need in adults can be transposed to the world of children.

To serve the basic needs of children (to play and develop competence) in a way that does not rob adults of their own satisfaction requires a supportive community. The other interpersonal features of life such as friendship must complement rather than compete with child rearing. For the child to flourish, the parent must have access to the social riches of family or family surrogates, kin and kith. Just as child and family are inseparable, both in interests and in functions, so family and community are wedded by a functional connection. Unless a society provides parents with the means to rear children, it will be faced with unhappy parents and inadequately prepared children, an unhappy mixture that directly threatens the goal of quality in the human experience.

It is reassuring to know that the fundamental needs of children and adults are relatively simple and basically unchanging. To meet those needs for the mass of the population—a quantum leap in happiness—is a challenge to the skill of society's professionals (such as social engineers, managers, politicians, and teachers) and individual citizens. This difficult task demands a more precise examination of the conditions that favor an intensive social investment by parents in their children without suffering psychological bankruptcy.

Making the necessary investment in children

Poverty undermines children's health and well-being (National Academy of Sciences, 1976), subjecting them to damaging stresses by placing them in threatening situations and by undermining the ability of their parents to give what children rightfully deserve—a finely tuned and affectionate responsiveness. Severe economic deprivation robs families of the social necessities of life, leading to social impoverishment. The pervasive presence of social impoverishment often interferes with nonmaterial factors related to the quality of life, such as social needs. Thus, social impoverishment is the most direct threat to human development.

The reality of poverty as a destructive social and psychological force is vivid in Sanger's (1938) account of her work with mothers living on the Lower East Side of Manhattan during the early 1900s:

> Each time I returned to this district, which was becoming a recurrent nightmare, I used to hear that Mrs. Cohen "had been carried to a hospital, but had never come back," or that Mrs. Kelly "had sent the children to a neighbor and had put her head into the gas oven". Day after day such tales were poured into my ears—a baby born dead, great relief—the death of an older child, sorrow but again relief of a sort—the story told a thousand times of death from abortion, children going into institutions. I shuddered with horror as I listened to the details and studied the reasons back of them—destitution linked with excessive childbearing. The waste of life seemed senseless. One by one, worried, sad, pensive and aging faces marshalled themselves before me in my dreams, sometimes appealingly, sometimes accusingly [p. 89].

When life is so impoverished that children are a burden, they tend to further impoverish rather than enrich the quality of life. As Wright made so clear in *Islandia*, only by establishing an adequate and stable material setting can there be the fullest development and expression of the psychological and social quality of human experience.

Thus efforts to design a sustainable society centering on the labor-intensive nature of child rearing must avoid naive sentimentality about "the good old days," as Schumacher (1973) observed with respect to the economic and technological spheres. It does not follow, however, that material investment can be substituted for psychological and social investment in the rearing of children. The only outcome from such a course can be a materialistic construction of reality incompatible with a sustainable society. The essence of development is the child's conception of the world and his or her ability to "discover, sustain, or alter its properties" (Bronfenbrenner, 1979b, p. 9).

A sustainable society required that people direct their developing competence toward cultivating renewable, nonpolluting resources. Chief among these "clean" resources is social intercourse, which Campbell (1976) found to be the primary reliable source of meaningfulness and satisfaction. This bodes well for designing a sustainable society, suggesting that such a society is compatible with "human nature" if it is built on labor-intensive enterprises that generate and sustain a comfortable social web, surrounding, dignifying, and supporting the individual human being. Children and child rearing must stand at the heart of such a web. They are the most reliable occasion for knitting people together in mutually satisfying socially productive work and play; the perfect vehicle for organizing a sustainable society.

To work out the implications of this principle for every aspect of economic, political, and social life clearly is no small task. Certain cultural and historical forces work against the necessary psychological and social investment in children. Severe economic stress is a poignant fact of life for at least one in six American children and their parents. Moreover, the demands of their parents' work socially impoverish many children. The necessary psychological and social investment has been diverted both by poverty and by affluence (Bronfenbrenner, 1974c), which makes many adults suspicious of the child's nature and belies claims that ours is a "child-centered" society. "The greatest single impediment to our improving the lives of America's children is the myth that we are a child-oriented society already doing all that needs to be done" (Zigler, 1976, p. 39).

The temptation to use material investment as a substitute for psychological investment is real and compelling. The Soviet Union tried creating boarding schools to provide "disadvantaged" children with high-quality, professional child care, but abandoned this compensatory intervention program when it became apparent that "you can't pay a woman to do what a mother will do for free" (Bronfenbrenner, 1978). Material investment seems an easy way out of making the necessary labor-intensive investment but is ineffective at best and developmentally damaging at worst. Similarly, in the United States in the 1950s, surveys showed that high on the list of reasons given for purchasing television sets was "to bring the family back together" (Garbarino, 1975). The result, of course, was physical togetherness but psychological apartness, parallel rather than interactive social experience.

The reservoir of public support for child rearing and family life is often stymied by the tantalizing proposition that parents can have their cake and eat it too—invest in their children and do their own thing as well. Unless their "thing" is child rearing, it can't and won't work. And to be effective, parents need a supportive social environment that cares for them as they care for their children, one that balances nurturance and guidance, consensus and diversity.

Family-support systems

In discussing the relative role of material versus psychological and social investment in child rearing, the concept of *support systems* inevitably arises. In the view of one pioneer researcher in this area, support systems are enduring social relationships that combine both nurturance and feedback (Caplan, 1974). They provide the individual with warmth and security in addition to guidance and direction. This joint function and meaning of support systems becomes particularly important when considering effective parenthood, where the protective function is particularly salient. Indeed, the main factor mediating between the parent/child relationship and the larger society is precisely the family's network of support systems. The richness, diversity, and strength of these support systems, which contribute nurturance and feedback to parent/child relationships, are some of the principal environmental determinants of the child's developmental robustness. In this respect, the good life for families resembles the political good life for communities: social pluralism both protects society from dangerous excesses and provides diverse and enriching experiences by combining consensus and diversity (Garbarino & Bronfenbrenner, 1976).

Although most of the public debate concerning the fate of children centers around the alleged decline of the American family, the issue actually lies outside the family, in the family's relation to the community. Understanding this relationship is a necessary precondition for looking at the condition and future of American families. The destruction of traditional sources of social pluralism poses a danger of social impoverishment, in which the support systems necessary for effective parenthood are undermined. Without these support systems, the parent/child relationship is jeopardized—hence references to "the decline of the American family."

Social impoverishment cannot solely be attributed to economic poverty. Other factors—such as geographic mobility, instrumental interpersonal relationships, and the erosion of neighborhoods—affect enduring patterns of behavior among family units. Geographic mobility strains and often breaks the functional relationships that underlie support systems. Although modern communications permit support systems to function over long distances, as in the case of weekly transcontinental phone calls to grandparents, such geographically dispersed social networks cannot have the same day-to-day significance as more concentrated, localized ones. Perhaps equally threatening, however, is the fact that geographic mobility may produce an adaptive cultural response in which short-term, immediate relationships become desirable in place of long-term relationships built on daily contact over an extended period. Geographic mobility may make it more difficult for children and parents to share a common history with those in their current support systems and to share experiences that build trust, understanding, and the motivation to provide nurturance and feedback. Thus, instrumental interpersonal relationships may play a larger role. Such relationships are inconsistent if not incompatible with genuine support systems that validate the intrinsic worth of the person.

The very notion of designing a sustainable society presupposes that alternative arrangements can be made even though it is not possible to recapture an idealized past. The promise of modern life, of course, is to permit social enrichment to grow out of material adequacy. Is this good life on the horizon? What does the future hold for children and parents?

Psychosocial investment

As was noted earlier, there is a deeply rooted tension—one might even say conflict—in the United States about children: the notion that American society is child-oriented is belied by thinly disguised resentment of children and by certain inevitable realities that place adults at odds with childrens' needs. As *Time* Magazine put it, "Those who detect a pervasive, low-grade child aversion in the United States find it swarming in the air like pollen" (Morrow, 1979, p. 42). Politically, children are losers (Featherstone, 1979; Zigler, 1976). The issue is really one of investment—how does society rank that which it values? Several important points can be made on this score.

First, most Americans retain a fundamental and unwavering commitment to parenthood, despite the declining birthrate (Glick, 1979). In a rather extensive review of childlessness in the United States, Judith Blake (1979) reports the results of a nationwide survey of adults dealing with the advantages and disadvantages of childlessness. She found that adults do not intend to be priced out of the parenthood market by the high economic costs of childbearing and child rearing, although they will limit the number of children they have. People do value children for their intrinsic worth, and this affirmation is the bedrock for the future (Blake, 1979). On balance, it seems clear that the primary investment in children, namely their conception and birth, is still being made—and will continue to be made in the future. Smaller families are still families and tend to be good ones at that (Lieberman, 1970).

This fundamental commitment to having children—at least, to having one child per couple—does not, however, guarantee the future. The quality of life for children in the future is by no means assured simply by the fact of them being born. The issue of enduring and appropriate psychological and social investment remains. In fact, the current thrust toward self-gratification and preoccupation with economic pressures makes quite real the possibility that adults will continue to have children yet not willing (or able) to make the necessary investment in child rearing. Some data suggest that this is a real problem.

A recent study by Bahr (1978) offers us a rare opportunity to compare adolescents' views of their parents in the same community over a 50-year span. It should come as no surprise that teenagers value fathers who spend time with them— in 1924, 63% of the girls and 62% of the boys felt that the most desirable attribute in a father is the fact that he spends time with his children; in 1977, these figures had risen to 71% and 64%, respectively. This change is small and reflects the unchanging nature of father/adolescent relations. What is of real interest, however, is a significant change occurring in how much adolescents value their mothers spending time with them. One presumes that to explicitly value this means that it is problematic, that it is an issue. In 1924, 34% of the boys and 41% of the girls placed a premium on having their mothers spend time with them. By 1977, the percentages had risen to 58% and 66%. Presumably this reflects the gradual departure of mothers from the day-to-day lives of their adolescents over a 50-year period, which corresponds directly with the tremendous increase in mothers working outside the home. These data complement others collected by Bronfenbrenner (1970) and his colleagues that show a continuing decline in the amount of active time spent by parents with their children and link this decrease to a variety of disturbing trends, including impaired social functioning and alienation.

Happiness lies in what Erik Erikson (1963) calls the issue about one's relation to the future, that of "generativity versus despair." One finds genuine happiness in psychological and social investment for the quality of the future. By investing in children, either directly, as a parent, or indirectly, one makes the world a better place for children, one invests in the future. How well does American society do—and how well can it do in the future—in making this investment a productive, happy one? The answer is to be found in the neighborhoods and institutional lives of adults.

Neighborhoods

Whether or not the intrinsic value of children will triumph over their burdensomeness depends in some measure on how supportive the family's neighborhood is. The quality of neighborhoods as contexts for family life has become a significant issue for students of community and human development. But the concept of neighborhood, so attractive in principle, has proven very difficult to define in operational, concrete terms. Kromkowski (1976) provided one of the best statements of what a good neighborhood is:

> A neighborhood's character is determined by a host of factors, but most significantly by the kinds of relationships that neighbors have with each other . . . a healthy neighborhood has some sort of cultural and institutional network which manifests itself in pride in the neighborhood, care of homes, security for children, and respect for each other [p. 228].

When stated this way, the significance of neighborhoods as support systems for families is clear and indisputable. A strong and supportive neighborhood makes the task of parenthood significantly more manageable.

Research on neighborhoods (Garbarino & Crouter, 1978a; Garbarino & Sherman, 1980) provides some insights into the way a family's social environment can affect the experience of parent/child relationships. Economically and demographically similar settings can present very different social environments, which can affect the quality of life for parents and children.

In a recent study, two neighborhoods were selected on the basis of their economic and demographic similarity and their (very different) rates of child maltreatment (Garbarino & Sherman, 1980). The rate of child maltreatment differed by a factor of 5. When these two settings were examined, it was found that expert informants ranging from elementary school principals to mail carriers saw the low-risk area as a healthy neighborhood and the high-risk area as a socially sick environment. Samples of families drawn from each neighborhood were interviewed. The families identified very different patterns of stresses and supports, patterns in the use and source of help, use of formal support systems, and evaluations of the neighborhood as a setting in which to raise children. Also, parents in the high-risk neighborhood reported high levels of stress in their day-to-day lives and a general pattern of "social impoverishment." The high-risk neighborhood—one in which neighbors do not help each other, in which there is suspicion about contact between parents and children, and in which the norms and behavior increase family weakness—was described in the following terms by professionals working in it:

> That's one of our heaviest caseloads, both as number of families and as problems within each family. Alcoholism is quite a big problem. There are mental health problems, a very high death rate, a high birthrate to unmarried mothers, poor nutrition. Medical knowledge is only of emergency care. Many of the girls are early school dropouts [Visiting nurse].

> There are probably a significant number of five- to eight-year-olds at school who got themselves up this morning. They may or may not have been at their own homes, but they got themselves to school and took care of their needs [Elementary school principal].

> We have the least amount of input from them compared to other centers. . . . We're not as close to that neighborhood. Nobody is [Director of community center].

> The women sometimes form a buddy system, but there is not a lot of interlinking between them. . . .They don't know very many people. They don't associate very much. They don't have a lot of family supports. They may be on bad terms with the family. This area is sometimes a hide-out for them. . . .There are a lot of teenage girls with their babies who want to get away from their families downtown [Visiting nurse] [Garbarino & Sherman, 1980, pp. 196–197].

When interviewed, mothers in the low-risk neighborhood rated their area as more than twice as supportive a place to rear children as did mothers in the high-risk neighborhood. What is more, they rated their children as significantly easier to care for in the low-risk neighborhood.

Creating and maintaining strong neighborhoods for families is one of the principal challenges facing efforts to design a sustainable society. All the elements of quantitative growth work against neighborhoods. Mobility is a threat, of course. Motorized transportation permits bedroom communities and undermines walking communities, which works against neighborhoods. Restrictive rezoning to produce residential ghettos also works against neighborhoods because a functioning neighborhood requires some commercial activity. Within cities, strong neighborhoods resemble strong small towns. The important question is whether or not the seemingly inexorable trends toward the destruction of neighborhoods will be permitted to continue. The answer will come in the public decisions concerning rezoning and mass transportation. The quality of life for children is determined in large part by progress in the life of the community.

Supporting community life

The design and delivery of human services, the nature of adult work, and the structure and function of educational institutions all have a significant effect on community life and the quality of life for children. Child services are delivered in a variety of ways and in different settings (see Chapter 1). How well can these programs and services be integrated into formal support systems and balanced with the informal "private-enterprise system" of human services that offers most help on a day-to-day basis? Models for integrating formal and informal support systems are being developed, and in fact, are in place in some communities (Garbarino & Stocking, 1980).

In the world of work, the issue is whether or not conflicts between the roles of parent and worker can be resolved in the favor of the former. The entrance of large numbers of mothers of young children into the workforce has produced a keen awareness of the need to rationalize the relationship between work and home, one that has not been resolved satisfactorily despite the fact that the Social Security Act provides single working mothers with child support. Providing adequate and developmentally enhancing day care for preschool children is another unresolved and highly charged issue. How this issue is resolved will have a bearing on the quality of life for children and, in fact, on the quality of children for life. When the world of work forces an adult (male *or* female) to choose between being a good parent and a good worker, children suffer, and ultimately their future is impoverished. A design for a sustainable society must address the need to establish norms about the world of work that will reduce its intrusion into family life. Freud observed that a well-adjusted person is distinguished by his (or her) ability to work *and* to love. Similarly, a high-quality society will arrange itself so that people can do both and do justice to both— assuming, of course, that equal opportunity for employment exists across the classes.

Besides play, by and large, children's work is school work. Research on school size suggests that large schools (enrollments greater than 600 in Grades 9 to 12) tend to become psychologically unsustainable (Garbarino, 1980a), creating depersonalization and a reduction of the effective social pluralism of the child's experience. Large schools tend to discourage participation, create elitism, encourage staff inflexibility, and most insidiously, alienate those students who are already academically marginal. Historical data on school size chronicle the decline of quality of life for children in their primary institutional setting. In this area, perhaps more than any other, there

Children's unsupervised activities sometimes lead to high-risk situations. Community support systems can help to lessen the dangers to children and to society as a whole.

has been an unthinking policy of growth that undermines and destroys socially desirable settings (small schools) on the basis of a warped sense of quantitative progress and use of economic models. The notion that big schools mean power and opportunity directly parallels the notion that an unlimited policy of growth means progress. The data suggest that a reverse of the 30-year trend toward large schools is possible. Just as escalating energy costs have given pragmatic impetus to "walking neighborhoods," these same forces will increasingly demonstrate the cost-effectiveness of small schools. Such schools can now be technology-intensive to permit an academically rich *and* character-building social environment.

All three areas—family, neighborhood, and the life of the community—are always in flux. Economic and demographic conditions may shift the direction of their influence, sometimes favoring supportive environments, sometimes undermining them. The constant issue is the stance taken by social policy.

A recent cross-national survey of public policy and public services for families (Kahn & Kamerman, 1975) concluded that the rhetoric in the United States proclaims the value and sanctity of children in family life; reality is something else. The United States provides nowhere near as many child-care services or cash benefits to protect child and family life as the European countries do. Former director of the Office of Child Development Edward Zigler (1976) echoes Kamerman and Kahn's judgment when he says "We think we care more than our actions would say" (p. 39).

In any case, public debate in the future must take into account the needs of children (and therefore their parents) in making decisions. For example, will corporate profit take precedence over the need of workers to have adequate time to care for their children? The suitability of policies regarding child care will be revealed not in grand pronouncements or even in major legislation, but in the day-to-day decisions that affect and shape the lives of families. This standard can be applied to the ideology of growth.

The relevance of children's issues to the growth policy debate

Social impoverishment—the denuding of those relationships that function as support systems providing nurturance and feedback—is a correlate of growth defined by quantitative product irrespective of psychological and social quality. If society permits the social impoverishment of parents' lives, it undermines the quality of life for children, and thus in effect, the quality of the future. Is it wise to keep destroying the social integrity of families by increasing the demographic and social homogeneity of neighborhoods, devaluing parenthood, overemphasizing the importance of material productivity rather than social responsibility as a criterion for personal value, increasing the instrumentality of social relations, divorcing work and home, and promoting large schools for their efficiency as mass producers? If the answers are no, then the growth-policy debate must come to terms with the possibility that conventional thinking (the quantitative-product orientation) is not socially helpful.

It is a great temptation to propose a nostalgic "good-old-days" solution, but for a modern rendering of traditional sources of social pluralism to succeed, a restatement of the developmental necessities of life is needed. As individual families struggle with this issue, institutions can make a vital contribution: they will decide how successful families are. If institutions are dominated by a quantitative orientation to growth, then families will be swimming against the tide. The future is a public-policy issue. Productive action is possible in at least four areas. These topics reflect an intermingling of action and ideology, of cause and effect, of shaping events and shaping minds. To design a sustainable society, progress must be made on each of the following fronts.

1. *National support for the family-impact analysis concept.* The scientific basis for evaluating the impact of change—particularly economic growth—is rudimentary. Needed is a kind of "social currency" that can be used to compute the costs and benefits to families of various policies and decisions. Investment in this area of research and development is a high-priority item on the agenda for would-be designers of a sustainable society (Johnson, 1978). (This chapter unfortunately reflects this lack of empirical evidence.)

2. *Neighborhoods as units for analysis and planning.* Local governments and corporate leaders need to become aware of the importance of thinking about neighborhoods—not simply individuals and communities—as units of analysis. Data-collection policies of the U.S. Census Bureau are already being changed to reflect this orientation, and in many ways adequate data are a precondition for intelligent policy. Growth policies must consider how existing neighborhoods may be affected as well as how new residential areas could be developed (National Commission on Neighborhoods, 1979). Unless planning and zoning decisions reflect such considerations, neighborhoods are doomed to be eroded and new developments will not occur.

3. *Public education.* Public opinion polls show support for the primacy of nonmaterial family-related "payoffs" (see Harris, 1978). The public supports family life and recognizes that family stability is a precondition for meaningful existence. There is a pressing need for public articulation of how personal and institutional decisions can tap these resources and respect the values they reflect. More research to investigate the relationship between home and work is needed so that the conflict between them can be resolved.

4. *Linking professionals and natural helping networks.* Natural helping networks provide effective human services as well as substantial psychological payoffs. Sustaining society socially requires a reduction in the specialization of formalized institutions. Also to be avoided are accountability evaluations that waste money and are used for political gain. Instead, greater sharing of helping functions among professionals and lay people should be encouraged (Garbarino & Stocking, 1980).

Conclusion

Children and their rearing are labor intensive, not energy intensive. A sustainable society, one that is ecologically sound, should therefore focus on children. Children benefit from a "small-is-beautiful" philosophy. Producing smaller schools can focus efforts to enhance the psychological and social circumstances of childhood, thus enriching the quality of human life generally. Directing institutional practice and policy toward families is imperative. This includes everything from giving priority to families in travel logistics to offering tax incentives for responsible parenthood. Children and their activities are appealing ways to shift recreational activities away from energy-intensive and materialistic consumption. Play is both developmentally important and socially enriching. Some people have lost sight of this in their efforts to make children's play more professional—witness the proliferation of costly and equipment-intensive sports. Family hikes and other "primitive" activities provide ecologically sound, psychologically satisfying, and developmentally enhancing alternatives to materialistic, energy-intensive activities. As pointed out earlier, because the only thing of real value adults have to offer children is their time and interest, it is a pleasant coincidence that such an investment is also a precondition for an ecologically sound and sustainable future society.

Summary

Historically, the quality of a society's human life in the future is inseparably linked to the well-being of its children today. Therefore, the well-being of children is the principal challenge faced by a modern society, particularly one that faces continuing economic pressures and has a history of developing products with little concern of what and whom they are for. Children and their needs provide a "labor-intensive" anchoring point for adult relationships and are intrinsically satisfying when set within a social context rich in enduring interpersonal relationships. The principal threats to the quality of social life are trends toward universalist rather than particularist systems for evaluating individuals, and materialist rather than social criteria for evaluating productivity. Large schools and socially isolated families, both of which undermine child development, are the contexts in which these two trends find their most dangerous expression. A sustainable society requires a profamily orientation to meet the needs of children and provide for the fundamental psychic needs of adults. A variety of implications for individual action and social planning are derived from this premise. Socially strong neighborhoods should be preserved and restored. School size should be reduced, thus rejecting the application of big business and management—a model long supported. And "family-impact analysis" should be used as a basis for guiding decisions in the public and private sectors.

4

Dynamics of Intervention: Toward Prevention

Chapter overview

The dynamics of intervention can best be understood by illustrating and analyzing intervention as a decision process. This chapter examines the factors that instigate intervention and the types, approaches, strategies, and techniques used. The chapter focuses on juvenile misbehavior, to demonstrate the multifaceted complexity of intervening in the lives of children and their families.

Issues to consider

How do attitudes, perceptions, and resources influence the intervention process?

How can interventions be classified, and what assumptions underlie them?

What are abnormal attributes, and what are the implications of their use in intervention?

What are the special characteristics of families who have juvenile children who misbehave?

What is the conceptual difference between "substantive justice" and "legal justice," and how does this difference influence the treatment of juveniles?

Why does society's attitude of parental authority and training for autonomy create problems for the treatment of juveniles?

What impact does the juvenile court have on families?

How successful is the juvenile court in correcting and preventing juvenile misbehavior?

What alternative intervention strategies exist to help families and retard juvenile misbehavior?

What should be the future thrust of intervention efforts?

Introduction

A study of the dynamics of intervention raises certain questions: Is the U.S. social services system equitable? Does the government neglect certain families? How can governmental services offer protection and nurturance to all who need them? Are needed services provided, for example, to families who have one parent, or a retarded child, or both parents working? Do minority families have equal access to such services? Should all families contribute to the government? As change in family forms escalates and as the number of children in society declines, the government is exploring ways it can "accommodate to the changing needs of families in order to help them adapt, cope, and rear children without undue burden" (Task Panel Reports III, 1978, p. 20).

The following general discussion of intervention decisions in terms of instigating factors, approaches, types, and strategies and techniques underscores the need for diversity urged earlier. Attentiveness to the implications of using labels also underscores this need. A case illustration can show how complex intervention is. The example chosen—the treatment of juveniles who are said to misbehave— demonstrates the use and consequences of labels, indicates the problems of interpretation within the American societal value and legal structures, and suggests the implications of intervention for families and child services in the future.

Intervention as a decision process

Historically, certain groups have been sanctioned to pass judgment on people and to try to change people's behavior and attitudes. In societies in which theological explanations of people have dominated, priests, shamans, or even witch doctors have helped people with personal problems and attempted to rectify behavioral deviations. In Western societies in the past, such disorders were often assumed to be manifestations of disturbances of the nervous system or biological structures. This attitude placed the major responsibility for dealing with problems on physicians, who searched for structural causes of "mental diseases" to impose "cures."

Only in the last three decades has the view been challenged that biological structures account for behavioral problems and represent mental illnesses. Alternative models of developmental dysfunctions (see Chapter 9), care-giving problems (see Chapters 5, 8, and 10), and family disturbances (see Chapter 7) have been developed based on scientific theory and empirical research. Consistent with this trend has been the belief that a wide array of specialists can promote change. This belief recently has evolved still further to include the idea that lay people also can promote change. This vastly expanded use of professionals, paraprofessionals, parents, and volunteers to intervene throughout life spans endorses the belief dramatically evolving lives and contexts can be mediated.

On the surface, intervention sounds both proper and potent. Why not intervene in the lives of people to help them? But this raises other questions. Should interventions be available to children only when their parents decide to seek or allow help? What role should the government have in decisions to intervene in the lives of families and children? How should interventions be evaluated?

Answers to these questions can be either simple or complex. For example, a mother ties her 6-year-old daughter to her bed, gags her, and says,

> "You filthy pig. I don't know what to do with a child like you. You're big enough not to wet your bed." A familiar smell of urine fills the room. The child's eyes are transfixed on some invisible point on the ceiling. "Oh! Why can't they [the welfare agency] just take you?" she stammers. "If they don't, I don't know what will happen to you next" [Author's files].

No doubt you are upset about the mother's behavior, annoyed with the agency for not removing the little girl, and perplexed as to why a 6-year-old would be bedwetting. In order to answer the question of how to intervene in this situation, many influential factors must be considered.

Instigating factors

Any helping process must clarify current attitudes and identify alternative courses of action to solve perceived problems. No helping process can be conducted without applying and influencing attitudes. Other factors—such as, severity of the problem and available resources—are also influenced by attitudes and affect the helping process.

Attitudes. Attitudes can be defined as "a combination of feelings and beliefs which result in a predisposition to respond favorably or unfavorably towards particular persons, groups, ideas, events, or objects" (Johnson & Matross, 1975, p. 52). Thus, attitudes consist of cognitive and affective components—information and an emotional response—that vary among individuals and groups.

Attitudes are purposeful because they help a person anticipate and cope with events by making certain reactions automatic. Many of us, for example, hold opinions about child abuse, the removal of a child from biological parents for foster-care placement, alternative child-care arrangement, and adoption. Likewise we form attitudes about children's roles and rights in society, the meaning of "good" parenting, and the role of the government in our lives. These attitudes can be manifested verbally or behaviorally, contemplated introspectively. Attitudes can facilitate or frustrate life. If attitudes promote environmental interactions that enhance growth and adaptation, or maintain levels of functioning, then they are useful and appropriate. However, if attitudes create more pain, trouble, and problems, then they are inappropriate.

An attempt to change people's attitudes often is included in attempts to alter people's behavior. We all engage in this process—trying to influence or being influenced—at some time or another. The following two examples show how all of us can be affected by others in our daily lives.

A liberal white middle-class student prides himself in participating in civil rights activities. He returns to school to find his roommate is a first-year lower-class Hispanic who keeps different hours and has different friends. They cannot even communicate well because neither knows each other's language well enough. The student becomes increasingly hostile toward his roommate and experiences guilt about mistreating someone who has been less advantaged. He chats with friends, his advisor, a counselor, and even a stranger he meets on a bus. Each person tries to influence his attitudes toward his roommate, Hispanics, and civil rights.

Or consider the situation of a 16-year-old girl whose friends and boyfriend convince her that she is in love. She agrees to engage in sexual relations, becomes pregnant, and must decide to have or to abort the child. She seeks consultation from her parents, her friends, her minister, her physician, and a counselor. Each person tries to influence her attitudes toward child bearing or abortion.

Changes in attitudes, however, do not necessarily mean behavior will change. Indeed, attitudes and behavior may be unrelated because of the multiplicity of motives, skills, and resources that also affect behavior. Johnson and Matross (1975) support this point:

> A person's verbal, intellectual, and social skills may affect how attitudes are expressed in behavior; a person may be against war and still vote for a prowar politician because he cannot understand the varied references the politician makes to his position on war; or a person may want to be friendly with another person, but not have the skills to express friendliness [p. 53].

Researchers (such as Mischel, 1968) have demonstrated that behavioral responses are influenced more by situations than attitudes. To explain behavior, we must ask, "What is the context? Who is present? What normative behaviors are expected? What alternative behaviors are available? And what are the consequences of certain behaviors?" A parent who has severe difficulty interacting with and rearing a dysfunctional child and who feels very guilty about the problem may behave quite competently when a special education teacher is present. Behavior, therefore, has many determinants, of which attitudes are one.

Professionals receive training to develop their own attitudinal and behavioral skills and to apply these skills. Interventions have become formalized in today's society, although each member is influenced by and influences others. Chapter 12 examines the attributes of professionals and their role in society. Professionals are the

Family forms such as single parenting and foster-care situations are changing at increasing rates, which challenges our child-service system and our attitudes.

major resource on which people rely to perceive their problems, determine intervention strategies and techniques, and help them overcome or cope with difficulties.

Perceived severity of the problem.   Adults may seek professional help when they are dissatisfied, cannot help themselves, or want change to occur. Intervention often involves other people or environmental factors. For example, a spouse may want a mate to participate in a drug counseling program, a person who has been in an accident may have to relearn how to walk and talk, or a child may be reported to have stolen something and his or her parents are required to appear in juvenile court. Adults assess not only their own intervention needs but also their children's needs, except in cases where parents are found incompetent or where law dictates policy (for example, public school attendance). (Children's rights are discussed in Chapter 11.)

Often intervention represents not a deliberate well-reasoned choice but a response to a crisis situation. Caplan (1964) defines crisis as "a short period of psychological disequilibrium in a person who confronts a hazardous circumstance that for him constitutes an important problem that he can for the time being neither escape nor solve with his customary problem-solving resources" (p. 18). Crises in families stem from both external and internal factors. For example, difficulties in holding a job, completing an education, or making friends may represent external influences. Internal triggers could be a fight with a mate, the crying of a baby, or an adolescent who does not listen. Other variables, also contribute to crises, such as health, stress, intelligence, and personality. For example, parents need to have both knowledge and good judgment to care for children. If they lack either ability, and if other factors such as poor health, emotional difficulty, or feelings of community isolation are present, a variety of crises can result, from unemployment to child abuse (Kempe & Kempe, 1978).

Professionals also perceive people and situations, then determine ways to mediate. As the discussion of treating juvenile misbehavior later in this chapter demonstrates, parents' and practitioners' perceptions often vary: parents may seek court intervention to solve a problem that professionals feel should be handled at home, with training and education..

Resources. Sometimes parents or service providers do not have the necessary resources to make the best or any intervention choice. For instance, a working mother places her 2-year-old in the care of a neighbor who may or may not meet the child's needs. Or an adoption agency may not have a large enough staff to explore the range of placements available for a child. Or a foster agency may spend a greater amount of time with initial placements than with replacements, because of an attitude that every child should at least have a chance to experience permanence.

The issue of resources goes beyond an individual level to encompass families, communities, and state and federal agencies. Often resources are interpreted to mean money, because it can be used to support people, materials, and facilities. Many factors influence the allocation of resources: societal values, public attitudes, legislation, and the political/economic climate. More specifically, the effectiveness of intervention programs or the establishment of strong support for certain programs often dictates whether programs will be initiated or continued. A wealth of evaluation procedures are used to determine intervention effectiveness (see Chapter 13) and professional accountability (see Chapter 12). Concern about resources is critical for the establishment and implementation of social policy for children and families (see Chapter 11). Thus, in making intervention choices for children, parents, professionals, and the citizenry need to coordinate their efforts (see Chapter 14). Intervention is no longer just a unilateral process between client and professional where service providers isolate themselves and set forth systematic objectives for solving particular problems for certain people. Intervention is no longer an informal process of getting service from others. Rather, the concept of intervention has grown into a complex, multifaceted formal process that must accommodate the demands of our rapidly advancing, technological, pluralistic, democratic society.

Approaches to intervention

Interventionists differ in their philosophies and attitudes about factors that account for problems. Some believe difficulties arise from biological variations among people, others, that social factors are the relevant determinants. Most believe in some combination, however, so caution is warranted in interpreting these approaches as ends of a continuum.

Structural approach. Traditional interventionists try to unravel the mysteries of human behavior by focusing on the analogy between physical and mental illness. Any personally disruptive, emotionally unpleasant, or socially unacceptable behavior is labeled a symptom and is accounted for by a person's past or hereditary makeup. This attitude dominated the legislative evolution of child-services (see Chapter 2).

Learning approach. Other interventionists assume that human activities and attitudes are learned. A useful definition of learning is "the process by which an activity originates or is changed through reacting to an encountered situation, provided that the characteristics of the change in activity cannot be explained on the basis of native response tendencies, maturation, or temporary states of the organism (e.g., fatigue, drugs, etc.)" (Hilgard & Bower, 1966. p. 2). This definition suggests that learning-oriented professionals are concerned with (1) the individual/environment relationship, (2) how behavior originates and changes as a result of individual/environment interactions, (3) the necessity for specifying reactions or observable

behavior, (4) the necessity for measuring aspects of situations, and (5) the
for a reliable and valid system for detecting change (for example, see G
Deutsch, 1977; Hultsch & Deutsch, 1981; Levy, 1970; see also Chapters 6 and 13).

When practitioners begin with the propositions that behavior, adaptive or
maladaptive, must be learned and that the proper study of behavior is the study of
relationships, they do not deal with behavior in isolation. Instead, they seek to
increase or establish desired responses, eliminate undesirable behaviors, foster the
generalization of newly acquired behaviors, and promote the maintenance of such
behaviors. This perspective and focus on processes of intervention programs are
supported throughout this book.

Types of intervention

The intervention process is concerned with determining how people are
functioning and how this functioning can be improved, with timing and sequencing of
procedures to maximize effectiveness, and evaluating to reduce failures and
perpetuate successful efforts. Four broad categories—correction, maintenance,
prevention, and optimization—can be used to describe types of intervention.
Although each will be examined separately, in actuality they are often used together.
For example, child-abuse programs attempt to correct the abusive situation, maintain
effective personal interactions among family members, prevent further abuses, and
optimize the development of the individuals involved.

Correction.   To correct a behavior or situation, intervention takes the form of
remediation (modifications to return an individual or situation to normalcy) or
rehabilitation (modifications to help the person or situation regain as much normalcy
as possible). The forms differ on two major dimensions: (1) *time*, remediation being a
quicker process than rehabilitation and (2) *functional level*, returning to "normal"
being associated with remediation, approximating normalcy with rehabilitation. The
assumption is that when a needed correction is unattended for too long a completely
"normal" state cannot be restored. A child without a proper diet, for example,
becomes malnourished, cannot resist disease, and may suffer brain damage. A child
who suffers prolonged abuse may have numerous physical problems, many of which
can be mended but that may persist or leave permanent damage.

Proper diagnosis, while critical for corrective intervention to be successful,
fosters a use of labels and perpetuates the concept of abnormalcy, which produces
other problems. The child who needs remedial reading becomes "the child who had
remedial reading." The drug abuser becomes the "ex-junky." Like a Scarlet Letter, an
"ex-" gets affixed to what deviates from a norm—once an adopted child always an
adopted child. (This discussion of labeling is continued later in this chapter.)

Maintenance.   Activities that support certain standards—legal, moral, or
social—are maintenance interventions. The U.S. legal system illustrates this type of
intervention because it seeks to maintain order. Historically, health, housing, income
supports, and education have received governmental support. The social context
always influences which areas will be maintained at what level of functioning for
which groups of people. As sociopolitical and economic factors alter, so too do these
forms of intervention (see Chapter 2).

Prevention.   Preventive strategies are designed to anticipate and influence
change in the developmental course of individuals and families. Effective preventive
intervention requires knowledge of the relationship among past, present, and future

factors. A goal or outcome must be specified, and the important antecedent or contributing factors must be identified. Timing becomes crucial, not only in terms of knowing when to do what for how long, as with the other interventions discussed, but also in terms of knowing how to sequence factors that influence a particular outcome. For example, immunization programs prevent illness and disease. Parent-training programs attempt to prevent child-rearing problems (see Chapter 10). Greater efforts are needed to identify specific goals, sequence activities, and determine the optimal duration of programs.

Optimization. Arranging conditions to maximize the positive constructive development of individuals and families is called optimization intervention. Such strategies are used to help people improve their own lives. For example, preschool programs are designed to help children acquire necessary skills and experiences for academic success. Interpersonal-skill training teaches people how to establish and maintain satisfying relationships. And programs for dysfunctional children try to capitalize on the children's functional abilities. Most optimization intervention consists of some form of education that is available during certain times in the individual's life span.

Selecting strategies and techniques

The type of intervention used depends on the target—a child, parent/child dyad, or family—and on what behavior or situation is involved. Child-service providers use either individual or group strategies. Individual-oriented approaches emphasize that problems are personal and that one-to-one interaction helps to maintain confidentiality. This form of intervention is often taken to correct specific behavioral or psychological problems such as depression, phobias, or aggressive acts.

Group approaches introduce more complexity. First, groups can be naturally or artificially constituted. For example, existing groups, families, or school classes of children may receive interventions. Or voluntary mutual-help groups can be constructed around certain criteria for specific purposes (for example, to help abusive families, parents, or children or to assist parents in their understanding of nutritional education).

Almost any newspaper or bulletin board provides evidence that groups as a medium for changing people are "in." About 5 million Americans have participated in groups aimed at personal growth or change at one time or another. Approximately 3 million others belong to self-help groups, and tens of thousands are engaged in group psychotherapy (Lieberman, 1975). Confrontation therapy, consciousness raising, encounter, Gestalt, marathon, Transactional Analysis—this litany of labels identifies just a few of the groups that currently abound.

Group intervention is not new. In the early 1900s, Joseph Pratt (1907) held classes for tubercular patients; Trigant Burrow (1927) used a group context to identify behavioral disorders and coined the term "group analysis," and Jacob Moreno (1953) developed psychodrama, which he used in group psychotherapy. These efforts, however, were isolated, and pragmatic concerns predominated. There was little interest in exploring the conceptual frameworks for using groups until after World War II. Then individuals began to shift from supporting the traditional intervention approach to endorsing the learning approach to problems or to a social rather than intrapsychic explanation of difficulties. Many practitioners feel this shift occurred because of the number of problems experienced by returning soldiers, resulting in "the jump from a dyad (a two-person interaction) to multi-person treatment situations an easy transition" (Lieberman, 1975, p. 437).

Why are groups so effective? Jerome Frank (1961) has extensively discussed the importance of hope as a factor for producing change in groups. Hope really means that a person believes he or she can change and can be responsible for such change. Group situations seem to encourage hope. Members see others succeed and hear others tell how they conquered problems.

Professional recognition that children seem to benefit most from a group strategy has stimulated a trend toward including the entire family as the intervention target. This approach, rather than focusing blame on any one family member, considers group dynamics to be the cause of the problem. Thus, as members learn to communicate, they start to believe that change is possible—that hope exists.

Whether a child-service worker employs a group strategy or a one-to-one approach, many intervention techniques are possible; for example, attitude modification, role playing, operant methods, fear reduction, aversion methods, self-management, and relationship enhancement. It is beyond the scope of this book to delineate all intervention techniques, but one fundamental area—interpersonal skills—deserves special emphasis.

Truax and Carkhuff (1967) have identified three rather distinctive interpersonal skills for enhancing the interaction of professionals and lay persons. Although these skills were advanced more than 20 years ago, they are still promoted today (for example, see Dugger, 1975; Kanfer & Goldstein, 1975; Mearig & Associates, 1978). The skills are genuineness, accurate empathy, and nonpossessive warmth. Table 4–1 summarizes how each is rated.

A genuine person is one who does not use roles or a professional facade in interactions. His or her personal feelings are not denied, but the other person (for example, a client or a co-worker) is encouraged to reveal him- or herself. Thus, both defensiveness and phoniness are absent.

Accurate empathy means being able to see and understand the other person's perspective. This understanding must be communicated in language, tone, and gesture to fit the other individual's mood. Accurate empathy lets the person feel accepted and supported, which fosters a more open exchange.

Nonpossessive warmth is acceptance without being judgmental or coercive. An unconditional positive regard is extended to the other person in both physical and nonphysical cues.

Regardless of what other techniques (such as interviewing, counseling, or psychotherapy) are employed, well-developed interpersonal skills help the professional in his or her role as an intervener. Society is placing a greater premium than in the past on these skills as factors for producing social change because more and more people are experiencing greater stresses and must make many more choices during their lives than in the past.

Proliferating labels

Many human-care services have been developed around an array of labels—retardation, mental illness, disadvantaged, deprived, autistic, emotionally disturbed, abused, and so on—that isolate people as abnormal, even if their condition is temporary (for example, people who are unemployed or institutionalized). Labeling takes place when behaviors or attributes occur too often or not enough in comparison

TABLE 4-1 Summary of interpersonal skills scales

Scale A   Genuineness

1	2	3	4	5

1. Clearly defensive; evidence of discrepancy between verbal responses and inner feelings.
2. Responds appropriately but in a professional manner rather than person to person. Gives the impression that his responses are made because they sound good rather than because they express what he feels.
3. Implicitly defensive, although little explicit evidence.
4. No evidence of facade or defensiveness.
5. Open to expression of feelings. Verbalization matches inner experiences. Accepts and recognizes contradictory feelings.

Scale B   Accurate empathy

1	2	3	4	5	6	7	8	9

1. Inaccurate responses to obvious feelings.
2. Slight accuracy in response to obvious feelings. Ignores deeper feelings.
3. Some response to obvious feelings or some concern with deeper feelings but inaccurate with regard to what feelings are.
4. Often accurate with obvious feelings; fairly often accurate with deep feelings, although spotted by inaccurate probing.
5. Always accurate toward obvious feelings; frequently accurate with deeper feelings, although occasionally misinterpreting them.
6. Always accurate toward obvious feelings; frequently accurate toward content but not toward intensity of deeper feelings.
7. Always accurate toward obvious feelings; frequently accurate with deeper feelings but occasionally misses in regard to depth. May go too far in direction of depth.
8. Always accurate toward obvious feelings; almost always accurate with deeper feelings, both in content and in intensity. May occasionally hesitate or err but corrects quickly and accurately
9. Always accurate toward obvious feelings and toward deep feelings, both in content and in intensity.

Scale C   Nonpossessive warmth

1	2	3	4	5

1. Actively offers advice or clearly shows negative regard.
2. Responds mechanically or shows passivity that communicates almost total lack of regard.
3. Indicates positive caring but in a semipossessive way. Sees himself as responsible for other person.
4. Clearly communicates a deep interest in and concern for other person's welfare. Other person is given freedom to be himself and to be liked for himself. Helper sees himself as responsible *to* other person.
5. Warmth without restriction. Shows deep respect and caring for other person, no matter how other person chooses to behave.

to societal norms or to one's own experiences or expectations. For example, a 3-year-old child who isn't talking as much as an older sibling did at that age may be called "quiet," "slow," or "dumb." Labels also are applied when behaviors or personal characteristics do not seem typical for a particular age and gender. A little girl 6 years old is not supposed to beat up children who pick on her; however, a little boy of the same age is encouraged—even taught—to fight for what is right. Children who deviate from such expectations may be called "tomboys" or "sissies."

Labeling places professionals in the role of enforcing cultural proscriptions about characteristics, behaviors, physical conditions, and states of being. According to Goffman (1963), the label *abnormal* has been sanctioned for three categories of attributes: (1) abomination of the body (physical deformities, disabilities, and chronic conditions), (2) blemishes of character (behaviors that deviate from social norms), and (3) physically or culturally inheritable characteristics (sex, race, religion, and nationality).

Ideals or expectations for optimal development and performance also exist. Parents are supposed to protect and nurture children, and teachers along with other professionals are supposed to assist in that process. Individuals are supposed to want to live in some meaningful satisfying way. These norms, however, can be violated if behavior is either maladaptive or maladjusted. A child who refuses to eat or sleep displays maladaptive behavior because his or her survival is jeopardized. A child who is antagonistic toward parents or peers demonstrates maladjustment. Thus, maladaptive behavior concerns behavior that hampers survival, while maladjusted behavior concerns behavior that hurts relationships.

If people are thought to deviate from a norm because of social factors, intervention often results. But when genetic characteristics are considered to account for these discrepancies, interventions often are not attempted. As recently as the close of the decade of the 1970s, the case was made that "some 20 million Americans suffer from mental or emotional disturbances, but fewer than one-third received help. The statistics show that there are 14 million persons in need of assistance who are not receiving service. The overwhelming proportion of this group is found among the minorities, women, and physically handicapped" (Task Panel Reports III, 1978, p. 231).

Although professionals may not consider these people either abnormal or ineligible for help, people categorized in such ways may be too embarrassed by the label to seek assistance. Regardless of why large segments of the population are not being served, the dilemma remains: people who need help are not receiving it. Evidence from all age groups suggests that labeling, whether positive (such as "precocious child") or negative (such as "juvenile delinquent") often becomes a self-fulfilling prophecy that is difficult, if not impossible, to reverse (Katz, 1979).

Most professionals use labels under certain conditions and for appropriate reasons. If they are confident of their diagnosis, they apply a label to a client's attribute or behavior. In addition, to the degree they feel a behavior is obtrusive (generalizing across situations or jeopardizing the adjustment or adaptation of the child) they will use labels. Often the strongest labels are applied when professionals feel parents are responsible for the problem, perhaps to impress on parents their ignorance or abuse so they will begin to modify their behaviors quickly. But labels can produce fear and guilt in parents, thus preventing them from obtaining help. Some parents fear that a label could cause them to lose their children; others are concerned about the intrusion into their family; still others become fearful because of their ignorance of what the label implies.

To illustrate the importance of how fear may not only delay intervention but also make it impossible, consider the following account:

> Ann, a 20-year-old mother of four children, lived in a small room that was unheated. There was no running water or electricity. The floor was made of dirt, with a firepit located in the middle. Her children, aged 5, 3, and 2 years, and 6 months, were kept in a playpen with boards placed across the top so they could not stand. Each child was taken out periodically to eat, to be taken to the outhouse, or to have diapers changed. The older children were not using language to communicate. They also had extremely long toenails and fingernails, some of which had grown together. Ann's appearance was quite similar. Her hair was matted, nails broken, clothing torn and soiled. Ann and her children were thin and pale, and suffered from some form of respiratory congestion.

The caseworker said that Ann qualified for food stamps and welfare and she would do what was necessary to see that Ann would receive them. She informed Ann that she would return next week. The following week the caseworker returned with her supervisor and told Ann that she would have three months to correct the situation of "child neglect." She would have to be a "better" mother or else her children would be taken away. They said someone would be returning each week to see how she was doing. One week later, the caseworker returned to find that Ann and her children were gone. Contacts were made in the area, and no one knew the whereabouts of Ann. The agency persisted in their efforts for several months, but the case was finally dropped [Author's files].

In their attempt to be helpful, the professionals seemed to frighten Ann so greatly that she took her children and left. After weeks of checking and chatting with her neighbors, it was discovered that Ann had no husband, had been raised in that shack herself, and was considered a good mother. As one older woman put it, "At least her kids don't die, like some others." Rather than "bulldozing" into the situation and telling Ann she should be a "better mother," the professionals should have explored the cultural environment and attempted to win Ann's trust. Perhaps these children will grow up "normal," but it is unlikely that we will ever know.

Professionals need to examine their motivations and values to decide whether reinforcing society's version of reality is appropriate or not. Will a label help or hurt? Rhodes (1978) says "[All] of us must individually go into ourselves and make our own decisions about how we serve and whom we serve" (p. 55). And, further, "[Perhaps] we might think of our clients in the existential reality of their social situation, as survivors, and our task as that of helping them to survive the pressures of their human condition" (p. 54).

The complexity of intervention

Intervening in the lives of people is more complex than simply a sequence of decisions on the part of involved parties. What roles do parents, professionals, and the government play in decisions to intervene in children's lives? What are the effects of different types of intervention in children's lives? These questions cannot be answered individually because each influences the others. To illustrate this idea and to portray the realistic difficulties associated with intervention, this section turns to a persistent problem in contemporary society—children's misbehavior.

Attitudes and perceptions of juvenile misbehavior

The Twentieth-Century Fund Task Force on Sentencing Policy toward Young Offenders (1978) reported that in an average year over the last decade 1.3 million minors appeared before the juvenile court. Of this group, on an average 60% were formally charged and 40% were identified as needing supervision. Although each state reports different average figures, to show the number of children involved per year and carried on the probation roster, let's consider some figures from New York City. Andrews and Cohn (1977) reported that on an average 13,000 new cases came before the court each year with approximately 10,000 carried on the books from one year to the next. (For a discussion of the high incidence of youth misbehavior, see Coffey, 1974; Cole, 1972; Eldefonso, 1973; Johnson, 1975; McLean, 1969; and Streib, 1978.)

As early as 1646, laws made it illegal for juveniles to engage in criminal acts. Traditionally, behaviors deemed illegal for minors were incorporated into definitions of delinquency. In the early 1960s, New York and California created a new

Many times a juvenile's misconduct is the result of relationship difficulties within the family.

jurisdictional category for non-criminal juvenile offenders (called PINS, or persons in need of supervision, in New York). Many other labels—child/minor/juvenile in need of supervision, (CHINS, MINS, or JINS); beyond-control child; ungovernable child; incorrigible child; unruly child; wayward child—apply from state to state. Such labels allow coercive judicial intervention in cases of juvenile conduct that would not be considered as misbehavior if engaged in by an adult.

Interpreting and treating juvenile misbehavior

Substantive or legal justice. The separation of the juvenile justice system from the criminal justice system emphasizes the distinction between substantive justice and legal justice, which has a controversial history in our society. Some social reformers have wanted fewer rules to guide children's conduct and have called for laws constructed to protect children from parental abuse. This approach relies on social norms and few laws and reflects an emphasis on substantive justice. Other social reformers have supported carefully delineated rules for minors, with misconduct behaviors and circumstances detailed by laws. This approach emphasizes legal justice. As a consequence of this debate, each state has the authority to determine laws directed toward juveniles. Many of these codes are too general or too specific about conduct and circumstances. The "unruly child" provision for the state of Ohio (Ohio Rev. Code 2151-022, Supp. 1975) illustrates the point by using in Items A–C such sweeping terms as "reasonable control" and "habitually truant," which create further difficulties in interpreting the law and judging juveniles. Do these terms mean the child should always be compliant, listening to all adults in authority? And what makes a behavior a habit—for example, skipping school once, twice, or three times? In contrast, the explanations offered in Items D, E, F, and G clearly define misconduct.

Legal codes that are specific facilitate the legal justice process. To illustrate, suppose a child has a history of running away from home. The state code is scrutinized to determine whether the child could be charged with a delinquent act—conduct that would be a crime if committed by an adult. Thus, the state's laws are consulted to find out (1) the state's position about the behavior, and (2) how an adult would be treated for such a behavior (in this case, the parallel adult behavior is desertion). In those states that support substantive justice for juveniles, however, statutory requirements are not even considered. The court does not focus on prior rules. A child is called *delinquent* only if this label helps promote personal welfare or the welfare of the state. This system is even more difficult to operate than one that has legal guidelines, because decisions solely rest on a judge's opinion.

Authority or autonomy.   Conceptually, the difficulty in developing laws for minors concerns the interpretation of parental authority and child autonomy. The conflict exemplifies points made earlier about attitudes and perceptions. The court wants to maintain parental dominance so children will learn and accept general cultural goals and conform to acceptable conduct. However, adult individuals are autonomous under the rules of law. Thus, proper child rearing must socialize children to exercise independent choice within societal norms. These two important concepts, authority and autonomy, pose problems in the majority of PINS cases (Katz & Teitelbaum, 1977). For example, the themes of authority and autonomy emerge as an area of conflict for the following PINS case:

> Johnny G., a somewhat retarded, chubby 14-year-old with a smile and a winning way, was brought into Juvenile Hall as being "beyond the control of his parents." This was his fourth time to the Hall for this "offense." Twice previously he had been placed on informal probation and had only recently completed his latest stint. Johnny's father is a 41-year-old truck driver and his mother is a 38-year-old housewife. There are no other children. The father says the problem is that Johnny sometimes steals from his parents, never goes to sleep at a decent hour, rarely gets up in time for school, and "just doesn't listen." . . . Both mother and father indicate that Johnny has no specific bedtime and that virtually [no] family rules are consistently enforced [Feeney, 1977, pp. 251–252].

In this case, as with many others, courts must exercise judicial power over children for noncriminal behavior because parents do not provide guidance. From the beginning of the juvenile justice system, many people have believed that child deviance is a result of parental error. When children are neglected or deviant, the government must provide care, as Judge Mack (1909) noted:

> The child who has begun to go wrong, who is incorrigible, who has broken a law or an ordinance, is to be taken in hand by the state . . . because either the unwillingness or inability of the natural parents to guide it toward good citizenship has compelled the intervention of public authorities [p. 107].

Because judges not only represented the authority of parents, but also were expected to parent the children coming before them, formal procedures in courts gave way to informal treatment of youth in which the state

> reaches out its arm in a kindly way and provides for the protection of its children from parental neglect or from vicious influences and surroundings, either by keeping watch over the child while in its natural home, or, where that seems impracticable by placing it in an institution designed for the purpose [*Commonwealth* v. *Fisher,* 213 Pa. 48, 62 Atl. 198, 1905].

Implications for families

Whether the court's activity as surrogate parent strengthened or weakened the American family is still debated today. Creation of a juvenile justice system has promoted the displacement of natural parents as caregivers of the young: parents have solicited court action for problems in their own behavior.

A spokesperson for the juvenile court movement, vanWaters (1925/1971) saw the society being saved by such intervention from the consequences of family decline. Some social reformers are less convinced of the rationale for judicial intervention in the lives of children and families. Teitelbaum and Harris (1977) feel the juvenile courts often have difficulty justifying their actions:

> Without convincing reason for concluding that incorrigibility reveals some abnormal development, without a theory that satisfactorily defines the kind of socialization expected, and without evaluation of the utility of judicial-correctional intervention in this area, courts are left with only the Fifth Commandment [Thou shalt honor thy father and thy mother] to justify and guide their actions [p. 35].

A complaint from an adult, usually a parent, initiates judicial involvement. In fact, in PINS cases the majority of complaints are made by a parent or another relative. Families that petition the court for PINS decisions tend to be poor, members of minority groups, or broken families. For example, in a 1972 sample of New York City PINS cases, Andrews and Cohn (1977) reported that the mean income of the families of the juveniles was less than $5000 and that more than half of the youths' families were on welfare. Racial minorities represented 85% of the group; about 80% of the youths came from broken homes. Andrews and Cohn concluded that such families do not have the resources available to help them cope with such family crises.

Can a coercive agency—a court—reduce this family tension? Parental reactions reveal that a public forum is disruptive. Children often humiliate parents in public by verbal hostility. Also, labeling of the child, either by the family or society, has negative consequences. For instance, evidence indicates that children labeled PINS are treated more severely than are delinquents by personnel such as intake officers and probation officers. Even after probation, youth report that their parents continue to label them with negative terms (Mahoney, 1977).

The observation by intake workers that PINS children are more troubled and come from homes with more difficult problems than other delinquents does not necessarily mean that PINS families are more pathological than other families. Rather, PINS families may just use the juvenile court more. Typically, in delinquency cases some adult other than a parent files a complaint. Once the complaint is filed this person does not have to deal with the situation any longer. Thus, PINS families may just be more visible because action is initiated by parents, which might make people's perceptions more negative.

Perhaps it is a positive step for parents to turn children over to a court. This approach may be the only and easiest way for children to divorce parents, as Mahoney (1977) notes:

> One of the most healthy and sensible things some adolescents can do is leave parents whose lives and relationships are confused, who are out of touch with reality, or who attempt to use the youths to meet their own emotional needs. Such youths need institutional support to move out, to obtain a "divorce" in some acceptable way from parents [pp. 173–174].

Implications for future intervention

Although numerous attitudes about the juvenile justice system could be presented, the main issue here is whether such intervention is effective. Does this type of intervention correct behavior? Does it prevent further negative conduct? To answer these questions, let us look at the sparse empirical data that exist.

In 1970 in Sacramento County, juveniles in violation of Section 601 of the California Juvenile Court Law were asked whether they wanted family therapy prior to court proceedings. It's interesting to note that of the almost 1000 cases only 36 petitions (PINS) were filed. These children and their families received family therapy. Therapists focused on family interaction (such as communication, decision making, and discipline techniques) rather than attributing the problem to the juvenile only, or solely to the parents. The problem was seen as a result of a system malfunction. The maximum number of sessions was five for each family, each session lasting between one and three hours. The counselors were available to families after these sessions, as well. All family members had to be present for each session.

Data were compared to a matched control group of PINS youths, and both groups were followed for the next year. Results indicate that, although about 50% of each group repeated violations, only 20% of the treatment group and 30% of the control group moved on to criminal offenses. Also, the cost per child to the probation department, which monitored both groups, was twice as high ($561) as the cost ($274) of treatment. The researchers argue that because of case overloads children were seen more frequently but for less time, which may explain the higher cost and even negative results of the control group (Baron & Feeney, 1972).

It appears that neither family therapy nor the judicial process was more effective in correcting misbehavior. However, the treatment group did perform fewer criminal acts than the control group. These results suggest that helping an entire family correct its interaction may indeed prevent an accused juvenile offender from criminal behavior. More research and greater efforts to expand and differentiate intervention strategies are needed to correct and prevent problem behaviors among juveniles in the context of their families.

Energies also should be directed toward identifying the specific group procedures that are effective for these families. Perhaps families with similar characteristics should form into groups so members gain support and receive challenges from similar others. Research (see Deutsch, 1975; Deutsch & Madle, 1975) on other variables such as empathic training and positive forms of social behavior suggests that similarity is crucial for people to feel comfortable in communications, promote concern and affective understanding, and develop alternative behavioral strategies that are generalized to home settings. This approach could foster the development of a new concept—families in need of service (FINS)—and produce many advantageous changes in the present jurisdictional system. Others argue for a voluntary group approach that would exclude professionals and would not only prove more effective than wardships and court-ordered commitment but also free resources for child-abuse and criminal cases (Gough, 1977).

Conclusion

Intervention is a complex process of making decisions that strives to produce change or to retain a status quo and involves lives at different levels of functioning and need. Essentially each of us is embroiled in the process by making decisions for ourselves and others or accepting others' decisions. Although often functioning at an informal level, people, other than professionals, intervening in lives is evolving into a more acceptable practice and viewed more positively by both professionals and laypersons.

With this prevailing attitude of the inclusion, not the exclusion, of others in the intervention process, we reexamined how the instigating factors—attitudes, perceived severity of the problem, and resources—influence specific types and strategies of intrusion into the lives of families that have juveniles who are supposedly unmanageable. The increase in incidence rates and the number of "unruly" children reflect a pervasive problem.

We have learned that labeling children as PINS can have negative consequences; that parents often initiate the process for the wrong reasons; and that a public forum is disruptive to the family system. Thus, corrective intervention is myopic and the emphasis on individual approaches over group approaches should be challenged. Considerations of other systems and programs of intervention can help in making effective applications and broadening individuals' perspectives in this area.

Perceptions and attitudes cause or can cure the matter. How should juveniles who misbehave be viewed? Where should blame be placed—on children, families, or society for perpetuating the negative stigmas and creating a service system that lacks family support? Perhaps we should not try to decide who is at fault but should instead devote intervention efforts toward the reorganization of resources to help families who live in increasingly stressful environments. The case rests. PINS can needle us or we can take action and apply what has been learned to other areas of intervention.

Summary

Intervention no longer is a unilateral helping process where service providers isolate themselves and set forth systematic objectives for solving particular problems for certain people. Intervention today is a multi-dimensional, complex, highly formalized process that must accommodate to the demands of today's rapidly advancing, technological, pluralistic, democratic society.

Changing intervention efforts from correction to prevention means changing prevailing attitudes about children and families. It means minor problems and severe crises can be avoided. Technology is on our side. Major strides have been made on numerous fronts. Empirical evidence mounts and glimmers with suggestions of effective approaches to avert rather than to correct. Our acceptance of individual and family diversity and pluralism may force continued efforts to develop a rich arsenal of alternative intervention types, strategies, and techniques to maintain optimal levels of functioning.

Interventions include correction and maintenance as well as prevention and optimization. Although they differ in their goals and sequencing, each type may alone constitute the intervention or be used in combination. Individual or group approaches are used with a wide variety of intervention techniques. In all approaches, however, interpersonal skills of genuineness, accurate empathy, and nonpossessiveness are highly valued by society and are critical for professional and laypersons alike.

Human-care services have developed around an array of labels that reflect diagnoses of (1) temporary abnormality, (2) atypical behavior or characteristics compared to the norm, and (3) maladaptive and maladjusted behavior. Three categories of attributes—abominations to the body, blemishes of character, and inheritable characteristics—have been socially sanctioned for using labels. Unfortunately, the third category is often used as an excuse for why intervention does not work or as a reason for not attempting intervention with large segments of the population. The use of labels often produces self-fulfilling prophecies for individuals. Professionals, especially those who use corrective intervention, need to be cautious with their use of labels because a negative stigma and genetic inferiority may be implied.

Codes that vary from state to state describe juvenile misbehavior and allow coercive judicial intervention among youth that is different from that applied to adults. Originally conceived as a form of substantive justice rather than legal justice, the juvenile justice system operates separately from the criminal justice system. Substantive justice is invoked when the welfare of the child and the safety of society are used to guide court rulings. When prior rules (existing statutes) are the focal point, decisions are based on legal justice. These two forms of justice contribute to both vague and specific use of terms to describe juvenile misbehavior. Legal justice relies on specifics, whereas substantive justice thrives on vagaries. Conceptually, the difficulty in establishing laws for minors also has reflected the courts' conflict between wanting to maintain parental authority while supporting the idea that child rearing should promote autonomy. Child deviance has been considered to be a result of parental error. Thus, judges have been asked to represent parental authority, and also to parent children directly, using informal court procedures to demonstrate their support.

Whether the juvenile court's activities strengthen or weaken the U.S. family is still debated today. However, the juvenile court system certainly does promote the displacement of natural parents as caregivers. Parents typically initiate the process by a complaint. Families seeking court action tend to be poor, members of minorities, and not intact. These families do not have the resources to help them cope with their children. The court is viewed as a solution to a crisis. Both parents and children report the court process as a negative experience. Some researchers believe it may serve as a vehicle for youth to obtain a "divorce" from unacceptable parents.

Few empirical studies have been conducted on the effectiveness of the juvenile court for correcting or preventing misbehavior, promoting family cohesion, or reducing family tensions. One study reported that family counseling was a more effective intervention technique than was the juvenile court process because fewer youth graduated to criminal offenses. However, the rates of repeated violations were about equal for those having undergone therapy and those on probation.

Further research is needed to determine the role group approaches could play with the juvenile justice system. Some individuals believe the judicial system should be revised to focus on the jurisdictional concept of family in need of service (FINS) rather than person in need of supervision (PINS). Others argue for a voluntary group approach to juvenile misbehavior, which would free court resources for cases of abuse and criminal misconduct.

We must apply other systems and approaches of intervention to broaden our perspective in this area concerning juvenile misbehavior as well as others. Group approaches and program accessibility have contributed to effective intervention efforts. We must network—form linkages within our child service system—so each area has the potential to benefit from another one. Isolated efforts, like a simplistic approach to intervention, must give way to cooperation and complexity.

SECTION **2**

Working with Children

The study of human development has always consisted of basic and applied research. Investigations of specific processes—perception, cognition, physical growth, and socialization—represent basic research efforts. Studies of human behavior and interactions at all levels—individual, family, community, and society—deal with the applied aspect of research efforts.

Some recent researchers (for example, Zigler & Muenchow, in press) assert that differences between basic and applied approaches are not that great. Zigler and Seitz (1980) find "a synergistic interplay between the worlds of the ivory tower and the real settings in which children spend their lives," contending that "society will benefit the most from social science when it represents a dialectic between basic and applied research" (p. 153). The purpose of this section is to present such a synergism or dialogue between basic and applied research that involves work with children, continuing to emphasize children in the context of family interactions and societal forces. Specific empirical evidence is presented along with intervention programs, strategies, and techniques used by various child service providers to intervene in children's lives.

This section addresses various complex issues that directly affect children and practitioners who work with them. For example, are children being treated as commodities to be bought and sold? What role should the government play in protecting children and providing them with permanent homes? Who should receive such services? How do other forces such as economics and legal policy influence service delivery?

Chapter 5 examines the broader social context that fosters attitudes toward alternative forms of child care and generates social policy about day care. Chapter 6 presents a model for analyzing child service programs, with early childhood education programs used to illustrate its application. Chapters 7 and 8 address protective and substitute services, confronting problems of definition, identification, types of intervention, and evaluation. Contemporary difficulties and future challenges also are discussed. Chapter 9 deals with the effect of legal, historical, and social attitudes on services for developmentally dysfunctional children. In November 1972, the

Congress passed the Education for All Handicapped Children Act (Public Law 94-142). Other laws require child service providers to individualize and formalize their intervention plans. Besides laws shaping our efforts, history and social attitudes have profoundly influenced the service delivery system for dysfunctional children.

Chapter 10 provides a detailed examination of parent/child interaction and intervention. Parents' roles in child services and the strategies for involving them in child intervention are delineated. The chapter then focuses on the dynamics of intervention: What influences children's cognitive and affective development? How do settings make a difference, and to whom—child, parent, or family? What role do communities play in child services? In answering these questions, the ramifications of applying an ecological perspective are confronted, and the important benefits of both basic and applied research are emphasized.

These discussions support the view that neither the developing child nor the family exists in isolation; rather, they interact with their context.

Children are influenced by the media, by the state of the economy, by the length of the work days, and by an industry's discussion about whether its employees must move from city to city every few years. Children are influenced by the availability or unavailability of satisfactory . . . care arrangements . . . The family is still seen as the primary agent of a child's socialization, but it is seen no longer as the sole agent [Zigler & Seitz, 1980, p. 156].

5

Perspective on Day-Care Services

Chapter overview

Often parents need arrangements for the care of their children. This chapter considers the broad factors that influence the nature, implementation, and evaluation of day care. The social context of day care is considered, and the delivery of day-care services is presented. Two key themes predominate the discussion: Who is responsible for child care? And who benefits from alternative child-care arrangements?

Issues to consider

Why does the term *day care* carry negative stigma?

How does family structure, family income, and teenage pregnancy influence day-care usage?

How is day care defined?

How does the social context influence this definition?

What are the general effects of day care?

How does research influence the social connotation of day care?

What are the similarities and differences in types of day-care services?

Which parents select what day-care programs, and why?

What is involved in planning, implementing, and evaluating day-care programs?

What are the problems with day-care services.

Introduction

Although the importance of adequate child care is usually not disputed, the following incidents illustrate reasons for and the benefits of day care for entire families.

> One mother who is suffering from phlebitis is not able to give her active three-year-old son full-time care but, with sufficient rest while he is away from home during the day, she can be relaxed and carry on well for the rest of the time. Her husband brings the child to the [day-care] center [Yoemans, 1953, p. 7].

> The oldest of Mrs. B's four children was four when this family came to the attention of the Seven Hills Neighborhood House in Cincinnati. Mrs. B felt that she was going to have to resort to desperate measures to solve her problems, and she told the agency director that she had decided to place her children in foster care. Beset by an inadequate welfare allotment, substandard housing (four children and herself in two rooms), marital difficulties, and full-time care of the children, Mrs. B was finding life "too much" for her. The day care center was suggested as a means of relieving some of her child care burdens so that she could reestablish herself [Hansan & Pemberton, 1963, p. 181].

Is day care needed? Who benefits from such services? What situations could be alleviated or avoided if children received supervised care away from home? Do such child-care arrangements enhance parent/child relationships and enrich the development of children and families? Steinfels (1973) and others answer these questions with a firm yes. For example, Keniston believes that day care often is the best choice for providing the care a child needs:

> Families with temporary problems such as the illness of a parent may need help caring for their children. Child care during the day in another home or a center is the remedy that

disrupts the family least; temporary foster care is more disruptive; placing children in institutions is most traumatic of all [Keniston & Carnegie Council, 1977, p. 141].*

Others believe the care of children should be the sole responsibility of the family, especially mothers. The Child Welfare League (1962) holds that "child care has always been a family responsibility and if the child's mother is unable to care for him the traditional solution has always been an approximation of maternal care . . . in the child's own home, involving other members of the family. This is customary and . . . natural" (p. 49).

Chapter 2 discusses the underlying values associated with this attitude of family being responsible for child care that prevails today as well as the factors—women entering the labor market and the sharp rise in the number of indigent children—fostering the need for some sort of child-care delivery service.

Many middle-class families also rely on day care. For instance, after a major survey of who uses day care in the United States, Ruderman (1968) concluded:

> Great numbers of normal, middle-class, intact, responsible families with working mothers need day-care services and even greater numbers of such families want it. In fact, as we get away from the problem situation cited in welfare documents [we can see] day care is primarily a childcare program on all levels of society for normal children and normal families [p. 341].

Of the families using day care today, however, a majority of them still are recipients of government funds. Perhaps this fact fosters the negative stigma still associated with day-care usage.

Factors influencing the use of day care

Family structure

There is today a pressing need for adequate day care (Fraiberg, 1977). More than 50% of working women have school-age children, over 30% of them with children under the age of 6 (U.S. White House Conference on Children, 1970). Although children younger than 5 have traditionally received alternative child-care arrangements, older children are in need of such care as well. Nearly 2 million school-age children are "latch-key children"; that is, they return home from school to an empty house each day (U.S. Department of Commerce, Bureau of the Census, 1970). Between 1950 and 1976 the percentage of working mothers increased from 14% to 39%. This single factor greatly promoted the need for day care. Approximately 900,000 children were enrolled in day-care centers during 1976–1977. Low-income families, many of whom are headed by single parents, constitute the largest proportion of families using this service (Deutsch, in press). Table 5-1 summarizes day-care enrollment by age composition for centers receiving federal monies to care for children from low-income families and for non-federally funded centers.

Family income

Day-care programs serve the needs of the poor and near-poor populations, and the rate of usage is directly related to parents' participation in the labor force. In 1978

*From *All Our Children,* by K. Keniston and The Carnegie Council on Children. Copyright © 1977 by Harcourt Brace Jovanovich. This and all other quotes from the same source are reprinted by permission of the publisher.

TABLE 5-1 Day-care enrollment by age composition

	Non-FFP centers		FFP centers[1]		All centers[2]
	Profit	Nonprofit	Profit	Nonprofit	
Children enrolled by age					
Two years or younger	42,700	33,700	13,800	31,600	121,800
Three years	51,800	57,600	22,200	72,500	204,100
Four years	62,300	74,800	25,300	95,300	257,600
Five years	45,500	51,700	19,600	71,200	188,000
Six years or older	36,100	33,900	10,400	45,700	126,100
All ages[2]	238,500	251,700	91,400	316,200	897,700
Percent distribution by age					
Two years or younger	18	13	15	10	14
Three years	22	23	24	23	23
Four years	26	30	28	30	29
Five years	19	21	21	23	21
Six years or older	15	13	11	14	14
All ages[2]	100	100	100	100	100

[1]Federal Financial Participation (FFP) Centers have at least one child enrolled whose care is paid for at least in part by federal funds.

[2]Totals may not equal sum of components due to rounding.

From *Day-Care Centers in the United States: A National Profile 1976-1977,* Department of Health, Education, and Welfare, Administration for Children, Youth, and Families, Office of Human Development Services. Washington, D.C.: Government Printing Office, 1979.

about 11.4% of the U.S. population was below the poverty level (an annual income of $6191), but rates varied widely among subgroups. For example, the poverty rate for White families (6.9%) was much lower than that for Black families (27.5%) and those of Hispanic origin (20.4%). Families headed by women with no husband present had a poverty rate of 31.4%, which far exceeded the rates for husband/wife families and families with a male head and no wife present (5.2% and 9.2%, respectively) (U.S. Department of Health and Human Services, 1980).

A child younger than 5 with a single, employed parent is about 30 times more likely to be enrolled in a day-care center than a child in a two-parent family in which only one is employed, and twice as likely as a child from a two-parent household with both parents working. Hispanics are four times more likely and Blacks are more than twice as likely as Whites to use relatives to care for their children; the ratio is much lower for Whites (U.S. Department of Health and Human Services, 1980). Table 5–2 summarizes day-care enrollment by funding, status of center, and background characteristics of children in 1976–1977.

Teenage pregnancy

Of the 1.1 million pregnancies that occurred in 1978 among women under 20 years old, 847,000 were unintended—86% of the pregnancies of unwed and 51% of the pregnancies of married women. The pregnancies of Black teenagers (70%) were more likely than the pregnancies of White teenagers (49%) to be unplanned. Among those who had had a first out-of-wedlock conception, 30% had a repeat pregnancy within two years. In fact, more than 50% of teenage unmarried mothers had one child under 5 living with them when they gave birth again (Guttmacher Institute, 1981).

The health, social, and economic consequences of teenage pregnancy are, in

TABLE 5-2 Day-care enrollment by funding, status of center, and background characteristics of children: 1976–1977

		Percentage distribution			
		Funded centers[1]		Nonfunded centers	
Characteristic	All centers	Profit	Nonprofit	Profit	Nonprofit
Annual family income					
Total	100	100	100	100	100
Less than $6,000	30	32	55	5	24
$6,000 to $15,000	43	45	36	45	48
More than $15,000	27	24	8	49	28
Race					
Total	100	100	100	100	100
White	63	74	44	81	67
Black	28	21	44	13	26
Other	9	5	12	6	7
Type of family					
Total	100	100	100	100	100
Two-parent	62	59	47	75	70
Single-parent	38	41	53	25	30

[1]Denotes centers that enroll at least one child whose care is paid for at least in part by government funds.

From *Day-Care Centers in the United States: A National Profile 1976-77*. Department of Health, Education, and Welfare, Administration for Children, Youth, and Families, Office of Human Development Services. Washington, D.C.: Government Printing Office, 1979.

almost every case, adverse. Babies born to mothers over 20 are more likely to survive than those born to teenagers. Maternal mortality rates also are higher among teenage mothers, especially those 15 and younger. And early childbearing devastates formal educational opportunities. For example, an extensive national study matched samples of 15-year-olds for race, socioeconomic status, academic aptitude and achievement, and educational expectations. When interviewed at age 29, those who became mothers or fathers before the age of 18 were two-fifths less likely to have graduated from high school. Looking at it another way, nearly all of these teenage parents received AFDC support, and currently nearly half of the AFDC expenditures are for households with women who had their first child during their teenage years (Guttmacher Institute, 1981; U.S. Department of Health and Human Services, 1980).

An expanding body of research indicates that family life or sex education programs or both can have a positive impact on the reproductive and sexual behavior of teenagers. These programs also can influence how adolescents view themselves and their abilities (Cooper, 1979). Numerous programs (for example, Deutsch & Yates, 1982a, 1982b) at both the high school and college levels have documented increases in knowledge and self-esteem as a result of participation in family life or sex education courses. When control groups were used, the noted increases for the treatment groups were significant in comparison (Cooper, 1979). These programs focused on the concept that people who feel competent and in control are better able to use information to guide their behavior, to make informed decisions, and to behave responsibly. (For a review of family life education teacher selection and preparation, see Cooper, 1982).

Individuals are able to incorporate the skills and knowledge attained from such programs into their personal and private lives. For instance, at Johns Hopkins Medical Institute in Baltimore, Maryland, staff members form close bonds with the young women and conduct classes on prenatal care, delivery, and child care. (For a discussion of parent-skill training see Chapter 10.) Results indicate that 85% of these mothers return to school and only 5 % are pregnant again in one year, compared to 10% and almost 50%, respectively, for those Baltimore teenage mothers who are not in the program (U.S. Department of Health and Human Services, 1980). Government concern is also evident: in 1978 the Department of Health, Education, and Welfare established the Office of Adolescent Pregnancy Programs that resulted from the Adolescent Health Services, and Pregnancy Prevention and Care Act of 1978 (Pub. L. 95-626, 92 Stat. 3595). This office continues to study the problems associated with teenage pregnancies, supports demonstration projects that provide services, and seeks ways to reduce teenage pregnancy rates. Such efforts are paralleled at state levels. For example, the California State Office of Family Planning, Department of Health Services, has supported a Family Health Education and Training Program conducted at San Diego State University in 1981–82. This program is founded on the belief that successful family-life education classes must be developed on a local level, built on a strong base of parent and community involvement. Because family-life education is a joint responsibility of home, school, religious, and community organizations, the program promotes a team approach, combining the resources and perspectives of all these groups to help self-selected communities improve their family-life education efforts. Such state support will be maintained over the next several years. Under the direction of Dr. Francine Deutsch, San Diego State University will continue to design, implement, and evaluate educational materials and to establish a California State University delivery system for present and future family-life educators. Perhaps as inroads are made in this area with a greater focus on preventive assistance, the rates of teenage pregnancy and possibly day-care usage will decline.

The social context of day care

Day care has been defined as "an organized service for the care of children away from their homes during some part of the day when circumstances call for normal care in the home to be supplemented" (United Nations, 1956, p. 18). The two major functions of such services are to care and to protect. Surrogate parents supervise activities in a safe place where food is provided. Although contemporary day-care facilities educate children, education historically has not been a goal.

With research evidence showing the benefits of early childhood enriching experiences (see Chapter 10), the conceptualization of day-care services altered. More than a decade ago, the Child Welfare League of America (1969) declared that "any form of day care should be designed as a developmental service that fosters the child's potentialities for physical, emotional, intellectual, and social development" (p. 9).

The government traditionally has supported day-care services to remedy economic difficulties, particularly during the Great Depression, World War II, and the War on Poverty (see Chapter 2 for an historical perspective on child care). Today, many people are questioning the government's support of such services. Belsky, Steinberg, and Walker, for example, believe that "industry should play a major role in sharing the burden of providing day care, since business benefits directly from the labor generated by supplementary child care" (in press). Others oppose government involvement on the grounds that it threatens family privacy.

Another major area of controversy also concerns whether day care should be a form of supplemental or substitute care. Day care as a form of parental replacement offends many individuals, perhaps because they feel it reflects their failure as parents.

Supplemental child care takes many forms and serves various types of families.

The inability to reach a consensus about the purpose of day care contributes to the lack of structure in the implementation, maintenance, and evaluation of programs. This in turn retards advancements in the quality of child care. "A 'system' of early child care in the United States can hardly be said to exist except as a serendipitous admixture of separate elements that together make up a patchwork of services bordering on the chaotic" (cited in Robinson et al., 1979, p. 37).

Other nations do not seem to have this difficulty regarding day-care services, primarily because they support unified values for rearing children and believe in governmental intervention into families. For example, in Hungary, "the care for children outside the family is almost exclusively the concern of the government" (Hermann & Komlósi, 1972, p. 10). In Sweden, "the role of the community is to support and complement the home in meeting the needs of children" (Berfenstam & William-Olsson, 1973, p. 16). For an excellent presentation of day-care services from a crosscultural perspective see *A World of Children: Day Care and Preschool Institutions* (Robinson, Robinson, Darling, & Holm, 1979).

Since the social context for day-care services has been inconsistent in its support, many questions remain: should the government provide day-care services for families to maintain a minimal level of organizational functioning, or should day-care services be available for all families or only certain families?

The effects of day care

In Chapter 10, a detailed analysis of the effects of day-care intervention programs on children, parents, families, and communities is presented. Here, we will broadly consider the impact of day care to form the foundation for our later discussion.

A valuable source of information regarding the potentially positive influence of day care has been the work of Israeli researchers who study children reared in kibbutzim, a communal living arrangement. A variety of factors in relation to receiving or not receiving group care have been examined: (1) impact on children of their parents being soldiers (Amir, 1969); (2) personality (Kaffman, 1965); (3) sex-role development (Rabin, 1970); and (4) moral attitudes (Rettig, 1966). This applied research indicates that group child rearing is producing healthy, productive societal members. The research also suggests that the effects of this extensive and even extreme form of day care on basic developmental processes are negative neither for children nor society (Beit-Hallahmi & Rabin, 1977). However, conclusions are complicated with many interactions noted.

Efforts have shifted from a preoccupation with the harmful effects of day care to identifying possible positive outcomes such as increased cooperation and altruism (for example, Rubenstein & Howes, 1979). Perhaps this shift indirectly suggests that the stigma once associated with giving up one's child to the care of a stranger is diminishing.

Delivery of day-care services

Day care serves about 11 million children younger than 14 for a substantial portion of a week. About 5 million school-age children, about 4 million preschoolers, and 2.5 million infants and toddlers spend most of their waking hours in some form of day care (Office of the Assistant for Planning and Evaluation, 1978).

Although day care can be conceptually defined quite succinctly, the delivery systems used are very diversified in terms of settings and programs. This diversity has created multiple classifications of day-care services. Kadushin (1980) and others divide day-care services along two lines—day-care centers and family day care, which occurs in homes. This text will discuss the three distinctive types of care developed by Belsky and his colleagues (in press)—center day care (CDC), family day care (FDC), and home care (HC). The latter two refer to out-of-home care and in-own-home care, respectively.

Types of day care

Center day care.   The major features typical of day-care-center programs are (1) they are on a fixed schedule; (2) they are licensed; and (3) they are run by professionals. Four areas receiving the most research concern are: (1) the number of children, (2) physical size of the environment, (3) children/staff ratio, and (4) the composition of the children. Researchers (for example, Kritchevsky, Prescott, & Walling, 1969; Prescott, 1965) have reported that, when centers consist of between 30 and 60 children, less emphasis is placed on routines and rules. However, when the number of children exceeds 60, professionals place much greater emphasis on control and are less cognizant of children's individual needs. In fact, in a recent study (Travers & Ruopp, 1978), group size was the most important factor that determined the quality of the day-care experience for children ranging from 3 to 5 years of age. Specifically, the staff interacted less with one another, controlled children less, and were more involved in praising, comforting, questioning, and other interactions with children when groups had fewer than 15 children. Children/staff ratio was found to have a minimal effect on the type of day-care experience for preschoolers. However, for infants and toddlers, as the ratio of children to staff increased, children displayed greater distress by crying and other behavior. Also negative behavior such as aggressiveness, destructiveness, and isolated behavior increased as the number of children per square foot increased (Rohe & Patterson, 1974).

Reviewing the literature on age of children in programs, Fein and Clarke-Stewart (1973) found that segregation and integration by age produce differential effects on children. In age-segregated groups, teachers are less affectionate and use less direct teaching, and children show more conflict and competition compared to age-integrated groups.

To say that one type of group composition is better than another is difficult because it depends on what experiences parents want for their children. Some parents may believe that opportunities to engage in and resolve conflicts are essential in order for children to learn to achieve and compete in today's society. However, other parents may believe that obeying orders via direct teaching and gaining experiences in displaying affect are of value for their children.

From the perspective of professionals, some educators feel that a mixed age group is a more realistic reflection of the world than a relatively similar age group. Others argue against such an experience because the public school system supports age-segregated classrooms. Thus, early childhood experiences may train children for skills for which they will not have opportunities for immediate transfer, resulting in penalities.

Family day care. The key features of family day care are: (1) flexible operating hours, (2) choice of caregivers, and (3) convenience. The two areas of controversy concern licensing and staff training. Does having a license and a trained professional staff produce positive program effects? Steinberg and Green (1979) found that, when formal training of caregivers is lacking, parents avoid placing their children in such homes. Thus, it seems, parents prefer a well-credentialed facility and staff. Parental preferences are supported by data. Carew (1979) compared 35 licensed and 25 unlicensed family day-care home programs (of these groups, 41 were supervised by a council). She reported that children in the unlicensed home experience were more unhappy, spent more time alone, and manifested more negative social behaviors than those children enrolled in licensed programs.

In-own-home care. A single caregiver and flexible scheduling highlight the features of in-own-home care. Observing 38 mother-reared and 27 babysitter-reared infants, Rubenstein, Pedersen, and Yarrow (1977) reported that "the overall pattern of results indicates that mothers provided a more stimulating and responsive environment than did substitute caregivers" (p. 530). However, when in-own-home care is contrasted to family day care and center day care, home-reared children demonstrate the least benefits in various developmental areas, such as cognitive and social (Clarke-Stewart, 1977).

Parental preference. Which type of day-care arrangement is preferred? More parents choose family day-care homes for their children than the other two care forms. About 3.4 million families use family day-care homes, 2.6 use in-own-home care, and 1.3 use center care (Belsky et al., in press). Belsky and his colleagues (in press) point out the strengths of family day care over the other care situations. Family day care provides individualized adult attention and a stable personalized relationship with a caregiver. Thus, data support parental preference for family day care.

Placement in programs

The degree of structure in a curriculum affects children differently. Prescott (1973) found that a structured curriculum, regulated by time periods for activities and types of activities, does not promote positive affective interactions between adults and children. Rather, the interactions consist of limit setting, and children seldom have opportunities for exercising their own autonomy and independence.

When making a placement decision, parents should be sure the day-care curriculum matches their goals for their child.

If parents want rule-obedient, compliant children, then they should select a structured program. If they desire self-initiation and affect from their children, then they should select a flexible curriculum. If all behaviors are desired, then parents should identify a structured curriculum that also permits some flexibility in children's activities.

At a general level, parents of different racial and ethnic groups exhibit preferences for different types of programs. Jaffee (1977) reported that Blacks prefer a structured curriculum with an emphasis placed on academic skills and discipline, while Whites seek out less structured programs that emphasize social and emotional skill building. However, circumstantial factors—health problems, family income, or program availability—dictate the placement of children in specific types of day-care situations. An important professional intermediary between parent and placement is the child-care provider, as the following incident demonstrates.

> The mentally ill mother and the four-year-old child were in such a constant state of friction that the father was afraid his wife would do some harm to the child in his absence at work. We [the staff] were able to arrange for the father to bring the little girl in the morning and call for her on his way home from work in the evening [Goddard, 1957, p. 32].

As this illustration indicates, day-care services indeed can be critical for a family's survival. Child-service providers must know the available community resources and be cognizant of why a child is being enrolled in a program. They not only can better help the child's development, but they also can assist parents either directly or by referral.

The ultimate decision to place a child in a day-care facility resides with parents. They should be sure that the curriculum matches their goals for their child. Interviewing the day-care staff and observing classroom activities help parents to arrive at a decision and help to reduce child turnover. Moving a child from program to program is not a positive experience because children often have difficulty adjusting to different people and environments. And, if child turnover is high, it is difficult to establish a smoothly running curriculum designed to enhance children's development. If a "swinging-door" policy is supported by the program staff (to obtain federal monies, for example), then professionals are not serving the best interests of children.

Consider the experiences of a family who just moved because both parents had obtained employment. They needed to place their 3-year-old son in a day-care facility as soon as possible.

> We looked through the yellow pages and called Garden of Eden [center day care]. The person from the program said our son David could be dropped off at 7 A.M. Monday morning. We never observed the program or chatted with the staff. After a week at the center, David became withdrawn. He was not interested in any of his usual activities. We called another center and enrolled him, and the pattern of our son's behavior was at first the same and then became worse. He would cry in the morning and say "I not go." We tried another center during the first month of our relocation. This time we visited the center before placing David. The director asked us questions, and we related our experiences. She suggested that David would be better in a family day-care home rather than a center with so many older children. She placed several calls and asked us to visit three family day-care homes before placing David. She suggested that David "visit" the homes with us and interact awhile prior to our deciding. Also, she advised us to ask David which one he would like to go back to.
>
> We three talked about the places we visited. David told us he wanted to go back to one in particular. We made the necessary arrangements. Although our son was happy now, he would still say "Lots of bad schools. I not go to a school." We wonder if he will ever forget about the bad experiences he had originally [Author's files].

Luckily for David, the director of a program took an interest in the problem of these parents, and the parents took the time to study the best placement for their child. Professionals and parents should work jointly to find the best placement for children.

Planning, implementation, and evaluation

Most of the material written about how to plan, implement, and evaluate day-care services focuses on the day-care center (see Auerbach & Rivaldo, 1975; Sciarra & Dorsey, 1979) and fits within the Federal Interagency Day Care Requirements (FIDCR) so funds can be received. According to these guidelines, day care must have not only an educational component but also a "social services component that supports family functioning" because it "is necessary to promote the well-being" of children (Department of HEW, 1975). Consequently, many professionals such as social workers, educators, nutritionists, and nurses are involved with day-care delivery. Rather than looking at the responsibilities associated with all of these roles, only global aspects will be considered: (1) needs assessment, (2) licensing and certification, (3) equipping the center, (4) organizing the children, and (5) evaluation. Chapter 6 presents a model for analyzing childhood programs, and Chapter 13 is devoted to evaluation.

Needs assessment. The first step in deciding whether a day-care center should be established is to determine community need. How many children and families are interested in such a service? Of these families, how many are willing to pay what amount? What are the ages of the children to be served? Do these children have any special characteristics, such as physical handicaps? After these questions are answered, these families need to be asked their preferred type of service and where they would like it located.

There are many ways in which this survey information can be gathered. Usually, it is collected via a questionnaire. This questionnaire can be mailed or a telephone survey can be conducted. Table 5–3 illustrates the type of questionnaire that can be constructed. Much time and energy are invested in this initial phase of planning. Such efforts should not be minimized because, without the support of parents and children, many good programs have failed.

Licensing and certification. Licensing represents an effort to protect the health and safety of children. In 1978, only 8000 (less than 25%) centers were licensed (Kadushin, 1980). Although at the federal level licensing requires that the staff hold certain credentials, a licensed program is no guarantee of quality or effectiveness. Besides FIDCR, states vary on what they require of a program in order that it be licensed (U.S. Senate Committee on Finance, 1974).

Whether early-child-care personnel should be certified or not has received considerable debate over the years. To date, most states require that day-care personnel be certified. Usually the State Department of Education is the office to contact for checking into certification requirements. A complete listing of certification requirements for each state can be obtained by writing to the Education Commission of the States, Denver, Colorado.

If certification cannot be obtained but a person is interested in getting a credential for child care, then becoming a Child Development Associate (CDA) may be appropriate. To earn this credential, an individual must be able to:

1. Set up a safe and healthy learning environment for young children
2. Advance children's physical and intellectual competence
3. Build children's positive self-concept and individual strength
4. Organize and sustain the positive functioning of children and adults in a group learning environment
5. Bring about optimum coordination of home and center child-rearing practices and expectations
6. Carry out supplementary responsibilities related to children's programs (Sciarra & Dorsey, 1979, pp. 35–36).

A representative from the Child Development Associate Consortium and three staff people assess the candidate to determine if a CDA credential can be obtained.*

Equipping the center. Preestablished criteria should be used to make decisions for purchasing center materials and equipment. These criteria should include: (1) utility, (2) suitability, (3) durability, (4) economy, (5) ease of maintenance, (6) safety, and (7) staff preference (Sciarra & Dorsey, 1979). The program goals or objectives will greatly determine types of purchases. For instance, if symbolic play is valued as a means for promoting role play and role enactment, then supplies that promote such activity would be purchased.

Organizing the children. The size of the group and how it is organized are determined by several factors: (1) licensing requirements, (2) physical space, (3) number of staff, (4) program philosophy, and (5) needs of children and staff (Sciarra & Dorsey, 1979). A major decision must be made about whether children should be age-integrated or age-segregated, depending on which type of transactions the staff wish to foster (see Chapter 6 for definitions of program specifications).

Assessing the program. The literature is voluminous with studies that evaluate the effects of different types of day care on children, families, and

*Child Development Associate Consortium, Suite 500, Southern Building, 805 Fifteenth Street, N.W., Washington, D.C., 20005.

TABLE 5-3 Child-care needs survey

Hello. My name is _____. I am calling for _____. We are conducting a survey so we can determine the child-care needs of our community. First, we need to know:

1. Do you have any children under 12 years of age?
   yes _____   no _____

[If no, then thank the person for helping us and terminate interview. If yes, then continue.]

2. What are their ages and are they boys or girls?

	Boy	Girl
0–12 months		
13–24 months		
25–36 months		
37–60 months		
in kindergarten		
in grade school		

3. What kind of child-care arrangements do you have for them?

	Boy	Girl
Parent provides care at home		
Another provides in-own-home care		
Cared for in another home in community		
Cared for half day in center		
Cared for full day in center		
Some combination of above		

4. How many days each week is _____ in someone else's care?

5. How many total hours each week is _____ in someone else's care?

6. For what reasons have you arranged for child care by someone other than you?
   a. employment/education/financial   b. for the child's benefit   c. personal reasons

7. What kind of alternative care would you arrange if you could have whatever care you wanted for your child [children]? Please answer yes or no for each type of care I will mention. [Mention each child's name before going through the list.]

	Boy	Girl
You provide care at home		
Someone else provides care in your home		
Care provided in another home in the community		
Center care provided halftime (less than 6 hours per day)		
Center care provided fulltime (more than 6 hours per day)		
Some combination of the above		

8. If the _____ were to establish a day-care program for your child [children], would you be interested in enrolling _____ for a morning session (3 hours or less), an afternoon session (3 hours or less), or the entire day (6 hours or more)? What meals would be required— breakfast, lunch, dinner? How many days per week would you want this service? How certain are you about your decision; do you feel that it's certain or that it's a possibility?

Age of child	3 hrs. or less A.M.	3 hrs. or less P.M.	6 hrs. or more (Full day)	Meals B	Meals L	Meals D	No. days per week	Degree of certainty C	Degree of certainty P
0–1									
1–2									
2–3									
3–5									
5–6									
6+									

TABLE 5-3 (continued)

---

9. Would you want transportation services if _____ participated?
   yes _____   no _____

[If no, omit questions 10 and 11.]

10. Would you use these services for
    a. dropping your child off?   b. picking your child up?
    c. for both dropping off and picking up your child?

11. Would these transportation services be *necessary* in order for _____ to attend?
    yes _____   no _____

12. If the day-care facility were located at _____, would this influence your decision?
    a. no   b. yes [direction of influence not specified]
    c. yes [positive influence]   d. yes [negative influence]

13. I'm going to read a list of possible features that our day-care program could have. Please tell me whether each would be of interest to you. [Not read for each child.]

	Yes	No
Emphasis on school readiness (for example, reading, arithmetic)	_____	_____
Emphasis on social skills (for example, planned opportunities to interact with children of different ages and backgrounds)	_____	_____
Emphasis on communication skills (for example, demonstrating or teaching ways to communicate)	_____	_____
Trips or visits to nearby places	_____	_____
Assessment of your child's health (eyes, ears, speech, and so on)	_____	_____
Transportation for your child at your convenience (choice of hours for pickup and delivery)	_____	_____
Opportunity for your participation in the program:		
as caregiver	_____	_____
on parent council	_____	_____
in family education (for example, lecture series, discussion groups)	_____	_____
helping with outings	_____	_____
helping with trips in the community	_____	_____

14. What would be your reason for enrolling your child?
    a. employment/education/financial   b. for the child's benefit   c. personal reasons

15. How much money do you presently pay for child-care assistance?

16. If you and _____ were to receive better services, would you be willing to pay more?
    yes _____   no _____

17. How long have you lived in this area?
    a. less than 1 year   b. 1–2 years   c. 3–4 years   d. more than 4 years

18. Do you plan to leave the community?
    a. no   b. yes, within 2 years   c. yes, 3 to 4 years from now
    d. sometime, but do not know when

19. Do you plan to have another child while you are in this community?
    yes _____   no _____

20. Would you consider using an infant center for your child-care arrangement?
    a. no opinion   b. no   c. yes

---

communities. Because of the invaluable role evaluation plays in the development and implementation of programs as well as social policy formation, this text devotes considerable attention to it. Specific program effects are detailed in Chapter 10, a formative user-based evaluation model is examined in Chapter 13, and needed evaluation changes are illuminated in Chapter 14. Throughout other chapters as well, the importance of evaluating child services emerges as a central theme.

Problems with day-care services

There are numerous problems with day care that go beyond the design and delivery of programs. These problems all relate in some way to the prevailing attitudes about day care. A negative attitude toward working mothers promotes a reluctance to support day-care services. How can the quality of day care improve when day-care needs and facilities receive such low visibility, especially compared to the needs of other groups such as emotionally disturbed children or juvenile delinquents? This section addresses two major problem areas—who is responsible for and who benefits from day-care services.

Who is responsible for day-care services?

The incongruity between societal goals and family child-care needs, and society's ambivalent attitudes toward working mothers and single-parent families, have produced a false notion about who is responsible for child care. The failure to develop high-quality day-care centers does not reduce the number of working mothers or single parents, but rather just produces inadequate day-care services. Attitudes that day care "undermines the American family" ignore the reality that day care actually can strengthen the family. Mothers and single parents can be gainfully employed. Problems in parent/child relations can be prevented. Children can remain in a community rather than be institutionalized or receive foster care.

The notion that day-care services are just a drain on the economy also is incorrect. Programs have been developed to hire welfare recipients as family day-care mothers (see Wade, 1970). For instance, the New York City Department of Social Services developed a Family Day Care Career Program in which mothers on welfare exchanged services, with those interested in job training (career mothers) having their children cared for by those interested in earning some money (day-care mothers). Data indicate that the majority of career mothers in this program did not return to welfare and the majority of day-care mothers earned enough money to reduce their dependence on welfare.

Day-care services are housed within the social-service system rather than the educational system because they were designed in response to a need precipitated by social-role changes. But day care is not restricted to a single function. The responsibility for day care must be balanced among three professional areas: social welfare, education, and health. Day care not only serves a social and health function but also extends education downward and outward. Younger children have opportunities to learn and older children have their school day lengthened.

That day care today is largely a commercial venture may be one reason why policy making for day care has been a struggle. Should day care be strictly a business venture? Would it not be better for day care to be a community investment of these three professions—social welfare, education, and health?

Who benefits from day-care services?

With so many people involved in the day-care system, different people believe different benefits are accrued. Parents see day care as a way to provide dependable and consistent care for their children, opportunities for interacting with children and adults, and learning and training experiences. Women's organizations view day care as the vehicle for emancipating mothers. Social workers consider day care as a way to protect and nurture children while parents are at work. Health professionals feel day care is a means for identifying and correcting health problems early and preventing problems in the future. Educators see day care as a way of compensating for problems that reduce learning. Developmentalists view day care as a time for optimizing children's potential in different areas of development. Government views day care as the mechanism for moving people off welfare. And industry looks at day care as a way to make members of families more capable and dependable workers. Since so many people have such different goals for day care, there is "competitive disagreement concerning who should control the day care 'turf'" (Kadushin, 1980, p. 300).

Conclusion

Day care could help compensate for the sometimes inadequate care children receive in their families. In 1977, for example, more than 20 million children under the age of 15 had not been immunized against one or more childhood diseases. Although 32 million received immunizations against diptheria/tetanus, polio, measles, rubella, and mumps, the figure of 20 million unprotected is staggering. The majority of this group were minorities or poor (U.S. Department of Health and Human Services, 1980). Day care could facilitate a shift from traditional models of health-care delivery and control dominated primarily by physicians to models that promote involvement by a variety of professionals. Because children's preventive health needs are rather predictable and most illnesses are quickly over, a great proportion of children's health care could be provided by high-quality nurses or other midlevel professionals at day-care locations. Even those children who have more serious health problems could be assisted by early diagnosis and referral.

Perhaps the deterioration of neighborhoods reduces the quality of care children and families receive. Since 1973 the Annual Housing Survey of the Department of Commerce has questioned residents about the physical conditions and services provided in their neighborhood as well as their overall attitude. From 1973 to 1976 opinions declined and support services were viewed more negatively, especially in terms of child-service accessibility (U.S. Department of Health and Human Services, 1980).

Although more research is warranted to understand the particular needs of different neighborhoods, the quality and accessibility of care should be improved for all family members. Also perhaps continued efforts to include families in the decision-making process that affects child care will help to identify intervention goals and establish priorities—essentials for the formulation of a coherent policy.

Summary

Whether children should be under parental care or the supervision of caregivers is still debated. Regardless, day care is needed and used. Working mothers and single parents utilize day care more than other families. With the increase in mothers in the labor force and teenage pregnancies, the use of day-care service has risen. Minorities and poor families also rely more on day care than do other groups.

Day care is easily defined as supplemental daily care in a variety of areas, but the social context determines the prevalent connotations associated with such care. A major area of controversy in the United States surrounds the purpose of day care. Countries that support unified values for rearing children and believe in government intervention into families do not debate the purpose of day care. These countries also provide research evidence showing the positive benefits of day care for both the individual and society.

About 11 million children younger than 14 participate in center, family, and in-own-home day care. Several factors influence the quality of care received at centers: (1) number of children, (2) physical space, (3) children/staff ratio, and (4) composition of groups of children. Day care also is characterized by flexibility of hours, convenience, and flexibility of caregivers. Parents prefer this form of care, and child-service providers find it promotes individualized attention from an adult. Parents, however, have different structural preferences for programs. Blacks tend to prefer a highly structured curriculum, whereas Whites seek less structure. Despite preferences, circumstantial factors often determine selection. Programs should be scrutinized by parents prior to placement.

The planning, implementation, and evaluation of a program involves: (1) needs assessment, (2) licensing and certification, (3) equipping the center, (4) organizing children, and (5) assessment of effectiveness. Numerous problems with day care extend beyond the design and delivery of programs to reflect the broader social context. Two major concerns deal with the questions of responsibility and benefits. Some consensus about these two issues must be reached and families allowed to participate in decisions that concern goals and priorities in order that a comprehensive day-care policy be formulated.

6

A Model for Analyzing
Early Childhood Educational Programs

Introduction
Generic program components
   Outcomes
   Transactions
   Antecedents
   Functional relationships
Application of theory to programs
   Maturationist approach
   Behavioral/environmental approach
   Cognitive/developmental approach
   Eclectic curriculum programs
Effects of theory and empirical research on
model programs
   Outcomes
   Transactions
      Child/material interactions
      Child/teacher interactions
      Child/child interactions
   Antecedents
   Functional relationships
Community influence
   Needs and values
   Participation and purposes
Conclusion
Summary

This chapter was written in collaboration with ELLEN A. SKINNER, Ph.D., as the senior author, while she was completing her doctoral degree at The Pennsylvania State University, College of Human Development. Skinner currently is at the Max Planck Institute, Berlin, Germany.

Chapter overview

Decisions are continually being made about the structure and functioning of educational programs for young children, on both a short-term and a long-term basis. Many sources of information are used to make these judgments that affect children. When professionals know what is needed to produce specific program outcomes, the potential for program success increases. The specification model for program analysis presented in this chapter allows for program comparisons and is applicable to a wide array of child services.

Issues to consider

How are program outcomes, transactions, and antecedents defined, and what functional relationships can be produced?

How does theory influence program development?

What controversy exists about program outcomes?

What are the characteristics of model programs—maturationist, behavioral/environmental, and cognitive/developmental?

What are the features of eclectic curriculum programs?

What are the effects of theory and research on model program components?

How can communities influence program development, implementation, and evaluation?

What are the benefits of a specification model for program analysis?

Introduction

Most child-service providers believe that experience can modify children's behavior and development, and that intervention efforts can correct current problems, prevent future difficulties, and optimize developmental processes. As members of this group, early-childhood educators select and organize experiences and interactions in preschool contexts to effect change. In making daily and long-term decisions about the structure of programs, educators use many sources of information—experience, insight, tradition, community and parent opinions, and theory and research—to plan, implement, and evaluate their programs.

Many practitioners, researchers, and theoreticians (Day, 1977; DeVries, 1974; Evans, 1975; Parker, 1974; Peters, 1977; Sigel, 1972) argue for explicit delineation of program dimensions, especially for programs providing similar services. They feel such specification allows professionals to examine the consistency among program assumptions, goals, and strategies. Sharing this information with staff and parents establishes communication networks and enhances commitment, both of which are critical for program success (Bissell, 1971, 1973). Specification also permits program adaptability to different geographical locations, staff, and families (Biber, 1977; Stallings, 1975). It facilitates program comparisons, which help professionals to select alternative methods for reaching similar goals (Bronfenbrenner, 1974a). Parents benefit because they can select programs congruent with their own values (Bissell, 1973; Trujillo, 1974) and their perceptions of their children's needs.

Since much of the theoretical and empirical efforts applying specification models for program analysis deal with early childhood education, this chapter will focus on these particular programs. However, other programs and professionals can benefit from its application as well. The potential for program success increases when professionals know what is needed to produce what outcomes for which participants. And, of course, demonstrating program success enhances support at many intervention levels: the government can better direct funding; organizations, lobbyists, and the public can argue with more credibility for financial support; communities can differentiate among programs more easily to direct families to receive help; families can renew their faith in the professionals and programs that influence their children; and children can benefit directly from the programs. Optimally, this information then feeds back into empirical and theoretical efforts, which further increases the likelihood of program improvements being made. Careful documentation also guarantees that experiences are shared and examined by other professionals, which can result in mutual learning and improved practice.

How can programs be delineated? What role does theory and empirical research play in the development of model educational programs and their specification? How can the community influence these programs? To answer these questions, the following sections use a formative evaluation model to examine program components in general and the specifications of early childhood educational programs in particular. Theoretical perspectives and empirical research are considered throughout this discussion. Then the broader context of early childhood educational programs are explored by pointing out community influences.

Generic program components

Components of preschool programs are identified to compare programs, to check the comprehensiveness and consistency of programs, and to identify underlying assumptions (Anderson, 1947; Day, 1977; Day & Parker, 1977; Evans, 1975; Peters, 1977; Sigel, 1972). A formative evaluation model will be used here to identify program components because of its potential applicability to other child-service programs (Provus, 1969; Stake, 1967). Discussion will be centered on three program components: (1) desired outcomes, (2) transactions needed to promote these, and (3) the antecedents and resources required for successful program implementation.

Outcomes

Outcomes are the changes a program attempts to produce in children, parents, student teachers, institutions, or communities (Berlack, 1970; Bronfenbrenner, 1974a; Peters, 1977; Peters, Golbeck, & Busch-Nagel, 1977). Outcomes describe which processes (cognitive, social, emotional, physical, motivational, or their relationships) should change in what way (attitudes, behaviors, dispositions, feelings) and to what degree (some absolute performance or skill; a normative shift or position). Day and Parker (1977) differentiate between two types of outcomes: goals refer to the global long-term aims of the educational process; objectives are the more immediate and specific changes a particular program seeks to produce. The important relationship between these two outcomes is often overlooked because educational goals are determined by values while objectives often reflect the pragmatics of the situation.

Transactions

Transactions are the particular experiences or interactions fostered to produce desired outcomes. Day (1977) observes that "it is the actual interaction of the child

Determining the success of early childhood education programs requires careful analysis of desired outcomes, transactions, and antecedent conditions and resources.

with his teachers, his peers, and the classroom materials that are directly related to the value of the program for the child" (p. 467). In planning programs, educators typically describe four types of transactions: child/material, child/teacher, child/child, and child/parent. Of course, many other combinations of interactions and experiences are possible.

Child/material interactions are characterized by static aspects of materials, including type, variety, flexibility, placement, manipulativeness, and structure, and by the procedures governing their use, including curriculum content, sequencing, activity periods, and initiation of use. Teacher/child interactions deal with instructional strategies, such as direct presentation, active games, supported play, and guided discovery, and motivational techniques, including initiation of contact with teachers, materials, or peers and limit-setting or disciplinary strategies. Child/child interactions depend on physical space and material organization, content and sequencing of curriculum, instructional strategies, and composition of the group. Child/parent interactions refer to the types of parental participation that foster the program goals and objectives (outcomes).

Educators also determine the specificity or latitude of transactions allowed (Day, 1977; Evans, 1975). They may decide that a wide array of transactions with fairly abstract common properties (often called *learning principles*) promote outcomes. Or they may delineate a very narrow range of preselected and sequenced activities (sometimes referred to as a *curriculum guide*) to achieve desired objectives. Most programs fall between these two extremes.

Antecedents

Antecedents are the conditions and resources needed to maximize success. Conditions concern competencies and characteristics of target children and their families, including socioeconomic status, temperament, cognitive level, sex, and entering abilities. Particular programs may aim at a target population or apply to all children (Goodwin, 1974; Peters et al., 1977; Rossi, Freeman, & Wright, 1979).

Resources describe settings, space, materials, staff, and money needed for successful implementation (Levin, 1975; Morris & Fitz-Gibbon, 1978; Peters, 1977). Some programs are effective only in certain communities and physical settings, or with certain budget structures (for example, nonprofit), but other factors, such as staff skills and abilities, must also be identified to implement a program (Bissell, 1973; Day, 1977; Evans, 1975).

Functional relationships

Planners must define the relations among outcomes, transactions, and antecedents (Stake, 1967). They should provide a rationale to explain why certain antecedents were identified and specific transactions were selected to produce outcomes in a target population. These relations should be theoretically and empirically rooted to facilitate program coherence and consistency, and to examine whether short- and long-term goals make sense in the context of contemporary society.

Application of theory to programs

Program outcomes, transactions, antecedents, and functional relationships often are based on assumptions deduced from theory. DeVries (1974) defines a theory as "an assumption, attitude, belief, or philosophy about human behavior" (p. 4). Parker (1972, 1974) and Peters (1977) emphasize the relevance of educational and child developmental theories for planning early-childhood education programs because they help in making decisions about goals, teaching strategies, curricula, and performance criteria.

Theories are characterized by their assumptions about developmental change: what changes, how changes occur, and why change happens. Kohlberg (1968) describes three theories that have been influential in education: maturationist, behavioral/environmental, and cognitive/developmental. A maturational orientation views development as the product of internal factors that unfold in predetermined, universal sequences. Behaviorally-oriented theorists believe development is additive and quantitative behavior change results from external environmental factors. A cognitive/developmental approach regards development as qualitative structural change that occurs because individuals actively seek and interpret their environments. An eclectic approach combines elements of each theory. Table 6–1 summarizes outcomes, transactions, and antecedents for four programs derived from these theoretical approaches, which are described in more detail below.

Maturationist approach

Educators using a maturationist approach to early education view development as the overarching goal of education. Assumptions about children's innate motivation and capacity for growth lead to transactions in which children select and guide their interactions with materials, peers, and teachers. Teachers provide a rich environment and structure interactions with children using generalized teaching principles such as guided discovery and supported play. Clearly, teacher selection and training are necessary for accurate program implementation (Denny, 1970; Lomax, 1972).

The Bank Street model illustrates a maturationist preschool (Biber, 1977; Biber, Shapiro, & Wickens, 1971; Shapiro & Biber, 1972). The ultimate aim of the educational process is to optimize development of competence, individuality, socialization, and integration. Objectives deal with enhancing children's ego strength (positive self-image, ability to deal effectively with the environment), autonomy

TABLE 6-1 Specification of program for four theories of development

Theory	Maturationist	Behavioral	Cognitive-developmental	Eclectic
Program	Bank Street	Primary Education Project	Piaget for Early Education	Montessori Method
Proponent(s)	Biber	Resnick	Kamii & De Vries	Montessori
Outcomes				
Goals	Optimize development (competence, individuality, socialization, integration)	Successful participation in school	Entire personality (intellectual and moral autonomy)	Academic and practical success
Objectives	Enhance self (ego, autonomy, integration) and cognition (abstract thinking, change)	Perceptual-motor, conceptual-linguistic, orienting-attending skills	Interaction with the environment (logical and socio-emotional)	Motor, sensory, language, academic skills
Transactions				
Child/teacher	Guided play, respond to child	Behavioral management techniques	Induce imbalance	Prepare and sequence activities
Child/material	"Spring-board activities" available; child-initiated, sequenced	Empirically devised, preplanned; teacher-initiated, selected	According to cognitive level	Self-correctional, specific
Child/child	Mutually supportive play, cooperation		Test new ideas	
Child/parent	Participation, decision making	Learns behavioral techniques		
Antecedents				
Conditions	All children	All children	All children	All children (especially disadvantaged)
Resources	Applies to each setting	Curriculum guide	Piagetian theory of child development	

(self-direction, true individuality, creativity, experimental attitudes), and integration of thought, feeling, and action (self-understanding, empathy). More cognitively oriented objectives include the development of: 1) facility with abstract symbols, 2) thinking and ordering processes, and 3) a sense of time and change in both natural and human-made environments.

In the maturationist framework, children are considered intrinsically motivated, capable of actively exploring their environment and able to initiate and engage in interactions to organize and interpret experiences. The teaching process attempts to stimulate, support, and guide the integration and expression of these developmental processes.

Prescribed transactions reflect the above principles of learning and teaching. Child/material interactions are initiated and sequenced by the child. The function and use of a variety of materials made available are expected to change with development. Also available are conventional language stimulation activities and "springboard activities" organized around children's concrete personal experiences. Teacher/child interactions generally take the form of guided play with adult support. Teachers create a healthy learning environment, observe children for relevant cues, and follow their responses in order to expand their thinking and learning. Each teacher is expected to facilitate children's development by generating a broad repertoire of instructional and motivational strategies based on the maturationist position.

Child/child interactions are promoted with a focus on mutually supportive play, cooperation, and respect for others. Parent/child interactions, viewed as central to a child's development, are encouraged through home and school visits.

Few specifications are made about antecedents, although lower socioeconomic groups are thought to need a particularly predictable environment at first so that children can clearly see the effects their actions can have. Research (M. Deutsch, 1966) shows that lower-class home environments tend to be cluttered with stimuli; many people occupy restricted spaces, and noise levels are high. By establishing environmental constancy, behavioral cause-and-effect relationships begin to be identified for self and others.

This adaptable program requires minimal resources and materials, reflecting the near-total autonomy of teachers in applying program principles to a particular community context. Teachers must be trained in both child-development principles and specific content areas and must be well skilled in their application to the setting to ensure program implementation.

Behavioral/environmental approach

Evans (1975) summarizes the position of educators who subscribe to behavioral assumptions. Long-term educational goals are to provide children the requisite academic and social skills to compete effectively in public schools. Objectives deal with preacademic skills (reading, math, handwriting, spelling) and social skills (self-confidence, independent decision making, cooperation). Teachers arrange systematic learning experiences by manipulating materials, structuring equipment, and sequencing activities. They select and administer reinforcement schedules to maintain desired behaviors. Curricula and instructional strategies are precisely specified and procedures are carefully delineated to evaluate individual and program progress.

An example of a behaviorally oriented program is the Primary Education Project (Resnick, Wang, & Rosner, 1977). The basic goal for education is successful participation in school programs. Gagné's theory of cumulative learning (1968) holds that competence in school activities can be taught and used to construct more advanced areas of learning. Target learning activities are perceptual-motor skills, conceptual-linguistic skills, and orienting-attending skills.

To achieve these objectives planners devise a sequence of activities (or curriculum guide), which includes behavioral objectives, a description of materials, an outline of teaching strategies, and evaluation techniques. Basic content areas include quantification, classification, and perceptual-motor activities. Instructional strategies and motivational techniques reflect the role of the environment: teachers select activities and initiate contacts with children. In general, teachers are responsible for setting up the classroom and adapting the designed activities for individual children within the behavioral framework set down. Parents are taught the general principles and specific techniques of behavior management. They are encouraged to work in the classroom and use these techniques at home.

Cognitive/developmental approach

Educators supporting a cognitive/developmental approach use Piaget's theory as a foundation for program development (Flavell, 1963; Ginsberg & Opper, 1969; Piaget, 1970). This theory prescribes content—stage-based development of cognitive structures and operations—and process—active cognitive construction through interaction with the physical and social environment.

The curriculum model of Kamii and DeVries extends Piaget's hypotheses about how development and learning occur, with the goal of education defined as the "development of the entire personality with particular emphasis on intellectual and moral autonomy" (1977, p. 392). The development of logical thought proceeds simultaneously with socio-emotional growth; both are fostered by interactions with the environment. Children are considered intrinsically motivated to act on their environment, but not all interactions result in development. Children must construct the relationships between their actions and goals and the effects on objects and information.

This viewpoint prescribes a learning environment in which a variety of materials and activities are available for exploration. Teachers must recognize how children think and the type of knowledge children are trying to construct and then expand on this existing knowledge by using various techniques. Teachers can ask questions, introduce new materials or goals, and use peer interactions as strategies for challenging children's thought—referred to by theorists as inducing cognitive imbalance or disequilibrium. Children encouraged to restructure, consolidate, and advance their understanding by testing out new ideas on materials and people, especially peers.

Since Piaget hypothesized that stages of cognitive development occur in the same sequence for all people, this program applies to all children. The key to successful implementation is to have trained teachers with a firm grounding in Piagetian theory and early educational practice. Although this framework does not prescribe specific curriculum activities, it views development as a reciprocal relationship between content and process. Thus, the learning of facts and skills provides the "raw material" on which current cognitive abilities act and later cognitive abilities are based.

Eclectic curriculum programs

No current theory of psychology, education, or development is comprehensive enough to provide a complete guide for all aspects of program development (DeVries, 1974). Therefore, all theory-based programs are eclectic to some extent; that is, they are not easily categorized into one of the three frameworks just described. These programs make assumptions from several of the frameworks or are derived from other approaches or theories.

The Montessori Program developed by Maria Montessori illustrates an eclectic curriculum. Long-term educational goals are academic and practical success. Short-term objectives fall into one of four areas of development: motor, sensory, language, and academic skills. Children are assumed to be intrinsically motivated to act on the environment and thus capable of selecting and pacing their own activities. However, spontaneous play activities are not considered necessary or even effective in promoting development. Instead, Montessori has constructed a variety of self-correctional materials that are sequenced according to difficulty. Learning is assumed to be a function of repeated interactions with the materials and a result of the contiguity between actions and effects.

Teachers help children develop their "natural powers" by preparing and sequencing intrinsically interesting activities. Although this approach was developed for economically disadvantaged children, it is applied to all children. For further descriptions, interested readers are referred to Concannon (1970), Evans (1975), Johnson (1965), Martin (1965), Naumann (1966), Rambusch (1962), and Standing (1966).

Effects of theory and empirical research on model programs

Outcomes

Some authors believe that theory and research cannot be used to identify educational outcomes—goals and objectives (Kohlberg & Mayer, 1972). They maintain that theory can influence how objectives are conceptualized but that "theories do not of themselves specify what the immediate or ultimate purposes of education shall be" (Biber, 1977, p. 428). Kohlberg and Mayer (1972), however, believe theory is still useful for educational programs, even though it does not prescribe goals: "theory can be used by those whose educational goals are related to and consistent with the content and explanatory principles of the theory" (p. 463).

To examine whether theory impacts educational outcomes for young children, Kamii (1971) identified the philosophies of various existing programs and looked at the objectives associated with each. Data indicate that programs derived from maturationist theories emphasize socio-emotional goals such as inner controls on behavior, pride in mastery, and effective interactions with peers and adults. Behavioristically oriented programs focus on objectives in the area of preacademic skills and language. Programs with a cognitive/developmental orientation deal with the development of logical thought and cognitive skills, such as classification, number concepts, spatial relationships, and language. It seems, therefore, that decisions about educational goals and objectives are more closely tied to theoretical assumptions than is apparent at first glance.

Regardless of which viewpoint is supported, individuals argue whether the long-term goal of education should be development or skill attainment (Day, 1977; Evans, 1974; Sciarra & Dorsey, 1979). This debate has also been characterized as the "content-versus-process" issue (Day, 1977; Evans, 1975), in which one side focuses on the attainment of specific skills and facts, assuming that their acquisition leads to the exercise of more general cognitive capabilities. The other side emphasizes the development of more general cognitive processes, assuming that the desire to use these processes will lead to the acquisition of bits of knowledge (for example, Biber, 1977).

Program planners recognize that in today's society educational attainment and development are not distinct entities but are profoundly interrelated. As a result, although some theorists (Kohlberg & Mayer, 1972) maintain that the purpose of education should be development and others (Anderson & Bereiter, 1972) emphasize academic skills, the current argument revolves around the empirical relationship between the two positions. Rhine (1973) evaluated 22 preschool programs in Project Follow-Through—a maintenance/intervention approach for those children who were initially enrolled in Head Start—and found that positive motivational attitudes and teacher support enhanced development and skill attainment. Self-confidence, curiosity, self-regulation, task mastery, and recognized accomplishment in skill areas promoted academic functioning in reading, language, and mathematics. Thus both goals—development (process) and skill attainment (content)—are interconnected.

The order and timing of objectives also reflect theoretical assumptions. The basic issue is whether development is continuous or discontinuous. The continuity perspective views development as changing only on quantitative dimensions, as the result of adding component parts. Program planners supporting this viewpoint, which is implicit in the behavioral/environmental approach, isolate prerequisite skills, carefully sequence objectives for each child, and empirically determine when acquisition levels are reached. A view of development as being discontinuous considers qualitative change as the result of transformation or integration of processes. Objectives usually differ in kind and children's developmental levels determine their ordering and timing. Activities are structured conceptually to relate to these objectives and are flexible to permit children to use a range of cognitive abilities. The cognitive/developmental approach exemplifies this perspective.

Different assumptions about the nature of change, therefore, lead to differences in the range and specificity of behaviors described by an objective. One program may require a specific, observable behavior for successful achievement of an objective. For the same objective in another program, behavior may not be seen as indicating change unless it is accompanied by other conceptually relevant behaviors.

In sum, theoretical assumptions influence: (1) overall goals for education, (2) the relative emphasis placed on a particular content area, such as cognition, language, or sensorimotor development, (Peters, 1977), (3) the degree of interrelationship conceptualized between these aspects (Day, 1977; Peters & Dorman, 1974), (4) the breadth, specificity, and sequencing of objectives (Day, 1977), and (5) the measurement of program outcomes (Peters, 1977).

Recognition of the importance of theoretical differences in programs was first reflected in the empirical research of Maccoby and Zellner (1970), who used program specifications to compare and contrast "treatment" types. They divided 22 programs included in Project Follow-Through into 4 categories: behavioral/environmental, cognitive/transactional, psychosexual/personality, and normative/maturational. Programs in these categories differed on theoretical assumptions, curricula, and instructional strategies. However, all model programs agreed on the importance of the following six points: (1) clear goals are needed to direct and to make consistent educational planning and curriculum delivery, (2) objectives must include a core of appropriate behaviors (attentional responses, task orientation, motivation to learn academic content), (3) objectives must include positive attitudes toward self and school (self-esteem, confidence, freedom from fear), (4) educational activities must be appropriate for the child's "readiness" level, (5) instruction must be individualized, and (6) all children *can* and *will* learn.

Transactions

Theoretical assumptions influence decisions about the interactions an educator believes will foster development or learning (Day, 1977; DeVries, 1974; Peters, 1977; Peters & Dorman, 1974). Again, these assumptions reflect orientations about the development of person/environment relationships: what a person starts with, and how and why development occurs. (See Overton & Reese [1973], Lerner [1976], and Looft [1973], for complete explanations of the various positions.)

Theorists differ with respect to their views on the innate nature of people (DeVries, 1974; Kohlberg, 1968). At one extreme are behaviorists, who view children as a compilation of learned behaviors, and as born with the capacity to respond to the environment. They see all motivation, personality, and cognitive characteristics as learned. At the other pole are maturationists, who view children as the product of an "unfolding" process and as born with the genetic preprogramming needed for characteristics to emerge. Between these extremes are cognitive/developmentalists, who believe that children are born with basic biological structures and regulatory mechanisms that allow them to select and interpret experiences and so construct their own pictures of reality. All three views recognize the relationship between maturation and learning; however, the emphasis given to each aspect influences educational practices as well as other related assumptions.

Beliefs about how and why development proceeds are associated with different theories. On the one hand, behaviorists see development as quantitative, with increments of learning added from external forces. For example, achievement motivation is seen as learned through environmental reward for independent and initiating behaviors (Crandall, 1963). The normal process of learning through trial and error is not considered necessary, since more carefully constructed sequences of experiences can lead to similar outcomes at a faster rate (Brainerd, 1978a). On the other hand, maturationists view development as an internally controlled unfolding process in which the child spontaneously seeks out and benefits from those aspects of the environment that will facilitate development (Wachs, 1977). As long as the elements necessary for normal development are available, children can use them with minimal assistance. Again, midway between these extremes are cognitive/developmentalists, who see development as the product of a dynamic relationship between the person's characteristics and abilities (particularly cognitive organization) and aspects of the environment. Children are viewed as self-motivated but not always seeking out or profiting from experiences designed to facilitate change.

Child/material interactions. Different assumptions about children and their development lead to the design of very different kinds of transactions to promote learning and development. Children's interactions with materials reflect the structure of experiences that educators believe will maximize learning (Bissell, 1973; Day, 1977; Featherstone, 1973; Mayer, 1971). Behaviorists hold that since children's spontaneous interactions with materials are not necessarily those that will foster development most efficiently, a tightly organized environment and system of external controls are needed to maintain appropriate interactions. They believe that readiness for certain experiences is empirically derived, allowing teachers to make available or direct children to relevant activities. The structure of material usage may be a product of the nature of the materials (for example, a sorting box), the reinforcement or instruction of the teacher (for example, "find the red circle"), or the system of norms and rules in the classroom (for example, bingo games are used according to the rules).

Maturationist educators construct environments to reflect their assumptions about how children learn, believing that a richly nurturant environment and a supportive rule system allow children to select and use interactions with materials to foster their learning. They assume that intrinsic motivation is a given, so only socialized behaviors must be learned. Children make decisions about readiness to learn. Thus, a wide range of age-appropriate materials are made available and used according to a self-initiation (or positive-response) rule system.

For cognitive/developmental educators, children's intrinsic desires to act on the environment ensure cognitively appropriate interactions with materials. Action is considered necessary but not sufficient for development (Gallagher, 1978). Therefore, interactions that induce conflict will be fostered by either the introduction of new materials or guidance in the use of existing materials. Sequence and timing of material use is primarily determined by children.

Child/teacher interactions. Children's interactions with teachers (instructional strategies and motivational techniques) also reflect assumptions about how development occurs (Bissell, 1973; Featherstone, 1973; Weikart, 1972; White et al., 1973). Behaviorally oriented teachers use more directive strategies because children must participate in selected activities in order to benefit from those experiences. Teachers assume an active initiating and limiting role so children can internalize these controls. Teachers tailor learning sequences for individual children by considering both skill level and reinforcement history, since the child will not necessarily select the most beneficial experiences. Motivational techniques involve modifying behaviors through selective reinforcement, modeling, shaping, and extinction.

Because of their assumptions about intrinsic motivation and self-guidance, maturationists allow children to select and use materials as desired. Individualization of instruction is a direct result of children's ability to initiate and maintain appropriate interactions. Teachers provide a supportive learning and social environment for children's growth. Of course, this involves limiting socially unacceptable behaviors and fostering social skills, although always within a framework of age-appropriate expectations and rules.

For the cognitive/developmentalist, teachers' motivation techniques are passive: initiation of activities originates in the child. However, the development that results from interactions is a product of children's activity in the environment, and then fitting these sequences together and applying them to other interactions. Teachers try to facilitate these processes through: question asking, prediction, suggestions, and other strategies.

Child/child interactions. The functions attributed to peer interaction by theorists influence its use in programs (Day, 1977). Behavioral programs typically do not ascribe special status to peer relations; peers are seen to function as models and reinforcement agents much as adults do. For maturationist programs, peer interaction is a primary socialization process and so typically a key objective and transaction. In cognitive/developmental programs, peer interactions are considered important because they provide alternative viewpoints and strategies.

Antecedents

Varying assumptions about antecedents cause educators to focus on different aspects of curriculum—entering skill level and reinforcement history; maturational level and socialization experiences; and cognitive developmental level (see DeVries, 1974 for a discussion of "readiness"). Specific theories of individual differences, especially those relating to personality and temperament, can lead to the identification of target populations for whom programs might be particularly effective. (See Nedler, 1977 for a description of a program about bilingual children, and Peters et al., 1977 for a summary of this position.)

Theoretical assumptions regarding resources result in different staff training and curriculum models (Day, 1977; Weikart, 1972). Behavioral programs typically focus on precise delineation of behavioral objectives; careful documentation of sequenced activities, required materials, and instructional strategies; and detailed prescriptions for evaluation procedures. Teachers are trained to set up classrooms within the prescribed framework and to adapt the behavioral principles and curriculum for use in their own classrooms. Teacher autonomy is restricted because the interactions children need for development have been prespecified.

Maturationist and cognitive/developmental teacher preparation involves the learning of basic teaching principles, the manifestation of which cannot be specified in precise behavioral terms. Discussion and modeling of concepts about desired types of curriculum experiences and instructional strategies and guided experience lead to a basic understanding of the goals and processes of education. These are then transformed by individual teachers when applied to particular settings, children, staff, and parents.

The issue of antecedents, therefore, can be divided into two questions: For what target populations or communities will transactions be effective in producing outcomes? And what resources are needed to insure implementation? Peters and colleagues (1977) addressed these questions by using the Cronbach (1967) aptitude-by-treatment interaction framework, which emphasizes the identification of abilities of each person in the target group and the individual use of resources for intervention strategies. Sometimes individuals can be grouped in treatments when certain abilities are held common. Evans (1975) notes that "different children will respond differently to any given educational method to the extent that their genetic makeup and past environmental experiences differ" (p. 394). Most model programs are designed for disadvantaged populations, but many maintain their effectiveness for all children. Occasional mention is made of transactions that may be needed for children with particular backgrounds (see Biber, 1977; Nedler, 1977), but most programs assume that individualization of instruction, translated differently for each model, deals adequately with individual differences.

Functional relationships

Three studies (Bissell, 1973; Soar & Soar, 1972; Stallings, 1975) used program specification to examine differences in program functioning and outcomes. The important utility of delineating programs, as you may recall, is for program comparisons. In their analysis of data from behaviorally and maturationally oriented programs, Soar and Soar (1972) concluded that the Follow-Through programs differed in two respects: behaviorally oriented programs exhibited structured learning and teacher-directed activity, while maturationally oriented programs emphasized free choice and pupil-selected activity.

Stallings's (1975) examination of seven Follow-Through model programs implemented at 36 sites revealed a number of variables that differentiated conceptually distinct programs. Two behaviorally oriented, one Piagetian, and four maturationally oriented programs were found to differ on four variables: adult reinforcement and praise, individual versus group performance, group size, and amount and variety of materials. He concluded that models contained unique features that were consistent across sites and congruent with specifications.

Bissell (1973) divided 12 Follow-Through model programs into 3 categories based on their conceptualizations: academic, cognitive discovery, and discovery. These correspond approximately to the behavioral, cognitive/developmental, and maturational categories described earlier. He found that the three types of programs could be differentiated on two variables: amount of preplanned discrete academic activities and frequency of teacher initiation and response. He also found that several factors were related to accurate implementation (defined as congruity between written curriculum and daily functioning). Specifically, programs with the most exact prescriptions of teacher behavior, classroom organization and activities, and so on were the most similar across sites. Academic programs were most successfully exported, followed by cognitive-discovery and then discovery programs, which include other processes besides cognition. In addition to specificity of written materials, other conditions maximized successful implementation: (1) adequate facilities and resource materials, (2) stable, well-organized staff model, (3) staff belief in and satisfaction with model, and (4) length of time since implementation began. A continuing theme in accurate implementation is the explicit delineation of key aspects.

Stallings (1975) also was interested in the functional relationships between particular types of transactions on the one hand and outcomes on standardized tests (Metropolitan Achievement Tests of Reading and Arithmetic, Raven's Colored Progressive Matrices, Intellectual Responsibility Scale) and child behaviors (absence, independence, task persistence, and question asking) on the other. Table 6–2 summarizes the outcomes associated with particular transaction types. In general, programs with systematic instruction and high positive reinforcement led to higher reading and math scores, whereas programs that included more exploratory materials, a more flexible classroom environment, and child-selection of activities resulted in increased nonverbal reasoning, independent working, and attendance rates.

The overall results of these studies demonstrate that, regardless of the specific model program used, good implementation leads to positive results that approximate specified goals and objectives (Evans,1975). While encouraging, these conclusions are qualified by several factors. First, the aspects that differentiate programs are not necessarily those that cause outcomes (Soar & Soar, 1972). Other unmeasured variables associated with measured factors may be responsible for changes, or combinations of variables may promote certain changes. Peters and colleagues (1977) argue that the effectiveness of transactions in influencing target behavior may be mediated by attributes of the target population. Secondly, effects obtained are almost always immediate, but their persistence and impact on later functioning are uncertain. Whether the problem of durability has implications for preschool programs or other educational and social services is not clear. Finally, the consistency with which transactions are fostered across community and geographical settings can affect the potency of transactions.

Community influence

Communities in which programs are located can influence the planning and implementation of programs. In the broadest sense, for a program to be supported in a particular location, the service provided must be needed (Trujillo, 1974; Peters & Dorman, 1974; Sciarra & Dorsey, 1979). More specifically, community members and parents influence programs in the following three ways: (1) their needs and opinions

TABLE 6-2 Summary of outcomes in seven Follow-Through model programs

Transaction type	Outcome (Program)*		
Child/material interaction			
1. Length of time in activity	Reading (O, K), Math (O, K)		
2. Informal experiences	Math (O, K)		
3. Exploratory materials	Cooperation (EDC, FW)		
4. Variety of materials	Cooperation (EDC, FW), Independence (EDC, FW), Raven's (EDC, FW, A, B, HS)		
5. Text books, programmed workbooks	Task persistence (A, K), Math (O, K)		
Child/teacher interaction			
1. Systematic instruction	Reading (O, K), Math (O, K)		
2. Feedback (reinforcement)	Reading (O, K), Math (O, K)	Absence greater	
3. Direct academic questioning		Absence greater	
4. Child-selected activities	Raven's (EDC, FW, A, B, HS)	Independence (EDC, FW)	
5. Child-initiated questions	Raven's (EDC, FW, A, B, HS)	Attendance greater (FW, A, HS)	
6. Teacher responsiveness	Question-asking (EDC, FW, B, K, HS)	Attendance greater (FW, A, HS)	
7. Child independence	Reading (O, K), Math (O, K)	Attendance greater (FW, A, HS)	
8. Individual (one-to-one) instruction	Question-asking (EDC, FW, B, K, HS) Task persistence (A, K)	Attendance greater (FW, A, HS)	
9. General conversation	Question-asking (EDC, FW, B, K, HS)		
Child/child interaction			
1. Small groups	Reading (O, K), Math (O, K) older children		
2. Larger groups	Math (O, K) younger children	Absence greater	
3. Child-selected group	Cooperation (EDC, HS, B)		
4. More peer interaction	Raven's (FW, EDC, A, B, HS)		
Overall attributes			
1. High flexibility	Independence (EDC, FW), Raven's (FW, A, B, HS, EDC)		
2. High structure	Internal success/external failure Internal failure/external success Internal success/internal failure (EDC)		

*Key to programs: *behavioral*   University of Oregon (O)   University of Kansas (K)
Piagetian   High/Scope (HS)   *maturational*   Far West (FW)   Bank Street (B)
University of Arizona (A)   Educational Development Corporation (EDC)

Based on "Implementation and Child Effects of Teaching Practices in Follow-Through Classrooms," by J. Stallings. In *Monographs of the Society for Research In Child Development*, 1975, 40.

can be reflected in program objectives; (2) their participation can provide resources and ideas for transactions; and (3) their existing social system can promote a context that influences both immediate gains and long-term effects.

Needs and values

A community and its participating families may have specific values and opinions about the identified objectives of the planners (Peters & Marcus, 1973; Stake, 1967; Taylor & McGuire, 1966). For example, Hoffman describes a needs assessment in which respondents indicated the following priorities: cognitive development, cultural pride, self-esteem, bilingual competency, and awareness of social, political, and economic pressures (cited in Trujillo, 1974). If programs are to be successful, parental objectives must be incorporated.

Several methods for soliciting community input have been identified (Peters & Dorman, 1974; Peters & Marcus, 1973; Hoffman, 1971; see especially Trujillo, 1974

Depending on which developmental theory is supported, programs will look different to observers and will satisfy different community and parental needs.

for program exemplars of community participation). Before a program begins, a community needs-assessment should be administered because the information gathered will help to make decisions ranging from the general, such as the type of program selected, to the particular, such as specific objectives desired. Sciarra and Dorsey (1979) detail the information needed to determine the number of families that will use a child-care service and the type of service desired, including number of appropriate-aged children, parents' willingness to pay, and location and type of program desired. In describing procedures to collect, record, compile, and analyze information, they emphasize brevity, understandable wording, and complete coverage of data. They contrast the pros and cons of questionnaire surveys (see also Peters & Marcus, 1973), telephone surveys, and small group meetings. See Chapter 5 for an illustration of a questionnaire used to collect community opinions.

Participation and purposes

Programs can be designed to view parents and community members not only as service recipients, but also as contributors and resources for programs (Wray, 1971). In fact, as Trujillo (1974) states, "Community participation means mutual initiative and involvement of persons from target area neighborhoods and the community at large, or special communities of professional people with the resources and skills to help with specific program problems" (p. 83-84). Parents and community members can extend the time, money, and skill of the staff in different ways: by donating materials, sites for field trips, or special presentations; by organizing demonstrations of skills or ethnic customs; by participating in the classroom as a teacher or teacher's aide.

Family participation also can extend a program's transactions into the home environment (see Bronfenbrenner, 1974a; Gordon, I. J., 1970; Nimnicht, Arango, & Cheever, 1977; Peters, 1977). Parent programs, direct instruction, workshops, demonstrations, and home visits can be used to promote desired program outcomes.

Parents can influence the particular educational transactions teachers provide by making decisions about curriculum content and staff selection (McInnerey, Durr, Kershner, & Nash, 1967). Interestingly, research shows that giving parents decision-making power in programs for their children can be an effective strategy for increasing their feelings of control, persistence, and positive attitudes toward education (Hoffman, 1971; Lally, 1971; Marshall, 1969). (Chapter 5 examines the evolving role of parents in child programs.)

Meeting the needs of a community and the needs of parents for participation does not mean just serving current interests; it also requires providing programs that build for the future. To achieve a positive long-range impact, programs should try to predict the needs of learners in developing communities within the societal context and help participants identify and reach their own goals.

Conclusion

Program planners design preschool environments that provide particular combinations of experiences for young children. The transactions selected depend on desired outcomes (short- and long-term) on the target population, and on available facilities, staff, and resources. Because of different assumptions and goals, program sponsors disagree about the most desirable program for certain children. The following three criteria can be used to measure the quality of any program regardless of ideology.

It is important to assess the coherence of program components. Given long-term goals for education and specific assumptions about children and their development, immediate program objectives must make sense. Likewise, antecedents and transactions must be consistent with outcomes. The functional relationship between components can be established by using theory or empirical research. It is the integrity of these links that defines a program's viability.

A second criterion is the extent to which the actual functioning of a program matches its planned operation. Accurate implementation of a program requires careful analysis of the elements that are essential to its success and provide materials (for example, written curriculum, teacher training and assessment, and formative evaluation) to ensure faithful reproduction of these elements.

A third criterion is the effectiveness of a program in delivering promised outcomes. Goals and objectives related to all transactions must be included and to be potentially achieved, outcomes, transactions, and antecedents must be specified and measured. See Chapter 13 for a model of program evaluation.

Various sources are available to aid in decisions about outcomes, transactions, and antecedents. Theory and empirical research, and community and parent opinion should be used by educators to produce plans for the operation of preschools. This process is complicated by many factors, one of which is that theory is notoriously difficult to translate into practice. Many theories do not adequately deal with the interrelationships among a child's biological, psychological, and social development, nor do they consider the relationships between the child and social, historical, societal, and physical environments. Also, practical constraints of time, money, staff, and community force educators to set priorities and make compromises.

Early childhood education, no matter how well planned and implemented, places inherent limitations on the effects produced. As Susan Gray observed, "An effective early intervention program for a preschool child, be it ever so good, cannot possibly be viewed as a form of innoculation whereby the child is immunized forever afterward to the effects of an inadequate home and a school inappropriate to his [or her] needs" (cited in Ryan, 1974, p. 136). Therefore, the development of quality preschool programs requires explicit delineation of program components and their evaluation within the societal context.

Judging the quality of programs always is a matter of opinions and values. Dialogues among educators, theorists, policy makers, and concerned citizens must continue. Although many viewpoints have been articulated (Evans, 1975) and serve to highlight complex issues, only by making assumptions and priorities explicit are intelligent discussions and choices possible. Given the powerful impact of educational experiences, decisions must be made wisely.

Summary

Youngsters receive education at earlier ages, in greater numbers, and for a wider variety of different reasons than ever before. Often parents view early childhood education as a way to ensure that their children will have the requisite skills for fostering academic success. They also may feel it provides an arena for socialization, especially when there are no siblings.

Professionals who believe that experience can modify children's behavior have built a labyrinth of programs, the complexity and variety of which sometimes make them appear as a convoluted maze. Because programs deliver different services, do not use similar measures, and vary in purpose, making comparisons is arduous. If the development of children is to be optimized, then perhaps the first task is to assess existing programs so that future planning can be directed.

A specification model allows a delineation and comparison of program components. By understanding program outcomes, transactions, and antecedents, professionals can more profitably share information among themselves and with the community. Documents describing philosophies, assumptions, and purposes can allow programs to be more consistently implemented. And the links among theory, empirical research, and application can be made with awareness of their implications.

Other positive effects can result. Families can renew their faith in professionals who can demonstrate the effects of programs on children. Communities can better identify which programs are available for which target groups. Even the government at a state or federal level could disperse funds more effectively. And, children will benefit, not despite what professionals do, but because of their purposeful efforts.

7

The Social Context of Child Protective Services

This chapter was written in collaboration with JAMES GARBARINO, Ph.D., as the senior author. Garbarino is currently Associate Professor of Human Development, The Pennsylvania State University.

Chapter overview

The abuse and neglect of children, which can result in both physical and psychological harm, is one of the urgent concerns confronting Americans today. Ways to protect children and help parents must be identified, implemented, and evaluated. This chapter examines child maltreatment within an ecological framework, which forms definitions of abuse and neglect, helps us understand causes and effects, creates the protective service system, and directs future efforts.

Issues to consider

How do contextual factors influence our definitions of child abuse and neglect?
What are the difficulties in diagnosing child abuse, neglect, and maltreatment?
What is the incidence of child maltreatment in the United States?
How can a family system dysfunction cause child maltreatment?
What conditions are necessary to produce child mistreatment?
How is child maltreatment reported and what problems surround reporting cases?
What is involved in determining and managing cases of maltreatment?
What are the problems with institutional maltreatment?
What are the characteristics of our present system of protective services?
What directions for the future are suggested by evidence about case treatment and intervention models?

Introduction

Dick and Sally are caseworkers for the Child Welfare Department in a medium-sized city. At any one time, each investigates and manages more than thirty cases of child abuse and neglect. They determine how dangerous family situations are and whether there are prospects for improvement. On any given day they may be asked whether a six-month-old is in danger of being murdered, a teenage mother is capable of caring for her two children currently in foster care, or a father who sexually molested his 10-year-old stepdaughter has progressed enough in a counseling program to let the girl return home. In the course of their work, they may be threatened by an irate father, bullied by a defense attorney, and worn to a frazzle by client and supervisor demands.

Dick and Sally, and thousands of others like them, are part of our society's system of child protective services, which provide help for abused or neglected children and their parents.

Lucy is a mother of three young children. Her husband works for the phone company and they are saving for a new house. All in all, her life seems to be in pretty good shape. However, there is one thing that bothers her these days, and that's her friend Betty. Betty also has three children and a husband who works for the phone company. Maybe that's why they became friends in the first place. Lucy likes Betty, but she is disturbed by the way Betty hits her kids. Sometimes the oldest one has bruises, and there was that time last month when the youngest one had a black eye. Betty said the little girl fell. Lucy wasn't really convinced, but how do you go about asking your friend if she beats her kids?

Across the country, half of the reports of abuse and neglect come to official attention through the efforts of friends, neighbors, and relatives.

Robert works for a federal agency in Washington, D.C. developing plans for the family-assistance program to deal with child abuse and neglect. The available money seems large on paper ($3.7 million). But after it's spread across the country and filtered through the bureaucracy, it seems to vanish. How can he devise a plan so that the money will reach families in greatest need? What route should he take and how can he justify his decision?

Significant differences of opinion exist about how best to spend the available federal money to improve child protective services—whether to emphasize research or demonstration projects, for example.

Elsie lives in rural New York state. She was born not twenty miles from where she lives today. Last Sunday after church she almost stopped to talk to the minister about her problem, but then didn't. That's just it. Is it her problem or should she mind her own business? The problem is her husband's sister, Maggie. Maggie lives down the road about six miles. There really isn't room for the four kids even if they kept the place clean, which they don't. None of the kids looks clean and they're always sick or getting hurt falling over the trash. Then to top it all off, Maggie left the kids with the seven-year-old in charge while she went out bar hopping. Elsie's husband says his family always does things their own way, but she wonders how those kids will grow up healthy the way they live. Whom can she talk to about her problem?

Many citizens are uncertain about what their responsibility is regarding child abuse and neglect, and how to go about fulfilling that responsibility. This uncertainty is exacerbated by the difficulty of defining and consequently identifying abuse and neglect. In fact, most experts agree that to conduct research on child maltreatment that is both scientifically sound and consistent with the real world of child protective services is a monumental challenge. The voluntary support of private citizens may be the key in providing the needed resources for an effective community response to the problem of child maltreatment.

Like nearly all significant human phenomena, child protective services exist in social contexts—institutions, neighborhoods, police stations, schools, and families. If we are to understand individual child protective service workers and their tasks, then we must understand their work world, including the allies they may call upon. What should children be protected from, and how many children need protection? What are the causes and effects of child abuse and neglect?

Child abuse and neglect defined

Defining abuse and neglect challenges practitioners, researchers, and theoreticians. One of the best analyses of child abuse (Parke & Collmer, 1975) concludes that none of the definitions is free of ambiguity.

Social and cultural factors

Definitions of child abuse and neglect differ as they take into account the following contextual factors: (1) the intention of the actor, (2) the act's effect upon the recipient, (3) an observer's value judgment about the act, and (4) the source of the standard for that judgment. Different emphases on these four elements—intentionality, effect, evaluation, and standards—form the controversy in defining child abuse and neglect.

Emphasis on effect and intentionality. The easiest definition of child abuse is: any behavior by a parent that results in injury to a child. The type of injury (physical or psychological) and parental intentions are ignored because judgments are based solely on the effect of parental behavior upon a child. What about a beaten child who escapes physical injury? This definition negates the abusiveness of the beating suffered. In other words, it lacks the concept of *standards*. So-called invulnerable children who thrive despite deprived childhoods, for example, would be exempt from this definition no matter how they were treated. However, children who were accidentally injured by parents would be classified as abused.

Other definitions of child abuse incorporate parental intentions. For instance, Kempe and Helfer define it as *"non-accidental* physical injury that results from acts of omission on the part of parents or guardians" (1975, p. 1). But this definition only considers physical injury, to the exclusion of psychological damage, which can and does occur (Kinard, 1979). However, it does not require that a parent intend to harm a child; therefore, parents who are ignorant can be called abusive. How do individuals become socially isolated where ignorance of society's standards for child care can flourish? Are communities accessories to this "crime" through tolerance or by ignoring such families?

Gil (1970) and others argue that force itself is abusive, even without specific physical injury. In his view, abuse is "intentional, non-accidental use of force aimed at hurting, injuring, or destroying the child" (p. 6). If "hurting" includes "causing pain," then this definition would call spanking abuse and would apply to most children (Gelles, 1978). Many researchers reject this definition because it is too broad, although they believe that the use of force against children is the core of the child-abuse problem in today's culture. Also they may not be able to envision a nonviolent style of child rearing.

Protective service workers are drawn into this debate over intentionality. Because these workers must make judgments, their own views on the use of physical punishment should be clarified through introspection and discussion with peers and respected authorities. Knowing where one stands on issues, what one's biases are, and what major values are addressed in an intervention area is of generic importance for all human service professionals (see Chapter 4).

Emphasis on evaluation and standards.   Community standards are used by some investigators to define child abuse. Parke and Collmer define it as "non-accidental physical injury as a result of acts (or omissions) on the part of parents or guardians *that violate the community's standards concerning the treatment of children"* (1975, p. 513; italics added). According to this view, community members can best interpret their norms and identify acts that violate those norms. Empirical evidence shows that while community standards vary, consensus about types and the seriousness of child maltreatment across ethnic groups does exist—for example, people agree about extreme abuse such as sexual assaults (Giovannoni & Becerra, 1979). The application of societal values at a community level is one way to judge child abuse.

Scientists who support an anthropological perspective view child abuse as a culturally determined label applicable to both behavior and injuries (Walters & Parke, 1964). They believe, for example, that facial scarification as part of a tribal ritual is not the same thing as sustaining facial scars from a violent argument. In their view, specific events and behaviors derive meaning from their cultural context, which determines what is normal and what is deviant. If scarification is typical for an age grade, then it is normal. This anthropological position suggests that the definition of child abuse must move beyond specific behaviors (and their physical consequences) because some may be culturally sanctioned.

Should cultures be limited in the types and degree of behavior toward children that they sanction? Some cultures, for instance, support harmful practices (such as infanticide). The American culture contains elements such as racism and sexism that harm children. How can features of cultures that are just style differences be distinguished from cultural "errors"—actions that are intrinsically harmful to children? And, once identified, what can or should be done about these actions?

Distinguishing legitimate differences in cultural style from practices based on anti-child values is a persistent dilemma. One anthropologist (Korbin, personal communication) recalls being questioned by native Hawaiian mothers about the "abusive" American practice of forcing infants to sleep in cribs and rooms apart from their parents. Is this child abuse or cultural difference?

The definition of child abuse must rely on authority beyond the opinions held by parents, which can be modeled after abusive parental behavior or incorrect assumptions about children. Thus, a legitimate definition of child abuse must include a second standard—our best scientific understanding of parent/child relations. This addition, however, does not negate the important role of culture in defining child abuse. For example, evidence demonstrates a connection between the use of physical punishment and impaired psychological development and social competence. However, the American culture so strongly supports the practice of physical punishment that only the most devoted child advocates would say that spanking in and of itself is abusive. Even empirical findings are equivocal about the effects of spanking on children. Defining some behavior as abusive, with the resulting implications about family life, must be based on a mixture of cultural standards and professional knowledge. The Hawaiian mothers' concern cited earlier is a good example. Thus, defining child abuse is admittedly a process of negotiation between culture and science, folk wisdom and professional expertise. Cultural differences do not in and of themselves imply abuse.

Diagnostic difficulties

Intentionality, effect, evaluation, and standards are emphasized in the following definition of child abuse: acts of omission or commission by a parent or guardian that are judged by a mixture of community values and professional expertise to be inappropriate and damaging. "Inappropriate" describes parental action; "damaging" covers its effect upon the development of the victim. Both are defined by a value judgment based upon community standards and professional expertise.

Inappropriate parental behavior may produce physical or emotional damage. But accurate prediction is difficult because victims usually suffer damage in many areas, and individual susceptibility to harm differs. Also, while each type of maltreatment is distinct in principle, in practice types of abuse overlap, especially when a troubled family is observed over a long period of time.

Abuse, neglect, or maltreatment.   Because child abuse is multifaceted in terms of damage and types displayed, the broader label *maltreatment* is more appropriate than the terms *abuse* and *neglect*. Acts of commission, in which adults actively harm children (the typical distinguishing mark of abuse), often accompany acts of omission, in which adults passively fail to provide necessities for children's growth and development (the primary characteristic of neglect). Neglect and abuse are often found in the same family, with some estimates putting their coincidence at 50% (Garbarino & Crouter, 1978a). They also may occur in sequence, as when neglect by one parent exposes a child to abuse by the other. (This often seems to happen in cases of sexual abuse.)

Issue of protection and standards. Which term—*abuse, neglect,* or *maltreatment*—is used is unimportant. The questions remain: how to protect a child or teenager from damage and exploitation, and how to enforce high standards of care for children and youth. The definition of child abuse given earlier articulates what parents and guardians (including the government) must do and what they may not do.

It also includes an awareness of development by incorporating the concept of appropriate rearing, which is different for young children than for adolescents. In fact, a fairly common parental problem is changing child-rearing habits. For example, teenagers are far more capable of abstract thought than are children and usually can independently evaluate their own motives as well as the motives of others. This capability demands that parents reason and consult with their adolescent children when making family decisions and setting rules. When adolescents initially assert their independence, disturbances often result even within otherwise smoothly functioning families (see Chapter 4 in Hultsch and Deutsch, 1981; Steinberg, 1977). Most parents eventually adjust to their adolescent children's concerns, needs, and problems. Those who do not are much more likely to abuse their teenagers. Protective service workers should be alert to the developmental dimension of abuse—the relevance and significance of individual characteristics shift as children get older— and to developmental changes in parents, which also influence parent/child interactions. Because some teenagers are more likely to be abused than others, professionals also must move beyond a focus on damage and corrective intervention to a focus on risk and preventive intervention.

Drawing a conclusion. There is no precise definition of child maltreatment, nor is there a conclusive list of defining characteristics that a professional can simply check with and check off in making a "diagnosis." Rather, to label behavior as abusive or neglectful is to draw a conclusion about its relationship to society's concept of the roles of a child and a parent in society and to scientific understanding of what helps children and what hurts them. This matter is not simply an academic point of little practical significance, of course. For legislators and jurists, it goes far toward explaining why it is virtually impossible to write "air-tight" child abuse and neglect laws that effectively curb the phenomena. For the child protective service worker, the problems in the meaning of child maltreatment must be dealt with on a daily basis, in the office, on the streets, in peoples' houses, and in the courts.

Incidence of child maltreatment

To perceive a problem as serious three factors must be considered: (1) primacy, (2) magnitude, and (3) severity (Manis, 1974). *Primacy* refers to a problem's role in producing or precipitating other problems. Poverty, for example, is a primary problem because it is implicated in a wide range of other problems. *Magnitude* refers to the frequency of the problem in a population, such as the number of cases of juvenile delinquency per 1000 families. *Severity* refers to the degree of damage or threat associated with a particular problem—for example, permanent brain damage leading to profound mental retardation. Child maltreatment is a serious problem because it reflects many thousands of families with a variety of problems that produce physically, socially, and emotionally impaired children and youth.

How many cases of child maltreatment are there? Of course, the answer to this question depends on the definition used—the broader the definition, the greater the numbers. Using the most narrow definition, one that includes only life-threatening physical assault, results in an incidence figure on the order of the thousands with perhaps an upper limit of ten thousand. Using a very broad definition of

Child abuse is more likely to be prevented when parents are able to adjust to their adolescents' needs and problems and when professionals are trained to deal with such developmental issues.

maltreatment, one that incorporates neglect as well as physical, emotional, and sexual abuse, the estimated incidence runs in excess of a million children.

How many children are victims of maltreatment? Fraser's figure (1979) of one million plus, an admittedly "soft" estimate, is based on many investigators' research and their best judgments. It includes Light's extrapolation (1973) from a national probability sample, which asked people if they were aware of cases of physical abuse. It further includes efforts by Sarafino (1979) to estimate the number of sexually abused children and youth and Polansky's (1976) estimate of neglected children. When these figures are added to the survey of parents by Straus, Gelles, and Steinmetz (1979) that dealt with all forms of domestic violence, the figure of one million per year seems reasonable and, if anything, conservative.

This large figure no doubt reflects multiple causes and effects of child maltreatment. What are the economic implications of intervention into the lives of these children? Fraser (1979) estimates if a figure of $8000 per effective treatment is used, one that seems reasonable based on existing approaches (Cohn, 1979), providing effective treatment for the annual number of child maltreatment cases would run on the order of $4 billion. To commit such financial resources to treatment programs that are not verified empirically is not likely, nor is it wise.

Family system dysfunction

Scholars and practitioners increasingly recognize that child maltreatment is the product of a multiplicity of factors (Friedman, 1976; Garbarino, 1977; Polansky, 1976). The sufficient conditions for child abuse and neglect lie in the daily experiences of the child, principally in the family, since members of the immediate family are perpetrators in some 90% of the cases, according to Gil's (1970) national survey of cases. In most cases, a recurrent pattern of child maltreatment requires the compliance or acquiescence of persons other than the parent/child dyad. Viewed this way, abuse is truly a family system dysfunction.

Normal and psychopathological abuse

A pattern of abuse is based on particular kinds of relationships between the victim/perpetrator dyad and others with whom they have or might have relationships. Two types of dysfunctions in the family system can generate abusive behavior. The first involves the psychopathological assault by parents, whether physical, emotional, or sexual. The simplest and least common form of abuse, derives from the parent's severely abnormal psychological functioning. The second stems from the psychologically "normal" abuse implicit in our culture's support of physical punishment and other forms of power assertion and authoritarianism within the family. This type of abuse is best understood as a process that initially magnifies small differences and deficiencies. These small asynchronies between child and care giver, mild control problems, forms of discipline, and slightly aversive interactions are multiplied over time until they are recognizable as deviant, dangerous patterns. In this way, psychologically normal parents are set up for abuse by the combination of our culture and their own special circumstances.

Friedman (1976) believes that distinguishing between abuse by normal adults and by sadistically psychopathological adults is essential for intervention efforts. After identifying the origins and characteristics of the family situation, the appropriate type of community support systems must be selected.

Situational incompetence

Abuse perpetrated by so-called normal individuals describes a form of situationally defined incompetence. These adults are not functioning properly in their caregiver roles, often because of social stress and lack of knowledge about parenting skills. Social stress usually occurs from societal factors outside the family, such as unemployment. But it can occur from the dynamics of family functioning, such as a child who just does not listen. Likewise, poor parenting skills are a function of external and internal factors. Job demands may be such that a parent has little or no time for interacting with his or her children. Or a mother and father may disagree over the best way to discipline a child with the result that no guidelines whatever are conveyed. Both stress and skills are process variables that shape interactions of family members. They also are relative in terms of time. Adults handle stress differently depending upon when it occurs, how long it lasts, and the ramifications of its influence on their particular circumstances. Similarly, parenting skills can vary. Some parents are extremely effective with children of a particular age. Competence in handling aspects of stress or parenting, like most forms of competence, depends upon the situation, narrowly defined by the family or more broadly defined by the community or the society.

As Green (1968) and others have shown, the key situational factor determining child abuse is the "match" of parent to child. Perceptions of stress and competence as well as expectations about how to handle them can vary between parent and child. Experimental laboratory research and studies in naturalistic settings have demonstrated that virtually anyone can be broken by some situations (Bettelheim, 1943; Milgram, 1974). Almost no one is immune to the role of child abuser when the discrepancy between support and demands becomes great enough, although people vary in the degree to which they act in an abusive manner. Some of us are "saints" and some "demons," but most of us are just people. This implies that some parents could have learned their abusive role, which then became part of their personalities.

Role problems

In contrast to researchers who seek to understand maltreatment as a personality malfunction, a sociological approach focuses on maltreatment as a problem with roles. Psychiatrists, however, usually view this as a character disorder.

The maltreatment of children stems from incompetence in the role of caregiver. Maltreatment, the culturally defined labeling of inappropriate behavior, can be excessive use of force, sexual misuse, emotional rejection, or inadequate provision of essential nurturance. The three factors that facilitate effective adaptation are rehearsal of the role, realistic and clear expectations, and congruence between the previous and the new role (Elder, 1977). These factors are particularly important for the transition to the parental role, depending in large measure on childhood experiences with parents, relatives, and teachers. These experiences go far in summarizing research findings concerning characteristics of people and institutions involved in mistreating children and youth, and societies that permit or even precipitate such maltreatment.

Parents who mistreat their children appear to have had little basis for rehearsing the role of caregiver, which in turn appears to be linked to their lack of empathy (Gray, 1978). They often were maltreated as children, did not have pets or siblings on which to practice being a parent, and have a history of social impoverishment. No wonder they have trouble learning the role of parent. Research continuously shows these adults lack knowledge about parenting and hold unrealistic expectations about children (Parke & Collmer, 1975).

The role of caregiver requires a reordering of priorities, especially the gratification of needs. The child must come first. Parents who mistreat their children are described as individuals who have trouble weighing their needs against their children's, and who receive little support in making appropriate choices (Justice & Justice, 1976). Often they represent the height of selfishness and possess the lowest self-concept. Incompetence in the role of caregiver, then, can be associated with internal forms of stress often brought about by this personal incongruity. A primary task of the protective service worker is dealing with these varieties of stress and mobilizing community support networks to mitigate against them.

Lives out of control

The more general problem related to child maltreatment is lives out of control, which can take many different forms. Young (1964) reported that in 88% of abusive families parents failed to take responsibility for making decisions. Others noted that abusing parents often perceive themselves as impotent in the face of forces both internal and external to the family. Justice and Duncan (1976) and others (Garbarino & Sherman, 1980) found that abusive families are characterized by enormous demands for adjustment, by events that disrupt roles and relationships and require stressful psychosocial and behavioral accommodations. Families involved in abuse seem caught up in a pattern of fundamental asynchrony, of chronic and acute mismatch between reality and their ability to effectively manage that reality. Such extreme mismatches occur in different areas separately or simultaneously. For instance, mothers and infants may not get along in the early weeks of life (Kennell, Voos, & Klaus, 1976); discipline may be both inconsistent and ineffectual (Young, 1964); and family members may not be able to agree about anything, from what to eat for dinner to when to visit grandparents (Parke & Collmer, 1975). The most promising treatment programs for these types of psychologically normal but socially pathological parents and families are those that create or restore effective life management, including effective child management.

The concept of lives out of control may best be thought of as a characteristic of a family's life-course development (Elder, 1977). The inappropriate timing and sequencing of important events that require role transitions may be crucial. An unwanted or unplanned pregnancy, either at the beginning or end of a family's child-bearing period, may interact with inadequate finances to produce a life crisis. Roles outside the immediate care-giving relationship such as in the world of work may be mismanaged or disrupted by social forces beyond parents' control, such as an economic depression. These events generate the kind of stress that often result in attempts to assert control through violence (acts of commission) or to surrender control through neglect (acts of omission). Linking such role malfunctions together to account for the maltreatment of children is a major, and largely unexplored, task for developmental research.

How do lives go awry? How do families get out of control? The weak link in the chain of events that normally supports families and protects children is social isolation. Isolation from potent, prosocial support systems places even the strong and competent in jeopardy, and often sends the weak or incompetent over the edge when stresses from within and outside the family conspire, as seems to be the case in most cases of child maltreatment. This imbalance of stress and support may take on new and special dimensions when adolescents are involved. Although empirical investigation is only beginning (Garbarino, 1980b), a major proportion of the cases of maltreatment involving adolescents as victims appear to be related to special characteristics of family interaction patterns associated with the normal crises of early adolescence—autonomy, authority, sexuality, and assertion. For this and other reasons, experts recommend that some specialization in adolescent abuse be built into the division of labor within protective service agencies (Fisher et al., 1979).

Necessary conditions for child maltreatment

Discussions of maltreatment generally neglect to distinguish between sufficient and necessary conditions for abuse. When this topic is treated, it is discussed peripherally to another purpose. Many researchers, including Bronfenbrenner and Mahoney

(1975), believe that for any particular sufficient condition to "cause" a specific effect, all relevant necessary conditions must be met. They reason that the absence of any required necessary conditions effectively disarms the sufficient conditions—for example, leaving out the firing pin of a rifle neutralizes the weapon. This is a critical issue in dealing with child maltreatment because approximately 25% of American's families are prone to becoming abusive as a consequence of some combination of child-rearing ignorance, unrealistic expectations concerning children, propensity towards violence, psychopathology, or the presence of a "special" child.

This 25% figure reflects several sources. Gil's survey (1970) found that over 22% of the adults sampled reported they could envision injuring a child at some point in their lives and nearly 16% had actually come very close to injuring a child in their care. Results of a study designed to provide a perinatal assessment of mother/baby interaction (Gray et al., 1976) concluded that 25% of the mothers have child-rearing attitudes and/or experiences characteristic of abusers. Work by Schneider and her colleagues (1976) in developing a screening questionnaire to predict potential problems in mother/child interactions also supports Gray's conclusion in identifying at-risk mothers.

Clearly, the sufficient conditions for child abuse are in abundant supply. According to recent reports (National Academy of Sciences, 1976), the number of families vulnerable to the conditions that produce the maltreatment of children is increasing. This vulnerability derives from changing patterns of family structure, as well as more general economic patterns and social conditions. More households with young children are headed by single parents who are likely to have low incomes and to experience a variety of unsupported social stresses. It is important that protective service workers understand how conditions cause vulnerability and translate into abuse and neglect so they can use their limited resources most effectively where the risk is greatest.

Cultural attitudes

There appear to be two necessary conditions for child maltreatment. The first is two-fold and involves the way a culture defines the rights of children. For a pattern of maltreatment to occur within families, there must be cultural justification for the use of force against children and a generally held belief that children are the property of their parents to be cared for or disposed of as those parents see fit. This becomes apparent, of course, most clearly in social and historical comparisons (Radbill, 1974). A culturally defined concept of children as the "property" of caregivers and care-givers' use of force against children and youth as legitimate appear to be essential components of child abuse and neglect—physical, sexual, and emotional.

As Albee (1979) has so persuasively argued, the central issue in mistreatment is the misuse of power. Garbarino and Hershberger (1979) concur that the ethical issue in child maltreatment concerns adult power and children's rights. Does the child have a right to integrity? And what powers are allied behind or against that right?

The validity of this proposition is supported by analyses of the history of child abuse (Radbill, 1974), the anthropological study of other cultures (Korbin, 1978), and analyses of the forces underlying violence in American society (Straus, Gelles, & Steinmetz, 1979). American society certainly fulfills the necessary conditions for child abuse (Lystad, 1975). In excess of 90% of parents reported employing physical force in the upbringing of their children in a survey conducted by Stark and McEvoy (1970), which was supported by the results of the national survey of families conducted by Straus and his colleagues (1979). In a sample of Los Angeles mothers, Korsch and his colleagues (1965) found that 25% reported spanking infants before the age of 6 months and almost half were spanking by the time the children were 12 months of age. Viano (1974) reported that two-thirds of the police, clergy, and educators polled condoned spanking. Laws clearly support the use of physical force against children. The Texas legislature, for example, in 1974 enacted legislation condoning "the use of force, but not deadly force, against a child younger than 18 years . . . (1) if the actor is the child's parent or stepparent [and] (2) when and to the degree the actor believes the force is necessary to discipline the child" (cited in Justice & Justice, 1976, p. 3). This law reflects both the historical role of violence in American civilization and the current trend to reinstate corporal punishment in the schools as a way of dealing with disruptive behavior by students.

Nonviolent cultures tend to avoid child abuse. Cultures in which children are "citizens" do not permit neglect (Tietjen, 1980). (The writings of John Nance—*The Gentle Tasaday* (1975)—and Margaret Mead—*Coming of Age in Samoa* (1961)— are relevant.) This is not to say that cultural support for violence or defining children as property are sufficient conditions for child maltreatment. There are nonabusive and nonneglecting adults in American society who condone the use of physical force to discipline children and who view children as property.

Isolation from support systems

Another necessary condition that promotes child maltreatment is isolation of the parent/child relationship from potent prosocial support systems (Korbin, 1978). This factor pertains to the relation of the family system or victim/perpetrator dyad to the community. That it is equally or more amenable to change than the deeply rooted cultural patterns outlined above is of special importance for child protective services, whose task is to create, maintain, and collaborate with family-support systems.

The concept of support systems has been developed and elaborated by several investigators. Caplan (1974) finds that a support system performs several critical social functions relevant to the dynamics of child maltreatment by acting as

> continuing social aggregates that provide individuals with opportunities for feedback about themselves and for validations for their expectations about others, which may offset deficiencies in this communication within the larger community context. . . . People have a variety of a specific needs that demand satisfaction through enduring interpersonal relationships, such as for love and affection, for intimacy that provides the freedom to express feelings easily and unselfconsciously, for validation of personal identity and worth, for satisfaction of nurturance and dependency, for help with tasks, and for *support in handling emotion and controlling impulses* [pp. 4–5; italics added].

The importance of such support systems increases, of course, as a function of the stressfulness of the family's external and internal environment and of the values of the individual. The unmanageability of the stresses is the most important factor. That unmanageability is the product of a mismatch between the level of stress, on the one hand, and the availability and potency of personal and social resources, chief among which are support systems, on the other.

Support systems function through social networks (Cochran & Brassard, 1979). While the concept of social networks has been developed and utilized by sociologists and anthropologists to describe complex communication webs, it has not generally been applied to the study of development. Recently, ecologically oriented students of development have begun to adapt the concept for assessing the support systems for families (Garbarino & Sherman, 1980).

Cochran and Brassard (1979) define the properties of social networks relevant to development as: 1) size and diversity of membership, 2) interconnectedness among members, 3) content of activities engaged in, and 4) directionality of contacts, more or less reciprocal. Studies of the social networks of families promise to identify practical applications of the concepts of social isolation and social integration and to describe how social isolation and the lack of support-system resources involve child maltreatment families. Therefore, the importance of social networks may give protective service workers a fulcrum around which to move neglectful and abusive families in the direction of adequate and appropriate child care.

The responsibility for social isolation is not entirely external to the individual. There is a difference between the lack of social supports and failure to use available supports. While the net result, social isolation, is the same, the implications for policy and practice are quite different. Elmer (1967) found parents who fail to use resources are particularly high on anomie; that is, they distrust and retreat from society. Lenoski (1974) reported that 81% of abusive families in his sample preferred not to seek help in resolving crises. Young (1964) showed that abusive parents attempted to prevent their children from forming relationships outside the home. Polansky and his colleagues (1979) found that neglecting parents felt they could not turn to anyone for assistance with day-to-day matters. Social isolation, like virtually all important human phenomena, is determined by an interaction of the individual and the environment.

Patterns of child maltreatment can occur only when families are isolated from communities and/or when they are not given feedback and support. Isolation may be structural (no social network) or cultural (a deviant network that tolerates or even condones maltreatment). For the sufficient conditions noted previously to result in maltreatment, they must occur in a context that permits the perpetrator/victim dyad to develop and be sustained.

Young (1964) found that 95% of severely abusive families had not established or maintained relationships outside their families. In this same study, 85% of the abusive families did not belong to or participate in any organized groups. Lenoski (1974) found that 89% of abusive parents having telephones had unlisted numbers, as opposed to 12% of the nonabusive parents. More than 80% of abusive families sought to resolve crises alone, versus 43% of the nonabusive parents. Straus (1980) showed that stress was linked to physical abuse when it occurred in the absence of participation in normal social groups such as clubs and churches. Polansky and his colleagues (1979) demonstrated a history of estrangement from normal social experience among neglecting parents. Giovannoni and Billingsley (1970) found that among a low-income group those who did not participate in the cooperative activities of the neighborhood, principally shared homemaking and child care, were more abusive and neglectful. Thus, the available research consistently links social isolation to child maltreatment (Garbarino & Gilliam, 1980).

What aspects of the community foster child maltreatment? Using statistical analyses to identify the socioeconomic, demographic, and attitudinal correlates of neighborhood differences in the rate of child abuse and neglect, specific neighborhood features promoting child maltreatment can be identified (Garbarino & Crouter, 1978a; Garbarino & Sherman, 1980). From these factors a pair of neighborhoods matched for socioeconomic level were chosen, one with a high risk of child abuse, the other with a low risk. Interviews with expert informants ranging from elementary school principals to mail carriers were used to develop neighborhood profiles. Samples of families were drawn from each neighborhood and interviews conducted to identify stresses and supports, with special emphasis on sources of help, social networks, evaluation of the neighborhood, and use of formal family-support systems.

The results lend support to the concept of neighborhood risk. Families in the high-risk neighborhood reported less positive evaluation of the neighborhood as a context for child and family development. They also revealed a general pattern of social impoverishment in comparison with families in the low-risk neighborhood. They rated the neighborhood lower, shared less, and discouraged interaction between their families and others in the neighborhood. The high-risk neighborhood was characterized by social isolation and a poor network of informal support systems. The low-risk neighborhood abounded in social connectedness and social resources.

This body of research, while useful, lacks a firm grasp on the sequence of events. How does social isolation develop as a characteristic of families? At least two contrasting patterns can be identified. The first includes families who form part of an "underclass" or deviant subculture—isolated rural families, mountain folks, people of Appalachia, and the like. They may remain outside of the normal support systems for generations. Pavenstedt (1967) called this group "the drifters." The second includes families who become alienated from community support systems through some event or series of events. Such a pattern may arise from moving, illness, the birth of a handicapped child, or severe reduction in income and the accompanying loss of social status (Elder, 1974). Other possible causes include the lack of inclination and ability of neighborhoods to provide the observation and resources essential to the feedback function and the inadequacy of social service systems in identifying high-risk families. For prevention and treatment to work, the "worlds of abnormal rearing" must be identified. A flow of information to and from these worlds must be established so that parent/child relations can be normalized.

The protective service system

Reporting child maltreatment

As we mentioned earlier, a major problem of child maltreatment is the family's relation to support systems. Support systems do not simply provide nurturance; they involve feedback as well. They tell families, especially parents, what is expected of them and guide them in what to do. They monitor and evaluate parents' behavior (Caplan, 1974). Obviously, informal support systems frequently provide such guidance. When informal feedback—from neighbors, relatives, and friends—does not enhance child protection, however, the formal systems—schools, the medical community, recreational leaders, and so on—enter the picture. A community's system for reporting child maltreatment to the formal network of human services, and ultimately to law enforcement agencies, functions as feedback for support systems.

Informal and formal reporting. What do community members do about cases of maltreatment? In a national opinion survey, a substantial proportion of individuals indicated that if they discovered people they knew were abusive, they would try to intervene to change the situation rather than report child abuse. This proportion was highest among groups with low education and among ethnic minorities. Direct action by citizens in their roles as friends, neighbors, and relatives is actually a central element in any community system of protective services. The likelihood of abusive parents seeking help increases when others know about the abuse. In fact, most states only require official reporting of suspected abuse and neglect by professionals. Roughly half of the officially reported cases, though, come from private citizens acting as concerned friends, neighbors, or relatives (Gil, 1970). Official reporting of child abuse becomes a critical feature of protective services when (1) reporting responsibility is accepted by the community and (2) appropriate protective action is taken in response to these reports.

The legal mandate for reporting child abuse began in the late sixties and early seventies, but only recently has reporting achieved systematic levels in most states (Garbarino & Crouter, 1978b). Since 1974, the American Humane Association has been contracted by the federal government to collect, collate, assess, and review reports of child abuse and neglect across the country. However, only some thirty-five states across the country are actively involved in reporting cases through this national clearinghouse. The reporting process is not systematic in many areas, particularly rural regions where interpersonal costs of reporting are very high and services are limited in scope and diversity (National Center on Child Abuse and Neglect, 1978).

Overreporting. The reporting process presents many dilemmas for individuals who seek to protect children from abuse and neglect. The public awareness campaigns, particularly in the early 1970s, emphasized reporting as almost the be-all and end-all of citizen responsibility, resulting in enormous increases in report figures. In Florida, for example, establishing a toll-free reporting hotline resulted in a one-year jump from cases numbering in the hundreds to cases numbering in the tens of thousands. Also in recent years, the number of reports across the country has risen into the hundreds of thousands. These well-intentioned efforts produced an actual net *reduction* in protective services because state governments did not provide the personnel to deal with increased numbers of reports. Thus, many reports of abuse and neglect often result in a lack of action because the protective services system is overburdened. Some critics, therefore, argue for narrowing the protective service mandate (Gelman, 1979) so intention efforts can reach the most extreme cases— really a corrective intervention posture rather than a preventive orientation.

Concern over confidentiality. A second dilemma concerns the question of confidentiality. Many people, including some professionals, refuse to report because of violating confidentiality of a friend, neighbor, or client. Often the implications of reporting are not within the control of the reporter whether layperson or protective service worker. After the report is made, a chain of events begins that can be more damaging than the problem itself. While this fear is often unfounded, enough "horror cases" exist in which reporting increased the problem or undermined supportive corrective intervention efforts. With these systematic problems in delivering effective remedial and rehabilitative services, Garbarino (1980b) and others argue for the need to shift attention towards prevention.

Case determination and management

Once a report is made, the protective service system, through its individual caseworkers, must make some determination about its validity. Typically, some reports are initially screened out and are not investigated on the grounds that they are obviously spurious or do not fall within the jurisdiction of protective services. Unfortunately, some cases in many jurisdictions are not investigated simply because of a lack of time and resources. A recent national survey of protective services offered to adolescents found that overburdened agencies are inclined to dismiss reports involving adolescents as victims so that they can concentrate on reports involving young children and infants as victims (Garbarino, 1980b). This is particularly disturbing because adolescents are reported as victims of abuse with the same proportion of frequency as other ages (Garbarino, 1980b). A study by Garbarino and Carson (1979) suggests that roughly half these cases involve a childhood history of maltreatment and half involve maltreatment that only began with adolescence.

Depriving older children of protective services may perpetuate the cycle of abuse as these adolescents grow up and have children of their own.

Case substantiation.   The central issue in case determination is whether it can be substantiated, meaning the evidence is sufficient for the caseworker to document and for it to stand up in legal proceedings if necessary. If a case is substantiated, then the agency is in a position to actively offer services. Agencies gain authority from the legal system when clients are mandated to accept services. When the evidence does not permit substantiation, even if the caseworker believes that abuse or neglect is present, then the protective service worker and the agency are left in a much more passive and less authoritative position. They may offer services, but these may be refused.

The barriers to gathering evidence necessary for substantiation include: (1) ambiguous inquiries (where the case cannot be determined with certainty); (2) unwillingness of participants to report on events (including the reluctance of children and teenagers to "rat" on their parents); (3) legal rules of evidence (what is admissable and how information may be gathered); and (4) the practical problems of time and energy. Protective service workers should be prepared for this kind of ambiguity and not expect a clear-cut, definitive mandate in many, if not most, of their cases. In fact, learning to deal with the emotionally charged ambiguities, double-binds, and "Catch-22's" of protective services is perhaps the greatest hurdle these individuals must overcome (Copans et al., 1979).

Coping with realities.   The gap between the ideal and the real in protective services is substantial and troublesome. Much is written about the noble missions of protective services: to save children, to remove them from damaging situations, and to restore families to more healthy functioning. This ideal is often thwarted by the realities of day-to-day case management. Often protective service workers lack a clear and powerful legal mandate to intervene, and instead must rely upon the voluntary cooperation of the client family in order to provide services. Rarely does time and money permit the kind of deliberate, thoughtful, and multidisciplinary team assessment of cases that most experts suggest is ideal. Communities vary in what services are available to families involved in abuse and neglect, and in how effectively referrals can be made to protective service agencies. Workers are often frustrated by legal or administrative time limits on the duration of services (often as little as sixty days from the time maltreatment is reported until it must be "fixed"). Client families may move and leave the legal jurisdiction of the agency. It was reported that nearly 25% of the cases were closed for this reason alone, and states rarely are able and willing to share information about specific cases (Garbarino, 1980b).

The need for referral.   Often protective service agencies must refer families to other human service agencies. Once referrals are made, however, the referring worker cannot ensure that the protective service mission was achieved. In fact, evidence shows that a majority of referrals made to agencies for service by protective service workers did not adequately achieve the purposes intended because of the client's refusal to accept the services offered.

Removing children from homes.   Protective service workers must deal with the issue of removing the child from the home. Although a simple, direct, and often publically supported tactic for protective services, removal of the child from the home to foster care is a cure that often proves to be worse than the disease. The ability of the foster-care system to provide adequate care and effectively to replace parents is challenged by researchers, practitioners, and parents (Emlen et al., 1977; Fanshel,

1975; Maas & Engler, 1959). In part for this reason, some communities around the country are seeking to establish diversion programs in which foster-care placement is averted, thus preempting the unfortunate chain of events following removal (Brown, 1978; Wald, 1976). These efforts go hand in hand with attempts to reform the foster-care system in the direction of permanent and precise planning for each child. Cases should not be permitted to slide so children are left in limbo with repeated placements and few, if any, opportunities for adoption (Emlen et al., 1977). With foster care, as much as if not more so than with protective services, the gap between the ideal (saving children) and the real (disrupting families) is particularly poignant.

Case treatment and evaluation

With all of these troubling issues of reporting, case determination, and case management, the question remains: how effective are various models of protective services?

The need for lay-oriented services. As part of a government-sponsored evaluation of 11 child abuse and neglect demonstration projects funded by the National Center on Child Abuse and Neglect, Anne Cohn and the staff of Berkeley Planning Associates determined essential elements of successful child abuse and neglect treatment (Cohn, 1979). The 11 programs studied served 1724 clients over a three-year period from 1974–1977. These cases resembled the typical protective service caseload in most respects—31% were single-parent families, 61% did not have an adult with a high school degree, and 56% had family incomes less than $5000.

Cohn's group found that fully 30% were reported to have seriously reabused or neglected their children while in treatment. Cases initially classified as serious (a third of the total cases) at intake were four times as likely to reabuse or neglect during treatment than were nonserious cases. This accentuates the need for expert intake work and concerted effort to protect the most seriously at-risk cases. In a separate analysis, Cohn reported that protective service workers with professional training and three or more years of protective service experience provided a better quality of case management.

The data, however, challenge conventional therapeutic approaches. Case managers accurately predicted future decreases in maltreatment for less than half of the clients served. Also, the most improvement was attributed to cases involving some nonprofessional treatment such as parent aides, volunteer counseling, and self-help groups such as Parents Anonymous. These families were positively evaluated in 53% of the cases (versus 39% for the professionally oriented treatment services). Lay-oriented services alleviated specific family problems such as stress and low self-esteem as well, although the success rate was only 35%. As might be expected, a lay-oriented approach was less costly and much more cost effective ($2600 per successful case versus $4700 for individual professional counseling). In addition, involvement exceeding seven months and smaller caseloads of 20 predicted greater treatment success.

Effects of stress. The unique stresses confronting protective service workers influence their delivery of services. In one of the few projects specifically designed to deal with this aspect of service delivery, Copans and her associates (1979) identified a range of common concerns and traps into which protective service workers fall and that result in the substantial burnout problem reported by most agencies around the country. They then designed a support system approach for protective service workers that improved their ability to cope with stress. This important innovation

Lay-oriented protective services, such as the provision of parent aides, can be both more effective and less costly than professional treatment.

can help individuals and agencies around the country cope with the real and challenging stresses of providing protective services.

Specifically, Copans and her colleagues found that expertise concerning child maltreatment is not enough to sustain child protective service workers; they need emotional support for their efforts and help in learning to deal with their feelings. Without these things, workers feel uncomfortable and make inappropriate decisions regarding case management. In fact, eleven sets of feelings and processes that frequently interfere with effective delivery of services were identified (p. 24):

anxieties about being physically harmed by angry parents and about the effects of a decision
denial and inhibition of anger
need for emotional gratification from clients
lack of professional support
feelings of incompetence
denial and projection of responsibility
the feeling that one is totally responsible for families assigned to one
the difficulty in separating personal from professional responsibility
feelings of being victimized
ambivalent feelings toward clients and about one's professional role
the need to be in control

Copans and her colleagues also reported that a regular support group was very effective in helping workers clarify and deal with their feelings. Concrete planning within the group complemented efforts to air feelings and led to more effective protective services. Most of what was noted earlier about social support systems and the role of parents applies to the role of child protective service workers. Few people can successfully fulfill the role of parent or child protector in social isolation. Thus, enduring relationships with potent, prosocial support systems for both abusive parents and professionals who deal with them must be enhanced.

Institutional maltreatment

While most of the published literature dealing with abuse and neglect concerns maltreatment by parents of their own children, experts have increasingly pointed their fingers at the serious problem of institutional maltreatment. A major social crisis in its own right is the abuse and neglect of children who are wards of the state, residing in detention facilities and residential treatment institutions for the mentally retarded, emotionally disturbed, physically handicapped or delinquent. Who is responsible for protecting these children? Who is responsible for protecting children who have been removed from their homes because of abuse and placed in foster care? As Aristotle asked two thousand years ago, "Who watches watchers, who guards the guardians?" That problem still has not been resolved.

Recent initiatives by the National Center on Child Abuse and Neglect (1978) to develop strategies and tactics for dealing with institutional abuse are just coming to fruition. Individual child protective service workers and their agencies may find themselves in extremely difficult situations as they attempt to cope with protective services for children who are wards of the state. Personal and institutional loyalties and the possibility of coverup are quite real here.

Alternative intervention models

The individual protective service worker is constantly faced with choices and decisions concerning what kind of protective services to offer. These individual decisions are influenced by, and to some extent constrained by, institutional and agency policies and practices, laws relating to protective services, available resources, and the models of service to which people subscribe. Wald (1976) argues that protective services must concentrate only on the most extreme cases of abuse, so that limited resources are not squandered and dispersed to the point of ineffectiveness. Such a view argues that it is better to do one thing well rather than everything poorly.

Clearly the mission of protective services in the last fifteen years has expanded from the narrowly conceived concept of child battering to the broader concept of child maltreatment. Can protective services effectively respond to this broad definition or must they retrench to a more narrow, focused mission? This question uses a false assumption, namely that the only way to offer protective services is through the conventional social-casework approach that relies upon corrective intervention.

Consultation model. Protective services can be preventive. Fraser (1979) and others argue that intervention in a rehabilitative or remedial mode is extremely costly and rather ineffective. A more effective view of prevention is one that emphasizes long-term consultative relationships with informal family support systems and that uses lay volunteers in the process of protecting children from maltreatment.

Where do most people get most of the help they need and receive on a day-to-day basis? Most of us rely mainly on friends, relatives, and neighbors. Just as our economy depends on the free enterprise system, so our social services are provided mainly by exchanges of assistance that are not professionally run. Recognition of this fact poses specific questions: what are the existing networks in which the family is already involved or might become involved? Are there individuals who are particularly adept at or interested in helping others in their neighborhood? Can they provide the missing link between professional responsibility for child protection and family responsibility?

By investing time and energy to become familiar with and trusted by an area's natural helping networks, professionals can use that relationship to enhance prevention, case identification, and treatment. A coherent strategy aimed at increasing professionals' access to communities' social resources, and communities' access to professionals' expertise is called the *consultation model*. Here professionals work with citizens and neighbors on behalf of children and their families (Collins & Pancoast, 1976).

Team approach.   Whenever possible, trained volunteers and self-help groups should be used. Self-help groups such as Parents Anonymous are effective and cost relatively little to operate. This combination makes them cost effective, a term that promises to be of increasing importance in coming years. Volunteers and self-help groups, no matter how well-trained and caring, are not going to solve all problems. No one specific strategy will. But they can handle many situations, thus freeing professionals for more serious cases. Professional resources also can be concentrated in a way that was rarely possible before. For example, in the Homebuilders in Tacoma, Washington, a team of counseling specialists rallies around a family in trouble when all conventional approaches have failed and family breakup is imminent. Therapeutic teams spend all their time with the family—up to six weeks, if necessary—trying to rescue parents and children from dysfunction so families can remain intact.

Conclusion

Consultation with informal helping networks is the most promising alternative model of protective services. If protective services focus on neighborhoods and family social networks rather than individual families, professionals who work in a consultative relationship with natural helping networks can perform both a preventive and rehabilitative function. This view is explained in detail in a book entitled *Protecting Children from Abuse and Neglect* (Garbarino & Stocking, 1980). Tactics appropriate to ecological intervention must be adopted and the balance of forces between the individual and environmental systems altered if children are to be truly protected.

If anyone is really "in the trenches" when it comes to helping high-risk families, it is the protective service worker. All the complexities and ambiguities of human services focus here with unmatched ferocity. The impulse to "rescue" children and punish parents is strong, almost undeniable. The challenge is to spare children and save families from misguided and inefficient behavior. Which is the greater danger? The question remains an open one, and must be answered on an individual basis by communities, families, and protective-service workers.

Summary

Practitioners, researchers, and theoreticians do not agree about the definition of child abuse and neglect because they emphasize different contextual factors: intentionality, effect, evaluation, and standards. This controversy creates difficulty in diagnosing abuse and neglect. All four elements are emphasized in the following definition: acts of omission or commission by a parent or guardian that are judged by a mixture of community values and professional expertise to be inappropriate or damaging. These acts should be placed under a broader label—child maltreatment—because child abuse and neglect are multifaceted in terms of damage and types displayed. However, the label is not as important as the issue—how to protect children and enforce standards. It is critical to support a developmental understanding of parent/child interactions because what is appropriate behavior at one point in time is not at another.

Child maltreatment is a serious societal problem with well over a million children affected. Efforts are made in determining the causes and effects. Some people believe child maltreatment results from family dysfunction in two types of processes. Parents can psychopathologically assault their children, or they can abuse their children within the cultural norms of power and force. More parents fall into the second category, with small asynchronies between caregiver and child evolving into seriously dangerous patterns over time.

Situational incompetence, role problems, or lives that are out of control can cause child maltreatment. Incompetence usually stems from social stress and a lack of knowledge about parenting skills. Internal or external reasons can account for parental incompetence, with effects varying depending upon when they occur and under what circumstances.

Parents who mistreat their children report little experience in rehearsing their roles when they were younger and unrealistic or unclear expectations about their children's behavior. They often were maltreated as children, have a history of social impoverishment, behave selfishly, and have poor self-concepts.

Many abusive families are out of control in many ways, all of which involve a mismatch between reality and their ability to manage that reality. These acute or chronic asynchronies can occur separately or simultaneously. Typically, inappropriate timing and sequencing of life events contribute to this lack of control. Social isolation sends weak families over the edge and places even strong families in jeopardy. This factor, coupled with the way culture defines the rights of children and the power of parents, form the necessary conditions for child maltreatment. Many times support networks are available, but parents fail to use them. Thus, it cannot be assumed that the responsibility for social isolation is entirely external to individuals. Research is needed to identify the sequence of events that causes social isolation and to explain why certain neighborhoods are more at risk than others.

Prevention of the conditions that produce maltreatment is more effective than identifying "high-risk" families and then preventing them from harming their children. But either approach is preferable to waiting until after abuse and neglect has occurred and then trying to correct it and prevent its reoccurrence.

Maltreatment is not a unitary phenomenon. As a result, the protective service system is complex and involves: (1) informal and formal reporting of cases, (2) case determination and management, (3) various treatments from the case worker therapeutic approach to a team approach, and (4) different forms of evaluation. Numerous problems abound. When too many cases are reported, the system overloads and they are not handled. Individuals may not report cases because they feel it would violate confidentiality. Documentation of cases often is difficult. Many cases are referred to other human service agencies with the abusive situation going uncorrected. Sometimes removing children from their homes is an easy solution that presents other problems associated with foster care. Professional protective services workers also are not immune to these dilemmas. They are affected by the stresses of their jobs and need assistance if they are to remain in the service delivery system. Burnout is high among this group.

If the protective service system is to be improved, efforts must be directed toward support networks, which benefit both professionals and families. Such an approach emphasizes a consultation model that utilizes family and community support systems, including lay volunteers. Whenever possible, a team approach also should be implemented so that professionals can concentrate efforts on more serious cases. All evidence points to the need for reorganizing protective services to focus on collectivities—families, neighborhoods, and communities—for people to work in consultative relationships within natural helping networks.

8

Substitute Child-Care Services

Chapter overview

This chapter discusses the similarities and differences in the process and problems associated with foster care and adoption. The impact of the professional social worker and the legal system on children and families also are considered.

Issues to consider

What are the differences between foster care and adoption?
What is the contemporary climate of foster care and adoption?
When do children receive foster care and what families are affected the most?
How do social workers determine foster-care placements, termination, and replacements?
How successful is the foster-care process?
What are the problems with foster care?
What is involved in the adoption process?
Why do people want to adopt children or become foster parents?
What state criteria exist for adoption?
What problems are related to adoption?

Introduction

Adoption and foster care are two socially sanctioned forms of substitute child care. Adoption involves a permanent change in family affiliation, matching up parentless children with childless parents. Adoption, in effect, creates a new parent/child relationship. Foster care, on the other hand, involves a change in the legal custody of a child. If a child's home situation is such that not even a minimal standard of social, emotional, and physical care are met, then a change in custody is warranted. This change produces major social and psychological adjustments. A child is separated, save for visits, from the biological family and needs to adapt to a foster family. A child also needs to accommodate to a new ecology—home setting, school, peers, and neighborhood. The person having custody must provide care—the child must be fed, clothed, sent to school, washed, loved, and so on. Typically, an agency gains legal custody of a child, then serves as an intermediary in placing the child with foster parents. The child, however, still legally "belongs" to his or her biological parents because they retain guardianship. This means only biological parents can give consent and represent the child in certain situations—for example, if surgery is needed, if the child who is underage wishes to marry or enlist in the armed services, or if legal representation is needed. Thus, the child can be returned to biological parents at any time because they "own" the child.

Historically, substitute-care procedures have treated children like commodities. For instance, in responding to applications for adoptions, adults during the late 1800s expressed the following preferences:

> The blue-eyed, golden-haired little girl was the desire of many; a few wanted a black-eyed brunette; or one "not too homely," definitely "not a redhead." One woman didn't care too much about "looks" but wanted assurance that the child "had not one drop of Irish blood." Disposition and health are defined: "clean, healthy, sensible and good dispositioned"; a "strict Christian, well dispositioned"; "light complexion, well disposed"; "a sunny German girl who can sing." One man requested a boy "possessing some form of

character. . . . It would be a home where no tobacco or whiskey would be tolerated. Please send five photographs."

Why they wanted a child was often expressed in terms of work; to wash dishes and run errands, to be a companion for an only child or an elderly person living in the family. [McCausland, 1976, p. 64].

Or, consider how a foster father used a young girl.

Frances, aged thirteen, recently made a personal application to a social agency stating that her foster father had been having sexual relations with her for the past two years. Upon investigation living conditions were found to be very bad. The foster mother corroborated the child's statements. Frances had been legally adopted in May 1918. She was sold to her foster parents by her mother for a quart of whiskey [Bremner, 1971, p. 142].

Fortunately, attitudes and actions about foster care and adoption have changed since these early days, but they still have a way to go. This chapter examines the contemporary context of foster care and adoption, exploring the basic differences between these two forms of substitute care. The process of each form of substitute care and related problems also will be discussed.

Foster care versus adoption

Substitute care in perspective

From the 1800s substitute-care agencies such as the Chapin Adoption Agency in New York, the Cradle Adoption Agency in Chicago, and the Children's Home Society in many states were trying to (1) establish their goals of protecting society, parents, and children; (2) confront issues and problems associated with placement; and (3) develop placement procedures and ways to handle unsuccessful placement.

People became concerned that these substitute-care innovations would encourage parents to desert or neglect their children. Why should parents feel guilty or attempt to provide adequate care when such care could be had elsewhere? Perhaps they would even adopt the attitude that it is their "duty to desert" so their children could receive better care.

It is difficult to determine whether data substantiate these fears. Records were not well maintained, and, even when they were, only the total numbers of children in foster care and adoptive care during each decade were noted. Interpretations, therefore, are difficult because the total number of children in society for each ten-year period was unrecorded. If totals were available, then we could make comparisons and see whether substitute care was higher during its initial implementation.

Statistics about the form of care, types of agencies, and types of children receiving care are available. From 1957 to 1975 the number of adopted children increased from 57,000 to 175,000. About half of the adopted children in 1957 were adopted by relatives. By 1975, however, this figure reduced to about one-fourth (Kadushin, 1980). There also are differences in public and voluntary agencies and the type of child adopted, as the Child Welfare League reports:

Whereas the very young, healthy child predominates among the children available through the voluntary agencies, albeit in reduced numbers, more than 60 percent of the public agency children are over one year of age and nearly a third are handicapped by physical disability, mental retardation, and other disabling conditions. Both types of agencies accept a disproportionate number of black children, and such children make up some 25 percent of the total number of children accepted for adoption in 1976. These children continue to be placed more slowly, so that a higher proportion of the accepted black children continued to await placement as compared with accepted white children [Kadushin, 1980, p. 470].

Similarly, the number of children placed in foster-care situations has increased. In 1933, there were 2.5 children per thousand in family foster care and 3.4 children per thousand in institutional foster care. By 1972, these figures reversed, with 3.6 in foster family care and 1.3 in foster institutional care. The rate for family foster care increased to 6 in 1977. Even these figures do not accurately reflect the number of children in foster care because informal forms of care are not included. Nor do they reflect the flow rate of children in foster care, because not used are the proportions of children receiving care compared to the total number of children, and the apparent decrease in foster-care placements can be explained by an increase in adoptions and a decrease in births. What is clear, however, is the trend of reduced placement in institutions and increased placement in foster-family homes. For instance, 47.2% of foster children were in foster-family homes, while 52.8% were in institutions in 1933. In 1972, only 20% were in institutions and 80% were in foster families (Kadushin, 1980).

The children receiving foster care today are older and have more difficult problems than their predecessors. When comparisons are made to the general population, there are more males than females and more Blacks than Whites in foster care. Kadushin (1980) feels that the need for foster care may increase despite a reduction in the population of children under 10. "A continuation of increases in marital disruption and out-of-wedlock pregnancies would suggest that a larger percentage of this small population of children may need substitute care. . . . This is particularly true for older and emotionally disturbed children" (p. 322).

Situations for substitute care

Finding permanent substitute-care situations for children so they do not have to undergo periodic adjustments is a growing concern. After children are in foster care for an extended period, greater efforts are made to terminate the rights of biological parents and to encourage foster parents to adopt these children.

With this emphasis on permanence, agencies involved in substitute care scrutinize the placement of children carefully. They also have developed a variety of ways to monitor how the child is cared for. The next two sections will consider the processes used for foster care and adoption. At this point in our discussion two questions are relevant: when is foster care appropriate, and when does the option for adoption occur?

Receiving foster care. If parents are unwilling or unable to care for their child even with the use of support services such as income maintenance or homemaker assistance, then foster care is appropriate. However, foster care can result from parent- or child-related problems. Parent-related problems, which are cited in about 75% of the cases, include parental neglect and abuse, abandonment, alcoholism, mental illness, marital conflict, emotional problems, and imprisonment. Child-related problems—mental retardation, physical handicaps, emotional disturbance, and "unruly" behavior—account for less than 25% of foster-care placements (Shyne & Schroeder, 1978).

Typically, parents seek placement because of child-related problems, seldom acknowledging their own difficulties (Phillips, Shyne, Sherman, & Haring, 1971, 1977; Jones, Neuman, & Shyne, 1976). Also, prolonged crises such as illness of the mother or prolonged unemployment of the father force parents to seek substitute

A variety of forms of substitute care are available for children, providing them with an array of interactions that aren't accessible through their biological parents.

care. According to Sauber and Jenkins (1966), children who receive placement are from "marginal families without sufficient resources to sustain themselves in the community when additional pressures or problems are added to their pre-existing burdens" (p. 61).

Consider the following.

> I felt very tired and sick, and I went to the hospital in my neighborhood where they told me I needed to be hospitalized immediately since I had hepatitis. I told them I had no one to take care of my children and the doctor took me to Social Services, and the children were placed. I have no friends in New York, and the only one to take care of my children was my mother-in-law and she was in Puerto Rico [Sauber & Jenkins, 1966, p. 82].

Unfortunately, single-parent families and minority families, especially those of the lower class, are forced to rely upon foster care more than other families. It seems that in an unsupportive context, parent-related problems are magnified. If the goal is to help strengthen the family unit, then additional ways to support families at local levels must be considered more fully. The Homebuilders Project in Tacoma, Washington provides such services to high-risk families and maintains contact to monitor usage. Only two to three families are assigned to each caseworker, who helps them cope with their problems. Evidence indicates foster placement is prevented (Slater & Harris, 1978). Other findings show that the Aid to Families of Dependent Children (AFDC) program successfully prevents foster placement (Jenkins & Norman, 1975).

Foster care as a form of substitute services will probably always exist. A single parent may be hospitalized suddenly, as was illustrated earlier, or a child's needs may override parental resistance (or even child resistance), as in the case of abuse and neglect.

Being adopted.   Children who are social or full orphans are candidates for adoption. Social orphans are children whose parents rejected, neglected, or deserted them. Full orphans are children whose parents died. In contemporary society, over 80% of children who are adopted were born out of wedlock. Only about .1% of all children for whom data exist were orphaned via parental death (Kadushin, 1980). The thrust of professional adoptive efforts is to find the best possible permanent family unit for these children and monitor the situation to determine its effectiveness. Although retaining the biological unit is preferred, as we discussed with preventive foster placement efforts, the adoptive family unit is highly valued. For many adults and children, this type of family unit is their only option.

Adoption may be an appropriate form of substitute care under the following conditions:

1. The biological parents are unable to care for the child because the family was never completely organized—as in the case of the illegitimate child.
2. The biological parents are unable to care for the child and are not likely to be able to do so in the future—as in the case of the child whose parents died or deserted him or her.
3. The biological parents have proved unable or unwilling to care adequately for the child.
4. Parents voluntarily relinquish their rights to the child.

Adoption is not appropriate under the following conditions:

1. The child with close family ties has parents or relatives who might be able to care for the child adequately in his or her own family home.
2. The child is so physically, mentally, or emotionally handicapped that he or she cannot live in a normal family setting, develop normal relationships with parental figures, and function adequately in a family (Kadushin, 1980, pp. 471-472).

Both foster and adoptive parents are no more or less parents than biological parents. As the Talmud says, "He who raises up the child is called 'father'; not he who begot the child."

The process of foster care

The foster-care process is multifaceted because it assesses, selects, and monitors foster families, biological families, and children. Professionals must determine needs of all three parties and help them with adjustment.

The agency's role

Assessment of people.   The first job of a foster-care agency is to identify potential foster parents. Usually, a social worker recruits and interviews potential parents. All methods of recruitment, from mass media campaigns to personal phone calls, are employed.

Why do adults become foster parents? Some women seek foster parenting in the belief that a main task of life is mothering. However, many of them only want infants because of a need to give and receive affection. Others want older children so they can contribute to the community (Fanshel, 1961) or increase family income without working outside the home (Rosenblum, 1977). Still others view it as a viable way to replace a sibling who died, ran away, etc. (Josselyn, 1952). Those adults who expect to be compensated in some way—emotional, social, or economic—are more successful in their quest to become foster parents. Long-term foster parents tend to be older, working-class people who receive strong agency support (Jones, 1975).

Numerous procedures have been developed to help agencies assess who will be good foster parents. Cautley and Lichtenstein (1974) created an interview schedule for applicants, and Touliatos and Lindholm (1977) developed a Potential for Foster Parenthood Scale, which attempts to determine the motivations of potential foster parents. Group homes require the greatest delineation of rules and regulations. The Child Welfare League of America (1959) specifies the standards of a group home from the number of children to the type of supervision. Typically, a married couple receives free room and board and a board rate for each child, or a salary. Various facilities—joined apartments or homes—can be licensed as group foster care homes.

Placement and parents.   After all the necessary information is collected during the intake process, a decision may be reached to place the child in a foster-care situation rather than trying to keep the child with the biological family. A written contract, the most important aspect of placement, represents a working agreement between foster parents and the agency and also may specify the frequency and type of visits with biological parents. Table 8–1 illustrates a short-form contract between

TABLE 8-1   Short-form contract between biological parents and agency

I, (Client), have stated my interest in regaining custody of (Child), and in order to work toward that goal, I agree to the following conditions:

1. I agree to visit (Child), every Wednesday from 1:00 P.M. to 3:00 P.M. in the (Child Welfare Agency) office.
2. I agree to meet with (Caseworker), every Wednesday at 3:00 P.M. in the (Child Welfare Agency) office to discuss my visits with my child, to review planning concerning my child, and to discuss changes in my situation as well as any other relevant matters.
3. I agree to participate in weekly meetings with a counselor from the County Mental Health Clinic.
4. I agree to keep (Caseworker) or (Child Welfare Agency) informed at all times of my whereabouts and home address.

I, (Client), understand that failure to meet the terms of this agreement may result in a petition for termination of parental rights to my child, (Child).

<u>   (signed) (Client)   </u>   <u>   (date)   </u>

I, (Caseworker), acting on behalf of (Child Welfare Agency), agree to assist (Client) in her efforts to regain custody of her child, (Child), and, in order to work toward that goal, agree to the following conditions:

1. I agree to have (Child) at the (Child Welfare Agency) office every Wednesday at 1:00 P.M. for visit with her mother, (Client).
2. I agree to meet with (Client) each Wednesday at 3:00 P.M. in the (Child Welfare Agency) office.
3. I agree to arrange transportation, upon request, for (Client) so that she can attend weekly meetings with the mental health clinic counselor.
4. I agree to maintain (Child) in foster care until a permanent plan can be accomplished for her.
5. I agree to keep (Client) informed of any significant matters relating to her child, (Child), such as illnesses, school progress, etc.

<u>   (signed) (Client)   </u>   <u>   (date)   </u>

It is jointly understood and agreed between (Client) and (Caseworker) that this agreement will continue in effect for a period of ninety days (unless jointly modified) and will be reviewed by (date), to evaluate progress toward meeting the stated goals.

From *Child Welfare Services* (3rd ed.), by A. Kadushin. Copyright © 1980 by Macmillan Publishing Co., Inc. Reprinted by permission.

biological parents and an agency. (See Stein & Gambrill, 1976 for systematic procedures used in developing contracts).

A contract protects all who are involved in the child's foster care and perhaps even more importantly, protects the child. The Guide for Parents of Children in Foster Care (New York City Department of Social Services, 1977) states that "parental rights and responsibilities go together. If you do not carry out your parental responsibilities you may lose or endanger your parental rights" (p. 1). Contracts allow the documentation of parental failure. Conditions that must be met for the child to return home and to remain in foster care are specified. If these conditions are not met, then evidence is available for petitioning the court to terminate parental rights or to place the child elsewhere (Phillips et al., 1971, 1977).

Placement and children. The social worker helps children adjust psychologically to placement in a foster home. Kadushin (1980) identified some typical areas of emotional difficulty children have expressed:

1. Feelings of rejection ("My parents don't want me"), which engender feelings of worthlessness
2. Guilt ("I am so bad that they had to get rid of me"), which leads the child to feel that he or she has contributed to breaking up the home
3. Hostility ("I hope they get hurt for having rejected me"), which reinforces the guilt, because hostile feelings, particularly against one's own parents, are a punishable offense
4. Fear of abandonment ("Will my parents want me back? What will happen to them while I am away?")
5. Fear of the unknown ("Where am I going? Will they like me?")
6. Shame (Why can't my parents, like other parents, take care of me?") [p. 349].

An often plaguing question that confronts the social worker is, Why me? The child often needs help to answer this question. By showing the child that love-hate feelings toward biological parents are not strange and that kinship ties to the foster family are possible without violating family loyalties, the question slowly can be resolved for most foster children. Essentially, children need help to understand that separation is not equated with rejection but rather is due to circumstances. To the extent that the community is understanding of the foster child's role, adjustment to placement is easier.

The foster parent's role

Foster parents are really partial parents because they guide the daily lives of children in interaction with the agency and, on occasion, with biological parents.

To illustrate the feelings of foster parents, the author's grandmother shared her experiences during the 1960s as a houseparent for a court-appointed group of nine 13- to 19-year-old boys who shared a double apartment in New York City. Circumstances made it impossible for most of these boys to be cared for by their biological parents or for the agency to return them to their homes.

> The bottom line is trust. They tested in the beginning about all sorts of things. Like the time one boy stayed out past curfew and did not call. My husband had the rule if you would be late you just had to call, but he didn't. We locked the door and he had to wake us up to get in. He felt badly and always called after that. Or the time when one boy sneaked out the window at night. My husband took him to the door and opened it, saying: "Look, this is the way people go in and out. You can go and come as you please in the evenings but be home by curfew." Or the time when a bedroom smelled of smoke. And it was one of the young

one's room besides. I told him, "look, if you want to smoke here is an ashtray and you smoke like you should, in the living room, you do not sneak or hide." You see they were all different boys, some stole, some had emotional problems. Many were in different homes and gave foster parents a lot of problems. Some were in institutions, too. I suppose they just had to see what we were like and whether we would love them.

After about a year, they began to trust us and saw we loved them. They asked for advice about who to date, where to go, what clothes looked good, and schooling. I so enjoyed these talks sometimes in confidence and sometimes with all the boys.

As the years went by, one boy became a teacher, another a lawyer, another a counselor, another a Bell Telephone supervisor, another a doctor; I can't remember it all. The agency said if one out of nine makes it, you are doing well. But most of all our boys made themselves into something. I get pleasure thinking about it.

Oh! Something else. My husband made a rule that everyone had to do some work when they were 16 years old even if it was an hour after school. The boys listened and got jobs. We helped find them work. We asked at places where we shopped. It was not that easy to do for all of them. They seemed to be pleased with themselves. Look, they had more money to spend for dates and things. I think this was an excellent idea. Young people should not just sit around. The boys that worked consistently a few hours after school did not have to do chores around the house; the younger ones took care of that. But their bedrooms and bathrooms, they always had to care for.

We had some rules, but life is not that simple. If a rule could not be followed, they just had to let us know. We understood. Talking is the important thing. My boys became good boys and became good men. After they left us, they would return to see the other boys. Or they would call us. To this day, some of them call to talk to "Mrs. D." and visit bringing wives and children.

Thus, the role of a foster parent can be very rewarding. Foster group homes provide older children with a family environment and therefore are used more frequently than institutional forms of care.

Caseworkers can be very helpful to foster parents who are having difficulty in their role because they know how foster children generally react to the foster situation.

[The caseworker] knows that fostering is largely a matter of trial and error, and that if a fostering fails, it may be because he has not selected the right child or the right foster home, or that the child was not yet ready for a fostering experience, or that the interference of the real parents has made the success of fostering impossible. But the foster parent does not have this experience of fostering as a guide. The foster parent . . . tends to feel that the success or failure of the fostering rests entirely on what the foster home has to offer to the child. To learn that this is not so will relieve the burden on the foster parents [Radinsky & Associates, 1963, p. 116].

The caseworker not only must reassure foster parents, but also must provide suggestions for problem situations and counsel those children who may need some assistance. With heavy caseloads, phone calls may become the best way to maintain contacts with foster parents after a personal one-on-one relationship is established.

Termination and replacement

Obviously, when foster parents no longer want to serve in their role, the foster placement is terminated. Other factors that lead to the termination of a foster-care arrangement include: (1) the child being returned home, (2) the child being adopted, (3) the child reaching an age of majority, or (4) the agency and foster parent deciding on a different placement, usually because the child has reached a certain age. Fanshel and Shinn (1978) reported that in about 75% of the cases studied a change in a child or a change in the biological family's capacity to care for the child was the major reason for terminating the foster-care service.

The average length of time in a foster-care family is about four years. Very few children (about 10–15%) receive such care for ten years or longer, and when this is the case more than one foster placement typically is used (Fanshel & Grundy, 1975). However, these studies are cross-sectional; that is, assessments are made at a specific time rather than over an extended period.

When the same children are followed over time (a longitudinal study), a different picture emerges. Jenkins (1967) tracked 891 New York City children. After all were placed, which took two years, foster care terminated for 54% after three months. By the end of a two-year period, 75% were no longer receiving foster care. A similar study (Fanshel & Shinn, 1972) over a five-year period confirms this finding that foster care is quite temporary. Of the over 600 children who were followed, 64%, a greater proportion of whom were White than Black, returned home at the end of five years.

When circumstances do not permit the child to leave foster care, as is often the case, caseworkers try to reduce the number of placements for a child so that he or she doesn't have to experience repeated separation and adjustments. When replacement is required rather frequently, children manifest more emotional problems with each subsequent situation (Eisenberg, 1965).

Replacement usually results from external and often unpreventable factors such as a foster parent's becoming ill or dying or a foster family's having to move. Replacement also happens to certain types of children—persistent thieves, truants, and promiscuous persons (Rosenblum, 1977).

In general, foster care is a stable form of substitute care. In a recent study (Shyne & Schroeder, 1978), 78% of the foster children had no more than two placements and about 70% of the group had only two caseworkers during their foster care. But the situation is quite different for older children and nonwhite children as will be examined in the section on problems with foster care.

Evaluation of the foster-care process

Young adults who received foster care during their youth are the primary respondents for evaluating the success of foster care. The majority of children who grew up with this form of care went on to become successful parents and workers. Factors that influence foster childrens' perception of the experience include the sex of the child and the emotional and interpersonal quality of the foster parent/child relationship. Males experiencing foster care have lower self-concepts than females, but adults who recalled that foster parents were supportive, fair, and loving are more successful in their societal roles as parents and workers. Thus the quality of the foster-care situation influences its success.

The effects of foster care on a child's development have been evaluated by several studies. In a major longitudinal study by Fanshel and Shinn (1978), baseline data on many variables such as intelligence, personality, and physical abilities were obtained on foster children, and updated data were obtained later. The researchers found no evidence to support the theory that the longer a child spends in foster care the more likely he or she is to show signs of deterioration. "Continued tenure in foster care is not demonstrably deleterious with respect to IQ change, school performance or measures of emotional adjustment" (p. 491).

Other studies compared children reared in foster homes with those reared in their biological families. A group of about 600 foster-care children from New York City were evaluated in terms of their physical and emotional problems and the circumstances requiring special attention. Results were compared to children home-reared in similar neighborhoods, and the two groups were found to be similar. Basically, "greater health risks [are] associated with poor inner-city minority group living" (Swire & Kavaler, 1977, p. 350), not with foster care.

Foster-family care experiences are not harmful to the development of a child, nor do they reduce the chances of being a successful adult. Even abused children showed remarkable improvements socially, emotionally, and physically under foster-family care (Kent, 1976).

Problems with foster care

The picture of foster care is brightly painted, but some looming shadows exist. There are three major problems with foster care: (1) children are placed in limbo; (2) some children are served and others are not; and (3) it is a back door to adoption.

Children in limbo

Many foster care children live in a "twilight zone," an in-between world: they are cared for by a family that cannot legally have them, but they "belong" to a family that does not or cannot do what is necessary to keep them. They are actually separated from their own biological family, but they cannot be adopted by their foster family.

Parents often initially try to alter circumstances so their children can return home. But as time passes with children in foster care, parents become distant. In a sense, their responsibility toward the child diminishes or atrophies completely. Research shows that these parents even alter their home environment so the reentry of a child would be impossible. They also assume types of jobs that would make care giving burdensome, if not impossible (Fanshel & Shinn, 1978).

Many individuals, from child advocates who want children to exercise their right to be adopted to the public who resent that tax money is used to support foster-care programs, are voicing their concern for the children in limbo, particularly those who entered the foster care system at young enough ages so they would have been likely candidates for adoption. But with the passage of time an optimal adoption placement becomes unlikely (Fanshel, 1979).

Numerous barriers block efforts to achieve permanent placement for foster children. To remove the legal barriers, laws need to be changed to terminate parental rights for a foster child who cannot return home or whose return is highly unlikely. Perhaps a child having a history of persistent neglect should be "freed" for adoption. Agency barriers need to be lifted. Certain children whose age, race, or handicaps reduce their chances of adoption need special consideration. Better monitoring procedures should be used for all children so they do not drift "in limbo."

Several projects have attempted to facilitate permanent family situations for children. The Oregon Project, which operated from 1973 to 1976, employed intensive systematic casework and efforts to terminate parental rights so children could be adopted. A caseworker's load was limited to 25 cases rather than the typical load of 50 to 60. Lawyers were employed full time for freeing children for adoption. Social workers received special training in the area of foster-care termination within the Oregon state legal system. The project focused on about 500 children, representing one-fourth of the state's foster-care children, who were in foster care for at least one year and were twelve years old or younger. After three years, about 80% of the children were no longer in foster care. About 30% of these children returned home, while 50% were either adopted or released for adoption (Emlen, 1977b).

The Alameda Project in California (Stein, 1976) was another effort to provide permanent care for foster children. Control and experimental biological families were identified. The experimental group received a variety of behavior modification techniques to alter situations so children could return home. Caseworkers were given a limited load of 20 randomly selected cases. All children received the typical services provided by the agency. At the end of a two-year period, a significantly larger proportion of foster children from parents in the experimental group returned home or were going to be adopted, compared to the control group. As with the Oregon Project, caseworkers' involvement and systematic planning and implementation efforts were critical for terminating parental rights or helping parents provide for their children's return.

The question remains: is permanence the important issue for good social psychological adjustment? After intensive interviews with parents and children, it was concluded that a legal permanent situation, either through returning home or adoption is not as important as a child's feelings of belonging somewhere, as his or her *perception* of permanence (Lahti, 1978). Kadushin (1980) disagrees.

> Despite these findings the logic is convincing that an adoptive placement, which combines legal and perceived permanence, is likely to offer the child a greater probability of stability than a long-term foster home not reinforced by legal sanctions, even if the intent is for the foster home to be permanent. A "marriage" through adoption has more factors conducive to permanence than "living together" in foster care [p. 389].

Serving some children and not others

Increasingly, certain children are more difficult to place and replace in foster care than others. These children typically are older, non-White, or handicapped. For instance, after studying 43 foster homes that cared for handicapped children, Arkava and Mueller (1978) found that these children were older, in placements longer, and experienced more replacements than other foster children. Foster parents of these children identified numerous problems: (1) care took a great deal of time and energy; (2) they felt confined because childsitters were hard to find; (3) specialized training was always needed to take care of children with different problems; (4) neighbors did not accept such children; and (5) educational resources were not available. Also, parents who take a handicapped child into their home report problems with their own children accepting the child. If handicapped children are to receive the same substitute care options as other children, additional resources should be made available for foster parents. Also, since such care requires far greater intensity, ways to allow for "time off" for these parents need to be explored.

Attitudes must change as well. Many communities develop zoning laws and other impediments that prohibit or discourage the establishment of foster homes for retarded children. For example, citizens of Scarsdale, a suburb of New York City, successfully resisted attempts to establish such a home in their neighborhood. The implications of these actions are great. These children need to be cared for, but where? Is placing homes together in "ghettos" in the children's best interest?

Problems exist in the placement of Black children, too. Many Black families are already caring for related and nonrelated children informally. Also, proportionately more Black children are in need of foster care than White children, as was mentioned earlier.

Attempts now are made for foster-care placement to perpetuate the child's cultural heritage. For instance, in 1978 Congress passed and President Carter signed the Indian Child Welfare Act, which gave Indian tribes more control over the care of Indian children. In fact, placement priority for a child is with a tribal family.

A back door to adoption

Foster parents are helpful conveniences for biological parents. But with a growing concern about children's welfare and especially with the permanence of placement, foster parents can be a threat to biological parents. An increasing number of foster parents adopt their foster children. Blood is no longer considered thicker than water.

The importance of an established relationship between foster parents and children is gaining priority in court cases. Courts are requiring not that the unfitness of biological parents be established for adoption to occur, but rather that biological parents prove that termination of their legal rights is not in the best interests of the child. Children's right to a continuous relationship is being protected more today than ever before (Egginton & Hibbs, 1975–1976).

This trend of more foster parents adopting children may result in increasing conflict between foster and biological parents. The conflict could take the form of advocacy groups protecting the rights of biological parents (Citizens Committee for Children, 1978). In one case, a mother was ill with multiple sclerosis and had to have her child placed in foster care. However, her condition, though terminal, improved and she requested the return of her child through a court proceeding. The foster parents also petitioned to adopt the child. The judge ruled that because the mother's life expectancy was shortened and a strong prolonged psychological relationship with the foster parents had been established, adoption was appropriate. Despite protesting groups on behalf of the biological mother, the court ruling remained unchanged (*Washington Star,* July 7, 1974, cited in Kadushin, 1980).

As a consequence of foster care becoming a "back door" for adoption in an increasing number of cases, biological parents may try to maintain contact with their children to establish that a psychological relationship exists. Foster parents may also try to alienate children from their biological parents. Foster care thus may become a "tug-of-love" situation for the children.

The process of adoption

Adoption is regulated by state laws, with the legal requirements varying from state to state. In some states, for instance, children who have reached a certain age (10 or 14) must consent to adoption. In other states, the child is not asked for an opinion. As a result of these differences, states have developed a uniform monitoring procedure to protect children who are transported across state lines for adoption. This agreement enables agency activities to be coordinated, provides for supervision of placement, requires a written report about the placement, and guarantees that children in transit are protected legally and financially (Brieland & Lemmon, 1977).

Legal procedures

The legal procedure for adoption begins when the adoptive adults file a petition with the juvenile, probate, or superior court, depending on the state. Usually, this petition is filed at a county level where the adoptive parents reside. The petition contains the potential parents' request for adoption, basic information about the child and themselves, and consent from the biological parents or other party (often the agency "surrenders" a child). The appropriate parties, including the children in some states, are notified. The court orders an official investigation of the circumstances. This investigation usually is performed by some public welfare agency, which makes a recommendation to the court. A closed court hearing is held in which the court meets the adoptive parents, child, and any witnesses. The petition for adoption is approved or denied based upon the "best interests" of the child. A court order approving adoption usually is either temporary or interlocutory, meaning that a trial period, typically six months, must be completed prior to the court's decree that the child legally "belongs" to the parents. Although annulling the decree is possible, once the final decree is issued, the child becomes the legal child of the parents. The child is given the parent's surname, a new birth certificate may be issued, and all proceedings are sealed legally. Alien children do not gain citizenship from adoption.

A major change in legal procedures concerns the father's role. Prior to the U.S. Supreme Court decision in *Stanley* v. *Illinois* (1972), natural fathers not living with their children were not consulted about the adoption of their children. Stanley, an unwed father who at one time had lived with and supported his children, was contesting the transfer of legal custody to the state after the children's mother died. The Supreme Court ruled in his favor. As a consequence, fathers must be given an opportunity to have custody or to surrender their children (Bodenheimer, 1975), which certainly can present problems for the agency investigating an adoption case. Time, energy, and effort must be demonstrated in attempts to contact birth fathers, the whereabouts of whom may be difficult to obtain. The agencies must determine whether or not an out-of-wedlock father ever accepted responsibility for his children. If responsibility is evident, then permission must be obtained for adoption to occur. However, in 1978 the Supreme Court decision in *Quilloin* v. *Walcott* upheld a Georgia law that said fathers of children born out of wedlock have no legal rights to challenge adoption if they never assumed responsibility for their children. This decision helps explain the trend of maintaining the foster parent/child relationship via adoption, especially in cases where biological parents abrogated responsibility for their children.

Thus, legal procedures for adoption are becoming increasingly child-centered. Adoptive parents and biological parents are scrutinized by the courts and welfare agencies. Mere blood ties are not evidence in and of themselves that a child belongs with his or her biological parents. It is hoped that the legal system will continue to move in the direction of children's best interests.

Attitudes and motives

Caseworkers play a key role in adoption decisions. These professionals assess applicants' maturity, their marital relationship, attitudes toward children, capacity for rearing a child, and whether their behavior in future interactions with an unknown child will be positive. Fortunately, professionals generally agree about the criteria for evaluating potential parents (Brieland, 1961; Brown & Brieland, 1975) Table 8-2 shows a rating sheet for prospective parents.

The motives of potential parents help caseworkers make decisions. Motives relating to a child's needs are received more favorably than those that focus on personal needs. For instance, adopting to save a marriage, to enable in-laws to become grandparents, to have someone take care of the parents during old age, or to replace a

TABLE 8-2 Some criteria in evaluating adoptive couples

Total personality	Feelings about children
Family relationships	Basic love for children
Work adjustment	Ability to deal with developmental problems
Relationship with friends	Sensitivity to and understanding and tolerance
Activity in community	of children's difficulties
	Ability to individualize child
Emotional maturity	
Capacity to give and receive love	Feelings about childlessness and
Acceptance of sex roles	readiness to adopt
Ability to assume responsibility for care,	Absence of guilt regarding infertility
guidance, and protection of another	Mutual decision to adopt
person	Ability to tell child he is adopted
Reasonable emotional stability	Attitudes toward biological parents and
Flexibility	illegitimacy
Self-respect	
Ability to cope with problems, disap-	**Motivation**
pointments, and frustrations	Desire to have more nearly complete life
	Desire to accept parental responsibility
Quality of marital relationship	Desire to contribute to development of
Successful continuance of marriage not	another human being
dependent on children	Desire to love and be loved
Respect for each other	
Capacity to accept a child born to other	
parents	

From *Child Welfare Services* (3rd ed.), by A. Kadushin. Copyright © 1980 by Macmillan Publishing Co., Inc. Reprinted by permission.

child who died of terminal illness would not be valued very highly. But motives such as helping a youngster contribute to society, making a child happy, giving love to another, or teaching a child to handle the world all would be viewed positively.

Applying for adoption

The trend for adoptive agencies today is to expand the list of potential parents by using a "screening-in" rather than "screening-out" approach. Applicants are screened in the following areas.

Health. Agencies require that applicants be physically and emotionally healthy. An applicant may have an infectious condition that the agency does not want the child to get. Poor physical health could jeopardize the applicant's earning capacity and consequently his or her ability to provide child care. Emotional health refers to a clear understanding of self in terms of strengths and weaknesses. Extremes such as overriding guilt or total independence are not considered to be good emotional health. Here, the testimony of others about emotional health is helpful for the agency to make a judgment.

Age. Individuals ages 35 to 45 are considered desirable for adopting an infant. Agencies believe that, if parents are too old, the child may be orphaned, sometimes for the second time; generational conflicts could arise; outside attitudes may be negative and difficult to handle for the child in an atypical family situation; and parents may not be able to interact actively with their children. Older parents, however, can more easily adopt older children.

Religion. Many states require that applicants have a religion and encourage placement of a child with people of the same religion as the biological parents.

Obviously, if the parents had different religions, then either could be selected. Religious affiliation of applicants usually is not a determinant for placement.

Financial stability.   Agencies look for financial stability rather than income of potential parents. Ensuring that the child will not place a financial strain on the family is one way to prevent problems from arising later.

Marital status.   Many agencies require that applicants be married for from three to five years, believing a married couple whose relationship has stood the test of time can provide the best climate for child rearing. However, many single people and homosexual couples also are adopting children. Relationship stability is now considered to be more important than marital status.

Marital relationship.   Agencies determine whether marital relationships are satisfactory. Are the husband and wife relatively happy? Do they accept their roles in various arenas such as household chores, decision making, and sexual interaction? The belief is that a happy twosome produces a happy family.

Infertility and adjustment to sterility.   Many states require proof of infertility as a prerequisite for adoption, reasoning that if a couple is fertile and parenthood is valued, they would have their own child. Also, the issue of supply and demand is considered. Only so many children can be adopted. Why should people who can have children deprive those who cannot? Also a refusal to give evidence of infertility is considered evidence of a poor adjustment to sterility, which could harm the potential parent/child relationship.

Capacity for parenthood.   Establishing a capacity for parenthood is the key for receiving approval for an adoption request. Even in the most liberal states that do not require meeting the above mentioned criteria, the concept of parental potential is critical. Applicants must know why they want to become parents and present a good argument for their potential parenting capacity.

Placing a child

Caseworkers want not only to identify potentially good parents but also to help children and parents adjust to their new relationship. Typically, with younger children, less assistance is needed than with older children. Discussions often occur with children and sometimes meetings are arranged with children and future parents before adoptions are finalized.

After placement, the trial period begins, for the protection of both parties. The caseworker wants confirmation that the child is placed with responsible parents in a positive family context. In the event that a child develops an unfortunate illness during this time, the agency can mediate with the court to remove the child, thus mitigating the trauma for parents and perhaps the child.

Adoptive parents view this trial period differently than agencies. Evidence (see Gochros, 1962; Zober, 1961) indicates that about half the parents from any group who recently adopted view the trial period as a time of probation in which their behavior and attitudes are under a microscope. One adoptive father reported:

> My wife was out of town on a planned trip that the agency was aware of. I was home with the infant and had gotten ill with the flu. Our daughter was due to go to the pediatrician for her monthly check-up. I tried to ready myself, but was too weak. Rather than risk changing the appointment, I called a friend and asked her to take the baby. I didn't want to do anything to jeopardize our final court decree. Those six months were like that. Like . . .

Oh! Like living in the shadow of fearing loss and that someone will find something wrong. I was so glad when our case was closed with the court. We all seemed to be more relaxed and happy [Author's files].

Evaluating placement

Judging the success or failure of adoption is difficult because many variables confound results and the timing of data collection varies widely. For example, data are gathered at various points during the trial period and are difficult to compare for interpretation. Rates of psychiatric treatment of adopted children are used to index placement failure, but comparable control groups are not established. Also, data gathered from independent adoption agencies cannot be compared to those from public agencies because the children they place tend to be older, handicapped, or foreign.

The success rate compared to some degree of rate of failure for adoption is high—65.7% of the placements are successful in providing children with homes and parents that result in good adjustment (see Table 8–3). What accounts for success:

TABLE 8–3   Recapitulation of adoptive outcome studies

Outcome	Number	Percent
Unequivocally successful Satisfactory Very good Good Successful Superior Low problems No symptoms or slight symptoms Excellent to fair Within normal range Very well adjusted	1,739	65.7
Intermediate success Not definitely unsatisfactory Fairly successful Indifferent Questionable Some problems Intermediate Average Moderate symptoms Not well adjusted	482	18.2
Unsuccessful Unsatisfactory Poor, low Problematic Unsuccessful Incapable High problems Problem child Disturbed	424	16.1
Total	2,645	100.0

From *Child Welfare Services* (3rd ed.), by A. Kadushin. Copyright © 1980 by Macmillan Publishing Co., Inc. Reprinted by permission.

parents, children, or both? What accounts for failure? Were certain problems present but undetected by the agency? And where do these problems manifest themselves, with parents or children? In order to gain some insight into the complex nature of these representative questions, we turn our attention to the problems related to adoption.

Problems with adoption

The problems associated with adoption go beyond violating legal guidelines (adopting a child through extralegal means on the "gray market"). Since adoption is not temporary like foster care, it perpetuates different problems for parents and children. First is the test of adequacy. Is the child good enough? Are parents good enough? Then there is the fear of rejection for both child and parents. This fear manifests itself differently for the more atypical or "hard-to-place" child. Such a label may make the situation a self-fulfilling prophecy for both parties. Then comes the problem of "telling the child." The scenario does not end there because now the child is confronted with questions of identity. So some adopted children embark on the journey searching for their heritage.

The gray market

One-fifth of the 17,000 children adopted in 1971 were part of the "gray market" (Kadushin, 1980). Agencies were not involved in their placement. Courts did not rule on behalf of the child's best interests. A probationary period did not exist. A final decree was not obtained. Information was not sealed. Rather, these children were adopted independently. Independent adoptions can take the form of biological parents making contact with an interested party or with an intermediary who makes contact with prospective parents. The intermediary sometimes earns a fee for "selling" the baby. Although little data document this procedure of independent adoptions, these adoptions do occur as routine "business transactions."

Gray-market adoptions are dangerous to children. Their rights are not protected. A good home is not guaranteed. Capable parents are not assured. Some caseworkers make placement errors, but their intentions usually are honorable and their track record is fairly good.

The gray market caters to the cash customer. The customer who can pay or make the most attractive offer to the person (intermediary or biological parent) negotiating the deal is the one who gets the child. Many people prefer going the independent route for adoption because it avoids "red tape." Potential parents do not have to be interviewed, petition the court, be investigated, be on probation, and so on, nor do they have to prove they are infertile or adjusted to sterility. In essence, they not only avoid a large bureaucratic system designed to protect the child, but also avoid any personal form of embarrassment that they might associate with adoption. Unfortunately, also circumvented is the opportunity for potential parents to explore all the ramifications and responsibilities associated with parenthood. Freedom to adopt means freedom from introspection as well as freedom from agency assistance.

Another possible problem with independent adoption is that there is no guarantee of confidentiality. All who are involved could at any time inform anyone of the situation. Hence, the adoptive parents could lose the control of telling their child. Also, upon learning that biological parents exist and records are not sealed, the adopted child may make a life-long cause of establishing his or her roots.

Other problems can occur, too. Parents may feel less adequate because they never

The gray market for adoption still persists and challenges us to develop a better monitoring system.

passed the agency screening. And children, should they find out, may feel less adequate because they were "purchased" rather than selected from among many. Either feeling could lead to fears of rejection for parents or child.

The gray market is disadvantageous for the biological parents, also. Often young women who have children out of wedlock surrender their babies without considering the psychological ramifications. Perhaps their immediate need was for money. Or perhaps they did not wish to embarrass their family or hamper any chances of obtaining a mate. Such a view is myopic. Since a child could reveal the situation at any point during his or her life time, they walk in the shadow of possible disclosure. The birth father's rights are violated as well. Perhaps he would have wanted the child at some point. But on the gray market, he is of little importance.

During 1974–1975, the Subcommittee of Children and Youth of the Senate Committee on Labor and Public Welfare held a hearing on "baby buying and selling" (U.S. Congress, 1975) in which much disturbing information was presented. There are baby farms where young women go to become pregnant and earn money (sometimes as much as $25,000) from the sale of infants. Some individuals try to convince women at abortion clinics to sell their children. Indeed, the gray market could be characterized as a black market. It presents a major problem for adoption and fosters a view of children as commodities to be bought and sold.

The test of adequacy

Parents who adopt are not referred to as "real" parents. Rather, society tells them they are second-class parents because they have not conceived a child. So from the beginning, adoptive parents may feel that their adequacy is being tested. Overcompensation may result in overindulging children—giving them too much or not disciplining them enough. Because they are made to feel inadequate, adoptive parents may be concerned about rejection by their child, who may want to find his or her "real" parents. This often occurs during the trial period and the process of telling the child.

Children who are adopted also may feel that they are being tested. They were rejected once by parents and certainly could be again. They may find fault with themselves, develop poor self-images, and feel they are second-class children.

What may be indicators of inadequacy may only be reinforced patterns of behavior. Because many adoptive parents worked with an agency, they have experienced professionals intervening into their lives. This may explain why they may continue to seek help when needed (Harper & Williams, 1976; Silver, 1970). Although adopted children compared to nonadopted children are referred more often for interventions, the percentages are not very high (15% or less) (Kadushin, 1980). Perhaps adoptive parents are concerned about their children because they were born to young women out of wedlock who were pregnant for the first time. Care during the pregnancy, whether nutritional or psychological, often was lacking, as evidenced by the high proportion of babies with low birth weights (Kadushin, 1980).

Rejection

Because they are difficult to place, minority children walk with the shadow of rejection before they are even adopted. Efforts are underway to place these children following guidelines similar to those used for foster care (Scott, 1976). Also, transracial adoptions are continuing to increase. In 1971, for instance, about 10,000 transracial adoptions took place (Kadushin, 1980).

Ladner (1977) argues that "a home and love are not enough to pay for loss of identity" (p. 86). However, evidence shows identity is not lost when a Black child is placed in a White home. Simon and Alstein (1977), in an interview study with 120 Black children in White homes, found that "Black children reared in the special setting of multiracial families do not acquire the ambivalence to their own race reported in all other studies involving black children" (p. 158). But the children in this study were an average age of about four, perhaps too young to confront their racial identity. Thus, while interracial adoptions may not be the ideal solution to the problem of rejection, they are at least one way of helping minority children to start their lives with acceptance rather than rejection.

Older children up for adoption have a life history that includes some form of rejection. The older orphaned child has lived with rejection for a number of years. The older child recently orphaned has established strong ties with biological parents. An older child who still "belongs" to biological parents has maintained ties with foster parents. Hence, these children are more likely than younger children to expect rejection again. Kadushin (1980) points out that older children "are more likely to test the adoptive parents' patience and endurance in order to prove their acceptability. The adoptive parents, thus, are in for a harder time and, at least initially, fewer satisfactions" (p. 541). Although adults can be rejected by their adopted children, typically rejection occurs from the agency. Individuals may not meet certain state requirements or reveal the "right" attitudes and motives to become applicants for adoption (Hochfield, 1963).

Telling the child

Informing a child that he or she is adopted is a difficult decision. Up until this point, efforts were made to integrate the child into the family and now the child will be differentiated. Many parents fear that the child will reject them.

Although telling the child may be difficult, the majority of scholars feel it is necessary (see Hagen, 1968; Paton, 1954; Schechter, 1960). Silence could mean the child is not accepted. Discovery through other sources may make the child feel deceived and hurt.

There are many ways in which a child can be told about his or her adoptive status without anxiety or apology. Telling a child he or she has been picked, however, can place undo pressure on the child. Also, it should not be overstressed or used as a label, as McWhinnie (1967) points out:

> None of the adopted children wanted their adoptive status shrouded in complete secrecy. . . . Equally they did not want constant references to it. They wanted something in between, where their adopted status was acknowledged without embarrassment and then overtly forgotten so that they were treated exactly as if they were the biological sons and daughters of their adopted parents [p. 249].

The search for heritage

Because adoptive parents legally are "real" parents, adoptive records are sealed. Biological mothers who have "surrendered" their children legally are protected from them intruding into their lives. But some argue that adoptive records should be opened to adopted children approaching adulthood, claiming that they have the right to know and learn about their biological parents (Sorosky, Baran, & Pannor, 1978). Numerous advantages are cited: adopted children can feel better knowing their roots; biological parents may be able to rid themselves of guilt; adoptive parents can feel reassured about their children's love; and an atmosphere of uncertainty can be lifted.

The disadvantages of finding out about heritage are numerous, too. Adopted children may not accept their roots. Biological parents may experience renewed guilt. Adoptive parents may feel rejected or never accepted. The Association for the Protection of the Adoptive Triangle (APAT) has been organized to support sealed records. Also, the Child Welfare League of America supports keeping records sealed in its Standards for Adoption Service (1973).

The people in this three-party system that suffer the most are adoptees. They feel a part of their lives is missing. After they discover who they "really" are, they report a sense of closure and feel even closer to adoptive parents (Jones, 1979; Sorosky, Baran, & Pannor, 1978).

If records are to be open, the question of open adoption is raised. An open adoption is one in which "the birth parents participate in the separation, placement process, relinquish all legal, moral, and nurturing rights to the child, but retain the right to continue contact and to knowledge of the child's whereabouts and welfare" (Baran, Pannor, & Sorosky, 1976, p. 97). Is it fair or right to have two sets of parents involved in the rearing of children? Who benefits from such a system? These questions merit further study and evaluation.

Conclusion

Foster care and adoption are two well-established ways to provide children with the love, care, nurturance, and protection needed to become healthy, well-adjusted adults, and to help adults fulfill their own needs, goals, and desires by becoming parents. But unless ways to overcome the problems associated with substitute care are developed, the number of children who can be cared for by foster or adoptive parents may diminish. With declining birth rates and increasing cleverness in circumventing the legal aspects of substitute care, a situation of high demand with little or no supply may be developing. Children are not commodities and should not be treated as such. In fact, perpetuating this attitude may be the crux of the problem. Children do not belong to adults. They are people with their own rights. Biological parents "owning" a child is not better than adopted parents "owning" a child. Children need parents and adults need children. The goal should be to maximize the match between parents and children and protect the next generation.

Summary

Foster care, a change in legal custody of a child, and adoption, a permanent change in family affiliation, are two socially sanctioned forms of substitute care that enable adults to serve in a parental role. Professionals work to find permanent substitute-care situations so children do not have to undergo periodic adjustments. Treating children like commodities is still a persistent problem today, as evidenced by the "buying and selling" of children.

Placement in foster care, often a form of corrective intervention, many times results from family crises, especially for minorities and the lower class. Despite political attitudes that hamper preventive placements, some high-risk families do receive social services. Foster care moves beyond mere placement to a multifaceted function. Professionals determine needs of children, foster families, and biological families. Agency functions are: (1) assessment, (2) placement, (3) assistance for adjustment, (4) determining termination, and (5) replacement.

The majority of children who grew up with foster care did so satisfactorily. Males have lower self-concepts than females, but individuals who recalled that foster parents were supportive, fair, and loving are more successful in their societal roles as parents and workers. Although the quality of foster care is related to its success, the following problems still exist: (1) children are in limbo; (2) only some children are served; and (3) it is a back door to adoption.

The process of adoption legally varies from state to state. A court petition requesting to adopt a child usually begins the process. The petition is filed, an investigation is ordered, and a closed court hearing is held. After an adoption is approved, a six-month trial period often follows. Procedures for adoption are moving in a child-centered direction. Biological ties are not enough evidence that a child "belongs" with those parents.

Potential parents' motivations and suitability for adoption are examined, with the following characteristics preferred: (1) good physical and emotional health; (2) age between 35 to 45 years (but older parents can adopt older children); (3) financial stability; (4) being married for three to five years; (5) satisfactory partner relationship; (6) adjustment to infertility; and (7) a demonstrable capacity for parenthood.

Although judging the success or failure of adoption is difficult because of the many variables, the success rate compared to the rate of failure for adoption is two to one. However, several problems are associated with adoption: (1) controlling the buying and selling of children; (2) testing parent and child adequacy with the trial period; (3) fearing rejection; (4) telling the child; and (5) searching for heritage. Efforts need to be directed toward solving these problems so children are no longer treated as commodities.

9

Services for Developmentally Dysfunctional Children

This chapter was written in collaboration with RONALD A. MADLE, Ph.D., as the senior author. Madle is currently Director of Training and Evaluation at Laurelton Center and Adjunct Professor of Human Development, The Pennsylvania State University.

Chapter overview

Children deviating from the norm have a history of being labeled and receiving different treatments. This chapter will examine the categories used to label these children, the purposes of noncategorical approaches, and the services provided. Then attention will be focused on the services needed by developmentally dysfunctional children.

Issues to consider

What are positive and negative features of labeling children as developmentally dysfunctional?

What is meant by the following terms: mental retardation, emotional disturbance, neurological impairments, learning disability, sensory impairments, and developmental disabilities?

How can noncategorical approaches to the developmentally dysfunctional better serve their needs?

How have services traditionally been delivered to developmentally dysfunctional children?

What contemporary services are available for dysfunctional children and what services do they need?

Introduction

More than ten million mentally and physically handicapped children and youth in the United States under the age of 18 are functionally impaired enough to require special services. In 1971, these children only received about half of the necessary services for an expenditure of slightly less than $5 billion by federal, state, and local programs (Brewer & Kakalik, 1979). Who are these children? What types of services do they need? How should these services be delivered? These are questions that child-service planners and workers must consider.

A decade ago most child-service personnel could ignore the problems of the exceptional child, who was segregated into special programs for service delivery. Not so today. Current laws and public opinion dictate that services for exceptional children be provided to the maximum extent possible under the current child-service delivery system. This means, of course, that increasing numbers of child service providers must understand the needs of exceptional children and develop skills working with exceptional children side by side with normal children.

Children who deviate significantly from developmental norms in at least one area of functioning receive any of a number of designations, such as exceptional, handicapped, special, and disabled. Under these broad classification labels, a large number of specific diagnostic categories are applied to these children—mentally retarded, emotionally disturbed, neurologically impaired, visually and auditorially impaired, and others. Regardless of the specific label or labels applied, these children require interventions to correct and compensate for problems and deficits.

The term *developmental dysfunctions,* often used to describe this group of children as a whole, refers to any enduring handicapping conditions that typically arise during an individual's growth period. This general term can be extremely useful or it can be used in a virtually meaningless and self-defeating manner (Chess, 1978).

This label can serve as a roadblock to a child's development. Sometimes children are placed in ill-suited programs or denied access to services for "normal" children that are a significant and important part of their lives. Even children who display extremely similar problems, such as autism and severe mental retardation, often are not served in the same setting. To be meaningful, the label *developmentally dysfunctional,* like any other, must serve as a starting point for careful analyses of children's strengths, needs, and limitations in each area of human functioning. Then tailored intervention plans can be developed and implemented to meet each child's needs (Smith & Neisworth, 1975). Thus, a label has the potential to expand service opportunities, not necessarily limit them.

Categories of developmental dysfunctions

Diagnostic categories summarize the salient characteristics of children with different types of dysfunctions. For example, a visually impaired child unquestionably has difficulty in receiving visual stimulation; however, virtually any other aspect of functioning may or may not be adequate. Children in this or any other diagnostic category demonstrate individual differences, as do normal children. Many times a child with one impairment has other problems as well. The challenge becomes to identify key features that are similar across problem areas so intervention efforts can be coordinated.

How can developmentally dysfunctional children be described? What are some of the salient characteristics of children who receive different diagnostic levels? How prevalent are certain disorders? Answers to these questions will provide a standard of comparison for this chapter's examination of some newer noncategorical approaches that are applied to developmentally dysfunctional children.

Mental retardation

Three classification systems are used in the United States to define mental retardation. Although these systems differ in relatively minor ways, they all emphasize a multidimensional definition that requires impairment to both intellectual functioning (cognitive component) and adaptive behavior (social-adaptability component). Retardation in the intellectual sphere is not sufficient for children to be classified as mentally retarded; they must also encounter significant problems in adapting and coping with their environment.

The American Association on Mental Deficiency (AAMD) defines mental retardation as "significantly subaverage general intellectual functioning existing concurrently with deficits in adaptive behavior, and manifested during the developmental period" (Grossman, 1977, p. 5). "Significantly subaverage" requires that a child score approximately 70 or lower on an intelligence test. This performance places the child's intellectual functioning two standard deviations below the mean of 100, which reflects the lowest 2.28% of the general population. This cut-off point is, of course, completely arbitrary. In fact, in earlier editions of the AAMD definition, the cut-off score was only one standard deviation below the mean (an IQ of approximately 85), which included 15.87% of the total population. Changing the cut-off point reduced the overall prevalence of mental retardation by about 14%. While such an alternative can have positive effects by removing stigmatizing labels, it also removed some individuals from programs and services beneficial for their development.

Early diagnosis of children's developmental dysfunctions provides the means to identify the types of services the children need in order to develop to their full potential.

Mental retardation generally is broken down into further subdivisions based on degree of impairment (see Table 9–1). At the highest level is the *mildly retarded* child, who differs from the normal child only in a slower rate of learning skills. These children are referred to as *educable*. In the IQ range from 40 to 54, children are called *moderately retarded* (or *trainable*). They evidence neurological impairment and demonstrate difficulty in learning skills needed for daily living. Many children in this category cannot even learn self-feeding and toileting skills until school age. At the lowest levels of functioning are the *severely* (IQ 25–39) and *profoundly* (IQ 24 or less) *retarded*. These children usually have significant physical and neurological handicaps and require intensive training to acquire self-maintenance skills such as toileting, self-feeding, and dressing. At the profound level, intervention strategies such as instruction-following and imitation must be intensively taught.

Mental retardation is the most prevalent of the developmental dysfunctions. According to Grossman (1977), the United States has over 3 million mentally retarded individuals under age 21 out of a total youth population of 103 million. The overwhelming majority of these children (over 2.6 million) are mildly retarded, with progressively fewer diagnosed at more impaired levels of functioning. Mental retardation clearly is a socially significant problem that must be considered in the development and delivery of child services.

Emotional disturbance

Emotional disturbance is a general term that refers to a wide range of conditions. Some emotional disturbance is merely a mild, transient reaction to stressful environmental conditions. Other forms are prolonged and profound disturbances that require life long services and support. In all cases, however, the outstanding feature is atypical socio-emotional behavior. The list of labels for various forms of emotional disturbance seems unending: adjustment reactions to childhood, infantile autism, childhood schizophrenia, psychosocial dysfunctions, behavior disorders, and phobic reactions, to name just a few.

TABLE 9-1 Developmental characteristics of the mentally retarded

Degree of mental retardation	Preschool (ages 0-5) maturation and development	School (ages 6-20) training and education	Adult (21 and over) and vocational adequacy
Profound	Gross retardation; minimal capacity for functioning in sensorimotor areas; needs nursing care	Some motor development present; may respond to minimal or limited training in self-help	Some motor and speech development; may achieve very limited self-care; needs nursing care
Severe	Poor motor development; speech minimal; generally unable to profit from training in self-help; little or no communication skills	Can talk or learn to communicate; can be trained in elemental health habits; profits from systematic habit training	May contribute partially to self-maintenance under complete supervision; can develop self-protection skills to a minimal useful level in controlled environment
Moderate (trainable)	Can talk or learn to communicate; poor social awareness; fair motor development; profits from training in self-help; can be managed with moderate supervision	Can profit from training in social and occupational skills; unlikely to progress beyond 2nd grade level in academic subjects; may learn to travel alone in familiar places	May achieve self-maintenance in unskilled or semi-skilled work under sheltered conditions; needs supervision and guidance when under social or economic stress
Mild (educable)	Can develop social and communication skills; minimal retardation in sensorimotor areas; often not distinguished from normal until later age	Can learn academic skills up to approximately 6th grade level by late teens; can be guided toward social conformity	Can usually achieve social and vocational skills adequate to minimum self-support but may need guidance under unusual social or economic stress

From "A Rationale for Degrees of Retardation" by W. Sloan and J. W. Birch. In *American Journal of Mental Deficiency,* 1955, 60, 258–264. Copyright 1955 by the American Association on Mental Deficiency. Reprinted by permission.

Different diagnostic systems are used to identify emotional disturbance and often conflict with each other. Some systems judge different types of childhood disturbances in the context of adult functioning, which are of limited value for working with children. The most refined diagnostic system, developed by the Group for the Advancement of Psychiatry (1966), is oriented to children and youth (Hobbs, 1975). Because it considers the sequences of developmental processes within the context of a child's family and community, this system recognizes that not all socio-emotional problems are "unhealthy." Some behaviors (truancy, getting into fights, stealing) and disturbances (fear of the dark, inability to speak, self-inflicted injuries) are viewed as adaptive responses to difficult circumstances, including impoverished housing, unemployed parents, alcoholic parent, and death of a parent.

Childhood emotional disturbance is estimated to affect 2% of the population, or about 2 million children (Kolb, 1973). Of these a large number have relatively mild problems that are limited to specific areas of functioning, such as psychosomatic problems of specific phobias, and require focused treatment. A few children (0.31%), however, manifest severe problems and receive a diagnosis of psychosis or autism, which is a specific form of psychosis. These children usually require an array of specialized services and are excluded from typical programs such as day care (Kolb, 1973).

Some professionals believe childhood psychosis consists of two predominant disorders, childhood schizophrenia and infantile autism, that have many features in common and only one difference—timing or onset of occurrence. Autism appears under age 6; schizophrenia occurs after 6. A listing of symptoms used to make a general diagnosis of childhood schizophrenia is displayed in Table 9-2. Regardless of debates over subtypes, scholars agree that severely disturbed children exhibit serious impairments in speech and social relationships, as well as bizarre motor behavior. In many cases, severe psychosis is very difficult to distinguish from profound mental retardation; the resemblance is often striking (Kolb, 1973).

TABLE 9-2   Nine basic symptoms of childhood schizophrenia

Severe and long-term distortion of interpersonal relationships
Unawareness of personal identity, manifested in self-mutilation and bizarre posturing
Extreme preoccupation with inanimate objects (or parts of them) without regard for their function
Ritualistic behavior aimed at maintaining an unchanging environment
Distorted responses to sensory stimuli as a result of abnormal perception
Excessive and illogical anxiety, often in response to common objects
Loss of, or failure to ever acquire, speech
Distortion of motor behavior (catatonia, hyperactivity, contortions, or ritualistic mannerisms)
Retardation in general skills with normal or exceptional ability in some areas

Neurological impairments

The term *neurological impairment* covers a substantial number of handicapping conditions with symptoms that include impairments in language, motor, and sensory functions, growth rates, and intellectual abilities. The reason often cited for these problems is a malfunction of the central nervous system, which often is caused by medically demonstrable brain damage. Unfortunately, in some cases this damage is presumed incorrectly, which hampers effective intervention efforts.

A large number of specific syndromes are associated with neurological impairments, including convulsive disorders, cerebral palsy, and multiple sclerosis. Epilepsy and cerebral palsy occur with enough frequency to have significant behavioral, educational, and social consequences (Hobbs, 1975).

Epilepsy.   About 0.5% of the American population suffers from the condition known as epilepsy, a variety of organic disorders consisting of irregularly occurring disturbances in consciousness (seizures or convulsions). In most cases, epilepsy is controlled by medication. Severe cases often are never controlled, except through extreme treatment such as surgical removal of a portion of the brain (Kolb, 1973).

Sometimes the root of the disorder can be determined, although about three-fourths of the cases have no identifiable cause (Kolb, 1973). Epilepsy ranges in severeness from grand mal, which involves generalized convulsions and severely impaired functioning during a seizure, to petit mal, which involves only a few seconds' lapse in consciousness and physical immobility.

Cerebral palsy.   Cerebral palsy (CP) is a group of disorders in which nonprogressive brain damage has occurred, resulting in motor disability. This impairment can range from barely perceptible to totally disabling. Children with CP frequently have difficulty walking and have impaired speech. These children are often viewed as "walking and talking funny." Although some children with CP do experience intellectual retardation, many score in a normal range of intelligence and demonstrate superior intellectual functioning.

Learning disability

Learning disability is a catch-all term used to describe children with disorders in listening, thinking, reading, writing, spelling, and arithmetic. The disorders of learning-disabled children frequently are very specific. A child may be very bright but never learn to read, or be able to read but not write. Another child may simply not be able to perform simple arithmetic, but exhibit no other problems. Excluded from this category are children whose disabilities are attributed to sensory impairments, mental retardation, or emotional disturbance. The terms used to describe learning-disabled children imply some type of underlying brain dysfunction, which rarely is identified. A commonly used term is *minimal brain dysfunction*, which suggests a neurological cause.

In addition to learning problems, learning-disabled children often exhibit hyperactivity, rapid emotional changes, attention problems, and impulsiveness (Clements, 1966). Because of the varied behaviors displayed, which can be of short or long duration, it is difficult to estimate the incidence of learning disability among children. The U.S. Bureau for the Education of the Handicapped (1971) has estimated that about 1%, or over 1 million children under the age of 21, exhibit some form of learning disability.

Sensory impairments

Visual and hearing impairments prevail as two primary sensory problems. Early detection and remediation are of the utmost importance because severe and generalized developmental problems such as mental retardation and emotional disturbance can result. Sometimes these impairments occur in combination with other dysfunctions.

Visual impairment. This term often is used to refer to children who have no measureable vision. At best their vision after correction with glasses is nonfunctional as a major channel for learning. These children must rely on braille as a major mode for reading and writing. Other visually impaired children who can perceive stimuli for reading and writing, although with great effort, are referred to as partially seeing. Current estimates indicate about 0.1% of all children have significant visual impairments (U.S. Bureau for the Education of the Handicapped, 1971).

Auditory impairment. Children who have problems with part of the ear or the nerve pathways to the brain are prevented from adequately hearing or perceiving levels of speech loudness. Two designations often used—deaf and partially hearing—are based as much on the impact on language development as the actual degree of auditory impairment. The deaf child's hearing loss precludes the normal, spontaneous development of spoken language unless it occurs after language has developed, while the partially hearing child has enough hearing during early childhood that some spoken language is developed. About 0.5% of American children possess a hearing loss so severe that it interferes with their educational and developmental progress (U.S. Bureau for the Education of the Handicapped, 1971).

Developmental disabilities

In 1972 a new, rather inclusive category of developmentally dysfunctional children—the *developmentally disabled*—was created by the Federal Developmental Disabilities Act. The act defines a developmental disability as one "attributable to mental retardation, cerebral palsy, or another neurological condition of an individual found . . . to be closely related to mental retardation or to require treatment similar to that required for mentally retarded individuals," (Guidelines for Programs and Services for Developmentally Disabled Persons, 1972, p. 7).

As defined, the population of developmentally disabled persons closely approximates that referred to earlier as developmentally dysfunctional. The latter term, however, incorporates some handicaps such as autism that may or may not be included in the former. While the term has significantly advanced the notion of a less categorical approach to problems of handicapped children, many individuals feel the definition should apply to those children whose handicaps have persisted and are expected to continue. Neisworth and Smith (1974) suggest that "developmental disability refers to significantly deficient locomotor, communicative, adjustive, or academic functioning that is manifested during the developmental period, and that has continued or can be expected to continue indefinitely" (p. 346).

In light of such criticisms, attempts have been made to revise the definition of developmental disabilities, with major implications for professionals and services. Professionals would attend less to handicapping conditions per se and more to the severity of particular problems of developmentally disabled children. Services could be identified, sequenced, and integrated for children who require sustained assistance in childhood and throughout adult life. More abundant support could be secured for those children who are neglected. More importantly, it is a needed first step for federal legislation to codify laws that provide funding for a large group of children on the basis of their service needs rather than their diagnostic categories. This may represent the genesis of a noncategorical approach to dysfunction, which could mean the abolishment of labeling and stigmatization of children and their families.

Noncategorical approaches

Although the Developmental Disabilities Act was a significant legislative step forward, much needs to be done before children are served on the basis of their needs rather than their labels. The field of special education, in particular, has significantly advanced models that deal with assessing children's needs in specific areas of functioning. Iscoe and Payne (1972) suggest that children may differ from what is considered "normal" along several basic dimensions: physical, adjustment, and educational. Each of these dimensions is further divided into three subcomponents that permit measurement and reveal areas that require special intervention:

I. Physical status
   A. Visibility of physical deviation
   B. Locomotion capabilities and limitations
   C. Communication capabilities and problems
II. Adjustment Status
   A. Peer acceptance
   B. Family interaction
   C. Self-esteem

III. Educational Status
   A. Motivation
   B. Academic achievement
   C. Educational potential

Based on a functional analysis of a child's status rather than type or cause of disorder, this innovative scheme is useful to describe and plan for services in all of the diagnostic groupings discussed previously.

This is not to negate the importance of diagnostic categories, which are highly useful in medicine or in research. However, they often muddle the delivery of services to individual children, especially those who were misdiagnosed or received more than one diagnosis. Misdiagnosis usually leads to mistreatment and multiple diagnosis typically results in confused treatments, many of which conflict and hamper change.

Noncategorical systems have the potential to profoundly affect the training of service workers. Instead of training people to work with mentally retarded children, for example, workers could be trained to work with a facet of a disability or with adjustment problems across a variety of settings. An emotionally disturbed child would no longer be referred for special services; rather, professionals specializing in relevant areas of disability would work in a team with other service providers to plan, implement, and evaluate needed services for the child in various contexts (Smith & Neisworth, 1975).

Traditional service delivery

Services for dysfunctional children are a relatively recent phenomenon. Historically, children who were malformed or in some way defective were left to die or be killed. Survival of the fittest was the rule. These types of children sometimes were preserved, but primarily for the amusement and benefit of others. Some served as court jesters to amuse royalty. Others were used by people to solicit alms. The religious atmosphere of the Middle Ages fostered an institutional approach toward dysfunctional children, who were taken in and cared for in monasteries. But just as the influence of religion waxed and waned, so, too, did the treatment of dysfunctional children, who sometimes were destroyed (Kanner, 1964).

The most recent era of services, one of training and habilitation, often is traced to the writings of John Locke, who felt that people were vastly influenced by their environments. One early effort to work with dysfunctional children was Jean-Marc Gaspard Itard's attempt to "educate" a wolf-child who was found in the forests of France. Much of the current work on education and training dysfunctional children traces back to Itard through people such as Montessori and Sequin (Smith & Neisworth, 1975).

During the 19th century various types of institutions were developed for the mentally retarded, emotionally disturbed, and other types of dysfunctional children. Not until the beginning of the 20th century, however, were special classes instituted for dysfunctional children. The last 50 years marked the growth of child guidance clinics, although this service deals more with mildly dysfunctional children than with the severely and profoundly dysfunctional. These three services—institutions, special classes, and child guidance/mental health clinics—remain as the most visible and frequent specialized services for dysfunctional children (Achenbach, 1974).

Far too many professionals, as well as the general public, have failed to consider the great similarity between the needs of dysfunctional children and those of other children in the development and delivery of services. The monolithic, specialized services designed for "special children" have often been considered the only viable means for intervening into the lives of dysfunctional children. Hence, the development and proliferation of special education classrooms and the large, centralized residential institution are two of the dominant methods for providing services, particularly for severely dysfunctional children. These forms of service delivery will be described in more detail later in this chapter.

Contemporary services

The era of "public awareness" starting in the 1960s has seen the most rapid and consistent change in services for dysfunctional children. Dysfunctional children have been recognized as having both human and protective rights, as well as a right to education and treatment. Court proceedings and legislation have called for accountability.

The 1970s witnessed dramatic changes in the delivery of services for developmentally dysfunctional children. No longer is the specialized, self-contained service considered the most desirable option for the provision of services. The trend is toward the integration of children into the same service systems as all other children use, with appropriate specialized support.

Normalization

The philosophical impetus for this change in service delivery derived primarily from the *principle of normalization.* This concept originated from practices and laws in the Scandinavian countries, particularly Denmark and Sweden (Bank-Mikkelson, 1969). Early statements about normalizaton emphasized the need for dysfunctional children, especially the mentally retarded, to be treated as much like "normal" children as possible (Nirje, 1969).

Wolfensberger (1972) redefined *normalization* for use in the United States as being the "utilization of means in order to establish and/or maintain personal behaviors and characteristics which are as culturally normative as possible" (p. 28). Wolfensberger feels that the means used to provide services for the developmentally dysfunctional should be similar to those for other people and service goals should produce behaviors as similar to normal as possible. The provision of culturally normative services is not sufficient; providers must demonstrate that services lead to desirable outcomes.

Attention to the provision of "normalized" services for exceptional individuals remains the most critical application of the normalization principle. This means that all people, whether "deviant" or not, should be integrated to the maximum extent possible into the service delivery system. Traditional segregated such models as the residential institution and the special classroom should be replaced with integrated services.

These thrusts toward integration of handicapped or dysfunctional children into normal services have been referred to as *deinstitutionalization* (residential integration) and *mainstreaming* (educational integration). In both cases, what began as a humanitarian principle (normalization) has been codified into law and litigation; court cases and recent legislation have demanded these types of integration to the maximum extent possible. These concepts and practices will be discussed in more detail later.

The *physical integration,* emphasized by the normalization principle only has

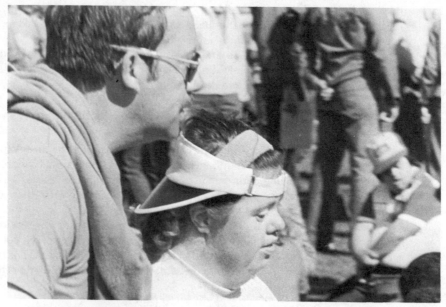

Deinstitutionalization and mainstreaming are two recent practices in the move toward normalization for developmentally dysfunctional individuals.

value when it leads to eventual *social integration* through increased interaction with and acceptance of developmentally dysfunctional children. It is possible to physically integrate children into a service without socially integrating them. For example, a dysfunctional child may receive physical health services from a family practitioner but, due to the scheduling of appointments, still not come into social contact with other children. Or the staff of a group home may decide to take its residents to an institution for a Christmas play rather than to the local school, or they may prohibit neighborhood children from playing on their playground. Without the social integration of children, normalization is not possible. Physical integration, however, is a necessary precondition; without physical exposure of dysfunctional children to other children, social acceptance and interaction cannot possibly occur.

Developmental model

Along with the principle of normalization has come the *developmental model,* which emphasizes the developmental rather than the pathological nature of these dysfunctions (Wolfensberger, 1972). This model presents the overall rationale for providing dysfunctional children with a general program of active treatment and training which employs many services. It has three underlying assumptions. (1) All human beings are in a constant state of change, which is a characteristic of life itself. To perceive dysfunctional children as physiologically or psychologically static is to deny them experience as *living* organisms. (2) Human beings change in predictable, orderly, and sequential ways, in compliance with specific stages. As with all organisms, individuals begin the life cycle with relatively little ability to cope with their environment and increase their competencies as they progress through the life span. (3) While the general sequence of developmental stages is established, individual (and cultural) differences in the details and rate of development are considerable. Such differences are the result of a complex interaction of the internal, external, and genetic environments of individuals, which begins at conception and does not cease until death. This model embodies the optimistic viewpoint that dysfunctional children, even if profoundly impaired, are capable of growth, development, and learning.

This view of the dysfunctional child as a developmental being has had important implications for service planning and delivery. Everything from the effects of nutritional factors upon neurological and intellectual functioning to the effects of sensory and experiential deprivation are viewed as important shapers of the individual's development. Therefore, a wide array of services must be included in an intervention plan for an individual child.

Individual program plans

The primary mechanism for implementing the developmental model for services for dysfunctional children is the *individual program plan,* which is now a formal part of many regulations and laws. Other terms that have been applied to this concept include individual education plans, individual treatment plans, and individual habilitation plans.

This approach requires that an individualized plan be developed for each child by a team of service providers who represent many disciplines. The function of this team is to develop a comprehensive, developmentally appropriate picture of the total child's strengths and needs. Once this is developed, the team establishes both long- and short-range goals for the child and determines which services will be needed to attain these goals. Then the responsibilities for providing services are fixed and "contracts" are made for the services to be provided. Once the plan is implemented, the team monitors progress toward the objectives and revises the plan as needed. The focus of this process is on the attainment of goals and objectives. It is not sufficient that a child receives services; progress must also be realized.

Generic services

In the past, the provision of one specialized service, such as education, often meant that other services were also delivered in specific settings. Such is the case with the severely impaired child who is placed in an institution. Another component of the individualized approach to service delivery for dysfunctional children is the increased utilization of generic services when appropriate. For example, retarded children who need specialized and intensive training to achieve certain skills can still remain in their homes, whereas in the past, they would have almost automatically been placed in an institution, receiving no assistance from generic services.

The acceptance of general service providers needs to be expanded. Most family physicians can deal with the normal health problems of dysfunctional children and only refer them to specialists when warranted. Day-care services can be provided to dysfunctional children without resorting to "special" centers for them (Neisworth & Madle, 1975). The available services for dysfunctional children are increased exponentially under this service model, allowing the integration and acceptance of these children in the community. It also frees space in specialized programs for the more severely impaired children who need them most.

Mediated services

Earlier approaches to dysfunctional children assumed that service providers had to be specially trained professionals and that parents and paraprofessionals had to be skilled to provide effective services. Parents can now be active participants in actually delivering services for their children, rather than merely trying to obtain them. For example, parents of children with crippling disorders who need occupational therapy are being trained to perform simple but critical daily exercises with their children. The parents of mentally retarded children are receiving training in how to toilet train their children and in how to adapt their home to meet the needs of the child (a residential service usually performed by institutions).

One of the important contributions of the developmental model is recognition that developmental dysfunctions are *ecological* in nature and involve all aspects of the child's environment (Smith & Neisworth, 1975). As a result, child-service providers specializing in dysfunctions now perform such tasks as parent training and consultation. It is no longer enough to know how to work with the child. The provider must now be able to work with significant people in the child's world to assist them in working with the child. Besides training, these special educators often need to maintain their support and supervision of those who directly provide assistance to the child.

Services needed

What types of services are needed by this population of developmentally dysfunctional children? Table 9-3 presents an overview of the variety of services needed for these children and youth. Although service needs for dysfunctional individuals do not end at age 18, we have truncated our discussion here in keeping with the scope of this book. In fact, an outstanding characteristic of developmentally dysfunctional children is that their handicaps are expected to continue well into adulthood.

Roughly the service needs of these children can be grouped into five areas: prevention, identification, residential, treatment, and education and training. As illustrated in the table, certain of these services are more important at some stages of a child's life than at others. In fact, vocational services are not included because they are primarily a need of dysfunctional adults. Also, although these services are discussed as being relatively discrete entities, they typically occur together in real life in the form of a comprehensive service system (Gelman, 1974). As mentioned earlier, the program plan should provide appropriate coordinated services in all areas. The isolated delivery of services is much less effective than a coordinated approach.

Prevention strategies

Preventive services are generally most important during the prenatal, infant, and preschool stages of a child's life. Unfortunately, while substantial preventive programs could drastically reduce the incidence of some childhood disorders, prevention is still a relatively neglected form of intervention. For example, about half of all visual and hearing impairments are due to genetic and prenatal disorders that could be prevented biomedically (Brewer & Kakalik, 1979).

Maternal health care, genetic screening and counseling, and immunization are the primary medical intervention strategies used during the prenatal period. A number of disorders based on heredity can be prevented through genetic counseling, which many times will result in a couple deciding to adopt rather than bear children. For example, Down's Syndrome, a form of retardation, many times more likely in mothers over age 35 (or under 16), can be prevented through this strategy. Still other

TABLE 9-3 Services for developmentally dysfunctional children

Services	Service agents	Service disciplines
Prenatal Prevention: Prenatal care, treatment of the fetus, genetic counseling, therapeutic abortion	Health agents: Primary physician, local health department, hospital, clinic	Physician, public health nurse, genetic counselor
Infancy and preschool Prevention (medical): Metabolic screening (PKU, immunization, routine medical care, nutrition)	Health agents: Primary physician, well-baby clinic (local health department, hospital)	Physician, public health nurse, nutritionist
Prevention (psychosocial): Stimulation, training, education	Child care agents: The home, adoptive home, adoptive agency, foster care (social service), child development center	Mother or mother surrogate, teacher and teacher's aide, social worker, volunteers
Identification and treatment: Screening, diagnosis, parent counseling, medical treatment, management, psychosocial treatment	Health and child-care agents: Well-baby clinic, primary physician, medical specialist, developmental evaluation clinic, home nursing service, mental health/mental retardation center	Public health nurse, pediatrician, psychologist, social worker, physical therapist, speech therapist, dentist, family
Residential services: Providing a stimulating place to live and develop	The home, adoptive home, foster care family, group home, institution	Parents and parent surrogates, social worker, institutional staff
Training and education: Self-help (feeding, dressing, toileting), language, cognitive, motor, socio-emotional training	Early childhood education agents: Childhood development center (generic and specialized)	Teacher, teacher's aide, psychologist, speech therapist
School age Identification and treatment Residential Training and education: Self-help (as needed), academic, social, motor, language, recreational, vocational, activities of daily living	(See Infancy and preschool) (See Infancy and preschool) Education and rehabilitation: Child development center; public school (elementary, junior high, senior high); vocational rehabilitation agency; employer	Teacher, teacher's aide, school psychologist, guidance counselor, speech therapist, vocational rehabilitation counselor, business and industry
Life span Case management and advocacy: Assuring that appropriate services are received and that the person's rights are protected	Mental health/mental retardation agencies: Mental health center; federal, state and local agencies; legal counsel; guardians; parents	Social workers, guardians, lawyers, volunteer advocates, family

Adapted from *Mental Retardation: Nature, Cause, and Management,* by G. S. Baroff. Copyright © 1974 by Hemisphere Publishing Corporation. Reprinted by permission.

disorders can be prevented through proper maternal immunization. One example is rubella, which can cause mental retardation, blindness, and other severe disorders if contracted by the mother during certain stages of pregnancy, especially the first trimester. Couples who have an Rh incompatability can minimize the risk of cerebral palsy and mental retardation in their laterborn children through an immunization procedure given within 72 hours after the birth of their first child.

Delivery emphasizes prenatal maternal health care. Since a large number of disorders are prevalent among mothers whose health care and nutrition during pregnancy was not adequate, this strategy can prevent many problems. Without proper prenatal care, the risk of premature infants with low birth weights and attendant childhood dysfunctions is drastically increased.

Shortly after birth, the newborns are screened for disorders that could result in developmental dysfunctions if left untreated. For example, infants are routinely screened for a medical disorder known as phenylketonuria or PKU. Children possessing this metabolic error will almost always be mildly to severely retarded if preventive treatment is not provided quickly. They also are predisposed to other problems such as seizures. With the prescription of a special diet low in phenylamines for about six years, however, the child will probably have normal intelligence.

During the remainder of the preschool period, preventive efforts concentrate on general child health. Screening for disorders such as vision and hearing impairments that could result in more severe dysfunctions if left untreated also is continued.

In the area of psychosocial prevention, which child service workers are more likely to be involved with, the primary thrust is on the enrichment of the parent/child relationship during infancy and early childhood. The preponderance of information on causes of certain childhood disorders such as retardation and emotional disturbance indicates that the environment greatly affects mental and emotional development. While preventive programs designed to deal with psychosocial factors differ in their details, they all emphasize providing children with warm care givers who should stimulate their development.

Identification and diagnostic assessment

Various types of identification services detect children who may be somewhat "different" from other children and provide specific follow-up assessment of their abilities and disabilities. Dysfunctional children are commonly identified through one of three mechanisms. The first of these methods is that some worker in the existing general service system—for example, the family physician or teacher—notices that a child has symptoms of some disorder. Such an observation may lead to further screening, perhaps of visual functioning, and lead to the diagnosis of a visually handicapped youngster.

The second general mechanism by which dysfunctional children are identified is that the family (or even the child) may express concern that something is wrong and seek assistance for the problem. One difficulty in relying on this type of identification is that parents frequently deny the existence of problems in their children. As a result, they may delay intervention until significant secondary problems have arisen, such as when a hearing impaired child begins to have difficulty learning language.

The last method of finding dysfunctional children is through formal screening or testing programs. Vision and hearing screening is typically a part of many health service programs. Another identification service of this type is the routine screening of newborns for PKU.

To be effective, early-identification programs must reach large numbers of people. Screening can be conducted at fairs, shopping centers, or ball games. Materials can be distributed to help parents track the developmental progress of their children.

For example, the HICOMP Project at Pennsylvania State University distributed a device known as "Jotty Giraffe" for parents to use in tracking their child's development much as it is used to track a child's physical growth. In this way children with developmental delays could be brought in for more extensive assessment to determine what type of services, if any, were needed.

Without proper and universal identification programs, no clear picture of the overall needs of the dysfunctional population can be drawn. The lack of qualified and valid identification services leads to distressingly frequent errors of both omission and commission. Another problem created by the relatively informal and nonuniversal nature of identification efforts is that rarely does the identification of dysfunctional children by one type of service (for example, the educational) result in identification by other service components.

Even the best formal identification programs such as vision and hearing screening is far from universal for school-age children and is virtually nonexistent for preschoolers. This is unfortunate, for early identification is especially important. The deaf child frequently needs early language development services and some types of progressive impairments could be halted before severe impairment occurs. Much of the identification continues to be done by parents, teachers, and others not specially trained to recognize symptoms of dysfunctions.

If identification services are so important, why are they so underdeveloped? One possibility is that many mildly impaired children receive specialized services, excluding those children most in need. A progressive shift of services for the mildly impaired from the specialized to the general system would open the way for more systematic identification programs and more effective use of both types of services.

Residential enhancement

Regardless of which services are provided to developmentally dysfunctional children, environmental settings must be enhanced. The overall condition of a child's home environment can either enhance or negate the effects of services in other areas. This is illustrated dramatically by the effects of placements in residential institutions on the functioning of the mentally retarded. Institutions have received considerable criticism because of the deplorable conditions in many of them (Blatt & Kaplan, 1966). In fact, recently a number of the larger institutions have been ordered closed by courts due to these conditions. But research has demonstrated that children who lived in impoverished home environments actually increased their levels of functioning when placed in institutions. Children from good family environments did exhibit rather severe decrements in functioning after institutional placement (Sarason & Doris, 1969).

When children are profoundly impaired, parents and professionals often institutionalize them. Some physicians also continue to recommend institutional placements for Down's Syndrome children at birth or shortly thereafter. This is disconcerting because considerable data show that home-raised Down's Syndrome children evidence significantly better functioning than those raised in institutions. Fortunately, the increased provision of supplemental services such as financial assistance, parent training, and day-care centers that accept dysfunctional children are making it possible for an increasing number of dysfunctional children to remain in their own homes. An especially helpful service to parents who raise their own dysfunctional child is *respite care* (Madle, 1978). This is an arrangement by some institutions and other residential settings to take care of the child for short periods of time, ranging from a weekend to a month so that parents can "get away," as it is difficult to find childsitters for handicapped youngsters.

When children cannot be raised in their natural home, the preferred option is either adoption or placement with a foster family. It is often more possible for foster families to raise dysfunctional children than either biological or adoptive families because the funding structure of many states provides financial assistance to foster families (Wolfensberger, 1971), while none is available to biological and adoptive parents.

Older children who are more than mildly impaired are still placed in group-care settings such as community residences, regional centers, and institutions. Until recently, the preferred placement was virtually always a residential institution. These institutions were typically large, understaffed, and impersonal—many with three to five thousand residents. The professional staff often were not qualified to handle severe impairments such as lower functioning, mentally retarded, and psychotic children. This situation is gradually changing. Increasing numbers of institutions are discharging residents to other settings. Staff-to-resident ratios are improving with the aid of various federal assistance programs such as the Social Security Act. Professional staff are becoming interested and trained in developmental dysfunctions.

Deinstitutionalization—placement in smaller residences for 8 to 20 people that are made available in local communities—is a recent trend. These residences, often known as "group homes," have been developed for all ages and specific types of children and adults (Madle, 1978). For example, a child development home for children 4 to 18 years old with no more than 6 mixed-age children and two houseparents provides a situation more similar to a family residence than can an institutional ward of 40 residents with 3 or 4 staff. While most group homes serve only as residences, several types are oriented toward intensive training and treatment. A behavior-shaping unit for example, concentrates on the development of daily living skills in moderately to severely retarded children (Madle, 1978).

Noninstitutional placements are conducive for children receiving other services such as education and training or health care outside of the home setting, as do normal children. In an institutional setting, all of these services are provided within the facility—a very unnatural and nonnormalizing state of affairs.

Medical and behavioral/adjustment treatments

Two types of treatment services—medical and behavioral/adjustment—are needed by dysfunctional children and their family members. The array of services for behavioral/adjustment problems is overwhelming. Both types of treatment service are available on an inpatient and outpatient basis. Most commonly, inpatient treatment is provided in residential institutions, with a limited proportion of services being provided in psychiatric units at general hospitals and community mental health centers. Typically, this treatment form is reserved for the most severe problems.

Milder adjustment problems are generally dealt with through outpatient treatment mechanisms such as community mental health centers, child guidance clinics, outpatient services of general hospitals, and day treatment centers. Unlike the inpatient service, the outpatient treatment allows other types of services to continue with little disruption. Family adjustment problems, which occur at a high frequency in families with dysfunctional children (Kurtz, 1978), are typically dealt with on an outpatient basis through family counseling and education.

The types of treatment services provided for dysfunctional children in these settings encompasses all available forms of counseling and psychotherapy, ranging from client-centered approaches to behavior modification. The treatment generally is behavioral in nature for severely impaired children because they lack both the intellectual and language development needed for verbal psychotherapies. The other treatment approach considered for this type of children is some highly structured forms of play therapy (Robinson & Robinson, 1976).

As mentioned earlier, this area of service has seen an increasing involvement of families and other significant people in the children's daily life in the treatment process. It is now fairly well accepted that adjustment and behavioral reactions can only be dealt with by recognizing that the total ecology of children's lives must be modified to successfully treat such problems. The primary focus is on teaching the significant people in children's social contexts to better help them cope with problems rather than relying on professional/child interactions (Williams & Gordon, 1974).

Educational and training programs

Developmentally dysfunctional children need education and training, just as other children do. Often their education and training will begin at an earlier age to try to compensate for their problems. Many times service will merge with the residential function. For example, the severely mentally retarded child who needs training in self-feeding will probably be taught in the home instead of a classroom. Special educational efforts for dysfunctional children did not always exist. Until the early 20th century most dysfunctional children were excluded from school or dropped out at a very early age. Once public education became mandatory and the needs of exceptional children were recognized, special educational arrangements were promoted and teachers were intensively trained. These arrangements often proved to be beneficial. For example, mentally retarded children often showed greater cognitive development when placed in special education rather than a regular classroom. Unfortunately, however, they also tended to show less progress in other areas of functioning, such as social and interpersonal development (Sarason & Doris, 1969). As is often the case with specialized services, the increased attention to one aspect of need overwhelms all the others. While the special education classroom still remains as a viable educational alternative in working with dysfunctional children, it is gradually falling into disfavor as the only means of providing education for these children (Deno, 1970).

Education has adopted a normalization concept called *mainstreaming* in which educational services for dysfunctional children are provided in the same setting as for other children whenever possible. The result is a graded series of educational alternatives that accommodate to a regular classroom. Special arrangements such as ramps for a wheelchair or modifications in instructional materials may be necessary. Or supplementary instruction from a specially trained teacher may be needed. Children who cannot be directly integrated into the classroom are placed in a special class on either a part-time or full-time basis. Most of the other educational arrangements, such as special day schools, homebound instruction, and institutional placement, are very segregated and allow for little interaction with nonhandicapped children.

For children with severe intellectual impairments, the educational curriculum places much greater emphasis on functional skills such as recognizing survival words (danger, stop) or preparing a simple meal than on academic skills. At the most severe levels of retardation, most skills taught are as basic as following simple instructions and imitation.

One of the more recent developments in educational services for dysfunctional children was the passage of Public Law 94–142, the Education for All Handicapped Children Act in 1975. The specific objective of this legislation was "to assure that all handicapped children have available to them, within the time periods specified . . . a free appropriate public education." This legislation was needed, since even with special classes many of the most severely impaired children continued to be excluded from educational services. Now even the most severely impaired child must be provided with an *appropriate* education.

Yet another goal of the federal government in the area of education of the dysfunctional is to secure the enrollment of preschool-aged handicapped children in federal, state, and local educational and day-care programs. Effective education of handicapped children must begin very early. To wait until normal school age to begin educational services is only to magnify dysfunctions as compared to normal children. Increasing numbers of preschool programs are being developed for handicapped youngsters. Many of these programs, especially those funded by the U.S. Bureau for the Education of the Handicapped, integrate handicapped and normal children.

The impact of high-quality early education programs for handicapped children can be highly significant. One indicator of this effectiveness can be seen in programs for young Down's Syndrome children (Hanson, 1977). As we mentioned earlier, these children are usually sent to institutions early in their life and function at a severely retarded level. But projects at the University of Washington and elsewhere showed that with proper early education, these children can learn to read by age three or four. By the time they reach school age, the children in the project are usually functioning at mildly retarded and even nonretarded levels. Such results are certainly at odds with the idea that these children should receive life-long institutional placements.

Conclusion

Providing services for dysfunctional children is an exciting, rapidly changing, sometimes frustrating arena. Dysfunctional children have for a long time been "stepchildren," receiving little attention from child services. What attention they did receive emphasized their differences. Services were developed to segregate them and they were treated as diagnostic categories rather than people. Recent changes in how developmentally dysfunctional children are defined and efforts to secure their rights within their environmental context have posed new dilemmas.

Who will serve as advocates for dysfunctional children? Advocacy basically is a process of representing the rights and interests of an individual or group in order to realize the rights entitled to by obtaining needed services and by removing barriers. Advocacy for developmentally dysfunctional children is difficult because responsibility is diffuse within a complicated service delivery system. Advocacy efforts, however, are occurring. In fact, parents of handicapped children have a strong growing network and have become a powerful force in advocating for their children. Most mental health/mental retardation programs assign staff to function as case managers for a number of dysfunctional children. These individuals ensure that children actually receive needed services.

Organizations such as the National Association for Retarded Citizens and the United Cerebral Palsy Association also serve as advocates for an entire subset of dysfunctional children. These groups secure new rights and services and have promoted legislation requiring services such as free public education for all exceptional children.

Parents, teachers, and others should be made aware of the advocacy role they can play. Much effort must still be directed at helping to integrate dysfunctional children into the usual services available for all children. Child-service providers must be trained to work with dysfunctional and functional children in the same context, and parents must be shown how the dynamics of social interactions can benefit all children. Once developmentally dysfunctional children are accepted more fully, services can be developed to better meet their needs.

Summary

More than ten million children under the age of 21 are functionally impaired and need services. Historically, these children were poorly treated and labeled in a variety of ways. Numerous labels—mentally retarded, emotionally disturbed, neurologically impaired, learning disabled, sensory impaired, and developmentally disabled—are still used to identify, diagnose, and treat these children. The term *developmental dysfunctions* refers to any handicapping condition or conditions that typically arise during the growth period of an individual's life span. To be meaningful, this label, like any other, must serve as a starting point for careful analyses of children's strengths, needs, and limitations in each area of human functioning.

A noncategorical approach, based on a developmental analysis of a child's status rather than type or course of disorder, is useful to describe and plan services in all of the diagnostic groupings discussed. In this innovative system, a child is assessed and described rather than assigned to some superordinate category of dysfunction. Diagnostic categories are highly useful in medicine and research, but they can hamper the delivery of services.

Based upon the principle of normalization, the means used to provide services for the developmentally dysfunctional should be similar to those for other people, and service goals should produce behaviors as similar to normal as possible. Providing culturally normative services are not sufficient; providers must demonstrate that services lead to desirable outcomes. This integration thrust, also called *deinstitutionalization* and *mainstreaming,* has been codified into law.

The individual plan in which a team of professionals determines each child's strengths and needs and monitors and evaluates progress is the primary mechanism for implementing a developmental model for services for dysfunctional children. Recently, generic services are relied upon whenever possible to encourage integration with nondysfunctional children. Parents are trained to assist their children's development.

Dysfunctional children need effective identification programs to diagnose problems as quickly as possible so appropriate interventions can follow; to ensure prevention efforts that will thwart any further complicating condition; to enhance their physical and social environments; to perform medical and behavioral/adjustment treatments; and to supply early education and training. These children need advocates even moreso than others, because responsibility is so diffuse within a complicated service delivery system. New rights and services (for example, public education for all exceptional children) have been secured, but additional efforts are needed to help integrate dysfunctional children into the usual services available for all children. As child service providers are trained to work with dysfunctional and functional children in the same context and to help parents and other workers deliver services, perhaps this goal will be achieved.

10

Parent/Child Interaction and Intervention

This chapter was written in collaboration with MEGAN SPENCER FLYNN as the senior author. Spencer Flynn is currently completing her Ph.D., Department of Psychology, The Pennsylvania State University.

Chapter overview

The changing role of parents in child-care services is scrutinized in this chapter. To understand the effects of child-care arrangements on parents and children, the effects of interaction and intervention are of primary concern.

Issues to consider

What contributed to parents using child services?

How has the parental role evolved in child services?

What strategies exist for involving parents in child interventions?

In what ways are home-based and out-of-home-based intervention strategies for child care different?

What are the purposes of the parent/staff coalition?

How do parent/child interactions and interventions influence children's cognitive development and social development?

How do settings make a difference in the behavior of children?

What are the effects of child-care arrangements on parents and families?

How can child-care arrangements affect the larger community?

What are some major cautions regarding supplemental and substitute child-care services?

Introduction

"Home, wanna go home." We have all heard this sad, sometimes heartbreaking child's refrain, often followed by wide-eyed silence, quivering lips, and tears. Home is a special place for little people. Why is it so unique? A home means something distinctive to young children because of mothers and fathers, special people who parent.

What happens to children when a large portion of their day is spent away from home, separated from their parents? Are they affected by prolonged separation? Are parents affected by limited contact? We are not yet sure how out-of-home child care arrangements influence children or families. However, due to sharp rises in the employment rate of mothers with young children and the increasing popularity of day-care programs, searching for answers to these questions is imperative.

> Changes will begin to be made only when we reorder our nation's priorities, realizing that social services cannot be treated as fringe benefits or stopgap measures, but are essential to our society's health. And among top priorities in social services is support for parents in protecting and nurturing their children's potential for development into competent, healthy adults [Provence, Naylor, & Patterson, 1977, p. 243].

The evolving parental role in child services

The Westinghouse Report (1969) and Bronfenbrenner's (1974a, 1974b, 1976) reviews of early-intervention effects reported that federally funded Head Start Programs of the 1960s did not produce the hoped-for increases in intelligence or school achievement of disadvantaged children. In fact, initial gains made by Head Start children declined after the first or second year of the program, dropped sharply on kindergarten entrance, and three or four years after the program terminated, fell within an IQ range of 90 or below.

Why did these programs fail? Several possible answers were entertained—all early-intervention programs were doomed to fail because the goal of creating equal opportunity for all was not possible; children were not enrolled at early enough ages, or parental involvement was missing. Perhaps the conclusion to be drawn is that enhancing children's development is more parent related than program related.

The quest for how parent/child interaction relates to intervention in children's lives began. Psychoanalytic theory (Ainsworth & Wittig, 1969; Bowlby, 1951; Goldfarb, 1943; Spitz, 1945) indicates that the mother/child relationship affects not only the quality of the attachment bond, but also influences subsequent child advancement in social, emotional, and cognitive development. Studies of middle-class mothers' teaching strategies revealed that the children of mothers who employ a specific style of interaction, cognitive or rational, perform more successfully than other children in school (Hess & Shipman, 1965; Streissguth & Bee, 1972; Tulkin, 1972; Zunich, 1962). Also, when mothers assume primary roles in intervention programs, their children produce higher rates of intellectual gain (Gordon, I. J., 1969; Karnes, Teska, Hodgins & Badger, 1970; Levenstein, 1970, 1971).

Society responded to this evidence by supporting parents' involvement in interventions for children. For instance, the 1968 Federal Interagency Day Care Guidelines mandated parent involvement in all phases of project functioning for government-subsidized Head Start Centers (Auerbach, 1975). These guidelines required each center with a child population of more than 40 to meet three criteria: (1) an opportunity for parental involvement in decisions concerning program functioning; (2) an opportunity for parents to observe and participate in the program; and (3) a policy advisory committee consisting of not less than 50% of parents of the child population (Honig, 1975).

Although each center was required by law to observe these guidelines, parent participation or staff responsiveness was not guaranteed, and the possibility that intervention programs could not outweigh home environments was not considered. Skepticism still prevailed. How could the parent/child bond contribute so much to optimize child development, when home-reared children displayed various difficulties in school settings? Thus, the role parents played in child intervention programs evolved slowly. As data emerged, researchers began to believe that the parent/child bond critically influences child development. Efforts were directed toward maximizing the effects of educational intervention by using home-based and parent-involvement strategies.

Child-care programs, whether viewed as interventions, socialization experiences, or a purchasable, convenient service, now recognize the necessity and right of parents to actively share in the formulation of policy and programs for their children. In response to recent research that points strongly to the overriding influence of the home on a child's future academic success (Clarke & Clarke, 1976; Clarke-Stewart, 1977; Thomas & Chess, 1977; White, Kaban, Attanucci, & Shapiro, 1978), many day-care and preschool services now include parents in their programs. But this adjustment has had less effect on children in group care than the specialized training of caregivers, which we will examine later in this chapter, and the pressure to lower adult/child ratios and group size, which improves the quality and quantity of interactions. Also, service providers who support different program models are focusing more on humanistic ambience in classrooms than they did in the past.

As discussed in the previous chapter and elsewhere in this book, the changing social context also helped to shape new forms of parent participation in child care.

The demand for quality day care (Featherstone, 1976; Provence, Naylor, & Patterson, 1977; Woolsey, 1977), and opportunities for paternal involvement in child care increased as a result of the women's liberation movement (Rossi, P. H., 1978). The rapid and continued rise in the divorce rate and the number of single-parent families, many headed by females with young children, also suggested the need for supplemental caregiving (Fraiberg, 1977; Rossi, A. S., 1977). In an inflationary economy, increased financial burdens on both one- and two-parent households produced demands for child care services as well (Sawhill, 1977). Schultz (1974), who linked child-bearing practices to economic change, cited the decline in the birth rate as evidence that as the price of a mother's time increases, the importance of time spent on child rearing decreases. Technological changes, high mobility rates, and loss of community support systems also have contributed to the overwhelming internal and external pressures parents confront in child rearing. Healthy, productive parenting can be a lonely, difficult job.

Strategies for involving parents in child interventions

How are parents involved in child interventions? How do professionals view such participation? To answer these questions, the thrust of parent-involvement strategies will be examined. Parent-involvement programs differ in their approach to the needs of children, families, communities, and the goals of society. Some strategies use different delivery settings, typically in-home or out-of-home. Others vary in the type of service offered; for example, parent education versus a parent/staff coalition. Parent involvement strategies also can be placed on a continuum reflecting the degree of parental activity (Gordon, I. J., 1969) and the degree to which the parent is viewed as central to the intervention. For a comprehensive analysis of preschool and intervention strategies that incorporate parenting components, see Day and Parker (1977), Honig (1975), and Robinson, Robinson, Darling, and Holm (1979).

Educating parents

Parents occupy one of the most important social roles in American culture. How is parenting learned, and how is it learned well? For future parents and for professionals the critical questions are: how is poor parenting prevented, and how is good parenting optimized?

Children learn characteristics of a parental role, often unconsciously, by observing their parents and the parents of other children. They attempt these roles in play and may even practice with younger siblings. Books and television programs also give children glimpses of parental behavior.

While children learn the rudiments of parenting, their involvement in rearing younger siblings is decreasing, especially for the middle class. More adults also report the transition to parenthood difficult without support systems (family, community, and society). They feel unsure about their behavior toward their children, what to expect from them, and how to avoid problems in the future. Many parents are receptive to information and want to apply it to their parenting role.

Parenting classes are a usual way to impart information to parents and to prevent future problems. Parent training focuses on disseminating knowledge of child development and parenting skills to ensure that future parents or those with infants will have adequate information to rear their children successfully. Programs are offered through baby clinics, colleges, hospitals, and other direct-service agencies. Since the rise in teenage pregnancy, parenting classes also are being given in high

In our culture, a parent occupies one of the most important roles for which there is no formal training.

schools. Support groups are established for new parents as well. Parents, often with infants in tow, meet to explore and to share their feelings and responsibilities as parents. In a sense, parent support groups are a compensatory form of parent education. They offer a substitute for the neighborhood and family networks that at times are so sadly lacking in the necessary support for parenting.

The 1950s era of Dr. Spock spawned a deluge of mass-media information on child rearing and child development. Magazines, television, newspapers, and books offer what some view as an overabundance of information on how to become a better parent, how to deal with specific behavior problems or typical developmental conflicts, and how to manage problems unique to working mothers.

A number of programs have been developed to train parents how to interact more effectively with their children in order to prevent and correct mental health problems and other difficulties. They also serve to support the positive aspects of existing parent/child interactions and optimize family relationships. These programs view parenting as a difficult, complex task that can be more constructively accomplished when parents use specific skills for communicating and setting limits with their children. Unlike parenting classes, which tend to impart general child development, nutritional, and medical information, parent training focuses on teaching techniques for parent/child interaction. Parents are trained individually, as a family, or in parent groups. All family members enrolled in a program should be active participants—practicing the skills both in class and at home. Central responsibility for the success of the program, therefore, rests with parents.

The Parent Effectiveness Training Program, or P.E.T. (Gordon, T., 1965), the Filial Program (Guerney, 1977, 1978), and Haim Ginott's (1965) strategies for constructive conversation are examples of parent training programs. The principles of Guerney's Filial Program and the P.E.T. Program are acceptance and empathy. Parents are trained in *active* or *reflective* listening, strategies designed to facilitate discovery, enhance the ability to identify the feelings behind children's statements, and accept children's feelings as real and important. It is believed that ignored feelings do not disappear; they simply go underground to re-emerge in a disguised and.less constructive manner. Both programs are based on the belief that more constructive parent/child relationships can be developed when the feelings behind negative or destructive behaviors are understood. The final goal of these and other parent-training programs is to build warm, trusting relationships between parents and children.

The comprehensive ideal

The bigger the better, include everything—this could be the motto of a truly comprehensive program. It also represents the American belief in the capacity to do it all and to do it better than anyone else. A comprehensive program would require the individualization and match of services with a family's needs, thus ensuring a suitable fit with the principles and unique demands of a pluralistic society with its many subcultures. It also would require that these tasks be carried out systematically under the umbrella of a single, comprehensive model. Services in an inclusive model would cover prenatal, childbirth, and postnatal care; medical, nutritional, and family health services; and parenting and child education components.

A comprehensive program almost demands the methodical supply of services to every individual throughout his or her life span. Available social services, while abundant, are not offered within a centralized system. Parents are responsible for finding and availing themselves of the child services they feel are appropriate. Social service agencies often perform this process of needs identification and service seeking for parents who are unaware of community resources or unable to carry out this process independently. Yet, to a great extent, parents are forced to find fragmented social services and piece them together to match family needs, frequently an exhausting, time consuming, and sometimes expensive process. Although comprehensive programs incorporating varied services do not exist, Head Start is viewed as a specific comprehensive program for children and families during the preschool period, especially for low-income persons. We will return to this issue from another perspective when we discuss the parent/staff coalition.

Home-based strategies

Home-based intervention strategies were developed primarily to optimize the educability and cognitive development of children from disadvantaged homes. The term *home-based* often is used to refer to all intervention strategies that view the parent rather than the teacher as the primary change agent. Here it will be used to refer to those programs that take place in the home.

Home-based strategies evolved in the hope that in-depth parental involvement in the educational process would produce long-term improvements in children's intellectual and academic achievement. This strategy, a planned variation of Head art, developed largely as an offshoot of the parent-centered perspective of the mid to late 1960s. Two variations of Head Start home-based programs are Developmental Continuity Programs and Home Start Programs.

The goal of home-based programs is to facilitate a parent's acquisition of the skills necessary for optimal parenting. The programs attempt to supply mothers from lower socioeconomic groups with teaching and child-interaction strategies that approximate those employed by middle-class mothers, or what has been termed the "hidden curriculum" of the middle class. Research by Hess and Shipman (1965) and others revealed that middle-class mothers, whose children often have higher intelligence and achievement scores, exhibit a high rate of responsive, face-to-face, verbal interaction with their children (Dandes & Dow, 1969; Rosenberg & Sutton-Smith, 1969; Tulkin & Kagan, 1970). Mothers from lower socioeconomic groups who employ these strategies also tend to have children with higher intelligence and achievement scores.

Home-based programs vary in the extent and type of support given to parents and the degree of actual parent involvement. Peters (1977) specified a number of critical elements for home-based programs: (1) structure, (2) individualization, (3) focus on the mother/child dyad, (4) shifting educational responsibility to the mother, (5) the motivation of the mother, and (6) the comprehensiveness of the family support system. Not all home-based programs meet these criteria. Few mothers, for example, respond positively to a trainer who is distant, authoritarian, and unresponsive to individual family needs. In fact, a critical component for a mother's successful involvement in a program and for the eventual gains made by a child is the relationship formed between the mother and the in-home trainer (Weikart & Schweinhart, 1979).

In-home interventions generally use either skills-training or attachment strategies. Trainers using a skills approach model behavior for mothers, while trainers in an attachment program support positive, constructive interactions between mothers and children. A skills-training program teaches mothers through the use of educational and play materials to instruct children in a developmentally appropriate manner. Mothers are encouraged to adapt training procedures to their situations and to their children's personalities (Powell, 1976). Attachment programs focus on the mother/child affective bond, which data show is critical for a child's cognitive and emotional development (Bromwick, 1976). Affective strategies attempt to foster warm, positive interactions between mother and child. Both training programs, however, emphasize verbal interaction between mothers and children and lend or give materials to mothers for playful and educational interactions with their children.

Recently, in-home interventions incorporate attachment and skill-training elements. Less time is spent on maternal observations of trainer/child interactions, and more time is spent on establishing positive relationships between mothers and trainers. The goal is that mothers will be primary agents of change, not only in theory, but also in practice.

Out-of-home-based strategies

Although out-of-home programs also center on mothers, they try to enhance the maternal self-concept in a setting other than the home. A good self-concept, which fosters self-confidence and role competency, is viewed as essential for mothers to optimize the development of their children.

Parents, generally mothers, meet in groups with a trained leader. Two possible advantages of group training outside the home are: (1) to give mothers the perspective and belief that they are responsible for positive changes in their children; and (2) to provide them with cohesive peer support. Peer support, the development of a maternal network, increases the effectiveness of the program and also enhances maternal self-concept.

In group meetings with mothers, trainers model positive, educational interaction strategies, and the constructive use of materials. Mothers role-play mother/child interactions and are given support, encouragement, and additional avenues for intervention. Medical, nutritional, child-development, and care-giving information are presented, as well as information on available community resources and employment and educational opportunities. Besides making materials available for home use, techniques for adapting ordinary home objects to educational purposes are shown. Group sessions generally support personal problem solving.

Parent/staff coalition

A common thread running through all parent-involvement strategies is the relationship among people. Regardless of what is done, where it is done, and what role parents play, the issue is human relationships—between parent and child, parent and trainer, and parent and staff. Efforts are directed to maintain or reestablish relations among people and their environments.

The parent/staff coalition uses relationships as the basis for parent involvement strategies. The coalition approach focuses on the building of a single, reinforcing, child-centered system and the establishment of mutually constructive goals between the parent and the child-care system. This approach is based on sound theory, but to date there is no research evidence that shows it works better than other approaches.

Although parent/staff contact in some form is an element of all child-care programs, the purpose and extent of interaction between parents and staff vary considerably. Traditional forms of interaction consist of the parent conference, intermittent parent group meetings, and the intake contact during which a staff member elicits information from a parent concerning a child's history and development. These techniques only vaguely address the issue of interactions and are not aimed at developing relationships. The goal of a parent/staff coalition moves beyond these superficial forms of interaction and seeks to establish bonds between people.

After the implementation of Head Start programs, parent involvement in decision making was advocated, then mandated as a critical component of community involvement and control. Parents made policy-making decisions concerning the implementation and evolving educational structure of the program. After early childhood intervention programs refocused their educational efforts on the parent, several new approaches evolved, engaging parent and staff as a team (Featherstone, 1976). The parent staff coalition—a joint socialization process—requires parent/staff input to maximize and support the efforts of both parties in a mutually satisfying child rearing process (Kappelman & Ackerman, 1977). Parents and educators are viewed as equally necessary in the education and socialization of children. As with other interventions, the mothers are viewed as the primary change agents.

A coalition approach is well-suited to American society, in which various ethnic, religious, and social groups hold differing values and standards of child rearing. A positive relationship between a parent and child-care worker permits both agents to learn from and adjust to each other and to construct the most educationally and socially sound program for every child. Positive relationships between parents and staff can also help children feel more secure in out-of-home settings.

The parent/staff bond is created by numerous techniques. Joint child assessment procedures during intake and throughout the program have been developed to allow parent/staff identification of each child's developmental level, needs, and problem areas in order to specify joint educational and social goals (Provence, Naylor, & Patterson, 1977). Parents frequently participate in: (1) special or ongoing projects, (2) the teaching process, and (3) decisions about program structure or goals. A single staff member is assigned care of only a few children and is responsible for daily or weekly contacts with their parents. This procedure decreases the fragmentation of information exchanged between parents and staff and creates a compensatory network to share child-rearing responsibilities. It increases the chance of bonding between children and special staff members as well. Assignment is based on child and parent match to the staff member and is altered accordingly when the child or parent requests it or when stronger bonds are established with another staff member.

A coalition approach has several advantages: (1) it allows parents and staff to agree on needed family services and to use fragmented social services in a comprehensive and appropriate manner; (2) it permits the establishment of child-care bonds that may be lacking in the community; and (3) it assists in federal government allocation of funding within the boundaries of community needs and resources. The parent/staff coalition also firmly supports the need for child-care staff to be competent, empathic, flexible, serious professionals.

There is little or no agreement on those factors that constitute an optimal child-care system nor on how to design and implement such programs. While American society has gradually moved in the direction of a child-centered approach offering an increasing number and variety of federally subsidized social services, there is much disagreement on the need for government-mandated child care. Americans generally are in agreement, at least theoretically, that a nation based on democratic principles of equality and equal opportunity should not abandon its children; that children should be able to develop in environments permitting the fullest realization of individual potential. Still to be resolved are how such environments are created and maintained for all children, how the cost of optimizing environments is managed on an individual or national basis, and how the rights and differences of citizens are protected in a process of optimization. Underlying each of these questions are the challenging issues of defining an optimal child-development environment and enacting appropriate policies. The parent/staff coalition, as it relates to each of these questions, may prove to be a very fruitful strategy for involving parents in child interventions.

The ecology of interaction/intervention

The remainder of this chapter will examine research pertaining to the effects of child-care strategies on children, parents, families, and broader social systems. This review will focus on intervention studies that directly involve parents in educational efforts directed toward the child and those that infer effects from increased or decreased parental involvement in child care.

Effects on children's cognitive development

Does early education make a difference in children's later school performance? The majority of studies investigating the effects of day care on the intellectual development of disadvantaged children show that the gains made by children progressively decline until, by grade one or two, they reach a level equal to those children who do not receive intervention (Bronfenbrenner, 1974a, 1974b; Caldwell, Wright, Honig, & Tannenbaum, 1970; Cochran, 1977). The data indicate that these programs enrich intellectual development for the duration of the intervention but do not engender permanent cognitive gains. The data also reveal that the programs reduce the negative influence of the home environment while in effect; however, the home environment has an overriding effect on the intellectual achievement of children no longer in the program.

Consequently, two alternatives are left. Children can be permanently removed from home environments deemed undesirable. However, who is able to identify undesirable homes consistently, without error? Removal of children from their homes requires moral, legal, and political decisions that are contrary to long-held democratic principles advocating the rights of the individual and the sanctity of the family. This implies that optimization of the development of children resides with the family.

What interventions improve the home environment? Research findings indicate that when the intervention focus is the home environment, specifically the mother, children have enjoyed intellectual gains, often of longer duration than those found in programs not involving the parent. In a series of studies by Levenstein (1970) and Levenstein and Sunley (1969) a "home visitor" (trainer) used interesting toys and modeled positive, verbal interactions with children in their home setting, which mothers then emulated. Children gained an average of 17 IQ points, which was sustained over a two-year follow-up period. Substantial IQ gains that remained four years after program termination also were reported in similar studies (Gordon, I.J., 1969; Gordon, I., & Breivogel, 1976).

The Early Training Project, an intervention program involving home and day care, followed children from initial intervention at age 3 through the fourth grade (Gray & Klaus, 1970). Children in the experimental group received half-day, center-based interventions during the summer months only. The core of the program for the experimental group was parent training. All parents in the experimental group received weekly in-home meetings with a trained home visitor. Two control groups received no intervention. The program terminated when children entered kindergarten. Although on final testing at grade four the children's IQ scores in experimental and control groups had declined, the experimental group still maintained significant gains on the Stanford-Binet test when compared to the other groups.

Karnes and associates (1970) attempted to separate the effects of in-home and out-of-home parent intervention. Twenty mothers from a lower socioeconomic group met weekly with a trainer for two years. The children ranged in age from 12 to 24 months at the beginning of the program. Post-intervention testing on the Stanford-Binet and the Illinois Test of Psycholinguistic Abilities (ITPA) revealed that when compared to a matched control group of 20 children, program participants gained an average of 16 IQ points, with language the area of greatest cognitive growth. Home trainers perceived mothers as the primary agents of change.

Until recently, the only long-term follow-up study undertaken in childhood intervention was a project begun by Skeels (1966) in the 1930s, which involved 13 children with a mean IQ of 64 and a control group of 12 children, mean IQ 86. All children in the study were living in the same institution for the mentally retarded. The average age of transfer to the institution was 19 months. Medical, birth, and family histories were similar for both groups and children did not exhibit signs of organic impairment. The experimental group attended a kindergarten as soon as they were able to walk and also were, in effect, "adopted" by an older girl in the institution or by an attendant.

Over a period of 5.7 to 52.1 months, the experimental group gained an average of 27.5 IQ points. The experimental period for the control group was 30.7 months with a mean IQ loss of 26.2 points. When the children in the experimental group reached a normal level of intellectual functioning, almost all were adopted and removed from the institution. The children in the control group remained in either an orphanage or state school for the mentally retarded.

Twenty-five years later, Skeels located the majority of his original sample. Impressive differences were found between the two groups of adults. Experimental group adults had completed more school and were married, employed in skilled jobs, and better adjusted. Control-group adults were employed in unskilled jobs and had completed an average of 3.95 grades in school; a third were either permanent or intermittent residents of an institution. While the life environment of subjects in Skeels's study certainly does not parallel that of disadvantaged children, results clearly show the fact that an improved and sustained environment make a lasting difference in people's lives.

Skeels's study gave impetus to the Ypsilanti Perry Preschool Project, a preschool intervention program antedating Head Start. This project is part of the Consortium of Longitudinal Studies headed by Dr. Irving Lazar and financed through the Federal Administration for Children, Youth, and Families. The Consortium was founded in the mid 1970s in order to trace the children in Head Start and similar compensatory programs. To date, the findings of the Consortium's longitudinal work substantiates the results of the Perry Preschool Project.

The Perry Preschool Project, in operation from 1962 to 1967, involved 123 children from lower socioeconomic homes. Children ages 3 to 5 received 1 or 2 years of a half-day preschool program 5 days per week and mothers were given weekly in-home training in which they assumed major responsibility for interaction with their children. The preschool and non-preschool control groups were tested at ages 3, 4, and 5, and at the end of the first through fourth school years and in grade eight (Weikart, Epstein, Schweinhart, & Bond, 1978).

Children entered the program in waves of 25 from 1962 through 1967. The last wave of children is now completing high school. Batteries of standardized tests administered to the children included the Wechsler Intelligence Scale for Children (WISC), Stanford-Binet, and California Achievement Test. Preschool assessment measures included the Peabody Picture Vocabulary Test, the Leiter International Performance Scale, a nonverbal IQ test, the ITPA, the Maternal Attitude Inventory, and the Cognitive Home Environment Scale. Testers were blind to the condition of the subjects. Self-reports, teacher reports, and parent reports also were assessed, and at grade nine, lengthy interviews were held with all parents and children (Weikart, Epstein, Schweinhart, & Bond, 1978). A post-high-school assessment scale is currently being developed for further follow-up.

A large portion of the data from fourth through eighth grades has been analyzed (Weikart & Schweinhart, 1979; Weikart, Bond, & McNeil, 1978). The children's IQ scores exhibited the same pattern found in other early-intervention projects—a sharp rise followed by a gradual decline. By grade three, IQ scores for children in the preschool and control groups were nearly identical. In contrast, the results of the California Achievement Test (CAT) were significantly different for the two groups. By grade six, CAT scores for the preschool group began to climb, while those for the

control group began to level off. By grade eight, the sco[...]
were more than a 1.0 grade equivalent ahead of the cont[...]
.004 level. The greatest CAT score gains in the presch[...]
language, and arithmetic. By eighth grade, 38% of th[...]
group required special placement, compared to only 1[...]

Weikart's group also has analyzed the cost of pr[...]
projected lifetime earnings, special-education savings[...]
parent. The total economic benefits amount to 248% [...]
preschool (Weber, Foster, & Weikart, 1978, p. 5) or a savings to [...]
$8,448 per child.

Although neither Skeels's study nor the Perry Preschool Project identify which factors produced the strong, positive changes in children's achievement, it seems evident that one to two years of a quality preschool program combined with an effective home program can make permanent changes in children's lives. Further research is needed to clarify whether it is home-based strategies, preschool experience, or some combination of these elements that positively influences child achievement.

Encouraged by these results, Congress budgeted a $150,000,000 increase for Head Start programs in 1977. Although funding was cut for other federally subsidized social services, the 1980 Head Start budget maintained the 1979 funding level. Continued funding of Head Start indicates government support of supplemental child care and responsiveness to the empirical work of social scientists.

Effects on children's attachment

A major concern of professionals who study child development is the potentially adverse effect of early preschool or day care on the formation of the mother/child attachment bond. Depriving the child of access to the mother may have a negative effect on the child's later emotional and intellectual development (Bowlby, 1951; Goldfarb, 1943; Spitz, 1945). Recent evidence (Kotelchuck, 1976) indicates that infants show similar patterns of attachment to the father as to the mother.

Generally, the quality of a child's attachment to the mother is assessed through the "strange-situation" experiment. The child is repeatedly separated from the mother in a strange context and the child's behavior on separation from the mother and on reunion is measured. Clarke-Stewart (1978) and others have questioned the accuracy of the strange-situation procedure as a measure of mother/child bonding.

In a review of attachment studies contrasting home-reared versus day-care-reared children, Belsky and Steinberg (1978) reported conflicting results. Several studies showed a stronger attachment by home-reared children, while others found stronger attachments in children reared in center day care. In two other studies, no differences were found. All of these studies used variations of the strange-situation procedure.

Kagan, Kearsley, and Zelazo (1978) examined the attachment behaviors of 65 children from ages 3½ months to 29 months. Half the children were reared at home and half were center-reared. No differences were found between the two groups. In a recent study, Roopnarine and Lamb (1979) compared 23 home-reared children, half of whom were to enter day care. The mean age of the children at the beginning of the study was 3.1 years. All the children were tested in the strange situation prior to enrollment in day care. The children who were to remain in home care exhibited less distress on separation than those who were to enter a day-care center. The day-care p evidenced less exploratory behavior on separation, and cried more frequently d remained closer to the mother on reunion. After three months in day care, there were few significant differences between the two groups. The changes in the behavior of the day-care group three months after enrollment in the program were significant. It is possible that the characteristics of parents who enroll their children in preschool or of the children to be enrolled differ from those who remain in a home environment. An alternate explanation, not entertained by the authors, is that the children who were to enter day care were informed of this fact, and therefore exhibited anxiety on being left by the mother at the initial testing session.

In their study of infants ages 12 to 15 months, Blanchard and Main (1979) found that the longer children were in day care, the less avoidance behavior they demonstrated toward their mothers. Children who tended to avoid their mothers also evidenced less social and emotional adjustment in the day-care setting. Much of the research evaluating day care and attachment has failed to correlate age at entry with length of enrollment in the program. Conflicting evidence may, in part, result from uncontrolled variables rather than the quality of attachment between mother and child.

Individual differences between children may determine a child's ability to adapt successfully to out-of-home care. Day-care studies have not investigated the positive or negative effects of regimented child-care programs that fail to account for differences in individual temperaments (see Thomas & Chess, 1977). While high-quality day-care programs may adapt to individual needs and temperaments of young children, a majority of nonprofit early-child-care centers have been judged inferior (Keyserling, 1972). Observational data from nine metropolitan day-care programs (Sheehan & Abbott, 1979) indicated that the staff are engaged in custodial care to the exclusion of individual attention. Nearly all the data on day care and intervention programs are derived from high-quality centers, operating on a half-day schedule with a high rate of parental involvement, high child-staff ratio, and low staff turnover. Very little information exists on the effect of the poor-quality, full-time, out-of-home care available to the majority of families who use child-care services.

Thus, the findings of day-care effects on mother/child attachment are equivocal. Continued research is necessary to determine how day care influences the bond between mother and child and its long-range effects on maternal attitude toward children. Also, investigations are needed to assess children's attachment to their fathers and to siblings.

Do settings make a difference?

To a certain extent, everyone's behavior alters with different people and places. Lately, investigators have examined how children's behavior is influenced by the home and the day-care environments, and the behavioral differences or similarities of mothers and substitute care givers when interacting with children.

Several recent studies investigated children's behaviors in various settings, the contrasting behaviors of mothers who cared for their children in a home setting, and staff behaviors toward children in high-quality day-care centers. Although the measures used in these projects assess child behavior, many of the results directly relate to differences in adult behavior.

Johnson (1979) compared the amount of time spent by 3-year-old children in social and nonsocial behaviors. Half the children were home reared, half day-care reared. Children in home settings spent significantly more time seeking a service, such as food or information getting, and conversing with their mothers. Children in day care spent significantly more time cooperating with adults, exploring, and passing time. Johnson (1979) concluded that group differences were a function of the demands made on children and adults, which related to the larger numbers of people in the day-care programs, which often are criticized for high child/staff ratios and frequent staff turnover.

The differences between children's home and day-care behaviors are significantly associated with competency. White et al. (1978) found that socially and academically competent children, when compared to less competent children, engage in significantly higher rates of conversation with their mothers and spend more time getting information from them. As noted in our earlier discussion of the "hidden curriculum" of the middle class, mothers who are involved in reciprocal verbal interaction with their children produce more academically successful children.

Rubenstein and Howes (1979) compared the behavior of 15 day-care and 15 home-care infants ages 17 to 20 months. Day-care infants, although they received the same degree of caregiver verbalization as home-care infants, were significantly less verbal than home-care infants. Mothers gave directions more frequently than care givers and talked more to their children independent of infants' verbal responses. In both the home and day-care setting, adult restrictiveness resulted in decreased rates in levels of mean developmental play for children. Infants in day care tended to exhibit higher overall developmental play levels, which were attributed to frequent, positive peer interactions. The authors suggest that peer interaction may help to offset the possible negative effects of early, prolonged separation from mothers.

Both center and home day care may have negative effects on child development if timed inappropriately with the developmental levels of children. There are indications that differences do exist in maternal versus caregiver behavior, even in high-quality day-care settings. It is critical that future investigations separate the influences exerted by the mother and the caregiver on the immediate and long-range development of children.

Effects on parents and families

Results of the few studies concerning the effects of early substitute child care on mothers, parents, and families are inconclusive. Also, as noted by Belsky and Steinberg (1978), there is no evidence concerning, "the ways in which day care affects the patterns of culture and subculture that serve as carriers of information, ideology, and custom" (p. 945). The nearly complete focus on the child has forced policy makers, professionals, and parents to rely on limited information. It may be conjectured that the effects of day-care and preschool programs are broadened or narrowed, depending on the larger systems within which children function and interact.

Researchers have long assumed that if the variables necessary for optimal development were identified, then substitute care givers could engage in optimizing behaviors and produce results similar to positive home environments. Such an assumption is questionable, for the mother/child dyad appears to be an especially potent bond (Kagan et al., 1978; Klaus, Jerald, Kreger, McAlpine, Steffa, & Kennell, 1972). Day care, while it may affect the mother/child relationship, does not alter the distinctive meaning of the bond for mother or child. Identical interactions engaged in by a substitute care giver simply may not have the same meaning for a child.

Conversely, it is also possible that when mothers perceive that the responsibility for nurturance, especially in infancy, rests on the shoulders of another, they may alter their attitudes toward their children.

Effects on attitudes toward children

Few studies have investigated changes in maternal behavior toward the child as a result of early, prolonged separation through substitute care giving. An infancy study by Klaus and colleagues (1972) found that mothers evidence less involvement with and responsiveness to their infants when separated immediately following birth. Routine hospital procedures permitting mothers limited contact with their newborns were believed to perhaps decrease the natural, immediate bond a mother might form with her child. Thus, the limited evidence indicates that early substitute care giving exerts a negative influence on maternal attitudes.

One new avenue of study focuses on the effect of early mother/child separation due to maternal employment. Hock's 1976 study of mothers' attitudes during the child's first year of life found no behavioral differences between employed and unemployed mothers. A more recent study (Cohen, 1979) investigated the maternal behaviors of employed versus unemployed mothers during the child's second year of life. Forty-four mother/child dyads were observed in a structured laboratory setting. Half the mothers were employed 2 or more days per week by the time their children were 6 months of age and half were not employed. Children of unemployed mothers verbalized more than children of employed mothers and received significantly higher scores on the Bayley Mental Scale and the Gesell Development Schedule. Receptive language scores did not differ significantly between the two groups. Unemployed mothers consistently gave higher rates of positive attention to their children, significant at the .02 and .002 levels. When intactness of the family was controlled, the differences between maternal groups still was evident. However, the differences found between intact families were inconclusive due to the decreased sample size. It is not clear what alternative child-care arrangements were used by the employed mothers in Cohen's study, a factor that may have influenced results.

Fowler and Kahn (1975) examined maternal attitudes toward children who were enrolled in an experimental day-care program early in the first year of life. Although both maternal attitudes and scores on Caldwell's Inventory of Home Stimulation increased in a positive direction from 11 to 18 months, both scores showed a rapid decline by 44 months. Several of the items on the attitude scale indicated that by the children's third year, mothers were less interested in their children's education and held a less positive attitude toward their children than before day care. While Fowler and Kahn's results cast a negative light on day-care effects and maternal attitudes, the recent results of the New York City Infant Day Care Study (Golden, Rosenbluth, Grossi, Policare, Freeman & Brownlee, 1978) indicate no systematic relationship either positive or negative between day care, family structure, and family functioning.

A number of earlier studies found evidence in favor of increased positive maternal attitude toward the child following intervention. Grodner and Grodner (1975) instituted a half-day preschool program for children ages 1 through 6 whose parents had a low socioeconomic status (SES). The program emphasized the teaching of parenting and educational skills and the enhancement of parental self-concept through joint parent/parent and parent/staff facilities, meetings, and program responsibility. Parental attitudes were measured before and after intervention using the Shoben Parental Attitude Scale. Parent scores then were compared to those of parents on a waiting list and those of a clinic staff. Postintervention testing revealed that the scores of parents enrolled in the program increased significantly over those of parents on the waiting list and were comparable to the attitudes of the clinic staff. Those parents were found to be less dominating, less passive, and more responsive to their children, exhibiting a more positive attitude toward child rearing. Morris and Glick (1975) and Karnes and associates (1970) also found positive attitude changes on the part of mothers six months after intervention. In many instances, however, maternal behavioral and attitude changes have been measured through written tasks that may not accurately reflect a true change in behavior within the home but rather the learning of specific responses.

In order to accurately assess the effects of day care on mothers' attitudes, more information concerning normative changes in maternal attitudes over time and in response to shifts in the child's development is required. It is possible that maternal interest in child education changes with the transition from home to preschool, preschool to kindergarten, and so forth. If this is so, decreased maternal interest may not be a negative indicator at certain points in the child's education. As noted by Bell and colleagues (1968, 1977), mother/child dyads are interacting systems in which the behavior of the child may exert a strong influence on the mother. Studies have not separated the interacting effects of mother/child dyads.

Marcus and Corsini (1978) found that parents of middle and lower SES groups hold different expectations of their children's abilities to perform successfully on achievement type tasks. Fathers and mothers of lower SES groups predicted a lower level of performance for their children than parents of middle SES children, even when the ability and performance levels of children in both groups were equal.

The most recent results of the previously discussed Ypsilanti Perry Preschool Project indicate that, even as late as the high school years, 51% of the parents of children who were enrolled in the preschool program are more satisfied with their children's school performance, while only 28% of the control-group parents were satisfied. Parents of children in the experimental group also desired more schooling for their children. Did improved school performance and behavior of children in the experimental group increase parental expectations or did the preschool experience influence parental aspirations, which in turn affected children? While there are no definitive answers to this complex question, it would seem clear that there is an attitude congruence and possibly a reciprocal influence between parent and child.

Effects on parental self-concept and behavior

What is the effect of the day-care experience on maternal self-concept and maternal behavior outside the family? Generally, it is assumed that enhanced maternal self-concept and feelings of effectance serve to strengthen positive parent/child interactions and allow mothers to act as constructive, motivated models for their children. Evidence for shifts in maternal self-concept have been inferred from changes in maternal behavior.

Studies by Morris and Glick (1975) and Karnes, Teska, Hodgins, and Badger (1970) showed that in-home intervention programs serve to increase a mother's belief that she is the primary educator of her child and that the positive gains shown by the child are a direct result of her abilities to teach her child successfully. These researchers speculate that maternal sense of competency and feelings of effectiveness may serve to positively influence maternal self-concept. In two studies completed by Lally (1971), mothers of children enrolled in preschool programs earned significantly more high school diplomas than did mothers in a control group. Karnes (1970) also found increased maternal community involvement and employment at the end of a two-year out-of-home program. Children in the program were not enrolled in a day-care program, indicating that perhaps the effects on maternal behavior were not simply a function of an increase in time available to the mother.

Steinberg and Green (1978) presented data that only 20% of the mothers using center day care felt they gained more information concerning child rearing and believed they were influential as parents than mothers using child-sitters or family day care. Preschool, family-day-care, or in-own-home programs that focus on the parent might produce much higher percentages of maternal perception of change or information gain.

Strengthening networks

Several other early-child-care effects relate to alterations of maternal behavior and interactions within the family. Because few studies intentionally have investigated variables external to the mother/child dyad, findings are incidental to research designs and, therefore, easily confounded. However, they do suggest that the influence of child-care arrangements may extend beyond the mother/child dyad to other family members, friendships, employment, and even the larger community.

Intervention studies suggest a broadening or strengthening of maternal peer networks within the community (Grodner & Grodner, 1975; Karnes, 1970; Morris & Glick, 1975). Mothers participating in out-of-home or in-home training groups seem to form supportive networks in terms of shared information, support, and child care assistance. Joint parent/staff facilities, such as those within community educational or health services, perhaps fulfill the same purpose, although not designed with network development in mind.

Meyers (1973) and Harrell and Ridley (1975) found that job and marital satisfaction increases as parents' satisfaction with child-care arrangements rises. There is some evidence, not well substantiated, that interventions centered on the mother and a target child may produce increases in academic performance for younger siblings after program termination (Klaus & Gray, 1970; Levenstein, 1970), producing what is called *vertical diffusion*. Mothers' increased parenting skills seem to influence nontarget children in a positive manner.

School personnel also may be affected by a child's altered behavior as the result of a preschool experience. Eighth-grade and high-school data from the Perry Preschool Project (Weikart & Schweinhart, 1979) show that while parents of experimental and nonexperimental children initiate school contact equally, teachers, though not aware of their student's participation in the program, tend to initiate fewer contacts with parents of the experimental children, which the authors interpret as the result of fewer school-related problems evidenced by the experimental children. Further data analysis, to be released soon, will help to confirm or refute this interpretation.

Research is needed to clarify the extended effects of various early-child-care arrangements on the entire family system, the extended family, and family friendship patterns. Future studies also must begin to investigate the influence of child care on the communities in which young children live and on the nature of parent and family involvement in the community, use of community resources, and employment patterns subsequent to day-care availability.

Mothers are increasingly participating in child-care assistance, which suggests that maternal peer networks within the community may be strengthening.

Proceed with caution—The light is yellow

There are a number of important factors that qualify the research findings in the field of early intervention and parent involvement in child care. Belsky and Steinberg (1978) point out several features that limit the scope of the available research. First, a major portion of the research in early child care has taken place in high-quality centers. A great number of day-care centers servicing children are not of high quality, and only 11% of parents with children under six years of age use day care or preschool services. Since almost all follow-up studies are discontinued during the elementary school years, there are little available data on the long-term impact or "sleeper effects" of early child care. Few studies specify the effect of various forms of child care on parents, families, or society. Questions abound concerning the reliability or usefulness of tests typically used to measure program outcomes and the "ecological validity" (Bronfenbrenner, 1977) of programs—that is, whether research-setting results can be generalized to other situations. Also, test measures differ from center to center, which makes comparisons between studies difficult; program implementation and staff/child relationships shift over time and are seldom investigated; and little data exist about how staff characteristics affect children, parents, or the structure of programs of varying quality.

Conclusion

A variety of sources have influenced the evolving form of early-child-care services in the United States. The changing political and economic climate in the United States and the traditional American beliefs in the family and individual rights have produced large-scale federally funded programs for young children and an increase in privately run preschool and home-care facilities. The efforts and concerns of parents, professionals, and special interest groups also have played an important role in early child care. A multitude of influences will confront future efforts to serve children.

Little is known about such fundamental issues at which critical environmental variables affect child development; optimal intervention and enrichment strategies; and the positive or negative influences of various early-child-care arrangements on children, families, communities, and society.

In the past few years, concern for early child care has been renewed, both in response to the longitudinal Head Start results and the possible broader influences of preschool child-care arrangements. It is hoped that this interest will serve as impetus to a better definition of child-care goals, a more explicit role of government in child rearing, and a more thorough exploration of the positive environmental variables that affect child development.

Research and application in these areas may permit a more comprehensive understanding of the potential optimizing influences of parents, families, child-service providers, and social networks on children. The issue of developing appropriate parental support systems and child-care programs then can be addressed more fully.

Summary

Direct parental involvement in child-care programs has increased over the last fifteen years as a result of theoretical contributions, empirical findings, and changes on a societal level. In 1968, the Federal Interagency Day Care Guidelines mandated parent involvement in all phases of project functioning for subsidized Head Start Centers.

Strategies for parental involvement in home and out-of-home vary as to: (1) parent education, (2) degree of activity, (3) the scope of involvement, and (4) parent/staff coalition role. Parent education classes, a form of preventive intervention, focus on imparting knowledge of child development and parenting skills to ensure that future parents or those with infants will have adequate information to rear their children successfully. Other programs train parents to interact, communicate, and solve problems more effectively with their children. These programs generally prevent and correct mental health problems as well as serve to maintain positive aspects of existing parent/child interactions and to optimize family relationships. Thus, parent training—individually, as a family, or in parent groups—focuses on teaching techniques for parent/child interaction.

Although society supports the concept of a comprehensive child-care program, child services are not offered within a centralized system. Home-based programs vary in the extent and type of support given to parents and the degree of actual parental involvement. Their goal is to facilitate a parent's acquisition of skills for optimal parenting and to develop a strong bond between mother and the in-home trainer. Attachment between mother and child is seen as critical to the cognitive and emotional well-being of the child. Out-of-home programs are similar to home-based programs with one major exception—the mother's self-concept is viewed as critical to her ability to optimize the child's development. A good self-concept is thought to foster feelings of self-confidence and competency. A variety of implementation methods are used.

The parent/staff coalition approach focuses on the building of a single, reinforcing, child-centered system and the establishment of constructive goals between the parent and the child-care system. It is believed that close, respectful relationships between parents and staff facilitate children's security in out-of-home settings and reinforce positive parent/teacher efforts. Numerous techniques are used to increase the parent/staff bond.

Child-care programs influence children's cognitive and social development. It seems evident that one to two years of a quality program combined with an effective home program can make permanent positive changes in children's cognitive abilities. However, the findings of day-care effects on mother/child attachment are equivocal. The setting often influences the effects of child-care programs on children and parents. In-home or out-of-home care that produces positive effects on child development can result in negative influences if timed inappropriately with the child's developmental level. Even in high-quality care settings, differences exist in maternal versus care-giver behavior. The influences exerted by mother/child and care-giver/child interactions on immediate and long-range child development need to be investigated.

Studies of the effects of early substitute/supplemental care on mothers, parents, and families are sparse, and the results mixed. For example, parents who enroll children in preschool programs hold higher expectations of schooling for their children and are more satisfied with their children's school performance. However, middle- and lower-class parents hold different expectations of their children's abilities to perform successfully. Lower-class parents tend to predict lower levels of performance for their children than middle-class parents, even when ability and performance levels of children are equal.

Child-care arrangements influence systems beyond the family. Mothers who participate in training programs form supportive community networks by sharing information and assisting others in child care. Also, as parental satisfaction with child-care arrangements rises, employment and marital satisfaction increases as well. Future studies must investigate the influence of child care on the communities in which young children live and on the nature of parent and family community involvement, use of community resources, and employment patterns subsequent to day-care availability.

Caution is warranted in interpreting these data. A number of programs are not of high quality. Little follow-up data exist. Reliability problems of test measures raise questions about "ecological validity." Also, test measures differ from program to program, making comparisons among studies difficult. Continued research, both basic and applied, is needed to understand the potential of optimizing influences of parents, families, child-service providers, and social networks on children.

Working for Children

Throughout our discussions, we have supported an ecological perspective for understanding children and families and the services they receive and need. We have advocated that parental participation be encouraged and community resources be available to assist adults in their roles as protectors and nurturers of children. This final section of the book highlights some indirect societal influences on families and children. So often these factors form the guidelines for working with children, affecting the destinies of families far more than direct services do. Once supported by society, these external influences are more difficult to change than elements of specific programs because they are rooted in historical attitudes and legal policy.

Chapter 11 focuses on child and family advocacy. What does advocacy mean? How can individuals serve in advocacy roles? How has the concept of *advocacy* been fostered by societal attitudes? How does it promote social policy for children and families? More questions than answers are raised—a reflection of today's complex, dynamically changing, highly technological society, which mitigates against simple answers to very complex issues, such as blaming parents for problems with children.

The role of professionals also has altered drastically in contemporary society. Chapter 12 illuminates the prevalent societal attitudes toward professionals, the meaning of professional self, and current dilemmas. Child mistreatment is discussed to illustrate the implications of professional disagreements.

Although tax dollars continue to be spent on delivering services to children and families, programs are riddled with pitfalls. Efforts to make programs accountable often take the form of determining whether programs succeed or fail, were used or not. Chapter 13 presents a model for evaluating the effectiveness of child services. This model has successfully been used to evaluate early childhood programs and is offered as a potential way to help determine accountability.

The concept of commitment, whether to a profession, an advocacy role, or a belief in a better future for children and families, forms the core for the concluding discussion in Chapter 14, which attends to controversial issues and the implications of solutions within an ecological perspective. Major themes presented throughout this book are synthesized and magnified for continued efforts on behalf of children.

11

Child and Family Advocacy: Toward Social Policy

Chapter overview

The establishment of a comprehensive family social policy constitutes a growing concern in this latter part of the 20th century. Advocates continue to raise issues and make changes in the lives of families and children. This chapter examines child and family advocacy within the context of family legal policy and children's rights, with emphasis on the development of social policy.

Issues to consider

What does advocacy mean and how has advocacy toward families and children changed?

What two directions has the child advocacy movement taken?

What rights do children have to education, religious expression, and due process?

What problems persist in trying to uphold children's rights?

How has a social policy for families evolved?

How do explicit and implicit family policies differ?

What factors impede the development of a family social policy?

Introduction

The following passage reveals some of the complexities and frustrations associated with child advocacy.

> Jimmy was almost five and suffered from leukemia with an uncertain prognosis. He usually took his necessary injections stoically and, in his own mind, probably hoped for better days. There was nothing he wanted more than to go to school. But his birthday was something like December fifth and the cut-off for kindergarten entrance was December first. (There was no preschool program in his community at that time.) The parents requested an exception to the age rule from the school administrators and the board of education. His pediatrician and school psychologist asked also. The response was that no exceptions could be made to the December first deadline; otherwise, many parents would be making similar requests. This child could wait, like everyone else, until the following September. The request procedure went on over a period of a month. . . .
>
> When the school rejection was definite, Jimmy's pediatrician arranged with a college student to have an hour session twice weekly with Jimmy. At this time they planted seeds, colored, worked with numbers, and read and made up stories together. Jimmy proudly referred to "his school." But, of course, it was nothing like a regular daily kindergarten program with a group of children, and he still looked forward very much to going to the "real school" in September.
>
> Jimmy died the following August [Mearig & Associates, 1978, p. 312].*

What feelings does this passage produce? Do you feel saddened by Jimmy's illness? Do you feel empathy for the parents, who are confronting the eventuality of their five-year-old son's death? Are you angry with the school administrators and school board that prevented Jimmy's admittance, at their support of a rule rather than a child? Are you confused as to why the pediatrician and school psychologist could not change the prevailing attitude? Or do you feel comforted that the pediatrician did find a college student who was willing to create a school atmosphere for Jimmy?

* From *Working for Children: Issues beyond Professional Guidelines,* by J. S. Mearig and Associates (Eds.). Copyright © 1978 by Jossey-Bass, Inc., Publishers. Reprinted by permission.

How could Jimmy's parents and the professionals have been better advocates for Jimmy? More generally, what does advocacy mean and what roles does it create? What are the prevailing attitudes and policies toward families and children? Whose rights are supported under what circumstances? This chapter addresses these questions by examining the concept of advocacy and attitudes and policies toward families and children. The desirability of a comprehensive social policy for children will be presented.

Definition of advocacy

An advocate is a person who actively supports or defends a value, an individual, a group or subgroup, or a change in legislation or attitudes. Such a person is an intercessor who pleads on behalf of X, in this case children or a particular group of children, such as abused children or children in foster homes.

A commitment to advocacy requires ego and emotional involvement to motivate a person to influence lives. This commitment can manifest itself formally in professional roles (for example, lawyers and lobbyists) or informally (for example, the pediatrician and school psychologist in the earlier account of Jimmy). In this diverse, pluralistic society, some of these efforts are valued and others are not by different people. Historically, social, political, and economic institutions and religious beliefs in the United States have dictated that parents serve as advocates for their children. In fact, legal doctrine assumed parents have a "natural" right to raise children as they deem appropriate.

With changes in social structures, advocacy attitudes and efforts have altered. Responsibility for providing children with education, health care, recreation, and other services, once the sole province of families, is now shared by other institutions that create new relationships and provoke changes. Persistent conflicts between children and authority figures and parents and institutions have produced an increase in advocacy efforts, which attempt to bridge the gap between individual grievances and social institutions. A new advocacy role, that of liaison to officials, legislators, coalition groups, community groups, and so on, has emerged. Advocates' attempts to improve situations often have required the redistribution of resources.

Advocacy has taken on a new and distinctive meaning in the last decade. The advocate not only establishes or supports cases, serves as liaison, and improves situations, but also lobbies to change systems, institutions, and laws. In this sense, advocacy means working with or against the systems that affect families and children. It can mean intervening to: (1) change a process such as budget allocation or legislation; (2) work for new procedures and institutions that strengthen families and protect children's rights; or (3) demand that existing legislation be enforced or funded. Advocacy strives for accountability of the systems that effect people's lives (Gross & Gross, 1977).

Professional and advocacy roles

Advocacy roles usually are assumed by special interest groups that organize around occupational responsibilities and settings (see Chapter 12) or by lawyers who work for particular organizations. Both groups have focused their efforts on legislative change to legally extend adult rights to children or legally identify children's special interests or needs. Seldom have families or children banded together on their own to legally serve their special interests or needs.

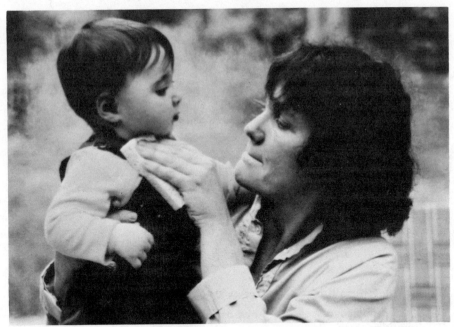

A child advocate is a professional and/or parent who is committed to supporting and defending children and who acts on their behalf in attempts to change legislation and attitudes regarding children.

Extending adult rights to children

With the socially entrenched attitude that parents have authority over their children, extending adult rights to them has been controversial and difficult to codify into laws. Consequently, courts seldom interfere with parents' decisions about their children's medical care, diet, religion, education, clothing, housing, discipline, and so on. Under certain circumstances, however, courts have declared older children to be wholly or partially emancipated from their parents. Full emancipation usually is granted in cases of marriage or enlistment into the armed services, but parental consent is required, too. Partial emancipation means a child has autonomy in specific areas. For example, the Supreme Court ruled in 1973 that a state could not make parental approval a precondition for abortion in the first trimester of pregnancy regardless of a girl's age (*Roe* v. *Wade*, 410 U.S. 113, 116). The majority of states, however, support the tradition of parental authority except in emergencies. Thus, extending adult rights to children has received little support, especially in the area of birth control and health care. Social problems—for example increases in teenage pregnancies—still persist and policies must be formulated to resolve them.

The thorny question arises as to whether a child should be able to refuse services that parents solicit or impose. Perhaps a child wants to refuse a new medical technique that parents have read prevents hyperactivity. Or perhaps a child wants to refuse immunization because of a fear of shots. In what areas or under what circumstances should children's opinions be considered?

Another issue is the role advocates of children and families should play in broader issues that concern environmental pollution, food adulterations, over-the-counter drugs, and nuclear accidents. Should the "Three-Mile-Island" children be told of possible negative consequences of radiation? Who is responsible for the "Love Canal?" What rights do those families and youngsters have?

Attempts have been made to tackle some of these broader issues for adults but not yet for children. For example, the Occupational Safety and Health Act (OSHA) of 1970, which states all workers must have a safe, healthy work environment, does not specify effects on worker's children, whether born or not. Keniston and The Carnegie Council (1977) believe standards should be made stricter to protect children and their families from pollution and other hazards:

> Child protection should go far beyond the traditional model of social workers looking out for neglected or poorly fed children to embrace a federal children's consumer and environmental watchdog agency that screens practices of private industry and government alike for their effects on children and communicates an early warning to parents and others who care for children . . . In the long run, nuclear power, disruption of the ozone layer, chemical additives, prescription and over the counter drugs, and industrial pollution may well present more pressing legal problems for whole generations of children [p. 210].

Protecting children's interests and needs

Child advocates have proposed a bill of rights for children that proclaims their entitlement to adequate nutrition, a healthy environment, continuous loving care, a sympathetic community, intellectual and emotional stimulation, and numerous additional prerequisites for becoming "healthy" adults (Rodham, 1976). To date, these rights are not recognized as legal rights under the law.

It is easier, of course, to focus on rights that are related to physical needs than psychological ones. For instance, what is continuous loving care and how can it be enforced? Legalization of this and other children's rights could create tremendous enforcement problems in an already vague legal system. The legal system itself could in turn undermine the effectiveness and even the integrity of such laws, nor is the law a panacea for a problem. "While the law may claim to establish relationships, it can, in fact, do little more than acknowledge them and give them recognition. It may be able to destroy human relationships, but it cannot compel them to develop." (Goldstein, 1972, p. 637).

The Children's Defense Fund (CDF) has been at the forefront of advocacy for protecting children's interests and needs. Modeled after the NAACP Legal Defense Fund, it is privately supported and staffed predominately by lawyers. It advocates basic rights for all children: education, privacy in relation to records, protection from research experimentation, adequate health care, and fair and humane treatment in the juvenile justice system. The CDF believes that because change for children is intensely political, involving money, power, and service, class-action suits are required to rectify inequities and to prevent bureaucracies from self-service rather than child service. The number of highly diverse individuals and groups working on behalf of families and children is growing at a rapid rate. For those interested in which organizations are involved and the scope of their activities, see Calabrese (1977).

Awareness, persistence, and allegiance

Professional or lay advocates must be aware of societal attitudes, the incidence of social problems, and appropriate agency officials and legislators to contact. Then they must order priorities and objectives, exhibiting flexibility in trying various approaches until one works. Numerous techniques to promote advocacy efforts are advanced. Sunley (1980), for example, suggests establishing a case of need through neighborhood surveys, expert testimony, and agency reports and publicizing the case through petitions, direct contacts with officials and legislators, demonstration projects, and the media. Sunley's observation that advocacy will be more effective when families support these efforts suggests the desirability of alignments between lay persons and child-service providers to enhance the probability of producing changes in family programs and policies.

Many dilemmas face professionals who work as advocates. What are their moral and ethical responsibilities? What risks should they take? How can their potential abuse of power be controlled? These questions are confronted in the next chapter, which examines professionalism.

Some changes in family legal policy have occurred, reflecting prevailing attitudes about the rights of parents and children and the ways to balance them. Legal policy has dictated the break-up of families in response to societal attitudes regarding parent/child relationships. The rejection of children by parents has caused much controversy, with blame placed on parents.

Family legal policy

The idea of children's rights independent of their parents recently emerged, which deLone and The Carnegie Council (1979) and Keniston and The Carnegie Council (1977) feel was inspired by the civil rights and liberties movements of the 1960s. Although children have been granted more legal rights and responsibilities by statutes and court decisions, the process occurs on a case-by-case basis. Keniston and The Carnegie Council (1977) suggests that jurisdiction affecting children should be more comprehensive in the form of a children's code "as a necessary foundation for determining the inevitable disputes that will arise in any set of relationships so complex as that of child, family, and state " (p. 185).

Family laws consistently have broken up families and confined children to institutional environments because of parental failure or a child's misconduct or handicap. Legal and social policies must redirect efforts to keep families together so children can identify with family life. Both basic and applied work reinforce the attitude that a relatively stable, supportive home environment is necessary for a child's healthy development (see Chapter 3).

It is an unfortunate fact in today's society that a large number of families are not stable; in fact, they frequently find themselves under a great deal of stress, victimized by outside factors such as unemployment, internal problems such as physical disability, mental illness, or alcoholism, or an interaction of both. The legal apparatus, rather than providing practical assistance in the form of income support, employment, child care, counseling, or training often declares these parents to be "unfit" and removes the children (see Chapters 7 and 8).

Societal rejection of parents

The families that are scrutinized and interfered with the most are minority, low-income, single-parent families. Since the majority of professionals who deal with these families have experienced a drastically different world socially, economically, and ideologically, they are apt to condemn all too quickly and lack awareness about the negative affects of institutional alternatives to which they readily condemn children. For example, Mnookin (1973) found court-ordered removal of children in about 65%

of the cases examined. In many other cases, legal policy requires removal for families to receive services. Removing children from their homes, however, usually costs the government more and benefits children less. With its current emphasis on punishment, the legal system has "no power or authority to order social agencies to help; its power is too often limited to watching, monitoring, checking-up, supervising, and ultimately taking children away" (Keniston & Carnegie Council, 1977, p. 189). Specific alternatives to this policy of removing children need to be delineated and removal implemented with more caution.

Should laws be enacted to ensure corrective intervention? What weight should be given to children's opinions? If a child is removed, should laws dictate the termination of parental rights so children can obtain a permanent home through adoption? Answers to these questions require acknowledging that externally impinging factors often place parents in crisis situations.

Parental rejection of children

When parents initiate the break-up of families, legal policy provides a mechanism to recognize separations and to reduce the negative effects on children. When dilemmas such as parental inability to control a child (see Chapter 4) or too many burdens with a dysfunctional child occur (see Chapter 9), society has sanctioned state custody for children. History suggests that the underlying assumption—"an unwilling parent is not a good parent" (Keniston & Carnegie Council, 1977, p. 192)—is wrong. Tragically, parents have given up or directly institutionalized children for the wrong reasons, the primary one being a lack of resources or support. For instance, many surveys show that the majority of institutionalized residents were admitted as minors and received no prior social services or evaluation (National Association for Retarded Citizens, 1968).

This situation raises profound questions: despite parental attitudes, do children have a right to their natural parents? Do parents have a right, no matter what the reason, to give up their children? True, a court cannot order parents and children to love each other, but it could provide assistance to those families who want to remain intact. It could ensure due process for those contemplating institutionalization. It could inquire into the lives of institutionalized children and determine whether they should receive another form of care.

Children without families

The treatment of institutionalized children is lacking in many respects. Isolated, large, and impersonal, institutions are overcrowded, regimented, and seldom adequately staffed. Despite these factors and the knowledge that children need strong bonds with adults for attachment and stimulation to develop, the treatment of children without families has been altered very little. It seems that society does not want to support children of so-called unfit parents with public funds. Parents, for the most part, are too preoccupied with their own children to invest energies in these abandoned children.

Only in the last few years have institutionalized children received any legal rights. Legal doctrine endowing these children with a "right to at least a minimum of what it takes to promote normal health and development" (Keniston & Carnegie Council, 1977, p. 197) has been interpreted to mean the right of treatment for mentally ill children, the right of rehabilitation for delinquents, and the right to care–a nourishing diet, protection from assault by staff and residents, some privacy in sleeping and bathing quarters, adequate education, medical care, and access to recreational and socializing experiences. This represents a good beginning, but much more can be done legally to protect these children from further deprivation and to nurture their development.

Attitudes, legislation, and interpretations

Society has advocated the attitude that children are incompetent and dependent upon parents who have widely diversified backgrounds, experiences, and expertise. Major social reforms, therefore, have been legislated to ensure the rights of all children and help society promote future productive, healthy generations of adults (see Chapter 2). Although there are no guidelines that limit parental involvement in their children's lives, indicating when state intervention should occur and considering the interests of children, courts have made major decisions that affect all families and children.

Children's rights to education

Every state in the United States has a compulsory education law, which means that children between certain ages, varying from state to state, are provided with an education and parents must let them attend school. Compulsory attendance laws attempt to strike a reasonable balance between the rights of children, parents, and those of the state. For instance, if a child fails to attend school because he or she lives an unreasonable distance from school and transportation is not provided, the child is not considered truant and parents are not guilty of violating the law. In fact, several states authorize that transportation be provided by the school or permit pupils to receive instruction outside of school, usually from a tutor or parent. Although such instruction, when legally permitted, should be carried out in good faith, efforts to monitor the process and assess children's development are problematic and unsystematic.

Sometimes parents contest the compulsory education law. In *Wisconsin* v. *Yoder* (406 U.S. 206, 1972), for example, several Amish parents challenged the Wisconsin compulsory education statute, claiming that the religious freedom of their children was being violated. The one child asked to testify did share her parents' religious views. Chief Justice Burger's majority opinion supported the right of the Amish parents to be exempt from the statute on the grounds that it violated their religious freedom. Although these children no longer had to attend school, Justice Douglas's minority opinion argued that the court ruling should apply only to the one child who testified because the interests of the other two children, not those of the parents, were in question. He concluded that children of sufficient maturity should express their own interests in future such cases. How maturity is reasonably interpreted will be difficult for courts to determine, especially when parent and child interests clash.

Interpretations of reasonableness in terms of children's rights for education have been handed down by the Supreme Court on many occasions. The Court assumes, for example, that compulsory education laws, which delegate to boards of education the power to make rules and regulations for the operation of schools, will be reasonable, but they often are not.

In recent years, the Court has heard an increasing number of cases concerning student conduct, activism, and individual rights. Cases often involve appearance (dress, haircuts, and so on) and free expression (for example, publications, demonstrations, and symbolic adornment). The Court's most significant statement concerning these issues was handed down in 1969 in *Tinker et al.* v. *Des Moines Independent Community School District et al.* (393 U.S. 503) dealing with students wearing black armbands in protest against the Vietnam War. School officials, informed of a planned protest against the Vietnam conflict, adopted a policy to suspend any student who wore a black armband to school and refused to remove it when asked. Five students were, in fact, suspended but were readmitted to school after the planned protest period ended. They then sought a federal district injunction to restrain school officials from disciplining them. The court held that the school's action was reasonable because it was taken to prevent disruption of regular school operations. The students appealed and the U.S. Court of Appeals upheld the decision. The U.S. Supreme Court overturned the lower-court decision, ruling that fear of disturbance should not override the fundamental right to freedom of expression. Since the students did not actually disrupt school activities and did not intrude in either school affairs or the lives of others, the Court ruled that they had the right to express their opinions.

Children's rights to religious expression

The issue of religion and individual rights in the schools has drawn considerable public attention in the 20th century. Under the First and Fourteenth Amendments, neither the federal government nor a state is free to establish religion or prohibit the free exercise thereof. In public schools, this principle has related to the issue of legality of Bible reading. Although Bible reading was permitted by half the states and prohibited in only a few states over the years, at the present time the Supreme Court of the United States has ended religious recitations in the classroom because they violate free exercise of religion and constitute an establishment of religion as defined by the First Amendment. Students are not required to participate in readings or prayers, nor may they be forced to witness such activities against their will.

The courts have also acknowledged the rights of students who neither practice nor believe in any religion. Even the most innocuous activities, such as the singing of religious songs, are held to constitute an imposition of religious tenets upon nonbelievers. Similarly, students choosing to be excluded from ceremonies or activities must respect the right of those who participate. Today's courts firmly uphold the privileges inherent in the First Amendment.

Children's rights to due process

In matters of procedural rights or due process students' rights to be heard are considered. Before students at a tax-supported institution of learning can be expelled or given a lengthy suspension for misconduct, they must be notified of the charges against them and some type of hearing must be scheduled. This hearing must be more than an informal review and must preserve the rudiments of an advisory proceeding. Witnesses and cross-examination must be present, and in certain instances presence of a lawyer is required. A high school senior, for example, faced with a charge of cheating that could result in denial of a state diploma, scholarship, and qualifying-exam privileges, would be considered to have the right to counsel. In a case of misconduct at a less severe level, a child who is suspended is entitled to a guidance conference to determine reentry but would not need a lawyer.

As a result of people's awareness of children's due-process rights, educational institutions have increasingly formalized their rules and regulations in student handbooks and catalogues. These documents set forth not only particular offenses but also the procedures used and the type of appeal system available.

Children's rights in procedural protections have been a substantial issue in the juvenile justice system. In 1967 the Supreme Court decided that the following due-process guarantees should be extended to children: (1) notice to both parent and child to have an opportunity to prepare a defense as well as a sufficient statement of charge; (2) right to counsel, and if the child is indigent, appointment of counsel; (3) privilege against self-incrimination; and (4) the right to confront and cross-examine witnesses. These legal guarantees extending the Bill of Rights to children represent the culmination of extensive advocacy efforts.

Social policies directed toward families and children are not creations of the 1980s—as we discussed in Chapter 2, intervention in the lives of children with and without families has occurred throughout history. But only recently has the concept of family policy been defined and its effects conceptualized.

Perspectives on family social policy

Rodgers (1973), a family sociologist, defines family policy as "how state action, government policies, are actually affecting families and the quality of life (p. 113)." Unfortunately, a definition such as this one that focuses on effects does not separate goals from implementation and evaluation. The effects realized may not be congruent with the objectives sought, and the degree of equity in the policies would be difficult to determine.

As early as 1968, Schorr attempted to focus on goals defining family policy as "consensus on a core of family goals toward the realization of which the nation deliberately shapes programs and policies" (pp. 143-144). Whose attitudes should form the consensus—the majority, the minority, or both? In 1969, Winston recognized that America's cultural diversity and history of unresolved social-reform issues provide obstacles to arriving at acceptable goals. Myrdal (1971) and others find difficulty in defining and constructing family policy as well as conceptualizing its effects reflect problems with interpreting equality.

Family policy "includes both the effects on the family of all types of public activities and the efforts to use 'family well-being' as an objective, goal, or standard in developing social policy" (Kamerman & Kahn, 1980, p. 62). Family policy encompasses both explicit and implicit consequences. In the category of explicit family policy are structured activities such as income maintenance, tax benefits, housing policies, and child welfare, some of which are available for families with certain characteristics; others, such as taxes, are imposed on all families. Implicit actions that affect families indirectly include decisions about building roads, industrial locations, and immigration regulations.

Consequences, purposeful or not, affect family members differently. Some interventions can benefit certain family members more than others, and others can impede the development of some members or the family as a unit, resulting in stress. Relationships and tensions should be monitored and may require additional interventions on behalf of the family (Kamerman & Kahn, 1980).

Empirical evidence supports the need to establish a comprehensive social policy for families and children, despite difficulties in determining specific goals and practices and in evaluating effectiveness. The relationship between family well-being and social policy was established in the Michigan longitudinal study of 5000 families in which factors such as income maintenance, employment, and housing were found to be critical for the well-being of families (Morgan, 1974). Developmental psychologists such as Bronfenbrenner (1974b) concurred, showing the effects of these factors on the lives of children and their future development. Kahn and Kamerman (1975) indicated how policies toward substitute care and toward special groups such as the handicapped need to be unified. Also, public concern about families and children reached a peak during the 1960s and early 1970s with the women's rights movement (see Myrdal & Klein, 1968; Ross & Sawhill, 1975).

In today's technologically advanced society, parents are becoming more and more powerless, not because they need reform or have failed but because most problems have moved beyond the individual and family level to broader levels–social, political, and economic. Professionals therefore must bring their attitudes, ideas, and policies in line with contemporary reality. When they continue to focus interventions on parents and children in isolation of their ecology, the wrong questions are promoted. Today is no longer a time to ask what parents are doing wrong. Rather, the question should focus on how to change social, political, and economic forces that victimize families.

This approach implies a new set of responsibilities. Parents and professionals must be committed to learn about what affects their family, how negative effects can be changed, and how problems can be prevented. In essence, adults must become advocates, raising questions and promoting policies that go beyond each case and comprehensively serve children and families for the future. To do this, people must become politically active at all levels, from PTA groups to Junior League to lobbying groups.

What might happen to children and families if a national policy that would interconnect scattered programs were implemented? Could, for example, day-care facilities offer frequent, mandated, and comprehensive health check-ups during the first several years of life? What if we established effective services to continue to monitor defects in children who at this point receive no follow-up assessments? Would advocating an integrated system reduce the presently widening gap between social change and social policy? These questions deserve serious consideration.

Overcoming impeding factors

Efforts must continue to overcome the factors that hamper the development of a comprehensive social policy. Three areas will be briefly considered here: bureaucracy, funding, and research.

The federal and state bureaucracy. Although the federal and state governments make proposals about programs for housing, health centers, day care centers, welfare services, and so on, actual decisions to implement such family programs are made by states. Passing legislation at either level is arduous and often impossible because of conflicting pressures from constituents, as evidenced by the inability of Congress to pass a comprehensive child-care policy since 1970. The awareness of citizen groups at all levels of government, however, have helped to expedite policy development because programs are not housed within one specific governmental structure. As was discussed in Chapter 2, numerous policies were generated as part of the Social Security Act. The Office of Education and Health and Human Services also oversees many programs.

Funding. A variety of problems have been associated with program funding. Chilman (1980), for example, argues that taxation policies must be examined because

A comprehensive family social policy that protects and nurtures children remains our choice to assist our society's future.

they relate to social policies and both affect the well-being of families. "Many serious inequities exist in the tax system, among them the antiquated taxing methods of localities (relying heavily on regressive property and sales taxes), tax loopholes and shelters available mostly to the affluent, and the recent easing of business and corporation taxes" (p. 78).

Theory and empirical research. An action-now approach has often been used to promote and develop social programs. For instance, during the early 1960s the Office of Juvenile Delinquency provided a vast system of opportunities for youth across many areas including work, education, cultural experiences, and camping (Cloward & Ohlin, 1960). The theory that deprivation causes delinquency was relied upon before empirical evidence was gathered. The massive and expensive programs that resulted were not very successful, and blame fell on scientists who generated the theory rather than on program planners.

This situation illustrates the need for continued efforts to encourage small-scale pilot projects that could offer support for theory, help produce a data base, and lessen public disenchantment with "ivory-tower" professionals. Demonstration projects, which are not as costly, promote an awareness of the complexity of problems and in the long run can further basic and applied efforts. Issues surrounding public sentiment about professionals are illuminated in Chapter 12.

Conclusion

Certainly it would be nice if protection and nurturance of children did not have to be legislated. But some parents deprive children of medical treatment, despite expert opinions that it is necessary. Others institutionalize children inappropriately as a way of ridding themselves of the parenting burden and responsibility. Fortunately, the majority of parents try to protect and nurture their children.

Laws represent some of the greatest advocacy efforts for children's and parents' rights. Erikson (1974) and others who are concerned with overlegislating view the government in the role of "superparent." But the American system is one of constantly shifting the fulcrum to balance the rights of children and parents with government intervention.

This issue of advocacy toward social policy is more complex than supporting or opposing legislative efforts. Some legislation is far too general, which presents problems of interpretation and possible inequities. Laws often are regarded as the panacea for solving problems or are applied in an extreme manner. Erikson (1974) suggests that schools are becoming overly regulated, hampering society's potential benefit from diversity and achievement. He raises the spectre

> of potential Chopins who must leave their pianos to participate in what is for them an inane classroom discussion of baroque music, of Olympic skating champions whose high school graduation diplomas are held up for lack of physical education credits, and of many other children who could learn inestimably more of what is important and useful to them in settings that the law now makes generally inaccessible during the prolonged period of compulsory school attendance [Erikson, 1974, p. 414].

Perhaps, the time has come when certain institutional regulations can no longer be blindly supported but rather should be challenged so children will be better able to adapt to their highly changing ecology.

Legal policy is but one element needed in a comprehensive social policy for children. Other factors must continue to be identified and inroads made in curtailing impeding factors. The cost of failure will be very high, as Keniston and The Carnegie Council (1977) observe:

> Failure to change today will lay on the next generation heavy social costs with a high moral, social, and financial price tag. On the one hand, they are the costs of human potential; on the other hand, they are the costs of trying to deal in the next generation with all the problems of crime, deep dissatisfaction, delinquency, and withdrawal that would have been prevented [p. 216].

Summary

All components of society–individuals, institutions, and government–continue to be perplexed about the proper programs and social policies to implement for families and children. Explicit and implicit policies do exist, however. U.S. history suggests that a policy be developed despite a lack of agreement over goals and impeding factors. Empirical evidence and scientific theory support this position.

Advocacy for families and children is growing. The advocate's purpose is to establish cases, serve as liaison, inform staff, build links between individuals and institutions, and improve situations, and to change systems, institutions, and laws. In this sense, advocacy means working with or against the systems that affect families and children. The Children's Defense Fund, a leader in the advocacy movement, uses class-action suits to rectify inequities and to prevent bureaucracies from self-service rather than child service. Other advocate organizations seek to legally extend adult rights to children or to legally protect children's special needs and interests. The rights of students are upheld under the First Amendment as long as they do not disrupt the educational process. Students can choose to be excluded from religious ceremonies, activities, or prayer, but must respect the right of those who wish to participate. Children's due process rights are supported by law as well. Children must be informed of rules and regulations not only at school, but also in the courtroom.

Laws also consistently have represented children when parents or guardians were considered "unfit." These laws have succeeded in breaking up families and confining children to institutional environments because of parental failure or a child's misconduct or handicap. Legal and social-policy efforts must be redirected to keep families together so children can identify with family life. Both basic and applied work reinforce the view that a relatively stable, supportive home environment is necessary for the healthy development of children.

In today's technologically advanced society, parents have become victims of social, political, and economic forces. A comprehensive social policy must focus on children and families in their ecology. Professionals must stop blaming parents and start changing external factors through advocacy efforts that include laypersons as well.

12

Professionals: No Promise of a Rose Garden

Chapter overview

The ways professionals interpret their roles, contexts, and power determine their relations to society. This chapter explores the relationship among professionals, society, and children. The meaning of professional self is a primary focus. Results from a major study about child mistreatment illustrate perceptual and procedural differences among professionals as well as between laypersons.

Issues to consider

What societal attitudes prevail about professionals, and why?
How does society contribute to the uncertainty of professionals, and what can be done about it?
What are the common professional settings?
What is meant by professional power and how is it abused?
How are professionals recognized?
How do professionals fit within the modern complexity of bureaucracy?
How do bureaucracies impose binds on professionals?
In what ways do professionals disagree, and what are the implications for practice and policy?
How should professionals intervene in children's lives?

Introduction

The following excerpt is from Des Pres's description of the volunteers in Albert Camus's *The Plague*.

> [They] pit themselves against the plague, with no conviction of success, but only determined not to stand idle while others suffer. Together, therefore, they organize hygienic programs, they tend the stricken, they dispose of the dead. They work twenty hours a day amid the stench and agony of the dying, spending themselves in that endless, empty time of day upon day, without the encouragement of visible progress, without the hope of a positive end in sight, and always with the knowledge that death may win. They carry on all the same, because "they knew it was the thing to do" [Des Pres, 1976, pp. 8–9].*

At the crux of being a professional is commitment despite all odds. Professionals need to feel they can produce changes, even within restricting conditions. They need an optimistic attitude in attempting to make a difference. If they become disillusioned, they become resigned to their fate; if they become cynical, they raise troublesome questions and create attitudes that indeed may make professional services disabling, as evidenced in the questions posed by McKnight (1978, p. 75).

> Why are we putting so much resource into medicine when our health is not improving? Why are we putting so much resource into education and our children seem to be learning less? Why are we putting so much resource into criminal justice systems and society seems less just and less secure? Why are we putting so much more resource into mental health systems and we seem to have more mental illness?

Cynical attitudes toward professional helpers should not be ignored, because

---

*From *The Survivor: An Anatomy of Life in the Death Camps* by Terence Des Pres. Copyright © 1976 by Oxford University Press, Inc. Reprinted by permission.

these attitudes are a part of the culture in which professionals function. A certain amount of cynicism toward professional helpers is neither harmful nor unwarranted, since it attempts to put professionals in perspective, reminding them of their own human fallibility. Professionals should work for and with people, not solely for their own benefit or personal gain. Nor should they treat the people served with condescension. Cynical concerns emerged from a history of experiences with professional arrogance. "Through an unwritten social contract, society gives special privileges to the professions. Professionals are believed to be people with special expertise. They foster implicit trust because of their dedication to high-quality services and commitment to people's welfare" (Shore, 1977, p. 359).

But society's fostering of privileged status for professionals has created an atmosphere of mistrust toward professionals in every field. Professionals represent the establishment (which is suspect in the first place) and are trained to intervene in the lives of others, which can be dehumanizing (Morse, 1978). That an occasional "rotten apple" does turn up argues not for a wholesale condemnation of the professions but for improving guidelines for professional behavior to promote proper training and to help monitor activities.

Professionals have had difficulty in deciding whose rights should be supported and under what circumstances when they intervene in the lives of children. Legally, whose rights should be supported—the rights of children, siblings, parents, or society? In the past, child-service professionals would ask a child which parent he or she wanted to stay with following a divorce. This type of decision has been removed from the professional child-services worker and placed with the courts. Thus, a professional helper's role is not as decisive as it once was (Morse, 1978).

The negative societal response toward professionals and the transfer of some of their authority, while an untenable situation for professionals, does reflect the struggle within the entire social-service enterprise. Just as parents do not necessarily act in the best interests of their children, neither do professionals necessarily know what is good for the people they help. Thus becoming a professional in today's changing society requires a realistic posture. Child-service providers must be aware of their own fallibility, realizing that they will not be able to love, care for, or help every client. They will likely not always make societal reforms. Nor will they be given a succinct list of professional commandments. Illusions about professionals have given way—no longer is there a promise of a rose garden.

Professionals and society

Professional roles

Often the term *professional* is misused or applied indiscriminately. For instance, an athlete who receives a salary and competes within a certain class of people or teams is called a professional, not an amateur. Those involved in prostitution, "the world's oldest profession," are not professionals simply because they are paid. People become professionals—teachers, lawyers, doctors, social workers, and so on—as a result of specialized training in a particular area, recognized as an occupational type and socially sanctioned as a profession. Professionals are a diverse group of skilled people who have achieved occupational roles that are organized around areas of knowledge—basic or applied.

The misconceptions about professionals often result from the value placed on income. It is thought that those people in competitive, high-paying jobs must be

Intervention in children's lives is complicated by the issue of rights—children's, parents', and society's.

professionals. To be successful financially supports long-standing societal values. According to Everett Hughes (1965),

> "profession" originally meant the act or fact of professing. It has come to mean: The occupation which one professes to be skilled in and to follow. . . . A vocation in which professed knowledge of some branch of learning is used in its application to the affairs of others, or in the practice of an art based upon it. Applied specifically to the three learned professions of divinity, law, and medicine; also the military "profession." From this follows later the adjective "professional," with the meanings now familiar [p. 2].

The essence of the professional ideal is to know and give advice that derives from special lines of knowledge and disciplines. With this license to profess comes certain behavioral expectations such as objectivity and emotional detachment.

Many professional roles result directly from technological and organizational changes. Emergent professions, far removed from the basic three of divinity, law, and medicine, need time to establish credibility. Some child-service providers have struggled to form an identity.

> Social workers earlier were at pains to prove their work could not be done by amateurs, people who brought their efforts naught but good will; it required, they said, training in case work, a technique based on accumulated knowledge and experience of human nature and its operation in various circumstances [Hughes, 1965, p. 5].

Professional settings

Professionals work in two primary settings—individual practice and organizations. Individual-practice settings promote professional autonomy and freedom. Although some lawyers and physicians maintain independent status, individual-practice settings in today's complex society are more likely to involve partnerships. Also many professionals practice in both independent and institutional arenas (Hall, 1975).

Professional organizations such as medical clinics, social-work agencies, and child-abuse agencies are represented by two subcategories. Some organizations are autonomous: members decide upon what norms they will follow, how behavior will be governed, what are the necessary administrative tasks, and so on. An organization such as a medical clinic that does not receive funds from governmental or private sources fits in this group. The second subtype, the heteronomous professional organization, exposes professionals to an external administrative framework. Heteronomous organizations include schools, welfare agencies, day-care centers, and other institutions that receive some type of outside support, either governmental or private.

The image of a professional as Florence Nightingale, Thurgood Marshall, or Jonas Salk does not apply to child-service professionals, most of whom are salaried employees working in an agency or institution. They seldom make autonomous decisions, and children's needs and interests are often pitted against those of the organization. The picture of the professional in today's society is really "the loyal bureaucrat" (McGowan, 1978, p. 155). The implications of this reality are significant: is it possible for child-service professionals to achieve occupational acclaim? Although many fantasize about their freedom in functioning for the sake of children, it is really counterproductive to live in such a dream world. The critical issue is how child-service professionals live with and shape the bureaucracies that make and administer the decisions.

Professional power

From a societal perspective, professional power is manifested in different ways. The power to make decisions that affect lives can be viewed as control over clients. In fact, professionals often exercise their power over themselves because they decide what to do, when, and how well they perform. Professionals' power essentially lies in their knowledge, training, and service. They develop and interpret knowledge and make it available to the public in some form. Professionals are central for service delivery. They are the core of the "knowledge industry" that is a key characteristic of modern nations. Recently the assumption that professionals know how to use their power was challenged, and new training (acquisition) and retraining (maintenance) guidelines are being contemplated (Freidson, 1974). For example, many professionals must periodically take examinations in their discipline to renew licenses, which often requires retraining first. An overreliance on examinations as indicators of ability may, however, result in further alienation. "The disposal of human beings by professional classification based on scraps of paper is symptomatic of the all too common alienation of professionals that spells abuse" (Polier, 1976, pp. 358-359). The greatest misuse of professional power concerns decisions about whether services should be withheld or granted. One of the most common ways to withhold services to children is through diagnosis and classification. Professionals often refrain from diagnosis and send those seeking help on a merry-go-round in search of a label. Such a search typically begins at the point of referral and frustrates both child and parents. The plight of Jimmy (Knitzer, 1978) illustrates the problem.

Two-year-old Jimmy was diagnosed as autistic by a child-clinic pediatrician, who referred him to a developmental center. There a psychologist informed Jimmy's parents that there would be an 8-month wait for a complete diagnostic workup. The diagnosis was confirmed but because the state did not consider autism to be a developmental disability the parents were referred to a mental health clinic, where a psychiatrist confirmed the diagnosis and informed Jimmy's parents that the clinic was in transition and unable to provide help. Jimmy would have to wait until he entered public school to receive any type of assistance.

The case of Jimmy goes beyond the problem of diagnosis and referral. Services were withheld from Jimmy because the providers involved were either misinformed or uninformed, functioning within the narrow frameworks of their respective agencies. Help was not given to Jimmy because no one took the responsibility to mobilize or integrate any services. Should child-service workers conduct "business as usual," ignoring what happens to children?

Fortunately, two major developments have helped to control professionals' potential abuse of power. One is the child advocacy movement, which was discussed in the preceding chapter, the other is the increasing demand for accountability. A vast number of regional, state, and national organizations and associations present specific guidelines for social-service providers.* Their policies specify ways in which professionals should deal with clients. Individual researchers also have generated methods—for example, treatment contracts consisting of "goal attainment scaling" (Kiresuk & Lund, 1976)—to enable accountability for professionals. Legislation has moved in a similar direction. For example, in Ohio a treatment plan must be written for each mentally retarded and mentally ill patient who is institutionalized (Ohio R. C. Sec. 15122.27). Written individualized educational plans must be produced for each handicapped child (Education for All Handicapped Children Act, Pub. L. 94–142, 1975).

Perhaps with this movement toward accountability, child-service providers will refrain from making definitive statements when they lack knowledge and will begin to interpret the guidelines of their profession individually rather than rely on agency interpretations. According to the American Psychological Association's (1977) ethical guidelines, psychologists are to "accept responsibility for the consequences of their work and make every effort to ensure that their services are used appropriately" (p. 13). The professional imperative is to think constantly about one's own values and their impact on others because "there are many exceptional situations in which the professional must go beyond the guidelines and make decisions based on personal conscience and . . . professional judgment" (Kessler, 1978, p. 147).

The professional self

Professional attributes

Competence or mastery of a domain of knowledge distinguishes professionals from other workers. Clients give them authority because they believe in their expertise and the efficacy of their judgment. Authority, then, represents the second attribute of a professional. The third attribute is the societally sanctioned privileges, such as increased income and increased flexibility and opportunity, of the professional following a training period and when professionally established standards are met. These sanctions usually take the form of licensing or accreditation by a professional body. Another sanction given to professionals is client confidentiality. By protecting the rights of clients, a professional's authority also is reaffirmed.

Professionals are also characterized by their support of a code of ethics that dictates appropriate behavior toward clients and colleagues. Ethical codes usually are

---

*Affiliations include American Association of Family and Marriage Counselors, National Association of Social Workers, American Sociological Association, National Association for Mental Health, American Educational Research Association, American Medical Association, American Home Economics Association, American Dietetics Association, American Psychological Association, and Child Welfare League of America.

enforced by the profession through removal from an association, censure, or informal ostracism. The fifth attribute of a professional is support of a professional culture, which includes following membership rules and regulations, maintaining knowledge qualifications, and practicing in appropriate locations in the sanctioned manner.

Finally, membership in a profession assumes certain personality dimensions. A professional should have a well-developed sense and appreciation of the profession. They should feel a sense of obligation to perform in the most competent way possible and to be open to continued growth and development. Thus, professionals should be people who work for the intrinsic rewards associated with the job rather than just extrinsic rewards such as money (Hall, 1975).

Qualifications are not enough

Many professionals view these six attributes—knowledge, authority, sanctions, code of ethics, professional culture, and obligation—as objects to be possessed. Such an attitude possibly represents the biggest misuse of professionalism. To be a professional means to be constantly questioning paths of action while dynamically interacting with children and families in a changing society. These attributes should not become a "magic circle" of protection and self-deception.

It also is unrealistic to treat each attribute separately. For instance, sanctions do not occur without knowledge; authority is not extended without sanctions and knowledge. In some sense, these three attributes are prerequisites for practicing. Following a professional code of ethics allows one to remain in business. For a professional to function with some peace of mind, commitment to the profession and obligation to clients are needed.

Professionals use these attributes as guidelines to define and interpret areas and issues throughout careers. Two constantly asked questions are: what must be done to receive social approval (sanctions) in terms of established professional guidelines? And what must be done to satisfy the "personal self" so one can function effectively as a professional? The bottom line actually is to be comfortable about decisions that affect clients.

Obtaining social approval by getting a license does not ensure that a budding professional has the necessary knowledge base for practicing. Likewise, as Danish and Smyer (1980) point out, it is wrong to assume that those who do not pass an examination are not competent. What professionals need is recognition of the complexities of their work. Carsten (1978), for example, took Forms 6 and 7 of the Professional Examination Service (PES) examination for psychologists seeking a license. Although Carsten, who had no college degree, did not pass the examination (she scored 55% and 60%, respectively, over 10% below the national mean of Ph.D. applicants), she could have crammed for it by attending one of those frequent preparation sessions advertised in the *American Psychological Association Monitor*. Carsten appropriately questions, "When consumers in Louisiana, California, Colorado, or New Jersey open the yellow pages to PSYCHOLOGIST, what will they get? What should they expect?" (p. 531).

It should be of no surprise that an exam does not ensure a knowledge base. Practical experience produces competency, a fact suggested by Flexner in 1910:

> There is only one sort of licensing test that is significant, viz, a test that ascertains the practical ability of the student confronting a concrete case to collect all relevant data and to suggest the positive procedure applicable to the conditions disclosed. A written examination may have some incidental value; it does not touch the heart of the matter [p. 169].

Although the evidence challenging examinations for professional licenses is scant, it does suggest the need for providing other safeguards for the level of professional quality. Perhaps assessments of performance that are sensitive to growth and development should be created.

Once professionals obtain a license, their colleagues seem reluctant to revoke it. For instance, in a period of a little over a year in New York State, only 16 of 1000 complaints of medical incompetence were reported by licensed practitioners (Pottinger, 1978). Koocher (1978) stresses that professionals do not see incompetence per se as unethical because it requires a relative judgment. "While statutory licensing bodies generally do have defined procedures for revoking the credentials they grant, rather dramatic evidence of incompetence or criminal behavior in the form of legal convictions or concrete inquiries to clients is usually necessary" (p. 13).

Professionals should realize that a license may be in neither their nor their client's best interests. Although it may be required for social approval, it should not be viewed as a testimony of competence, which develops through acts that are the result of training or retraining. Nor should it be viewed as a testimony of commitment, which evolves and changes through experience.

Since "these are times that try professional souls" (Morse, 1978, p. 17), child-service providers must decide what their personal and professional values are. Morse (1978) suggests that, especially in situations of risk, professionals need to weigh the potential benefits and harm to client and self. Weighing alternatives has become critical for survival and for maintaining a sense of commitment. The professional environment is subject to modifications in the larger society as well as within its own subculture.

> "We used to feel assured about who was the patient; now even the question of who is sane depends on definition and perspective. Earlier we thought we knew the methodology to be taught to would-be helpers. Now almost every method has advocates, and at times, it seems that anything goes" [Hersch, 1968, p. 506].

Codes of ethics for professionals also are not sacrosanct; they always are subject to revisions. Comparing the two versions of the Ethical Standards of Psychologists (American Psychological Association, 1953; 1977) illustrates how codes can change. In 1953, Principle 14 said "Test scores, like test materials, are released only to persons who are qualified to interpret and use them properly" (p. 59). But in 1977, Principle 14 encouraged openness: "The client has the right to have, and the psychologist has the responsibility to provide, explanations of the nature and purposes of the test results in language that the client can understand" (p. 14). Because disclosure rules are not given for every situation, decision making often is at an individual's discretion.

Professionals follow a model of self-monitoring. This freedom can be abused, as discussed earlier, but it also can establish a strong set of values that produce commitments and competence. Although the government at any level defers to professionals for judging whether or not an individual is qualified, it does exercise some control over their activities. The government serves as a mediator in disputes between and among professionals—for example, it supported organized medicine's refusal to allow clinical psychologists to deal with nervous and mental disorders (Freidson, 1970). The government also is involved in regulating the delivery of services. For example, the 1972 Social Security Act included a provision for establishing Professional Standard Review Organizations (PSROs), which were charged with reviewing whether services offered by individuals or institutions are necessary, appropriate, and of a sufficiently high level of quality to be paid for by the government.

For professionals to be successful, they must continue to seek personal growth and development and to view their roles as continually changing and evolving.

Professionals do not function in a vacuum. They often operate within agencies and interact "for the client's best interest." The following case study (Knitzer, 1978) typifies the difficulties they confront. The social worker, convinced that the mother was abusing one of her children but lacking sufficient evidence, convinced the mother to file a petition to have her two teenage daughters declared incorrigible by the court. That way they could be removed without evidence of abuse.

> In the petition [the mother] said that the girls did not always go to school and that sometimes they stayed out late. She said she felt she needed some help with them. At the court proceeding, the judge, relying solely on the caseworker's testimony that the girls should be removed from the home, ordered them immediately sent to the children's shelter. No one from the schools was ever asked about the girls, nor was there ever any discussion with the mother about how she might deal with the problem without removing the girls. After the court session, the mother and her daughters were visibly shocked. The mother said she had no idea this could happen, and repeated she had just wanted some help. . . .
>
> The sisters remained in [a community] shelter for two months, until a foster home could be found for them. They had been in that home for just three months when the foster mother complained that she had wanted to have only children under ten. The girls then returned to the shelter for another two months, until there was space in a group home. By this time, the girls, average students, had fallen badly behind in their school work. Throughout this period, the mother visited the girls regularly, and often, when she left, both she and the younger child were crying. . . .
>
> The mother's questions about when she could have her daughters back went unanswered. A year later, however, the social worker who originally encouraged the mother to petition the court said that at that time she was new to the community. She was no longer sure she did the correct thing in separating the girls from their mother [pp. 78–79].*

*From "Responsibility for Delivery of Services," by J. Knitzer. In J. S. Mearig and Associates (Eds.), *Working for Children: Issues beyond Professional Guidelines.* Copyright © 1978 by Jossey-Bass Inc. Publishers. This and all other quotes from the same source reprinted by permission.

In this situation, the judge behaved the most irresponsibly. He did not request testimonies from various professionals. He did not talk with the girls or their mother. He did not inquire about the best possible placement for the children, if indeed removal from their home was the right decision. The social worker's behavior also could be criticized because responsibility was assumed prematurely. When professionals do not assess children's needs and the best possible alternatives, intervention can not only be inappropriate, but also irreversible. Often the goals and actions of an agency conflict with client needs and professional values.

Bureaucratic binds

While professionals should periodically engage in self-examination and professional renewal, they often find themselves in bureaucratic settings that discourage such activity and produce conflicts that usually involve values, practice, and employer demands. Potential conflict areas between professionals and bureaucracies have been identified by McGowan (1978):

1. Bureaucracies are based on a hierarchical authority structure, whereas professions employ a self-monitoring model.
2. Professionals are expected to put client needs first, whereas organizational loyalty is a priority for bureaucratic employees.
3. Organizations are goal-oriented, whereas professions tend to emphasize process or proper use of knowledge and technique.
4. Responsibilities of bureaucratic employees are carefully delineated and staff are expected to separate work obligations from personal life, whereas professionals are expected to place professional obligations above personal needs.
5. In bureaucracies, separation is made between policy making and administrative functions, whereas these roles are not distinguished in professional behavior [p. 157].

In a bureaucracy, a person occupying a senior position is assumed to have greater expertise and authority but often makes decisions that may not be appropriate. There are several reasons for this situation. Promotions in bureaucracies often are based on seniority. The person there the longest gets the most power. Also, as people engage in a profession over time, they tend to apply the same solutions to new problems, ignoring changing contexts. A supervisor is removed from the client situation and the community and does not know all the subtleties of the case or the best possible referral. Sometimes the best solution might break an organizational rule or regulation such as a working parent having to drop a child off at a day care center early. While the teachers may be willing to trade off who arrives early, the principal says no because the situation may "snowball"—other parents may want the same privileges and other teachers might want additional pay. As a consequence, the parent withdraws the child, who is then made to stay home in the care of an older sibling. Thus, convincing one's supervisor of a professional opinion often is necessary for appropriate intervention to occur.

Another area of potential conflict for professionals involves their emphasis on process and the bureaucrat's emphasis on products. Bureaucrats often reward professionals who treat clients within the agency's rules and regulations rather than those who allow exceptions for the particular needs of clients. With the emphasis on products and results, bureaucracies in many instances provide services to a small well-defined target group likely to succeed rather than generalizing and adapting the services to include more people in need.

Since roles and responsibilities for staff are defined clearly in organizations, people may be reluctant to tread on one another's turf. This can create a situation in which 'things fall through the crack" or the "buck is passed." To meet client needs, professionals often have to step over their role boundaries or violate an organizational rule such as providing service for an at-risk person who cannot pay. Roles, responsibilities, and rules usually are established so the organization can function efficiently. Child providers whose prime concern is effective service for clients may experience difficulty in such settings.

Professional disagreements

Just because professionals have similar attributes, it cannot be assumed they will agree whether to intervene or how. Nor will problems necessarily be perceived in the same way. In fact, at the levels of both practice and policy individuals of the same as well as different professions disagree.

Child mistreatment, an arena in which numerous professionals are involved in interaction, illustrates the impact of professional disagreement on both policy and practice. Historically, four key professionals—lawyers, pediatricians, social workers, and police—handle cases of child mistreatment, although teachers and child-care workers are becoming more and more involved in this area. At a policy level, lawyers and pediatricians support a legal perspective, while social workers and police support a social-service perspective. This difference is rooted in the persistent conflict between the rights and needs of children and rights of parents. The types and degree of severity of mistreatment that justify removing a child from his or her home constitutes the heart of the controversy. The debate concerns the relative harm that may result from staying in the family situation versus being separated from it. The major issue is how immediate and certain harm is if a child is left with parents. On the one hand, the law makes the child's needs paramount, while it supports family privacy. On the other hand, the social-service perspective recognizes the importance of the child's emotional and psychological well-being.

Professionals' perceptions of child mistreatment. A few studies (Boehm, 1962; Billingsley, 1964) have tried to identify specifically the degree of professional disagreement in perceptions of child mistreatment. Recently, Giovannoni and Becerra (1979) examined where professional agreement and disagreement exist about child mistreatment and what degree of perceived seriousness prevails, raising questions that are both quantitative and qualitative. They used a vignette technique consisting of verbal descriptions of parental actions and the consequences—for example, "The parent banged the child's head against the wall. The child suffered a concussion" (p. 105). These 156 vignettes were presented by graduate social-work and sociology students to 71 lawyers, 113 social workers, 50 police, and 79 pediatricians from the Los Angeles area. Each person was asked to rate a vignette on certain criteria. Thirteen classes of child maltreatment were used to construct the vignettes:

> Cleanliness of child
> Clothing with reference to discomfort from cold
> Drugs/alcohol used by family members
> Educational neglect in terms of child's truancy and failing grades
> Emotional neglect (parents' verbal abuse, favoring one child over another, ridiculing, and so on)
> Fostering delinquency through parental acts of stealing

Housing (unsafe, overcrowded, dirty, unsavory neighborhood)
Medical neglect brought about by parental failure
Nutritional neglect in terms of degrees of over- and underfeeding
Parental sexual mores depicted by parental sexual activity
Physical abuse (types of physical assault)
Supervision (leaving the child alone or with an unreliable person)
Sexual abuse (sexual activity between parent and child)

The major findings indicate that there was no consensus about the seriousness of the incidents of mistreatment. Police and social workers most often agreed (73% of the time) and rated incidents as more serious than either lawyers or pediatricians. Lawyers disagreed the most with all other groups (about 45% of the time) and rated the incidents as less serious. They agreed with pediatricians about 50% of the time. Incidents that were acknowledged as mistreatment were: parental role failure in physical care of the child, neglecting care-giving responsibilities, and physical assaults. Social workers, physicians, and police were most concerned with nutritional care.

In terms of the nonphysical domains, social workers and pediatricians agreed on the level of seriousness, but police and social workers did not with either the previous two groups or with each other. However, across categories social workers and police held more similar views. Pediatricians were paired with lawyers most often. Parental experience or sex made no difference in ratings of seriousness.

The area of child abuse is obviously ridden with opinions and pronouncements. The inference to be drawn from the above findings is that community perceptions should be gathered. Just as perceptions of child abuse vary from community to community, so does the level of perceived seriousness. Giovannoni and Becerra (1979) reasoned that if community perceptions were available, then professionals could uphold the values of a community rather than impose their own (or use those of an agency).

The emergent theme of this extensive study is "the importance of 'protecting cultural differences'" (p. 158). From social-service and legal perspectives, respect for cultural diversity remains paramount.

> Community standards for child care reflect changing public attitudes and different views among different groups regarding what is essential for the child and what jeopardizes his well-being and future development. What may be considered neglect or abuse in one community, or for one group of children, may not be so considered in another. The point at which individuals in a community may take action, and the situations which are tolerated, will often differ from community to community and within communities [Child Welfare League of America 1973, p. 8].

Community perceptions of child mistreatment. To investigate community perceptions of child mistreatment, Giovannoni and Becerra (1979) selected 687 White, 129 Black, and 117 Hispanic parents from the Los Angeles area to respond to the vignettes. Comparisons were made with the ratings from the four professional groups.

Community members rated all incidents as more serious than any of the professionals. The White sample rated 94% of the vignettes as less serious than did the Black or Hispanic groups. Hispanics also rated vignettes portraying physical injury, sexual abuse, and drug/alcohol abuse as more serious than Blacks. However, Blacks rated matters dealing with nutrition, health care, cleanliness, supervision, education, housing, and clothing higher than Hispanics.

None of the lay respondents discriminated between the emotional and physical realms of abuse. The investigators suggest that this may reflect the general lack of knowledge about emotional abuse. Community respondents did distinguish among different types of mistreatment, identifying roughly the same categories as did professionals.

When socioeconomic status (SES) was assessed, different perceptions emerged. Lower SES groups saw mistreatment as more serious than did higher SES groups. Blacks, regardless of SES or sex differences, demonstrated the greatest consensus with their perception of the failure to provide supervision as the most serious parental mistreatment. On the other hand, Whites were the most heterogeneous in their perceptions. SES and sex differences presented an extremely diverse picture of Whites' perceptions of child mistreatment. The factors of sex and SES were uniform for the Hispanic group—the lower the income, the greater the perception of seriousness—and women rated mistreatment significantly higher than men.

Disagreement between professionals and laypersons. Comparing the two data sets, it appears that professionals do not impose their values on communities in terms of child mistreatment. Although they make finer discriminations of mistreatment than do laypersons, as was mentioned previously, consensus did emerge on one dimension—everyone viewed sexual abuse as the most serious child-abuse offense.

Perceived seriousness and intervention. The next question raised by Giovannoni and Becerra was: does perceived seriousness influence intervention? They studied 949 families who came to the attention of the protective systems in four California counties during 1975–1976. Agency workers were asked to note the reasons and behavior that lead to protective action. In 459 cases, physical injury was noted, with 50% also reporting sexual assault. Numerous other reasons such as nutritional, medical, and educational neglect, and lack of parental supervision were reported, but no category constituted more than 15% of the number of cases.

Results demonstrated that seriousness of mistreatment and parental attitude influenced the court dispositions. Positive parental attitudes even in the face of serious mistreatment such as sexual assault, failure to provide, physical injury, and inadequate environs encouraged the judgment that the situation could be safely managed at home. Court options provided were services to the child and family in their own home or voluntary foster-home placement.

Usually police or social workers, who view mistreatment most seriously, serve as the primary screeners of protective cases. Whether these primary professionals can learn to discriminate cases of mistreatment more finely will greatly be influenced by laws. More precise definitions may provide a starting point for legislative reform, with members of diverse ethnic groups having full representation at all phases of the definitional process. Giovannoni and Becerra (1979) concluded that until that time, the "definitional process cannot be a just one, and the definitions will remain inadequate" (p. 261). Child-service workers should be cognizant of the perceptions and related intervention choices of their colleagues and the people they are trying to help.

Professionals and children

Consent to a course of action in child services is another critical concern for professionals who work for children. What does consent mean? How is consent used to alter children's lives? How can it be used by professionals to not only protect but also enhance the rights and interests of children?

The meaning of consent goes beyond making decisions. If a parent or professional takes no course of action, then this indecision is a type of consent—a consent to do nothing. As in the case study cited earlier, the parents of Jimmy finally consented to wait until he entered school for help. Giving consent for a child to enroll in a program or receive a service is a decision that should be made on the child's behalf. Care should be given as to whether the experience is as "culturally natural" or "unrestrictive" as possible (Wolfensberger, 1972). Thus, if a child could benefit from a foster-home environment, then the child should not be placed in an institution. But many services rendered on the behalf of children do not follow these guidelines (Schrag & Divoky, 1975).

Consent serves the interests of children, parents, and professionals. Parents do not have to consent to inadequate or risky procedures, they can withhold consent until all their questions are answered. For the child-service provider, consent places the decision making power, in essence the right to self-determination, in the hands of clients. To gain consent, they must carefully explain to parents what will or can be done. Cooperative relations with parents is essential for helping children. Biklen (1978) speaks of consent as

> a legal concept that has been referred to and implicitly defined in court cases and in legislation. It has three major aspects: capacity, information, and voluntariness. All three elements are equally relevant to any consent procedure or decision. Simply stated, one must have the ability to give consent in order to do so; one must have adequate information to do so in a knowledgeable way; and one must be free from coercion or any other threat to one's voluntariness [p. 99].*

Capacity refers to how people acquire information and remember it. Because children are usually considered incompetent under the law, parents are asked to receive and process information on their behalf. When conveying information to parents, child workers should not pass judgment that a parent is competent or not competent. The issue is, given the information provided, is a parent able to make a decision? If a service provider questions the decision-making ability of a parent, then a lawyer or court should be consulted. It is also important to explain intervention procedures to older children, letting them know what to expect. This procedure usually enhances intervention effectiveness, allays anxieties or fears, and supports the rights of a child as a person.

In order to assess a caregiver's capacity for making a decision, a service worker must evaluate what information is pertinent or available and how the information should be presented. Different types of intervention will, of course, require that different levels of information be provided. For instance, if medical intervention is required, then caregivers (and the child) should be told about possible physical risks and reactions. If an educational program is suggested, then the possible psychological and behavior effects should be explored openly. When the proper information is not presented, as in the case study cited on pages 212–213, a parent often makes a decision that is not only potentially inadequate but also irrevocable.

Biklen (1978, p.105) asks, "Are caregivers making a free choice, or are they being coerced by the lack of options, by a fear of speaking up against a professional, by the provisions of inducements?" Issues of use or abuse of professional power come to the fore here. Sometimes coercion can be subtle. For instance, during the 1960s, many parents wanted to enroll their retarded children in the Willowbrook State School,

---

*From "Consent as a Cornerstone," by D. Biklen. In J. S. Mearig and Associates (Eds.), *Working for Children: Issues beyond Professional Guidelines.* Copyright © 1978 by Jossey-Bass Inc., Publishers. This and all other quotes from the same source reprinted by permission.

which was doing hepatitis research, but the waiting list was at 400. There were no other community services available. If parents signed a form saying they would "voluntarily" admit their children who would then be injected with a substance to induce hepatitis, then they did not have to wait for long periods to place their children in the institution. Obviously the coercive element was the lack of services available in the community.

Service providers must go beyond the mere guidelines of providing information so parents are capable of making a voluntary decision on behalf of their children. This is especially important with interventions that may require risk or that are irreversible.

> In situations where there is risk and irreversibility associated with the procedure, a child should always have an impartial advocate to give or withhold consent. Unfortunately, this has not always been the case in social services' dealings with children, where one professional often is expected to function *in loco parentis* in a subjective sense and at the same time look out for the agency's best interests [Biklen, 1978, p. 106].

Issues of consent make the professional's role with children unique in contrast with other clients. The concept is evasive, just as the attributes that define the professional self are. Having to seek consent can be beneficial to professionals because it may make them more aware of the possible consequences of their actions. Also, clients can increase their awareness of services because of their cooperative role in granting consent. The giving or withholding of consent, if applied properly, can be the professional's best tool.

Conclusion

In recent years child services have grown tremendously. Parents are relying more on professionals than families and friends. Professionals have a variety of educational experiences and have met the needed requirements for entrance into their fields. However, qualifications alone are not enough. As the range of services and the number of problems have increased, many child-service workers function in formal bureaucratic contexts and must deal with numerous conflicts. Parents complain about being ignored, mistreated, deceived. They often feel frustrated, angry, powerless. Service providers are more likely than administrators to receive these complaints, which usually are directed toward the bureaucratic structure. No doubt parents have many legitimate reasons for protest, but child-service professionals should not personalize this blame. They need to learn how to function within complex organizations, while not violating their professional attributes and potential for growth. This is possible when professional identity is viewed as an interactive developmental process. They need to be open to change at all levels, from societal (for example, social policy) to personal (for example, retraining).

Professionals need to care about children and families without suffering their pain. Those who cannot remain detached from others' problems "burn out," no longer able to function in their role. These individuals also need to care about their professions. They should help exercise quality control by developing new guidelines that determine entry and continuation in a profession. They can assist young professionals directly in a supervisory or training role or indirectly through modeling.

The child-service system, whether bureaucratic or societal, ultimately translates into people with varying perceptions, values, and goals. It is the way in which each individual interacts that can promote the quality of human life or destroy it.

Summary

Society's attitudes toward professionals has fostered privileged status, arrogance, and commitment, but these attitudes also have promoted cynicism, uncertainty, and mistrust among people in need of help. The uncertainty is exacerbated by the courts' difficulty in deciding whose rights should be supported under what situations. Illusions about professionals are beginning to give way in today's changing society.

Professionals are individuals who have achieved an occupational role organized around areas of knowledge. They work in two primary settings—individual practice and organizations—and manifest power either in relation to clients or to themselves. The greatest misuse of power concerns decisions about whether services should be withheld or granted. Diagnosis and classification are two ways to withhold services. Professional abuse of power is controlled by increasing demands for accountability.

Professional attributes are: (1) knowledge, (2) authority, (3) sanctions, (4) code of ethics, (5) professional culture, and (6) obligation. Professionals should view their roles as constantly changing and continue to seek personal growth and development.

Bureaucratic goals and objectives emphasize products, while professionals strive for improving process. Thus, conflicts often result. Disagreements can also occur among professionals in their perceptions and choice of intervention at both policy and practice levels. For example, in a recent study, perceptions of child mistreatment varied among lawyers, pediatricians, social workers, and police, with police and social workers agreeing most often. Incidents acknowledged as mistreatment were: (1) parental role failure in physical care; (2) neglecting care-giving responsibilities; and (3) physical assaults.

Since professionals work in communities, it is important to see how their perceptions agree with those of laypersons. A study of perceptions about child mistreatment showed that Whites saw abusive acts as less serious than did Blacks or Hispanics. Blacks felt neglect dealing with nutrition, health care, cleanliness, supervision, education, housing, and clothing are serious mistreatments. Hispanics rated physical injury, sexual abuse, drug/alcohol abuse as the most serious offenses against children. Sex and SES differences influenced the perceptions of Whites more than those of the other two groups. Blacks demonstrated the greatest consensus. For Hispanics, the lower the income, the greater the perception of seriousness, and women rated mistreatment significantly higher than men.

Professionals do not seem to impose their values on communities in terms of mistreatment. Consensus between professionals and laypersons emerged on one dimension—sexual abuse was seen as the most serious offense. However, perceived seriousness also influences intervention. Positive parental attitudes mitigate against removing a child from the family.

Since types of child mistreatment are related to social contexts, which change over time, professionals need to be aware of differences in communities. The primary screeners—police and social workers—set the system in motion, with court dispositions reflecting the "serious" label attached to mistreatment.

Finally, obtaining consent when intervening into children's lives is critical. When information is shared, issues for consideration are: (1) care giver capacity, (2) the child's level of development, and (3) avoidance of coercion. These areas are even more critical when interventions require risk or are irreversible.

Improving child services means that providers must: (1) view their identity as an interactive developmental process; (2) be open to change at all levels; and (3) care about children and their professions. Ultimately, commitment to people and their diversity will enhance children's lives.

13

Formative User-Based Evaluation of Child-Service Programs

This chapter was written in collaboration with ELLEN A. SKINNER, Ph.D. as the senior author, while she was completing her doctoral degree at The Pennsylvania State University, College of Human Development. Skinner currently is at the Max Planck Institute, Berlin, Germany.

Chapter overview

Determining program effectiveness is a necessary feature of all forms of service delivery. Often, however, evaluation follows the completion of a program and has no impact on program structure or functioning. This chapter illuminates one model of evaluation—formative user-based. Its process orientation permits the developmental improvement of ongoing programs. Examples of the questions this evaluative mode raises illustrate both its potential application across child-service programs and its positive consequences for service delivery systems.

Issues to consider

What features characterize formative user-based evaluation?
What dimensions are used to specify ideal programs?
How are deductive and inductive methods used in the program specification process?
What procedures facilitate program specification?
How are individual, observational, and standardized assessments employed to measure actual programs?
What are the strengths and weaknesses of these assessment approaches?
How is factual information gathered and retrieved, and what are some potential problems?
How are evaluation results used for program and evaluation improvement?

Introduction

Evaluation is a word that often strikes terror in even the most diligent and conscientious program planners. They may envision people in white coats poking through records and clicking their tongues disapprovingly. The entire staff waits breathlessly to see if their program "passed." Then, upon hearing the good news, all sigh with relief and return to business. Such reactions reflect the aversion we all have to being judged, especially in the case where program funding or continuance is affected by evaluation.

The function of evaluation has a history of intense debate. Evaluations are used to make judgments about the performance of professionals (Glass, 1969; Scriven, 1967), provide detailed descriptions of programs (Stake, 1967), plan or improve programs (Provus, 1969; Rossi, Freeman, & Wright, 1979), and detect cause/effect relationships and generalizations (Cronbach, 1963). Types of evaluations that accomplish any one of these aims are easy to find. Large-scale evaluations that make multiple comparisons of various factors have been conducted to determine the impact of educational programs like Head Start (Cicerelli, 1969) and televised instruction like Sesame Street (Ball & Bogatz, 1970; Bogatz & Ball, 1971). Evaluation results also have been combined with basic developmental research and used by investigators such as Bronfenbrenner (1974a, 1974b) to derive generalized explanations of developmental processes.

Individuals also disagree about the models that outline processes and procedures for reaching evaluation goals (for example, Goodwin, 1974; House, 1978; Popham, 1975; Stake, 1976; Worthen & Sanders, 1973). Although discussions continue, two points can be inferred: the range and flexibility of evaluation efforts are tremendous, and the choice of a specific set of evaluation goals restricts the conclusions that can be drawn.

Throughout this book the role of *process* for child-service providers and programs has been stressed. Therefore, it is appropriate to introduce a generic form of evaluation that focuses on process—formative user-based evaluation. Although it is not within the scope of this text to make an exhaustive review of evaluation procedures, an approach with potential application across child-service programs is presented. Formative evaluations continually assess process, providing feedback for the improvement of ongoing programs (Scriven, 1967). This type of evaluation often is contrasted with summative evaluation, which is product-oriented and judges the overall success of a program. Although summative evaluations often are used to determine a program's funding or continuance, they rarely are designed to improve the delivery of services.

Formative evaluations may be conducted either by experts external to the program or by staff. User-based evaluations reflect economic reality: continued evaluation can be assured only by the active role of staff and supervisors. Although expert help may be essential for initial planning and periodic monitoring of evaluations, procedures should maximize existing resources and minimize expenditure of additional time, money, and effort. The numerous advantages of formative user-based evaluations include: (1) the commitment of program staff to the conscientious completion and use of evaluation efforts; (2) the sensitivity of evaluation designs to long-term or slow changes; and (3) the potential for program improvement using assessment of process (Bernstein & Freeman, 1975; Coulson, 1976; Franklin & Thrasher, 1976; Provus, 1969).

This chapter explores the answers to two questions: what are the characteristics of formative user-based evaluation, and how can this type of evaluation be developed and used?

Characteristics of formative user-based evaluation

Formative user-based evaluation seeks to developmentally improve ongoing programs. In this case, development implies continuous changes; improvement occurs by increasing the match between a program's ideal and actual functioning. Evaluation can maximize program improvement to the extent that it meets two criteria—utility and validity. Utility in this context means that professionals must use evaluation results when making decisions about their programs. Validity refers to the accuracy of the match between program and evaluation, both in terms of content (what is looked at) and process (how it is measured).

Utility of evaluations

A substantial literature documents how evaluation efforts and program decisions can function independently (Cox, 1977; National Institute for Mental Health, 1971; Rein & White, 1977; Rossi & Williams, 1972; Weiss, 1972, 1973). Evaluation results are only used if (1) they answer questions professionals consider relevant; (2) the answers are in an understandable form; and (3) the results are available before program decisions are made. Because professionals pose different questions, each evaluation is unique in terms of information collected, format selected, and time required (Hawkins, Roffman & Osborne, 1978; Patterson, 1971; Rossi et al., 1979). However, to the extent that outcomes, transactions, and antecedents of different programs overlap, evaluation results can be compared (see Chapter 6).

One advantage of formative user-based evaluation is that it increases the program staff's commitment to the conscientious completion and use of evaluation efforts.

Validity of evaluations

Valid information refers not only to issues of design and measurement, but also to issues of match. To be valid, criteria for evaluation must match program ideals (Kamii & Elliot, 1971) and measurement schemes must match program structure and resources. The one perfect set of goals or measurement instruments cannot be found because validity is determined only by the relative value various tools have for particular programs.

The classic example of mismatch between program and measurement occurred when evaluators for Project Follow-Through attempted to use standardized tests (for example, Metropolitan Achievement Tests, Intellectual Achievement Responsibility Scale, Raven's Colored Progressive Matrices) to measure the effectiveness of the Educational Development Center's (EDC) programs. According to EDC, evaluators overlooked the primary goals of independence, self-esteem, and intrinsic motivation. Results, although consistent with Follow-Through's evaluation, did not match EDC's philosophy or goals (Burris & Chittendon, 1971; Stanford Research Institute, 1971, 1973). Thus, a final goal of formative user-based evaluation must be developmental improvement of the evaluation plan. If an evaluation does not provide valid information or if results are no longer used, it must be modified.

The process of formative user-based evaluation

The model of evaluation presented here is derived from the work of Provus (1969), Stake (1967), Suchman (1967), Peters (1977), and Rossi, Freeman, and Wright (1979). Its application to educational programs produces a series of related questions about services provided: (1) The ideal program—What are desirable program outcomes? What can be used to produce these? What antecedent resources and conditions are required for these transactions to be effective? (2) The actual program—Are suggested strategies producing desired outcomes under prescribed conditions? (3) Differences between ideal and actual programs—Why is the program not performing optimally—that is, not matching the ideal? What changes are most likely to improve ongoing services?

Each set of questions dictates a step in the process of evaluation. First, individuals must translate their ideas into a specification of the ideal program's functioning in terms of antecedents, transactions, and outcomes. Second, the content and process of a measurement scheme must be designed to assess the day-to-day functioning of the actual program. Finally, raw information must be transformed and combined with other inputs for altering both program and evaluation. Figure 13–1 presents a model showing the interaction of these elements. Clearly, conscientious completion of each phase ensures an evaluation that will yield meaningful information upon which key program decisions can be based.

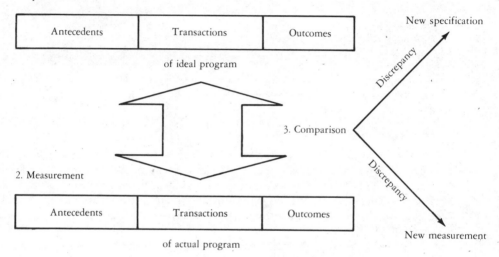

Figure 13–1 Model for Program Evaluation

Specification of the ideal program

According to the proposed model, the structure and function of the perfect program can be described when professionals specify three program components: (1) desired outcomes; (2) transactions that promote outcomes; and (3) antecedent conditions necessary for transactions to be effective. Table 13–1 summarizes these dimensions.

Outcomes. To specify program outcomes, a professional must fully describe the nature and targets of changes a program desires to produce (Bronfenbrenner, 1974a; Berlack, 1970; Peters, 1977; Peters, Golbeck, & Busch-Nagel, 1977). Targets for change are recipients of the service, which in preschool programs, for example, typically include children, parents, and student teachers. However, programs of broader scope may desire to influence the community or institution of which they are part (Goodwin, 1974). Describing the nature of change must deal with what changes and how changes are shown. Outcomes may be in multiple areas and expressed through many channels. The patterns that changes exhibit can vary as well. Influence may be immediate or delayed, long- or short-term, and generalized or specific to situations. Each desired outcome specifies the particular combination of who and what will be changed.

TABLE 13-1 Specifications of the dimensions of the ideal program

Outcomes	Transactions	Antecedents
1. Who changes— child, teacher, parent, supervisor, institution, community? 2. What changes— attitudes, behaviors skills, dispositions, abilities? 3. How does it change— short vs. long-term, generalized vs. specific, temporary vs. permanent, immediate vs. delayed? 4. How much change is desired—skill levels, unit change, readiness?	1. Who interacts— child, teacher, parent, supervisor? 2. With what or whom— materials, space, peers, teachers, schedule? 3. How do they interact— frequency, persistence, intensity, affect, variety, creativity?	1. What are necessary conditions? a. Who— children, parents, teachers? b. What— demographic information, attitudes, abilities? 2. What are necessary resources—physical space, materials, staff, money, time?

Individuals also must specify changes they wish to avoid (Berlack, 1970; Stake, 1967). These can take the form of either negative outcomes or absence of positive behaviors. For example, although promoters of motivation-oriented programs do not consider outstanding academic achievement in the first year of school (as indexed by grades) to be a major program goal, neither do they believe that their programs interfere with academic achievement. Hence, educators may occasionally choose to assess outcomes, the presence of which add little information about program effectiveness but whose absence indicates need for program change.

Specifying how much of a change is desired must occur as well (Coulson, 1976; Klein & Kosecoff, 1973; Rossi et al., 1979). As Coulson (1976) asks, "What is the benchmark against which program performance can be evaluated?" (p. 9). There are two ways to deal with this issue, one relative and one absolute. Ideally, educators would like to discover whether programs produce more change than would be expected to occur if participants were left alone; obviously, approximations of this ideal must be made. Normative information about particular processes in comparable populations, logical reasoning about prerequisite skill levels, and expert opinion may be combined to form estimates of the magnitude of change desired to meet goals (Klein & Kosecoff, 1973; Peters, 1977).

Transactions. Transactions, which focus on interactions and strategies, detail the dimensions of day-to-day functioning of a program that should produce desired outcomes. Analysis of ideal transactions allows professionals to explain and measure interactions. For example, ideally judges are to use informal procedures with juveniles in need of supervision and are to function as parent surrogates. The careful description of the desired interactions between judges and juveniles guides the choice of measures and the degree of satisfaction with actual interactions.

As with outcomes, planners must specify unintended and undesirable transactions—that is, interactions that might inhibit or interfere with positive change. Transaction information is essential to answer process questions (Bernstein & Freeman, 1975; Ciarlo, 1977; Coulson, 1976; Goodwin, 1974; Rossi, 1978; Williams & Elmore, 1976). Evaluation research, for example, shows that educational programs can be differentiated by transactional variables, which exert varying influences on outcomes (Bissell, 1973; Peters et al., 1977; Miller & Dyer, 1975; Soar & Soar, 1972; Stallings, 1975).

Specifying transactions is an easier task if relationships among program participants are close, because desired outcomes for one participant form the basis for successful interactions with another. A case in point is the foster-parent/child dyad. Desired outcomes for children—healthy, happy, socially adjusted, and so on—require that foster parents use strategies with children that are consistent and supportive (see Chapter 8). Thus, the correct application of these strategies produces the desired transactions for children.

Antecedents. Identification of outcomes and transactions are qualified by a third variable—antecedents (conditions and resources) required for strategies to produce outcomes (Stake, 1967). Conditions index the competencies and characteristics of participants prior to an experience. With foster care, for example, hard-to-place children tend to be older or handicapped. Particular resources and conditions are necessary for optimal transactions (see Chapter 8).

This information explains in part the differential effectiveness of transactions and generality of outcomes. Within programs, strategy effectiveness may be mediated by characteristics of participants (Peters et al., 1977; Goodwin, 1974) or limited by inadequate resources. Clearly, decisions for program improvement must take such factors into account. Between programs, professionals concern themselves with the question of generalizability (Coulson, 1976). In the case of child abuse, for instance, with what group of children and families, and under what circumstances, can professionals expect specified transactions to eliminate child mistreatment? Should special programs be developed for high-risk families who do not have community support networks?

Whenever possible, it is desirable to specify those characteristics of participants that render certain transactions more potent for producing change (Rossi et al., 1979). For example, educational programs designed to improve intellectual achievement of children from low SES groups posit various deficiencies that must be remedied to improve performance. The Becker–Engleman model identifies a lack of specific skills; the Demonstration and Research Center for Early Education isolates quality of parent/child interaction. Program goals and strategies differ accordingly. Upon further specification of relevant attributes, implications for transactions and outcome patterns become clear (see Chapter 6).

The specification process

Many of the methods that theorists suggest for formulating program objectives are equally valid for specifying relevant transactions and antecedents. Overall, researchers agree that consensus and commitment are essential for evaluations to be implemented and used optimally (Berk & Rossi, 1976; Wholey, 1977). Methods to formulate outcomes, transactions, and antecedents can be classified as deductive or inductive.

Deductive methods. Deductive methods derive program features from general assumptions or propositions. Programs can be based on educational, child-development, or psychological theories (Butler et al., 1971; DeVries, 1974; Kamii, 1971; Parker, 1974; Peters, 1977; Peters, Cohen, & McNichol, 1974) or derive aspects from empirical research (Rossi et al., 1979).

Often programs reflecting a deductive method support social values such as protecting children and strengthening the American nuclear family. For instance, studies that examine how different professionals, communities, and judges perceive child mistreatment and the related degree of seriousness show the relationships between perceptions and intervention decisions that attempt to support societal ideals. You may recall from the discussion in Chapter 12 that removal of a child from a home situation was only suggested in extreme cases of abuse such as sexual assault.

The difficulty with many child programs, whether substitute services, protective services, or day care, is in the interpretation of society's values. Specific programs such as those generated from a theory and based on prototypic models are much easier to evaluate even though difficulties in specification exist.

Inductive methods. Methods such as curriculum analysis (Baker, 1972) where educators analyze existing materials and reconstruct the underlying assumptions, objectives, and transactions illustrate the inductive method. Also, survey methods (Peters & Marcus, 1973; Stake, 1967; Taylor & McGuire, 1966), which gather opinions of relevant groups (parents, teachers, program planners, community leaders), are used to induce aspects of a program. (Chaper 5 presents a needs assessment questionnaire for making child-program-planning decisions.)

The government and agencies greatly support the inductive method. Reams of information about specific types of people are obtained. In and of themselves, figures on the number of unwed teenagers, children in need of supervision, hard-to-place children, adopted children, and so on are only useful for focusing efforts and resources. The inductive method only becomes meaningful when experts can use research, theory, and experience to deduce appropriate intervention strategies to correct or prevent problems. Hence, both inductive and deductive methods should be employed to derive child services. Even when these methods are implemented, the process of trying to establish social policy for children and families is difficult (see Chapter 11).

Recommended procedures. Since even experienced professionals may have difficulty articulating outcomes, transactions, and antecedents for program development, three techniques are recommended. First, the ideal participant must be described: What would they do, say, think? How would they respond to various situations and people? What is an ideal program? How will participants perform the year following such a program? Five years later? Ten years later? The ideal profile identifies and clarifies assumptions about optimal functioning.

When antecedents are specific as to target groups, identifying the ideal is easier. When parents select services the issue of the ideal is less complicated. But when services must be imposed, as in situations of child neglect, professionals seem to refrain from describing the ideal, in this case the ideal family, even after extensive study.

Likewise, how can the ideal community—one that has a certain type of resources—be identified? Perhaps, as was mentioned in Chapter 7, each community must be inductively analyzed to deduce the type of support systems that would ideally benefit members.

External factors such as inflation and unemployment often prohibit the luxury of speculating about goals. For example, the minimal standard of living set for families shifts as economics and opportunities for employment change. Thus, many goals are relative to their social and historical contexts (see Chapters 1, 2, and 3).

A second technique can aid in the generation of undesirable outcomes. Imagine the consequences of the most extreme form of intervention. For instance, programs that promote cooperation must be wary of conformity. For teachers, conscientious planning may be purchased at the price of spontaneity. One must be aware that there can be too much of a good thing.

Many intervention techniques attempt to prevent additional problems or avoid problems altogether. In foster care, for example, there is concern about permanency rather than just placement. In the case of child abuse, entire families rather than just parents are treated in efforts to prevent further problems. In general, efforts are made to involve parents in child-service delivery whenever possible, which should not only increase the likelihood of successful intervention efforts but also reduce factors that may interfere with interventions.

A third technique focuses attention on behaviors or characteristics that have been neglected because time, opportunity, or interest in their development was not provided. For example, programs that schedule only periods for individual activity may not allow the development of group skills. To illustrate this point more broadly, much literature on the impact of stress has been conducted over the last decade. Stress can result in mental and physical aberrations such as suicides and increased incidence of heart attacks (Hultsch & Deutsch, 1981). Though it has been shown that experience in dealing with stress helps people learn coping strategies (Lieberman, 1975), most interventions aim to reduce stress; little attention is directed toward training children to adapt to stress as part of a regular educational effort. Training programs do exist for high-risk groups, but are not abundant. With increasing rates of suicides among children, a major corrective intervention effort is needed.

Seldom are resources allocated for fostering behaviors or characteristics that are not critical for survival. Perhaps with new focus on prevention rather than remediation or rehabilitation, this arena will be evaluated more carefully and inroads will be made in optimizing the development of children, families, and communities.

In the final analysis of an ideal program, professionals, parents, and government officials must assimilate all of this information and put it into perspective. Provus (1969) suggests several logical criteria that may aid in this analysis: clarity, internal consistency, comprehensiveness, and compatibility with other programs with similar goals. After the information has been synthesized, professionals can submit written program specifications to experts and community members for a "test of completeness" (Provus, 1969; Lindbloom, 1969). This checking procedure assures planners that interpretations were correctly made and assures relevant groups that their opinions were heard and valued. Professional organizations or the local or federal government could serve as a final clearinghouse to reduce the likelihood of duplicated services and to increase efficiency.

Measurement of programs

Answers to questions of what is to be measured, and when, are derived from program specifications. The question of selection and use of measurement instruments also is derived from program goals and resources, including type and number of staff, expertise and training levels, and duties and responsibilities. Researchers have rightfully been concerned with the need to develop evaluation instruments that reflect program goals (Goodwin, 1974; Kamii & Elliot, 1971; Minuchin, Biber, Shapiro, & Zimiles, 1969; Stephens, 1967). As Evans (1974) cautions, "The value of measures . . . depends on the purpose for which they are being used" (p. 301). Thus, evaluators search for and catalogue measures appropriate for particular programs such as early childhood educational programs (see Evans, 1974; Goodwin, 1974; Kamii, 1971; Morris & Fitz-Gibbon, 1978).

For the development of a formative user-based evaluation, measurement selection is determined by additional criteria. Just as an evaluation's validity is enhanced when specifications and assessments are well matched, an evaluation's utility depends on matching assessment procedures with program resources (staff, skills, and schedule). Thus, program specifications and resources must be used to dictate assessment formats.

Different kinds of assessments provide different kinds of information and place varying requirements on providers and recipients of services. Four of the vast array of assessment types will be discussed: interviews, observation, standardized assessments, and factual data. Each is critiqued with reference to formats, results, and demands on program resources. Evaluation instruments such as observational schemes and interviews often are similar in format to intervention strategies. Developing a functional evaluation system, therefore, can directly help service delivery (see Chapter 4).

While they differ on format and type of information generated, the four assessment types—interview, observation, standardized assessment, and factual data—have certain properties in common. First, they can be used to collect information from a variety of sources, including children, parents, teachers, and community leaders. Second, they can be useful during any phase of program implementation—antecedents, transactions, or outcomes. Finally, each places demands on staff in terms of its development and use. These general principles are summarized for each measurement type in Table 13–2.

TABLE 13–2   Outcomes, structure, and staff demands of four assessment types

Measure	Format	Outcome	Structure	Development	User training
Interview	Structured dialogue	Opinions, perceptions, attitudes	High—questionnaire	Difficult	Easy
			Low—discussion	Easy	Difficult
Observation	Systematic recording of behavior	Behavior, behavior sequences	High—checklist	Difficult	Easy
			Low—definition	Easy	Difficult
Standardized assessment	Standard materials, instructions	Underlying attribute	High—test situation	Difficult	Easy
			Low—test situation	Easy	Difficult
Factual information					
Demogrphic data	Interview questionnaire	Facts	High	Easy	Easy
Unobtrusive data	System of collection	Program involvement	High	Easy	Easy

Interview assessment. Interviews generally are conversations in which a professional presents a set of issues to which a program participant responds. Issues can be of any form, from specific questions to general topics; answers can range from selection between alternatives to open-ended monologue. Parents can be questioned about their attitudes toward child rearing (Baumrind, 1971), their knowledge of the program, or their satisfaction with their child's progress. Students can evaluate the effectiveness of their own training for producing certain skills (Rossi et al., 1979) or they can make self-judgments about strengths and weaknesses. Children can be asked their opinions about activities, field trips, or classroom rules (Kamii, 1971; Lavatelli, 1970).

Various interview assessments have been constructed to elicit a range of opinions, attitudes, and perceptions. However, if existing instruments are not appropriate, the professional may decide to develop one that will serve his or her precise purpose. Often the rough draft of an interview can be formulated simply by identifying and systematizing current questions or issues. More structured interviews may require considerable thought and modification to ensure that items accurately communicate the intent behind the questions.

As questions become less exact and answers more open-ended, an increase in interviewer skill and experience is required to elicit meaningful data. Tape recorders and verbatim written records are only a temporary solution. Staff must be trained to recognize and record aspects of answers that reflect issues or areas of concern.

Observational assessment. Essentially, observations refer to the systematic examination and recording of behaviors or behavior sequences. Specific observational schemes vary in how the participant is observed and what content and behaviors are isolated. Observation is ideally suited for the detection of short- and long-term behavior changes in context—for example, a day-care center, foster homes, or courtroom. Verbal and nonverbal behavior toward a child and adult's use of praise and encouragement during a teaching session are two examples of behavior that can be isolated.

A wide variety of observational systems have been developed for use in measuring different behaviors (Evans, 1974; McReynolds, 1968; Schoggen & Schoggen, 1971; Simon & Boyer, 1970; Verma & Peters, 1975). Depending on the scale and scope of the instrument desired, the behavioral coding and observational format will vary. Format possibilities include rate and frequency counts, checklists, structured ratings, anecdotal records, narrative, and diaries. Typically, more specific behavioral codes are harder to develop but easier for staff to learn than are less structured codes. Two codes developed to measure self-help skills will illustrate this point. Specific self-help behaviors that occur in a target classroom setting, including such items as "puts on coat with no adult help," "throws away cup and napkin with no reminders" could be itemized on a structured checklist, which observers would use to record the occurrence of each type of behavior. Generating the list is time-consuming; user training is minimal. In a less structured coding system, observers would be given a general definition of self-help skills (such as "spontaneous occurrence of self-help behavior in the absence of adult supervision"). While this scale can be developed quickly, considerable instruction and experience is required to achieve a consensus about what constitutes self-help behavior and adult supervision.

Operationally defining behaviors often is difficult, as evidenced by the complexity of contextual factors—intentionality, effect, evaluation, and standards—used in defining child abuse and neglect (see Chapter 7). Depending on the degree to which each factor is stressed, different child-maltreatment behaviors will be observed. This difficulty exacerbates the problem of identification, the first step in any effective approach to child services.

Standardized assessment. This type of assessment is characterized by standard instructions, materials, and scoring procedures. For preschool children, assessment materials can be objects or pictures, responses can be verbal or nonverbal (Peters, 1977). For adults, standardized measures include traditional tests and rating

Identifying the behavior common to various activities (such as self-initiation in the case of self-help skills) will often aid staff in the learning of a specific structured observational code.

procedures. Standardized assessments are available for a variety of attributes (Evans, 1974; Kamii, 1971).

The results of such assessments are usually interpreted as indices of underlying traits or dispositions such as curiosity or moral reasoning that may mediate behavior across a variety of situations and vary depending upon when the assessment was made. The methodological rigor needed to construct valid standardized assessments makes impractical the development of unique measuring instruments. Luckily, a wide assortment of valid measures exist, although certainly aspects of development can be identified for which no generally accepted measurement tool is available.

Providing users with detailed instructions and standard materials assures consistent administration of procedures. Additionally, participants must be desensitized to the test-taking situation. For children, a gamelike format and placement of assessments in an unthreatening situation can minimize anxiety. Sensitivity to the many factors (for example, pacing) that influence adult performance should alter administration procedures and influence the interpretation of results (Hultsch & Deutsch, 1981).

Factual information.　Objective factual data can be of two types: demographic or unobtrusive (see Rossi et al., 1979, for examples with children). *Demographic data* denote facts about children, families, professionals, programs, or communities regarding factors such as age, sex, birth order, socioeconomic status, number of parents, and length of time in the community. These facts, which often are collected during intake interviews, provide valuable information about relevant antecedent conditions.

Nondemographic factual information is termed *unobtrusive data* (Webb, Campbell, Schwartz, & Sechrist, 1966) because collection does not necessitate direct contact with participants. Unobtrusive data—for example, the numbers of children receiving immunization shots or the number of visits to a social worker—can be useful in indexing program involvement and the use of services. These easily tabulated indices help explain differential program effectiveness.

Collection of factual information usually requires setting up a system to gather, record, store, and retrieve data (Cernea & Tepping, 1977). Demographic data may be acquired via questionnaires or interviews. The simplest example of unobtrusive data collection is attendance taking. One system for recording parent involvement in a child program is to require parents to sign a sheet that has been posted on the observation-booth door.

Much headway has been made in the development of retrieval systems that house factual information on the national level. For instance, a highly sophisticated computerized information retrieval system was developed by the Interagency Research Information System (IRIS) (Social Research Group, 1979). This system facilitates agency cooperation and reduces repetitive efforts of service recipients, but it also raises a concern about the misuse of information, especially with regard to an individual's right to privacy. With continued technological and legal advances, it is likely that its use will be carefully monitored and controlled (see Chapter 11).

Assessment scheme.　The final phase of planning an evaluation is organizing the measurement process. This assessment scheme details what is assessed, measurement instruments used, individuals involved, and time and preparations required. Evaluation procedures can be organized by an overview assessment scheme— a plan that follows each portion of the evaluation developmentally, providing professionals with a clear working guide and a comprehensive summary of the proposed evaluation. In addition, actual evaluation efforts can be monitored, eliciting valuable information about whether the evaluation is effectively implemented.

Table 13-3 presents an overview format listing all assessments along two dimensions: program participants and assessment timing. Within those two dimensions, professionals can place the relevant aspects to be measured and the proposed measurement tools in order of priority. For critical features, more than one type of assessment should be used. For example, if an important goal for teacher training is social reinforcement, the aspects to be measured include not only whether teachers can define the term (as measured by a standardized test) but also whether they can use the skill with different children (which requires observation) and

TABLE 13-3   Overview evaluation assessment scheme

	Before (dates) Antecedents	During (dates) Transactions	After (dates) Outcomes		
			After program begins	After program completion	Much later
Children	Priority #1 Instruments Priority #2 Instruments	Priority #1 Instruments Priority #2 Instruments	Priority #1 Instruments Priority #2 Instruments	Priority #1 Instruments Priority #2 Instruments	Priority #1 Instruments Priority #2 Instruments
Child-service providers					
Setting					
Supervisors					
Community					
Institution					

recognize its importance in classroom functioning (collected in an interview). Whenever feasible, the use of multiple measures is advised to assure a comprehensive assessment of important aspects.

Timing of assessments is determined by program specifications (Caro, 1971; Coulson, 1976; Evans, 1974; Fortune, 1972), information about the minimum time needed to produce effects, and knowledge of behavior stability and durability. Typically, an evaluation of antecedents (resources and participant conditions) happens prior to program implementation, process measures of transactions are monitored more or less continuously, and outcome variables are looked at in time for key decisions but not before effects have had a chance to accrue.

The developmental plan (see Table 13–4) details the preparations necessary for assessments to proceed on schedule. Essentially, they are developed backward from the target date, specifying each step and allowing time for its completion. Preparations for evaluating an early childhood educational program would include identification or development of appropriate instruments, training of users, and practical activities such as procuring space, scheduling assessments, and duplicating scoring sheets.

The assignment of roles is appropriate at this point, both for carrying out tasks within each timeline and for monitoring the completion of each step (Rossi et al., 1979). This guarantees that practical problems such as overload of certain personnel and scheduling conflicts can be identified and solved prior to program implementation. Additionally, overlap of various aspects can be eliminated to increase efficiency. The development of these organizational charts should help produce a valid, useful evaluation that answers the questions raised and matches staff and the program structure for which it was developed.

Evaluation results

The comparison between ideal and actual program functioning provides the basis for program improvement. Once the ideal program is specified and characteristics of the actual program measured, the process of interpretation

TABLE 13-4 Developmental evaluation plan

	Prior to start	Continuous throughout	End of 1st & 2nd quarters	End of program
Outcomes				
Motivational— curiosity, etc.	Interview, individual assessment	Observation	Individual assessment	Interview, individual assessment
Emotional				
Social				
Cognitive				
Physical				
Etc.				
Transactions				
Social environment— teachers, peers, rules	Interview, individual assessment	Observation	Individual assessment, self-report, expert rating	Interview, individual assessment, self-report, expert rating
Physical environment				
Etc.				
Antecedents				
Demographic	Interview	None	None	None
Autobiographical	Interview			
Personal	Interview			
Individual	Individual assessment			
Etc.				

translates discrepancies into concrete suggestions for change. Two phases of interpretation are considered: (1) translation of raw evaluation data into usable information, and (2) the use of this information for pinpointing problems in program and evaluation and generating solutions.

Translation of raw results. Condensation of raw results depends on the particular questions being asked (Suchman, 1967). Questions about overall performance or attitude (for example, parents' feelings about the program) can be answered by looking at group averages. Questions about behaviors or opinions of subgroups (for example, children with a particular temperament type) can be assessed by dividing participants into groups on the basis of some characteristic and comparing each group's performance. To monitor change over time (for example, a teacher's acquisition of group skills), a participant's behavior or disposition should be considered across several assessments.

Within these constraints, specific guidelines or criteria for data summarization can be established. Weekly and monthly reports, charts, graphs, and checklists are useful vehicles for data summarization. Structural supports for completing transformation processes can take the form of convenient information storage (notebooks, files) and scheduling blocks of time for data summarization. Finally, if staff members can see their results being used for making meaningful decisions, their consistent cooperation will be maximized.

Program improvement. A program is successful when outcomes are in the specified direction and reasonably greater than could be expected in the program's absence. Ultimately, the information accepted as evidence of this conclusion reflects a value judgment (Stake, 1970). Many evaluations conclude that a completely random, controlled design is necessary to rule out competing hypotheses (Rossi et al., 1979).

Although conclusions necessarily are limited without these controls, practical realities often require the use of more approximate methods.

The following types of standards can be used to compare program outcomes: (1) pretests of program participants on the same dimensions; (2) national test norms for populations comparable to program participants; (3) absolute standards of performance, often called criterion-referenced standards (Klein & Kosecoff, 1973); and (4) the judgement of experts derived from previous experience or substantive expertise (Coulson, 1976; Rossi et al., 1979, Provus, 1969; Stake, 1967). Coulson (1976) suggests that in some cases participants can be arrayed along a dimension of program exposure or intensity (as indexed, for example, by attendance or participation). If a program is effective, participant outcomes should be influenced by involvement.

Decisions about effectiveness also can be made on the basis of expenditures. Cost-benefit and cost-effectiveness models compare estimates of benefits (tangible and intangible) and costs (direct and indirect) to make statements about proportional savings or costs per substantive unit change (Rossi et al., 1979). Often the local or federal government uses these models to make decisions about which new and existing programs should be funded.

In addition to statements about accomplishment of goals, service providers should examine what's working, what's not working, and why. Conclusions about what is working can facilitate decisions about which transactions to keep and promote and which may be trimmed for efficiency's sake. Additionally, professionals should be responsible for communicating characteristics of environments, strategies, and interactions found effective in promoting certain outcomes.

The process of evaluation described here is designed to detect discrepancies between ideal and actual program functioning. However, improvement requires more than problem identification; solutions also are needed. Solutions can be generated only when evaluations can determine why goals aren't being reached. Three basic classes of problems generally account for a program's failure to produce desired results: (1) designed strategies are not being properly implemented in the program; (2) goals or strategies are not appropriate for participants with certain characteristics; or (3) strategies used in the program are not effective in influencing target behaviors. Each of these conclusions identifies a different problem and generates alternate solutions.

A general scheme for discovering why a program is not producing a desired outcome involves systematic elimination of each of the above possibilities. First, the adequate implementation of strategies must be checked. If, for example, teachers are not using planned curricula or supervisors are not modeling desired behavior according to specifications, then strategies are not receiving a fair test. Observations, teacher competence assessments, curriculum plans, and other transaction data can depict actual program functioning, which then can be compared to ideal transactions. The extent to which desired strategies are being implemented thus can be determined (see Datta, 1977; McLaughlin, 1975; and Rossi, 1978, for examples.) If transactions are reliably occurring, however, the educator can check to see whether strategies are totally ineffective or only ineffective for subgroups of participants. Perhaps outcomes only appear for children who are most deprived or most motivated. Unobtrusive and demographic data plus antecedent assessments of ability and attributes provide possible answers to this question.

Finally, if accurately implemented strategies are producing no effects, the strategies either are not effective or more time is needed for change. Outside sources of information are often useful for answering these questions. Other programs with similar strategies may provide perspectives on the reasonableness of timing and outcome expectations.

To determine whether strategies are ineffectual or more time is needed, planners must actively interpret the pattern of results, with evaluation simply as one more information source (Cox, 1977; Patten 1975). Sometimes practical constraints will dictate which possible cause of a problem is tested first. Even if it becomes evident that specified transactions affect only certain subgroups, it may not be realistic to replace all children not belonging to the group. One practical option is to concentrate the effective strategies on these children and try variations for other children. Likewise, strategies that show little effect may be maintained because of their impact on staff morale. Just as the identification of problems requires the blending of thought, experience, and evaluation results, so does the generation of solutions necessitate practical as well as theoretical considerations. Solutions should be implemented carefully and systematically.

Evaluation improvement. The validity and utility criteria examined earlier can be used as ideal outcomes for formative user-based evaluation. Developmental improvement of evaluation tools demands an understanding of why goals were not met. Three typical program evaluation problems are:(1) planned evaluation strategies are not being properly conducted; (2) strategies planned are not appropriate for particular programs; or (3) strategies planned are not effective for gathering required data.

The first problem can be detected by monitoring assessment activities. Are planned evaluation strategies conducted accurately and consistently? Are summarized results available when needed? Are overview and developmental charts followed? If the evaluation is proceeding precisely as planned and results are still not useful or valid, perhaps the strategy is not appropriate for the particular program. It is important to achieve a match between program specification and areas of measurement and between a program structure and types of measurement. Match can be assessed by careful reconsideration of the formative evaluation process, by cross-checking evaluations of similar programs, or by consultation with experts. Finally, assessments chosen may not be good indicators of program dimensions, calling for more careful specification of program aspects and multiple or alternative measures.

Unintended outcomes of using formative evaluation also must be scrutinized. Even ideal evaluations can create stress for participants, in terms of both time and anxiety. Assessments may strain relationships between observers and participants. Parents may feel their privacy is invaded. Children may tire of answering questions. Open-ended interviews, group and personal discussions, and special attention to vulnerable children may be required to detect and remedy feelings of aversion. Of course, unintended outcomes also may be positive. Specification of program ideals may enhance staff focus and cohesion; simple awareness of program objectives may improve staff performance. Measurement schemes may facilitate observation and communication skills. "The single most important finding from interaction analysis research for early childhood educators is that student teachers who are taught interaction analysis are generally more indirect, supporting, and accepting of their pupils than student teachers unfamiliar with this approach" (Goodwin, 1974, p. 296). Participating in the steady improvement of a program for children and their families and in generating information that may be useful to other child-service providers seems to bring a special satisfaction to professionals (Coulson, 1976).

Conclusion

Formative user-based evaluations have a history of successful implementation for early-childhood educational programs with a behavior orientation (Evans, 1975). Program goals usually are explicit and measurement schemes, although complex, can be derived more or less directly from program specifications. Acceptable strategies and their uses are prescribed. Evaluation results, although not always labeled as such, typically play a central role in decisions about key program aspects.

More process- or motivation-oriented programs (see Evans, 1975) usually have not employed evaluation and measurement as systematically. This is no accident: some proponents of process-oriented programs do not think evaluation has much to offer their programs (Rhine, 1973). Even those who support evaluation point out that exact specification of goals, transactions, and antecedents is problematic and instruments for the measurement of key program aspects are severely lacking (Kamii, 1971). Consequently, information about effective and ineffective program aspects are not communicated.

The process of formative user-based evaluation can be applied to various child-service programs. Constructing an evaluation that matches a program's content to its structure may solve some of the intervention problems. Also, program comparisons can be made, and positive and negative features of programs can be determined, documented, and shared.

Summary

Examples drawn from child-service programs illustrate the complexity of actual evaluation procedures. A formative user-based process of evaluation provides specific information about what works, what does not, and why. Documented information then feeds back into programs as reflected in alterations of outcomes, transactions, and antecedents. This process becomes useful to staff in terms of their structure and functioning; to children, who directly receive services; to families, who often seek information for program selection; to communities, which attempt to meet the needs of their members; and to local, state, and federal government agencies, which rely on evaluation results for funding and continuance decisions.

Formative user-based evaluation also reflects key themes suggested throughout this book. A developmental view of evaluation, supported within the dynamic interaction model considered in Chapter 1, not only allows for change but also promotes change by its support of continued reassessment of specifications. Since social contexts at all levels are constantly altering, such an evaluative mode can accommodate to them. By supporting both deductive and inductive methods for delineating program outcomes, transactions, and antecedents, societal values can be incorporated in the evaluation process. Although plurality may make this process difficult, ideally the model presents the possibility for moving toward some cohesive social policy for child services. This assessment process incorporates and values all sources of information, encouraging the attitude that theory, empirical research, and applied practices are of equal importance. This system also solicits the opinions and values of service recipients, which are critical for program effectiveness and for the establishment of social policy.

Formative user-based evaluation will never be a panacea for alleviating the problems associated with intervening in the lives of children and families. But it may be the vehicle to help correct the fragmented delivery system and to prevent further disorganization, inefficiency, and ineffectiveness. To the extent that the learning, experiences, and thoughts of laypersons and professionals converge, the process of formative user-based evaluation can optimize scientific understanding and service to children and families. The success of this process for early-childhood educators encourages other service providers to grapple with the challenges of formative user-based evaluation.

14

Commitment

Chapter overview

Ecological and developmental perspectives are used to challenge the present and contemplate future designs of child-service programs and policies. Choices are made either to maintain the status quo or to extend thinking, feeling, and behavior to serve children and families with a sensitivity to society's increasing complexity.

Issues to consider

How can ecological and developmental perspectives assist child-service program and policy designs?

Why should dimensions of social change be included in child-service program and policy planning?

What moral responsibility is associated with the delivery of child services?

How can designs for the future include the "good life"?

What role can professionals have in planning, implementing, and evaluating child services?

Why is commitment critical for the effective delivery of child services?

Introduction

Child services constitute a diverse, complex social arena with political, economic, and moral undertones that evoke intense controversies and contradictions. Considered separately, each critical issue or problem projects some inkling of the intricacies of the larger context in which child services operate. But these individual elements have little meaning outside themselves. Thus this book used information about individual programs, issues, and problems in order to analyze similarities and differences and explain the inception and evolution of certain relationships and conflicts. Since educational programs, the responsibility for child care, and the meaning of minimal standards are not viewed in the same way, certain assumptions and techniques of analysis were employed to clarify and organize perspectives.

A developmental perspective shows that the potential for change persists throughout time. Accordingly, Chapters 1 and 2 addressed the ways in which different age groups are treated in society, the dynamics of child/family/society interactions, and the interrelationships of factors that influence particular programs and systems of service delivery. Chapters 3 and 4 contemplated an alternative to enhance the quality of life of children and the intervention mechanisms available to accomplish such goals. Chapters 5 through 10 examined in-depth changes related to specific programs, services, and parent/child interactions. Finally, the concept of change was considered from three vantage points: (1) advocacy and the meaning of social policy, (2) professionals and their roles as change agents, and (3) evaluations and ways to enhance program effectiveness.

Each person who has reached this juncture in the book no doubt has different perspectives and various perplexities. Many may expect some form of termination— a concise list of what we know or need to learn about child services; specific recommendations about the training needed to assume different professional roles; or at least some indication of specific modes of action for improving parenting, programs, or service delivery. Most people have learned to expect closure—do's and don'ts, rights or wrongs, or at least some means to differentiate and substantiate beliefs.

What have *you* resolved? Is our society getting better or worse? Do you consider societal change to be progress, or do you believe that change produces regressions and unnecessary problems? Who fashions change: saints, geniuses, and prophets, or ordinary men and women—parents and professionals, practitioners and researchers?

Your views on these issues influence your perspective about relationship issues, which are an important element in the delivery of child services. Your point of view about interaction dynamics may be pessimistic, optimistic, or somewhere in between. Do you believe struggles for dominance by participants in the child-service system (parents, children, professionals, government) will persist? Can and should decisions be made to determine the parameters of child care, areas of responsibility, and professional boundaries? Who should make these decisions, and how long should they operate?

Genuine acceptance of the developmental perspective advanced throughout this book involves, at a minimum, acknowledging the likelihood of societal change, and at a maximum, accepting some role in the change process. Ultimately, each of us— student, parent, and/or professional worker—has the potential to assist children to function as healthy, productive individuals. New roles and ways to maximize rewards and minimize punishments occur constantly over generations. This capability should help us acquire flexibility in our service of children, which then requires "getting outside ourselves" so our subjective beliefs may be observed, tested, and open to challenge and change.

And so, this final chapter returns to the developmental point of view and extends an ecological perspective to raise certain fundamental questions, to confront some societal issues, and to challenge personal and professional commitments to child services.

Society and social change

Social order

Society is stratified into categories based on age and gender, divisions of labor, and access to resources. Institutions and agencies maintain appropriate behaviors and attitudes of different age groups. History shows, however, that as privileged ranks emerged, typically those with more resources had more power over their distribution. Thus, economic considerations dominated social reform efforts. Women with no other means of support were allowed to enter the labor force and day facilities were established for the care of children. Economic growth was thought to provide each citizen with equal opportunities. The term *individualism* began to be used in reference to specialization. Children were tracked early in school and advances were made in health care and nutrition for children.

This hierarchy further supported individual differences—special children and families were identified to receive funds and legal systems codified and defended the rights and privileges of different groups. These differences promoted competition among individuals and institutions, even though often those involved were unwilling or unable to compete because they lacked knowledge, time, and other necessary resources.

Today, the poor and the weak still have difficulty challenging the rich and powerful, but they are forming groups and finding advocates who can help them gain power, especially through laws, referral systems, and class-action suits. Advocacy has taken on a new and distinctive meaning in the last decade. The advocate not only establishes or supports cases, serves as liaison, and improves situations, but also lobbies to change systems, institutions, and laws. In the field of child services,

Ultimately, each of us (student, parent, and/or worker) has the potential and the responsibility to help children function as healthy, productive individuals.

advocacy efforts mean working with the systems that affect families and children. In today's highly technological and rapidly changing society, advocates strive for accountability in systems that affect people's lives.

Advocates, whether professionals or parents, neither can nor should assume sole responsibility for changing the social order. Social change takes place in the context of how societal resources are used, managed, and distributed. In the broadest sense, all facets of society contribute to social change and reflect its consequences. Future changes in this ecological framework seem inevitable, for people will continue to use skills and knowledge (technology) to satisfy needs as they improve their access to resources. Further, the notion that advancements produce positive changes still prevails.

Why, then, are changes in child services so problematic? History shows lack of agreement over goals and problems. In fact, the service-delivery system is riddled with value conflicts and ambivalence toward recipients and providers as well as particular programs.

Social and political differences exacerbate those conflicts, directing questions from the general to the particular, the abstract to the concrete. How much federal and state monies should support services? What level should serve as a minimum standard for services? Which children should receive what type of foster-care arrangement? How can early-childhood programs become more effective? How many dysfunctional children can one teacher include in a classroom to promote learning for all children? Essentially, the inability to organize priorities makes answering these questions a formidable task.

Immobility

The inability to establish priorities and the increasing technological complexity could be used by parents and professionals to forestall change in service delivery. History shows that frustration exacerbates dichotomies and stereotypes. People are eager to focus blame for child abuse, foster-care difficulties, or child neglect. Parents are subjected to microscopic investigation used to generate a myriad of characteristics to explain parental failure, producing ill will and antagonism on the part of others. Interventions are reduced to secondary importance; professionals are pressured and parents expect quick corrective remedies; and many children are further victimized.

Complexity need not enhance feelings of frustration. Rather than using impotence as an excuse for shifting blame from parents to society, professionals and parents should accept their incapacities, acknowledge their complex reality, and gain needed information about children, adults, and their social contexts. Services could then be appropriately designed for families, neighborhoods, and communities, resulting in a balance between complex forces that enhance, support, and reduce stress among individuals and social systems.

Moral responsibility

Underlying many social, economic, and political disagreements that separate people and impede future planning and commitment is the extent to which free will or determinism is thought to shape the human condition. People who support free will often resist explanations of human behavior, asserting that to place individuals with all their varied emotions, attitudes, values, and behaviors into scientific hypotheses or, worse yet, simulated computer programs threatens their humanity. Determinists, on the other hand, believe in external forces beyond human control and tend to see human activities as predetermined by biological laws, instincts, or fixed ideologies. This approach locks people into trends and outcomes that are viewed as inevitable. Believers in self-determination, however, hold humans responsible for their activities and future.

Obviously, individuals and societies are limited by capabilities. The degree to which forces beyond human control are assumed to cause events is relative to prevailing knowledge. Early humans used religion and even magic to explain and cope with their worlds, but today people increasingly rely on science to explain nature's mysteries. The increase in the human capacity to intervene in the lives of individuals and structures of society reflects a shift from a total reliance on natural forces to an increasing reliance on people in relation to their environment. North (1976) observed that "Whatever we do to the natural and social environments today will affect the way we think, feel, and act tomorrow. This is how we shape the future bit by bit—often so slowly and imperceptibly that we altogether fail to perceive how the hard times befalling us are part of our own doing" (pp. 55–56).

This book has supported the rights of individual integrity and family privacy while still valuing the collective good. Two key questions continuously emerge, producing standoff debates: can the well-being of a society be achieved without limiting the possibilities of individual self-fulfillment, and can a society achieve successful outcomes when a substantial number of members are frustrated and alienated? Definitive answers are neither possible nor necessary. Achieving a balance of goals between the individual and the society is needed to instigate change in society's sociology, economics, and politics. For instance, the increase in single-parent and two-provider families in the last few decades has contributed to alterations in values, aspirations, and expectations—for example, support of working women and government funding of alternative child-care arrangements. Each person has the responsibility to let opinions be heard and actively participate in the social-change process.

The legal system is a fertile area for participation. Laws consistently have represented children when parents or guardians were considered "unfit." These laws have succeeded in breaking up families and confining children to institutional environments because of parental failure or a child's misconduct or handicap. Legal policy efforts could be directed toward keeping families together so children could identify with family life and develop into healthy adults.

Laws have been allowed to rule people rather than the other way around. People hide behind laws as if they are the savior of all of society's dilemmas, problems, and difficulties. Laws can obscure complexities because they foster an adversary perspective, which has helped to deter efforts to improve child services and rekindle wornout controversies.

Designs for the future

Despite a history of disagreements and debates, people's determination to improve their lives persist. People change where they live, the conditions under which they live, their expectations, and so on. People's motivation to attain the "good life" is determined greatly by their perceived access to resources and opportunities for promoting self-esteem, and by positive reinforcements. Individuals must see that their efforts provide them with an increasing quantity of resources.

Even at a societal level, quality and quantity are intertwined. The resources available depend on the size of the population making demands, which in turn provokes changes. How these resources are allocated affects the quality of life of the entire population. Although individuals, families, groups, and even societies differ with regard to what they value, how values are implemented behaviorally influences who gets what and who pays what cost. These values reflect the responsibility each member assumes in a given society.

Communities seem ready to assume responsibility for extreme situations such as with abusive families (Elder, 1977). A substantial proportion of respondents in a national opinion survey indicated that if they knew about family-abuse problems, they would then try to help. This proportion was highest among groups with low education and among ethnic minorities (Gil, 1970), which has important implications especially in urban settings (see Chapter 7).

Research

Information is lacking about the sequence of events that promote stress and impede the inability to cope with life, resulting in social isolation. Why do families fail to use available services? How can social scientists assist families in exchanging services? How can the humanistic intentions of community citizens be transformed into realistic and competent action? An ecological perspective not only helps us understand the broader organization of society but also offers an opportunity to explore the complicated interactions of events and stresses in varied family situations and to eventually help people help themselves.

It would be ideal if children could be raised in stable, loving families that provide emotional support, social stability, and strong stimulation for enhancing their development. The truth is, society probably never will be able to provide the needed intervention to ensure the "good life" for all children. Instead, a little here and a little there is modified in the hope that children with problems or who live under adverse conditions may be helped. Rutter (1979) and others propose studying successful children reared under adverse circumstances rather than focusing on corrective

Studying children reared under adverse circumstances may help society to provide the needed intervention to ensure the "good life" for all.

intervention to enhance the quality of life. These efforts, they feel, have a greater potential for developing preventive intervention and a comprehensive social policy.

Children who experience all sorts of sources of risks—for example, parental criminality, poverty, child abuse, low intelligence, or large family size—do not always evidence antisocial behavior or poor mental health as adults (Rutter, Quinton, & Yule, 1977). In fact, over 25% of these children in one longitudinal study showed none of these behaviors. Some children not only survive their highly deprived and stressed environments, but "come through unscathed" (Rutter, 1979, p. 50). This study indicated that boys more than girls are damaged by family disruption and discord; irritable children are the target of parental criticism; and poor parental supervision produces more negative behavior than strict and consistent practices. Particular factors in the child's ecology beyond the family mediate the effects of stress. Children who feel positive about school and achieve better scholastically withstand the impact of stresses. Whether these children are constitutionally more resilient has yet to be determined, and the implications for children who are not achieving academically are not known.

Scope of opportunities also serve as mediators of stress. Although these data are speculative, deprived children who have special options for the future, such as attending college, do not perpetuate their family life system. If options are not available, youth from disadvantaged homes tend to marry young, produce children early, and imitate many parental child-rearing practices. Interventions providing options for the future might prevent the self-fulfilling prophecy (Rutter, 1979).

Continued empirical investigations of children's responses to stress and mediating factors may provide the information needed to help children survive their situations and prevent further problems. This effort may actually lead people toward "the good life" by changing a long-standing tendency to treat symptoms without locating causes. We may rid ourselves of simplistic notions that a welfare program will eradicate proverty or that prison sentences will reduce crime. None of these efforts confronts the ecological complexity of the problem that inspired them.

Programs and policy

Many social-service programs were founded on the assumption that growth, improvements, and advancements could be made in systematic ways. By the 1960s, however, it became clear that professionals had an inadequate understanding of planning, to say nothing of their comprehension of the dynamics of institutional structures and functioning. Although society's success is still measured by Gross National Product (GNP) rather than other indicators, it may be time to devise additional barometers to determine program and policy effectiveness.

A cost-benefit approach, derived from a preoccupation with economic factors, may not be suited for measuring programs and determining policy success. Often the costs and benefits of programs and policies are poorly defined and create confusion as to which precedes which. Also, difficulties arise in deciding who pays the costs, who receives the benefits, what should be included in the evaluation, and how a dollar figure can be placed on all variables. What dollar value, for example, should be placed on immunizing a child or raising an intelligence-test score (Zigler, 1973)?

The specification model presented in Chapter 13 may provide a way to reconceptualize goals for programs and policies, to determine levels of transactions, and to identify important antecendents associated with particular groups of people and settings. Because of social complexity, programs and policies could be directed toward enhancing individual competency relative to particular environments, enabling children and families to cope with the vast array of external factors. Zigler and Trickett (1979) propose that assessments be developed in four areas: (1) physical health, (2) motivational and emotional variables, (3) achievement, and (4) cognitive ability. Such an approach could be applied beyond the individual level to families and communities and used as indicators of program and policy effectiveness.

It is difficult to identify a foolproof plan that will adequately meet the challenges facing child-service professionals. But with careful examination, they may be less blinded by partisan ideologies and approaches, enabling them to focus on human problems and relationships and on social, political, and economic processes. Promoting social competence may not be the only answer, but it does respond to ecological changes, thus supporting a developmental perspective.

Technology permits spectacular planning and offers previously unexplored opportunities for change. For instance, the University of Illinois has developed the

PLATO system, a computer simulation program that contains a vast amount of demographic data from most countries. Historical data can be used to generate an array of variables—growth rates, GNPs, employment, day-care usage, which then can form equations to predict future situations for individuals, families, and even societies. In essence, this system manipulates all the possible antecedents and transactions imaginable to simulate outcomes (Wallia, 1970). Though in its infancy, this system has the powerful potential to precisely specify problems, correct conditions, and determine levels of maintenance for what and whom.

Using a system such as PLATO, we could move beyond our immediate ecology to a broader world ecology by answering such questions as: How have our policies improved or worsened the world situation? How have policies of other societies helped or hampered our efforts toward "the good life?" What are the most serious problems in the world today and what solutions are realistically possible? This is no more a pipe dream than was the possibility of the automobile, airplane, or satellites before their invention. What this system offers is prediction and control to enhance individual and societal well-being far beyond our previous time frames. The challenge confronting all of us is whether we choose to commit resources to produce a better future for our children.

Conclusion

There is reason to be optimistic about our capacity to deal with stress and complexity. True, conflicting social values and confusion about who is responsible for care giving have mitigated against building a formal comprehensive policy dealing with appropriate support services. But as a society we value endeavors that may eliminate human pain and increase human potential, and we have begun to face the long-term implications of economic instability and social complexity.

The groundswell of heightened stress experienced by families and children in the 1980s has produced some support for families and networking for communities. As social scientists further obtain empirical evidence and develop interventions to help persons deal with life situations on their own, as public consciousness about stressful events and actions increases, and as growing community-based networks establish themselves, then will we see our optimism rewarded.

While it will not offer quick solutions to pervasive and insidious problems, research is performed in specific contexts that allow precision in delimiting choices and indicate probable outcomes of certain behaviors. Investigations and analyses of children's stressful situations in various contexts can lead to a better comprehension of what may produce positive family relationships and community coherence. That knowledge may equip people to deal more effectively with the special situations of subgroups regardless of race, socioeconomic status, or political beliefs. Child-service providers must confront the problem of stress with the special contribution of research.

Dewey's prediction that "what we do in the next few years for and with our youth will determine in later years what they do with and to the institutions in which they find themselves" (1935, p. 9) is relevent to prognostications about the future of child services. The future, with its seductive technologies, perplexing problems, and intriguing issues, challenges child-service professionals to serve all children and families with sensitivity to the increasing complexity of our ecology.

References

Achenbach, T. M. *Developmental psychopathology.* New York: Ronald Press, 1974.

Aid to Needy Families, 42 U. L. C. A. §§ 601–644, 1935.

Ainsworth, M. S., & Wittig, B. A. Attachment and exploratory behavior of one-year-olds in a strange situation. In B. M. Foss (Ed.), *Determinants of infant behavior.* London: Methuen, 1969.

Albee, G. *Politics, power, prevention, and social change.* Paper presented at the Vermont Conference on the Primary Prevention of Psychopathology, June 1979.

American Psychological Association. *Ethical standards of psychologists.* Washington, D. C.: American Psychological Association, 1953.

American Psychological Association. *gstandards for providers of psychological services.* Washington, D. C.: American Psychological Association, 1975.

American Psychological Association. *Revised ethical standards of psychologists. APA Monitor,* 1977, 8, 13–14.

American Psychological Association. Comments on kids. *APA Monitor,* 1979, 10, 11–12.

Amir, Y. The effectiveness of the kibbutz-born soldier in the Israeli Defense Forces. *Human Relations,* 1969, 22, 333–334.

Anderson, J. The theory of early childhood education. In N. Henry (Ed.), *Early childhood education.* Chicago: University of Chicago Press, 1947.

Anderson, V., & Bereiter, C. Extending direct instruction to conceptual skills. In R. Parker (Ed.), *The preschool in action.* Boston: Allyn & Bacon, 1972.

Andrews, R. H., Jr., & Cohn, A. H. PINS processing in New York: An evaluation. In L.E. Teitelbaum & A. R. Gough (Eds.), *Beyond control.* Cambridge, Mass.: Ballinger, 1977.

Aries, P. *Centuries of childhood.* New York: Random House, 1962.

Arkava, M. L., & Mueller, D. N. Components of foster care for handicapped children. *Child Welfare,* 1978, 57, 339–345.

Auerbach, A. B. Parents' role in day care. In D. L. Peters & J. Beker (Eds.), *Day care: Problems, process and prospects. Child Care Quarterly,* 1975, (special issue) 180–186.

Auerbach, S., & Rivaldo, J. A. *Rationale for child care services: Programs versus politics* (Vol. 1). New York: Human Sciences Press, 1975.

Bahr, H. Change in family life in Middletown: 1924–1977. Paper presented at the annual meeting of the American Sociological Association, Chicago, August 1978.

Baker, E. L. *Using measurement to improve instruction.* Paper presented at the convention of the American Psychological Association, Honolulu, Hawaii, August 1972.

Ball, S., & Bogatz, G. *The first year of Sesame Street: An evaluation.* Princeton, N. J.: Educational Testing Service, 1970.

Bane, M. J. *Here to stay: American families in the twentieth century.* New York: Basic Books, 1976.

Bank-Mikkelsen, N. E. A metropolitan area in Denmark: Copenhagen. In R. B. Kugel & W. Wolfensberger (Eds.), *Changing patterns in residential services for the mentally retarded.* Washington, D. C.: President's Committee on Mental Retardation, 1969.

Baran, A., Pannor, R., & Sorosky, A. D. Open adoption. *Social Work,* 1976, *21,* 97–100.

Baroff, G. S. *Mental retardation: Nature, cause, and management.* New York: Hemisphere, 1974.

Baron, R., & Feeney, F. *Preventing delinquency through diversion: A first-year report.* Davis: Center for the Administration of Criminal Justice, University of California, 1972.

Baumrind, D. Current patterns of parental authority. *Developmental Psychology Monographs,* 1971, *4* (Whole No. 1, Pt. 2).

Beit-Hallahmi, B., & Rabin, A. I. The kibbutz as a social experiment and as a child-rearing laboratory. *American Psychologist,* 1977, *32,* 532–541.

Bell, R. Q. A reinterpretation of the direction of effects in studies of socialization. *Psychological Review,* 1968, *75,* 320–342.

Bell, R. Q., & Harber, L. V. *Child effects of adults.* New York: Wiley, 1977.

Belsky, J., & Steinberg, L. D. The effects of day care: A critical review. *Child Development,* 1978, *49,* 929–949.

Belsky, J., Steinberg, L. D., & Walker, A. The ecology of day care. In M. Lamb (Ed.), *Childrearing in nontraditional families.* Hillsdale, N. J.: Lawrence Erlbaum Associates, in press.

Berfenstam, M., & William-Olsson, I. *Early child care in Sweden.* London: Gordon & Breach, 1973.

Berk, R. A., & Rossi, P. H. Doing good or worse: Evaluation research reexamined. *Social Problems,* 1976, *22,* 337–343.

Berlack, H. Values, goals, public policy, and educational evaluation. *Review of Educational Research,* 1970, *40,* 261–278.

Bernstein, I. N., & Freeman, H. E. *Academic and entrepreneurial research.* New York: Russell Sage Foundation, 1975.

Bettelheim, B. Individual and mass behavior in extreme situations. *Journal of Abnormal and Social Psychology,* 1943, *38,* 417–452.

Biber, B. A developmental-interaction approach: Bank Street College of Education. In M. C. Day & R. K. Parker (Eds.), *The preschool in action: Exploring early childhood programs* (2nd ed.). Boston: Allyn & Bacon, 1977.

Biber, B., Shapiro, E., & Wickens, D. *Promoting cognitive growth from a developmental-interaction point of view.* Washington, D. C.: National Association for the Education of Young Children, 1971.

Biklen, D. Consent as a cornerstone. In J. S. Mearig (Ed.), *Working for children.* San Francisco: Jossey-Bass, 1978.

Billingsley, A. The role of the social worker in a child protective agency. *Child Welfare,* 1964, *43,* 472–492, 497.

Bissell, J. S. Planned variation in Head Start and Follow Through. In J. Stanley (Ed.), *Compensatory education for children, ages 2 to 8.* Baltimore: Johns Hopkins Press, 1973.

Bissell, J. S. *Implementation of planned variation in Head Start.* Vol. 1: *Review and summary of the Stanford Research Institute Interim Report: First year of evaluation.* Washington, D. C.: Office of Child Development, U. S. Department of Health, Education, and Welfare, 1971.

Blake, J. Is zero perfect? American attitudes toward childlessness in 1970's. *Journal of Marriage and Family,* 1979, *41,* 245–265.

Blanchard, M., & Main, M. Avoidance of the attachment figure and social-emotional adjustment in day-care infants. *Developmental Psychology,* 1979, *15,* 445–446.

Blatt, B., & Kaplan, F. *Christmas in purgatory: A photographic essay on mental retardation.* Boston: Allyn & Bacon, 1966.

Bloom, B. S. *Stability and change in human characteristics.* New York: Wiley, 1964.

Bodenheimer, B. M. New trends and requirements in adoption law and proposals for legislative changes. *Southern California Law Review,* 1975, *49,* 11–109.

Boehm, B. An assessment of family adequacy in protective cases. *Child Welfare,* 1962, *41,* 10–16.

Bogatz, G. A., & Ball, S. *The second year of Sesame Street: A continuing evaluation* (Vol. 1). Princeton, N. J.: Educational Testing Service, 1971.

Bowlby, J. *Maternal care and mental health.* Geneva: World Health Organization, 1951.

Brainerd, C. J. Learning research and Piagetian theory. In L. S. Siegel & C. J. Brainerd (Eds.), *Alternatives to Piaget.* New York: Academic Press, 1978. (a)

Brainerd, C. J. *Piaget's theory of intelligence.* Englewood Cliffs, N.J.: Prentice-Hall, 1978. (b)

Bremner, R. H. (Ed.). *Children and youth in America.* Vol. 2: 1866–1932. Cambridge, Mass.: Harvard University Press, 1971.

Bremner, R. H. (Ed.). *Children and youth in America.* Vol. 3: 1933–1973. Cambridge, Mass.: Harvard University Press, 1974.

Brewer, G. D., & Kakalik, J. S. *Handicapped children.* New York: McGraw-Hill, 1979.

Brieland, D. The selection of adoptive parents at intake. *Casework Papers, NCSW-1960.* New York: Columbia University Press, 1961.

Brieland, D., & Lemmon, J. *Social work and the law.* St. Paul, Minn.: West, 1977.

Bromwick, R. M. Focus on maternal behavior in infant interventions. *American Journal of Orthopsychiatry,* 1976, *46,* 439–446.

Bronfenbrenner, U. *Two worlds of childhood.* New York: Russell Sage Foundation, 1970.

Bronfenbrenner, U. Is early intervention effective? In *A report on longitudinal evaluation of preschool programs* (Vol. 2). OHD-75-25. Washington, D. C.: U. S. Department of Health, Education, and Welfare, 1974. (a)

Bronfenbrenner, U. The origins of alienation. *Scientific American,* 1974, *231,* 53–61. (b)

Bronfenbrenner, U. Reality and research in the ecology of human development. *Proceedings of the American Philosophical Society,* 1975, *119,* 439–469.

Bronfenbrenner, U. Research on the effects of day care on child development. *Toward a National Policy for Children and Families.* Washington, D. C.: National Academy of Sciences, 1976.

Bonfenbrenner, U. Toward an experimental ecology of human development. *American Psychologist,* 1977, *32,* 513–531.

Bronfenbrenner, U. Who needs parent education? *Teachers College Record,* 1978, *79,* 767–787.

Bronfenbrenner, U. Contexts of child rearing: Problems and prospects. *American Psychologist,* 1979, *34,* 844–850. (a)

Bronfenbrenner, U. *The ecology of human development.* Cambridge, Mass.: Harvard University Press, 1979. (b)

Bronfenbrenner, U. What shapes children? *Forum,* 1979, Spring/Summer, 12–13. (c)

Bronfenbrenner, U., & Mahoney, M. The structure and verification of hypotheses. In U. Bronfenbrenner & M. Mahoney (Eds.), *Influences on human development.* Hinsdale, Ill.: Dryden, 1975.

Brown v. Board of Education, 347 U. S. 483(1954).

Brown, E. G., & Brieland, D. Adoptive screening—New data, new dilemmas. *Social Work,* 1975, *20,* 291–295.

Brown, F. Crisis intervention as a treatment strategy in child abuse and neglect programs. Prepared for the Child Abuse and Neglect Curriculum Development Project. Paper presented at meeting of National Association of Social Workers, New York, May 1978.

Burris, A. M., & Chittendon, E. A. *Analysis of an approach to open education* (PR-70-13). Princeton, N.J.: Educational Testing Service, 1971.

Burris, M. E. State of the industry. Paper presented at the Food Marketing Institute, in Dallas, Texas, May 1979.

Burrow, T. The group method of analysis. *Psychoanalytic Review,* 1927, *14,* 268–280.

Butler, A., Gotts, E., Quisenbeny, N., & Thompson, R. *Literature search and development of an evaluation system in early childhood education: Behavioral objectives* g)Final Report). Washington, D. C.: U. S. Government Printing Office, 1971.

Calabrese, D. Where to get help, materials, and information. In B. Gross & R. Gross (Eds.), *The children's rights movement: Overcoming the oppression of young people.* New York: Anchor Books, 1977.

Caldwell, B. The fourth dimension in early childhood education. In R. Hess & R. Baer (Eds.), *Early education: Current theory, research and action.* Chicago: Aldine, 1968.

Caldwell, B. M., Wright, C.M., Honig, A.S., & Tannenbaum, J. Infant care and attachment. *american Journal of Orthopsychiatry,* 1970, *40,* 397–412.

Campbell, A. Subjective measures of well-being. *American Psychologist,* 1976, *31,* 117–124.

Caplan, G. *An approach to community mental health.* New York: Grune & Stratton, 1964.

Caplan, G. *Support systems and community mental health.* New York: Behavioral Publications, 1974.

Carew, J. Observation study of caregivers and children in day care homes: Preliminary results from home observations. Paper presented at Biennial Meetings for the Society of Research in Child Development, San Francisco, April 1979.

Caro, F. G. (Ed.). *Readings in evaluation research.* New York: Russell Sage Foundation, 1971.

Carsten, A. A public perspective on scoring the licensing exam. *Professional Psychology,* 1978, *9,* 531–532.

Cautley, P. W., & Lichtenstein, D. P. *Manual for homefinders: The selection of foster parents.* Madison: Center for Social Services, University of Wisconsin Extension, 1974.

Cernea, M., & Tepping, B. J. A system for monitoring and evaluating agricultural extension projects. Washington, D. C.: World Bank, 1977.

Chess, A. An introduction to developmental disabilities. In B. A. Feingold & C. L. Banks (Eds.), *Developmental disabilities of early childhood.* Springfield, Ill.: Thomas, 1978.

Child Welfare League of America. *Standards for foster family care.* New York: Child Welfare League of America, 1959.

Child Welfare League of America. *Day care report.* New York: Child Welfare League of America, 1962.

Child Welfare League of America. *Standards for day-care services.* New York: Child Welfare League of America, 1969.

Child Welfare League of America. *Standards for adoption service.* New York: Child Welfare League of America, 1973.

Chilman, C. S. Public social policy and families. In C. E. Munson (Ed.), *Social work with families: Theory and practice.* New York: Free Press, 1980.

Ciarlo, J. A. Monitoring and analysis of mental health program outcome data. In M. Guttentag & S. Sarr (Eds.), *Evaluation studies annual review* (Vol. 2). Beverly Hills, Calif.: Sage, 1977.

Cicerelli, V. G. *The impact of Head Start. An evaluation of the effects of Head Start on children's cognitive and affective development* (Report to the U.S. Office of Economic Opportunity by Westinghouse Learning Corporation and Ohio University). Washington, D. C.: U. S. Government Printing Office, 1969.

Citizens Committee for Children of New York City, Parents' Rights Unit. *Responding to grievances of parents with children in foster care.* New York: Citizens Committee, 1978.

Clarke, A. M., & Clarke, A. D. B. *Early experience: Myth and evidence.* New York: Free Press, 1976.

Clarke-Stewart, A. K. *Child care in the family: A review of research and some propositions for policy.* New York: Academic Press, 1977.

Clarke-Stewart, A. K. Recasting the lone stranger. In J. Glick & A. K. Clarke-Stewart (Eds.), *The development of social understanding.* New York: Gardner Press, 1978.

Clarke-Stewart, A. K. *Child care in the family.* New York: Academic Press, 1979.

Clements, S. *Minimal brain dysfunction in children* (Public Health Service Bulletin No. 1415). Washington, D. C.: U. S. Department of Health, Education, and Welfare, 1966.

Cleveland, H., & Wilson, T. *Human growth: An essay on growth, values, and the quality of life.* Aspen, Colo.: Institute for Humanistic Studies, 1978.

Cloward, R., & Ohlin, L. *Delinquency and opportunity.* New York: Free Press, 1960.

Cochran, M. A. A comparison of group day and family child rearing patterns in Sweden. *Child Development,* 1977, *48,* 702–707.

Cochran, M. A., & Brassard, J. Social networks and child development. *Child Development,* 1979, *50,* 601–616.

Coffey, A. R. *Juvenile justice system: Law enforcement to rehabilitation.* Englewood Cliffs, N.J.: Prentice-Hall, 1974.

Cohen, S. Maternal employment and mother-child interaction. *Merrill-Palmer Quarterly,* 1979, *24,* 189–197.

Cohn, A. Essential elements of successful child abuse and neglect treatment. *Child Abuse and Neglect,* 1979, *3,* 491–496.

Cole, L. *Our children's keepers: Inside America's kid prisons.* New York: Grossman, 1972.

Collins, A., & Pancoast, D. *Natural helping networks.* Washington, D. C.: National Association of Social Workers, 1976.

Concannon, J. A review of research on haptic perception. *Journal of Educational Research,* 1970, *63,* 250–252.

Cooper, L. *Family life and sex education: A summary of facts and findings.* Santa Cruz, Calif.: Planned Parenthood, 1979.

Cooper, M. L. *The selection and preparation of family life educators: A review of the literature.* San Diego, Calif.: Family Health Education and Training Program, 1982.

Copans, S., and Associates. The stress of treating child abuse. *Children Today,* 1979, January–February, 22–35.

Coulson, J. E. Problems and approaches in education and program evaluation. Paper presented at the annual meeting of the American Educational Research Association, Chicago, May 1976.

Cox, G. B. Managerial style: Implications for the utilization of program evaluation information. *Evaluation Quarterly,* 1977, *1,* 499–508.

Crandall, V. Achievement. In H. Stevenson (Ed.), *Child psychology.* Chicago: University of Chicago Press, 1963.

Cronbach, L. J. How can instruction be adapted to individual differences? In R. M. Gagne (Ed.), *Learning and individual differences.* Columbus, Ohio: Merrill, 1967.

Cronbach, L. J. Course improvement through evaluation. *Teachers College Record,* 1963, *64,* 672–683.

Dandes, H. M., & Dow, D. Relation of intelligence to family size. *Child Development,* 1969, *40,* 641–646.

Danish, S. J., & Smyer, M. A. The unintended consequences of requiring a license to help. Unpublished manuscript, College of Human Development, The Pennsylvania State University, 1980.

Datta, L. Does it work when it has been tried? And half full or half empty? In H. Guttentag & S. Sarr (Eds.), *Evaluation studies annual review* (Vol. 2). Beverly Hills, Calif.: Sage, 1977.

Datta, L., McHale, C., & Mitchell, S. *The effects of the Head Start classroom experience on some aspects of child development: A summary report of national evaluations 1966–1969.* (76-30088) Washington, D. C.: U. S. Department of Health, Education, and Welfare, 1976.

Day, M. C. A comparative analysis of center-based preschool programs. In M. C. Day & R. K. Parker (Eds.), *The preschool in action: Exploring early childhood programs* (2nd ed.). Boston: Allyn & Bacon, 1977.

Day, M. C., & Parker, R. K. *The preschool in action: Exploring early childhood programs* (2nd ed.). Boston: Allyn & Bacon, 1977.

Day Care and Child Development Reports, December 17, 1979, 8(23), 1.

deLone, R. H., & The Carnegie Council on Children. *Small futures: Children, inequality, and the limits of liberal reform.* New York: Harcourt Brace Jovanovich, 1979.

Denny, M. Provision for individuality in schools for young children of 3 to 7 or 8 years. *International Review of Education,* 1970, *16,* 96–99.

Deno, E. N. Special education as developmental capital. *Exceptional Children,* 1970, *37,* 229–237.

Despert, J. L. *The emotionally disturbed child—then and now.* New York: Robert Bunner, 1965.

Des Pres, T. *The survivor: An anatomy of life in the death camps.* New York: Oxford University Press, 1976.

Deutsch, F. The effects of sex of subject and story characters on preschoolers' perceptions of affective responses and intrapersonal behavior in story sequences. *Developmental Psychology,* 1975, *11,* 112–113.

Deutsch, F. Classroom participation of preschoolers in single-parent families. *ojournal of Social Psychology,* in press.

Deutsch, F., & Madle, R. Empathy: Historic and current conceptualizations, measurement, and a cognitive theoretical perspective. *Human Development,* 1975, *18,* 267–278.

Deutsch, F. & Yates, G. *Developing family life education programs: A three-unit curriculum model.* San Diego, Calif.: Family Health Education and Training Program, 1982. (a)

Deutsch, F. & Yates, G. *Family life education program development: A one-unit curriculum model.* San Diego, Calif.: Family Health Education and Training Program, 1982. (b)

Deutsch, M. Early social environment: Its influence on school adaptation. In F. Hechinger (Ed.), *Preschool education today.* New York: Doubleday, 1966.

DeVries, R. Theory in educational practice. In R. Colvin & E. Zaffiro (Eds.), *Preschool education: A handbook for the training of early childhood educators.* New York: Springer, 1974.

Dewey, J. Youth in a confused world. *Social Frontier,* May 1935, 2–9.

Dugger, J. G. *The new professional: Introduction for the human services/mental health worker.* Monterey, Calif.: Brooks/Cole, 1975.

Education for All Handicapped Children Act, Pub. L. 94-142, 89 Stat. 773, 1975.

Egginton, M. L., & Hibbs, R. E. Termination of parental rights in adoption cases: Focusing on the child. *Journal of Family Law,* 1975–1976, *14,* 547–580.

Eisenberg, L. Deprivation and foster care. *Journal of American Academy of Child Psychiatry,* 1965, *4,* 243–248.

Eldefonso, E. *Law enforcement and the youthful offender: Juvenile procedures* (2nd ed.). New York: Wiley, 1973.

Elder, G. H. *Children of the Great Depression.* Chicago: University of Chicago Press, 1974.

Elder, G. H. Family history and the life course. *Journal of Family History,* 1977, *1.*

Elmer, E. *Children in jeopardy.* Pittsburgh: University of Pittsburgh Press, 1967.

Emlen, A. If you care about children, then care about parents. Address to the Tennessee Association for Young Children, Nashville, November 1977. (a)

Emlen, A. *Overcoming barriers to planning for children in foster care.* Portland, Ore.: Regional Research Institute for Human Services, Portland State University, 1977. (b)

Emlen, A., Lahti, J., Downs, G., McKay, A., & Downs, S. *Overcoming barriers to planning for children in foster care.* Portland, Ore.: Regional Research Institute for Human Services, Portland State University, 1977.

Erikson, E. *Childhood and society* (2nd ed.). New York: Norton, 1963.

Erikson, R. A. On states as "super parents" of school children. *Intellect,* 1974, *102,* 414.

Evans, E. Measurement practices in early childhood education. In R. Colvin & E. Zaffiro (Eds.), *Preschool education: A handbook for the training of early childhood educators.* New York: Springer, 1974.

Evans, E. *Contemporary influences in early childhood education* (2nd ed.). New York: Springer, 1975.

Fanshel, D. Studying the role performance of foster parents. *Social Work,* 1961, *6.*

Fanshel, D. *Foster parenthood—a role analysis.* Minneapolis: University of Minnesota Press, 1966.

Fanshel, D. Parental visiting of children in foster care: Key to discharge? *Social Service Review,* 1975, *49,* 493–514.

Fanshel, D. Preschoolers entering foster care in New York City: The need to stress plans for permanency. *Child Welfare,* 1979, *58,* 67–87.

Fanshel, D., & Grundy, J. *Computerized data for children in foster care: First analysis from a management information service in New York City.* New York: Child Welfare Information Service, 1975.

Fanshel, D., & Shinn, E. B. *Dollars and sense in the foster care of children: A look at cost factors.* New York: Child Welfare League of America, 1972.

Fanshel, D., & Shinn, E. B. *Children in foster care: A longitudinal investigation.* New York: Columbia University Press, 1978.

Featherstone, H. *Cognitive effects of preschool programs on different types of children.* Cambridge, Mass.: Huron Institute, 1973.

Featherstone, H. Introduction. In D. Davies (Ed.), *Schools where parents make a difference.* Boston: Institute for Responsive Education, 1976.

Featherstone, J. Family matters. *Harvard Educational Review,* 1979, *49,* 20–56.

Feeney, F. The PINS problem—A "no fault" approach. In L. E. Teitelbaum & A. R. Gough (Eds.), *Beyond control.* Cambridge, Mass.: Ballinger, 1977.

Fein, G. G., & Clarke-Stewart, A. *Day care in context.* New York: Wiley Interscience, 1973.

Fisher, B., Berdie, J., Cook, J., Radford-Barker, J., & Day, J. *Adolescent abuse and neglect: Intervention strategies and treatment approaches.* San Francisco, Calif.: Urban and Rural Systems Associates, 1979.

Flavell, J. H. *The developmental psychology of Jean Piaget.* New York: Van Nostrand Reinhold, 1963.

Fleming, V. *America's children 1976: A bicentennial assessment.* Washington, D. C.: National Council of Organizations for Children and Youth, 1976.

Flexner, A. *Medical education in the United States and Canada, Number 4.* New York: Carnegie Foundation, 1910.

Fortune, J. Problems and approaches in education program evaluation. Paper presented at the annual meeting of the American Educational Research Association, Chicago, May 1972.

Fowler, W., & Kahn, N. The development of a prototype infant and child day care center in metropolitan Toronto. (Ontario Institute for Studies in Education, Ontario, Canada, Year IV, Progress Report). December 1975.

Fraiberg, S. *Every child's birthright: In defense of mothering.* New York: Basic Books, 1977.

Frank, J. *Persuasion and healing.* Baltimore: Johns Hopkins Press, 1961.

Franklin, J. L., & Thrasher, J. H. *An introduction to program evaluation.* New York: Wiley, 1976.

Fraser, B. The problem of child abuse: The future. *Reporter* (Region VII Child Abuse and Neglect Resource Center), 1979, *1,* 1–4.

Freidson, E. Dominant professions, bureaucracy, and client service. In W. Rosengren & M. Lefton (Eds.), *Organization and clients.* Columbus, Ohio: Merrill, 1970.

Freidson, E. Professions and the occupational principle. In E. Freidson (Ed.), *Professions and their prospects.* Beverly Hills, Calif.: Sage, 1974.

Friedman, R. Child abuse: A review of the psychosocial research. In Herner & Company (Ed.), *Four perspectives on the status of child abuse and neglect research.* Washington, D.C.: National Center on Child Abuse and Neglect, 1976.

Gagné, R. M. Contributions of learning to human development. *Psychological Review,* 1968, *75,* 177–191.

Gallagher, J. M. Reflexive abstraction and education: The meaning of activity in Piaget's theory. In J. Gallagher & J. A. Easley, Jr. (Eds.), *Knowledge and development.* Vol. 2: *Piaget and education.* New York: Plenum Press, 1978.

Garbarino, J. High school size and adolescent social development. *Human Ecology Forum,* 1973, *4,* 26–29.

Garbarino, J. A note on the effects of television viewing. In U. Bronfenbrenner & M. A. Mahoney (Eds.), *Influences on human development* (2nd ed.). Hinsdale, Ill.: Dryden Press, 1975.

Garbarino, J. The human ecology of child maltreatment: A conceptual model for research. *Journal of Marriage and the Family,* 1977, *39,* 721–736.

Garbarino, J. The role of schools in socialization to adulthood. *Educational Forum,* 1978, *42,* 169–182.

Garbarino, J. Changing hospital childbirth practices: A developmental perspective on prevention of child maltreatment. *American Journal of Orthopsychiatry,* 1980, *50,* 588–597. (a)

Garbarino, J. Meeting the needs of mistreated youths. *Social Work,* 1980, *25,* 122–127. (b)

Garbarino, J. Some thoughts on school size and its effects on adolescent development. *Journal of Youth and Adolescence,* 1980, *9,* 19–31. (c)

Garbarino, J., & Bronfenbrenner, U. The socialization of moral judgement and behavior in cross-cultural perspective. In T. Lickona (Ed.), *Moral development and behavior.* New York: Holt, Rinehart, & Winston, 1976.

Garbarino, J., & Carson, B. *Mistreated youth versus abused children.* Unpublished manuscript, 1979. Division of Individual and Family Studies, College of Human Development, Pennsylvania State University, University Park, Pa. 16802.

Garbarino, J., & Crouter, A. Defining the community context of parent-child relations: The correlates of child maltreatment. *Child Development.* 1978, *49,* 604–606. (a)

Garbarino, J., & Crouter, A. A note on assessing the construct validity of child maltreatment report data. *American Journal of Public Health,* 1978, *68,* 598–599. (b)

Garbarino, J., & Garbarino, A. C. Where are the children in utopia? Paper presented at the Second National Conference on International Communities, Omaha, Nebraska, October 17, 1978.

Garbarino, J., & Gilliam, G. *Understanding abusive families.* Lexington, Mass.: Lexington Books, 1980.

Garbarino, J., & Hershberger, J. K. Child maltreatment and the problem of evil. Unpublished manuscript, 1979. Division of Individual and Family Studies, College of Human Development, Pennsylvania State University, University Park, Pa. 16802.

Garbarino, J., & Sherman, D. High-risk families and high-risk neighborhoods. *Child Development,* 1980, *51,* 188–198.

Garbarino, J., & Stocking, S. H. *Protecting children from abuse and neglect.* San Francisco: Jossey-Bass, 1980.

Gelles, R. Violence toward children in the United States. *American Journal of Orthopsychiatry,* 1978, *48,* 580–592.

Gelman, S. R. A system of services. In C. Cherington and G. Dywbad (Eds.), *New neighbors: The retarded citizen in quest of a home.* Washington, D.C.: President's Committee on Mental Retardation, 1974.

Gelman, S. R., Governmental intrusiveness in the family: A continuing dilemma. *Children and Youth Services Review,* 1979, *1,* 147–175.

Gil, D. G. *Violence against children: Physical child abuse in the United States.* Cambridge, Mass.: Harvard University Press, 1970.

Ginott, H. G. *Between parent and child: New solutions to old problems.* New York: Avon Books, 1965.

Ginsberg, H., & Opper, S. *Piaget's theory of intellectual development.* Englewood Cliffs, N.J.: Prentice-Hall, 1969.

Giovannoni, J. M., & Becerra, R. M. *Defining child abuse.* New York: Free Press, 1979.

Giovannoni, J. M., & Billingsley, A. Child neglect among the poor: A study of parental adequacy in families of three ethnic groups. *Child Welfare,* 1970, *49,* 196–204.

Glass, G. V. The growth of evaluation methodology (Research Paper No. 17). Boulder: Laboratory of Educational Research, University of Colorado, 1969.

Glick, P. *The future of the American family.* Washington, D.C.: U.S. Government Printing Office, 1979.

Gochros, H. *Not parents yet—A study of the postplacement period in adoption.* Minneapolis, Minn.: Division of Child Welfare, Minnesota Department of Public Welfare, 1962.

Goffman, E. *Stigma.* Englewood Cliffs, N.J.: Prentice-Hall, 1963.

Goldberg, S. R., & Deutsch, F. *Life-span individual and family development.* Monterey, Calif.: Brooks/Cole, 1977.

Golden, M., Rosenbluth, L., Grossi, M., Policare, H., Freeman, H., & Brownlee, E. *The New York City infant day care study.* New York: Medical & Health Research Association of New York City, 1978.

Goldfarb, W. The effects of early institutional care on adolescent personality. *Journal of Experimental Education,* 1943, *12,* 106–129.

Goldstein, J. S. Finding the least detrimental alternative. *Psychoanalytic Study of the Child,* 1972, *28,* 637.

Goodwin, W. Evaluation in early childhood education. In R. Colvin & E. Zaffin (Eds.), *Preschool education: Handbook for early childhood educators.* New York: Springer, 1974.

Goranson, R. E. Media violence and aggressive behavior: A review of experimental research. In L. Berkowitz (Ed.), *Advances in experimental social psychology* (Vol. 5). New York: Academic Press, 1970.

Gordon, I. J. *A home learning center approach to early stimulation.* Gainsville, Fla.: Institute for the Development of Human Resources, 1969.

Gordon, I. J. *Parent involvement in compensatory education.* Urbana, Ill.: ERIC Clearinghouse on Early Childhood Education, 1970.

Gordon, I., & Breivogel, W. *Building effective home-school relationships.* Boston: Allyn & Bacon, 1976.

Gordon, T. *P.E.T. parent effectiveness training: The tested new way to raise children.* New York: New American Library, 1965.

Gough, A. R. Beyond-control youth in the Juvenile Court: The climate for change. In L. E. Teitelbaum & A. R. Gough (Eds.), *Beyond control.* Cambridge, Mass.: Ballinger, 1977.

Gray, C. Empathy and stress as mediators in child abuse: Theory, research, and practical implications. Unpublished doctoral dissertation, University of Maryland, 1978.

Gray, C., Cutler, C., Dean, J., & Kempe, C. H. Perinatal assessment of mother-baby interaction. In R. Helfer & C. H. Kempe (Eds.), *Child abuse and neglect: The family and the community.* Cambridge, Mass.: Ballinger 1976.

Gray, S., & Klaus, R. The early training project: A seventh-year report. *Child Development,* 1970, *41,* 909–1124.

Green, A. Self-destruction in physically abused schizophrenic children: Report of cases. *Archives of General Psychiatry,* 1968, *19,* 171–197.

Grodner, B., & Grodner, A. Children, parents and community: The peanut butter and jelly preschool. *American Journal of Orthopsychiatry,* 1975, *45,* 215–251.

Gross, B., & Gross, R. (Eds.). *The children's rights movement: Overcoming the oppression of young people.* New York: Anchor Books, 1977.

Grossman, H. J. (Ed.), *Manual on terminology and classification in mental retardation.* Washington, D.C.: American Association on Mental Deficiency, 1977.

Group for the Advancement of Psychiatry. *Psychopathological disorders in childhood: Theoretical consideration and a proposal classification* (Vol. 4), GAP Report No. 62. New York: Group for the Advancement of Psychiatry, 1966.

Guerney, L. *Parenting: A skills training manual.* State College, Pa.: Institute for the Development of Emotional and Life Skills, 1977, 1978.

Guidelines for programs and services for developmentally disabled persons. *Federal Developmental Disabilities Act.* Washington, D.C.: U.S. Government Printing Office, 1972.

Guttmacher Institute. *Teenage pregnancy: The problem hasn't gone away.* New York: Author, 1981.

Hagen, C. *The adopted adult discusses adoption as a life experience.* Minneapolis: Lutheran Social Service of Minnesota, 1968.

Hall, R. H. *Occupations and the social structure* (2nd ed.). Englewood Cliffs, N.J.: Prentice-Hall, 1975.

Hansan, J., & Pemberton, K. Day-care services for families with mothers working at home. *Child Welfare,* 1963, *42.*

Hanson, M. J. *Teaching your Down's syndrome infant: A guide to parents.* Baltimore: University Park Press, 1977.

Harper, J., & Williams, S. Adopted children admitted to residential psychiatric care. *Australian Journal of Social Issues*, 1976, 2, 43–52.

Harrell, J., & Ridley, C. Substitute child care, maternal employment and the quality of mother-child interaction. *Journal of Marriage and the Family*, 1975, 37, 556–565.

Harrington, M. *The other America*. New York: Penguin, 1971.

Harris, L. Importance and satisfaction with factors in life. *Harris Survey*, November 23, 1978.

Hawkins, D., & Hawkins, F. Leicestershire: A personal report. *Elementary Science Study Newsletter*, 1964, June, 1–3.

Hawkins, J. D., Roffman, R. A., & Osborne, P. Decision makers' judgments: The influence of role, evaluative criteria, and information access. *Evaluation Quarterly*, 1978, 2, 435–454.

Helfer, R. E., & Kempe, C. H. (Eds.). *The battered child* (2nd ed.). Chicago: University of Chicago Press, 1974.

Hermann, A., & Komlósi, S. *Early child care in Hungary*. London: Gordon & Breach, 1972.

Hersch, C. The discontentment explosion in mental health. *American Psychologist*, 1968, 23, 497–506.

Hess, R. E., & Shipman, V. C. Early experiences and the socialization of cognitive modes in children. *Child Development*, 1965, 36, 869–886.

Hilgard, E. R., & Bower, G. H. *Theories of learning*. New York: Appleton-Century-Crofts, 1966.

Hobbs, N. *The futures of children*. San Francisco: Jossey-Bass, 1975.

Hochfield, E. Across national boundaries. *Juvenile Court Judge Journal*, 1963, 14.

Hock, E. Alternative approaches to child-rearing and their effects on the mother-infant relationship. 1976. (ERIC Document Reproduction Service No. ED 122–943).

Hoffman, D. B. *Parent participation in preschool daycare*. Atlanta, Ga.: Southeastern Education Laboratory, 1971.

Honig, A. S. *Parent involvement in early childhood education*. Washington, D. C.: National Association for the Education of Young Children, 1975.

House, E. R. Assumptions underlying evaluation models. *Educational Researcher*, 1978, 1, 4–12.

Huessey, H. R., & Cohen, A. H. Hyperkinetic behavior and learning disabilities followed over seven years. Unpublished manuscript, College of Medicine, University of Vermont, 1975.

Hughes, E. C. Professions. In K. S. Lynn & Editors of *Daedalus* (Eds.), *The professions in America*. Boston, Mass.: Beacon Press, 1965.

Hultsch, D. F., & Deutsch, F. *Adult development and aging: A life-span perspective*. New York: McGraw-Hill, 1981.

Hunt, J. McV. *Intelligence and experience*. New York: Ronald, 1961.

Iscoe, I., & Payne, S. Development of a revised scale for the functional classification of exceptional children. In E. P. Trapp & P. Himelstein (Eds.), *Readings on the exceptional child*. New York: Appleton-Century-Crofts, 1972.

Jaffee, C. *Friendly intruders: Child care professionals and family life*. Berkeley: University of California Press, 1977.

Jencks, C. *Inequality: A reassessment of the effect of family and schooling in America*. New York: Basic Books, 1972.

Jenkins, S. Duration of foster care—Some relevant antecedent variables. *Child Welfare*, 1967, 46, 450–456.

Jenkins, S., & Norman, E. *Filial deprivation and foster care*. New York: Columbia University Press, 1975.

Johnson, D. W., & Matross, R. P. Attitude modification methods. In F. H. Kanfer & A. P. Goldstein (Eds.), *Helping people change*. New York: Pergamon Press, 1975.

Johnson, H. The effects of Montessori educational techniques on culturally disadvantaged Head Start children. 1965. (ERIC Document Reproduction Service No. ED 015 009).

Johnson, R. L. Social behavior of 3-year-old children in day care and home settings. *Child Study Journal*, 1979, 2(9).

Johnson, S. *Family impact seminar, program statement*. Washington, D. C.: Institute for Educational Leadership, George Washington University, 1978.

Johnson, T. A. *Introduction to the juvenile justice system*. St. Paul, Minn.: West, 1975.

Jones, E. O. A study of those who cease to foster. *British Journal of Social Work*, 1975, 5, 31–41.

Jones, M. Preparing the school age child for adoption. *Child Welfare*, 1979, 58, 27–34.

Jones, M., Neuman, R., & Shyne, A. W. *A second chance for families: Evaluation of a program to reduce foster care*. New York: Child Welfare League of America, 1976.

Josselyn, I. Evaluating motives of foster parents. *Child Welfare*, 1952, 31, 2.

Justice, B., & Duncan, D. F. Life crisis as a precursor to child abuse. *Public Health Reports,* 1976, *91,* 110–115.

Justice, B., & Justice, R. *The abusing family.* New York: Human Sciences Press, 1976.

Kadushin, A. Children in foster families and institutions. In H. Maas (Ed.), *Social service research: Review of studies.* New York: National Association of Social Workers, 1978.

Kadushin, A. *Child welfare services* (3rd ed.). New York: Macmillan, 1980.

Kaffman, M. A comparison of psychopathology: Israeli children from kibbutz and from urban surroundings. *American Journal of Orthopsychiatry,* 1965, *35,* 509–520.

Kagan, J., Kearsley, R., & Zelazo, P. *Infancy: Its place in human development.* Cambridge, Mass.: Harvard University Press, 1978.

Kahn, A., & Kamerman, S. *Not for the poor alone: European social services.* Philadelphia: Temple University Press, 1975.

Kamerman, S. B., & Kahn, A. J. *Social services in the United States.* Philadelphia: Temple University Press, 1976.

Kamerman, S. B., & Kahn, A. J. Explorations in family policy. In C. E. Munson (Ed.), *Social work with families.* New York: Free Press, 1980.

Kamii, C. Evaluation of learning in preschool education: Socio-emotional, perceptual motor, and cognitive development. In B. Bloom, J. Hastings, & G. Madaus (Eds.), *Handbook of formative and summative evaluation of student learning.* New York: McGraw-Hill, 1971.

Kamii, C. A sketch of the Piaget-derived preschool curriculum developed by the Ypsilanti early education program. In S. Braun & E. Edwards (Eds.), *History and theory of early childhood education.* Worthington, Ohio: Jones, 1972.

Kamii, C., & DeVries, R. Piaget for early education. In M. C. Day & R. K. Parker (Eds.), *The preschool in action: Exploring early childhood programs* (2nd ed.). Boston: Allyn & Bacon, 1977.

Kamii, C., & Elliot, D. L. Evaluation of evaluations. *Educational Leadership,* 1971, *28,* 827–831.

Kanfer, F. H., & Goldstein, A. (Eds.), *Helping people change.* New York: Pergamon, 1975.

Kanner, L. *A history of the care and study of the mentally retarded.* Springfield, Ill.: Thomas, 1964.

Kappelman, M., & Ackerman, P. *Between parent and school.* New York: Dial Press, 1977.

Karnes, M. B. *Research and development program on preschool disadvantaged children* (Vol. 1, Final Report). Bethesda, Md.: 1970. (ERIC Document Reproduction Service No. ED 036 663).

Karnes, M. B., Teska, I. A., Hodgins, A. S., & Badger, E. D. Educational intervention at home by mothers of disadvantaged. *Child Development,* 1970, *40,* 925–935.

Karnes, M. B., Zehrbach, R. R., & Teska, J. A. Conceptualization of the GOAL (Game Oriented Activities for Learning) curriculum. In M. D. Day & R. K. Parker (Eds.), *The preschool in action: Exploring early childhood programs* (2nd ed.). Boston: Allyn & Bacon, 1977.

Katz, A., & Teitelbaum, L. E. PINS jurisdiction, the vagueness doctrine, and the rule of law. In L. E. Teitelbaum & A. R. Gough (Eds.), *Beyond control.* Cambridge, Mass.: Ballinger, 1977.

Katz, I. Some thoughts about the stigma notion. *Personality and Social Psychology Bulletin,* 1979, *5,* 447–460.

Kempe, C. H., & Helfer, R. E. *Helping the battered child and his family.* New York: Lippincott, 1975.

Kempe, C. H., & Helfer, R. E. *The battered child* (2nd ed.). Chicago: University of Chicago Press, 1974.

Kempe, C. H., & Helfer, R. E. *The battered child* (3rd ed.). Chicago: University of Chicago Press, 1980.

Kempe, R. S., & Kempe, C. H. *Child abuse.* Cambridge, Mass.: Harvard University Press, 1978.

Keniston, K., & The Carnegie Council on Children. *All our children.* New York: Harcourt Brace Jovanovich, 1977.

Kennell, J., Voos, D., & Klaus, M. Parent-infant bonding. In R. Helfer & C. H. Kempe (Eds.), *Child abuse and neglect: The family and the community.* Cambridge, Mass.: Ballinger, 1976.

Kent, J. T. A follow-up study of abused children. *Journal of Pediatric Psychology,* 1976, *1,* 25–31.

Kessen, W. Ambiguous commitment. *Science,* 1976, *193,* 310–311.

Kessen, W. The American child and other cultural inventions. *American Psychologist,* 1979, *34,* 815–820.

Kessler, J. W. Potential errors in clinical practice. In J. S. Mearig (Ed.), *Working for children.* San Francisco: Jossey-Bass, 1978.

Keyserling, M. D. *Windows on day care.* New York: National Council on Jewish Women, 1972.

Kiesler, S. Federal policies for research on children. *American Psychologist,* 1979, *34,* 1009–1016.

Kinard, E. M. The psychological consequences of abuse for the child. *Journal of Social Issues,* 1979, *35,* 82–100.

Kiresuk, T. J., & Lund, S. H. Process and outcome measurement using goal attainment scaling. In G. U.

Glass (Ed.), *Evaluation studies, review annual* (Vol. 1). Beverly Hills, Calif.: Sage, 1976.

Klaus, M., Jerald, R., Kreger, R., McAlpine, W., Steffa, M., & Kennell, J. Maternal attachment—importance of the first post-partum days. *New England Journal of Medicine*, 1972, 286,460–463.

Klaus, R. A., & Gray, S. W. The early training project: A seventh-year report. *Child Development*, 1970, 41, 909–924.

Klein, S. P., & Kosecoff, J. *Issues and procedures in the development of criterion-reference tests.* Princeton, N.J.: Educational Testing Service, 1973.

Kleinfeld, A. J. The balance of power among infants, their parents, and the state. *Family Law Quarterly*, 1970, 4, 409–410.

Knitzer, J. Child advocacy: A perspective. *American Journal of Orthopsychiatry*, 1976, 46, 200–216.

Knitzer, J. Responsibility for delivery of services. In J. S. Mearig (Ed.), *Working for children.* San Francisco: Jossey-Bass, 1978.

Kohlberg, L. Early education: A cognitive-developmental view. *Child Development*, 1968, 39, 1013–1062.

Kohlberg, L., & Mayer, R. Development as the aim of education. *Harvard Educational Review*, 1972, 42, 449–498.

Kolb, L. C. *Modern clinical psychiatry* (8th ed.). Philadelphia: Saunders, 1973.

Koocher, G. P. Credentialing in psychology: Close encounters with competence. Paper presented as part of a symposium on Licensing, Accreditation, and the Public Interest at the annual meeting of the American Psychological Association, Toronto, Canada, August 1978.

Korbin, J. Very few cases: Child abuse in the People's Republic of China. Paper presented at the annual meeting of the American Anthropological Association, Los Angeles, November 1978.

Korsch, B., Christian, J., Gozzi, E., & Carlson, P. Infant care and punishment: A pilot study. *American Journal of Public Health*, 1965, 55, 1880–1888.

Kotelchuck, M. The infant's relationship to the father: Experimental evidence. In M. Lamb (Ed.), *The role of the father.* New York: Wiley, 1976.

Kritchevsky, S. E., Prescott, E., & Walling, L. *Planning environments for young children: Physical space.* Washington, D. C.: National Association for the Education of Young Children, 1969.

Kromkowski, J. *Neighborhood deterioration and juvenile crime.* South Bend, Ind.: South Bend Urban Observatory, 1976.

Kurtz, P. D. Family approaches. In J. T. Neisworth & R. M. Smith (Eds.), *Retardation: Issues, assessment and intervention.* New York: McGraw-Hill, 1978.

Ladner, J. *Mixed families: Adopting across racial boundaries.* New York: Doubleday, 1977.

Lahti, J. *A follow-up study of the Oregon Project.* Portland, Ore.: Regional Research Institute for Human Services, Portland State University, 1978.

Lally, J. R. *Development of a day-care center for young children: Progress report* (PR–156–C6). Syracuse N. Y.: Syracuse University Children's Center, 1971.

Lavatelli, C. *Piaget's theory applied to an early childhood curriculum.* Boston: American Science & Engineering, 1970.

Lenoski, E. F. *Translating injury data into preventative and health care services: Physical child abuse.* Unpublished manuscript, School of Medicine, University of Southern California Los Angeles, 1974.

Lerner, R. M. *Concepts and theories of human development.* Reading, Mass.: Addison-Wesley, 1976.

Lerner, R. M., & Spanier, G. B. A dynamic interactional view of child and family development. In R. M. Lerner & G. B. Spanier (Eds.), *Child influences on marital and family interaction.* New York: Academic Press, 1978.

Levenstein, P. *Final report to Children's Bureau. Verbal interaction project.* New York: Freeport, 1971.

Levenstein, P. Cognitive growth in preschoolers through verbal interaction with mothers. *American Journal of Orthopsychiatry*, 1970, 40,426–430.

Levenstein, P., & Sunley, R. Stimulation of verbal interaction between disadvantaged mothers and children. *American Journal of Orthopsychiatry*, 1969, 38, 116–m21.

Levin, H. Cost-effective analysis in evaluation research. In M. Guttentag & E. L. Struening (Eds.), *Handbook of evaluation research* (Vol. 2). Beverly Hills, Calif.: Sage, 1975.

Levine, M., & Levine, A. *A social history of helping clinic, court, school, and community.* New York: Knopf, 1970.

Levy, L. H. *Conceptions of personality.* New York: Random House, 1970.

Lieberman, E. J. Reserving a womb: Case for the small family. *American Journal of Public Health*, 1970, 60, 87–92.

Lieberman, M. A. Group methods. In F. H. Kanfer & A. P. Goldstein (Eds.), *Helping people change.* New York: Pergamon, 1975.

Light, R. Abused and neglected children in America: A study of alternative policies. *Harvard Educational Review,* 1973, *43,* 556–598.

Lindbloom, C. E. The science of muddling through. In E. U. Schneier (Ed.), *Policy making in American government.* New York: Basic Books, 1969.

Lomax, D. A review of British research in teacher education. *Review of Educational Research,* 1972, *2,* 289–326.

Looft, W. Socialization and personality throughout the life-span: An examination of contemporary psychological approaches. In P. Baltes & K. Schaie (Eds.), *Life-span developmental psychology: Research and theory.* New York: Academic Press, 1973.

Lystad, M. H. Violence at home: A review of the literature. *American Journal of Orthopsychiatry,* 1975, *45,* 328–345.

Maas, H., & Engler, R. *Children in need of parents.* New York: Columbia University Press, 1959.

Maccoby, E., & Zellner, M. *Experiments in primary education: Aspects of Project Follow Through.* New York: Harcourt Brace Jovanovich, 1970.

Mack, J. The juvenile court. *Harvard Law Review,* 1909, *23,* 104–122.

Madle, R. A. Alternative residential placements. In J. T. Neisworth & R. M. Smith (Eds.), *Retardation: Issues, assessment, and intervention.* New York: McGraw-Hill, 1978.

Mahoney, A. R. PINS and parents. In L. E. Teitelbaum & A. R. Gough (Eds.), *Beyond control.* Cambridge, Mass.: Ballinger, 1977.

Mahoney, M. A. *American families: Decades and centuries of change.* Unpublished manuscript, Dept. of Human Ecology, Cornell University, 1976.

Manis, J. Assessing the seriousness of social problems. *Social Problems,* 1974, *22,* 1–15.

Mann, H. The third annual report of the Board of Education. In H. Mann, *Life and works* (Vol. 3), 1868.

Marcus, T., & Corsini, D. A. Parental expectations of preschool children as related to child gender and socioeconomic status. *Child Development,* 1978, *49,* 243–246.

Marshall, D. R. *The politics of participation in poverty: A case study of the Board of the Economic and Youth Opportunities.* Unpublished doctoral dissertation, University of California at Los Angeles, 1969.

Martin, J. Montessori after 50 years. *Teachers College Record,* 1965, *67,* 552–554.

Mayer, R. S. A comparative analysis of preschool models. In R. H. Anderson & H. B. Shane (Eds.), *As the twig is bent: Readings in early childhood education.* Boston: Houghton Mifflin, 1971.

McCall, R. Challenges to a science of developmental psychology. *Child Development,* 1977, *48,* 333–334.

McCausland, C. L. *Children of circumstances: A history of the first 125 years of the Chicago Child Care Society.* Chicago: Chicago Child Care Society, 1976.

McGowan, B. G. Strategies in bureaucracies. In J. S. Mearig (Ed.), *Working for children.* San Francisco: Jossey-Bass, 1978.

McInnerey, B. L., Durr, B., Kershner, K. M., & Nash, L. A. *Preschool and primary education: Annual program report to Ford Foundation.* Harrisburg, Pa.: State Department of Public Instruction and Welfare, 1967.

McKnight, J. Professionalized service and disabling help. In I. Illich (Ed.), *Disabling professions.* Boston: Boyars, 1978.

McLaughlin, M. W. *Evaluation and reform: The Elementary and Secondary Education Act of 1965/Title I.* Cambridge, Mass.: Ballinger, 1975.

McLean, G. R. *We're holding your son.* Old Tappan, N.J.: Revell, 1969.

McReynolds, P. An introduction to psychological assessment. In P. McReynolds (Ed.), *Advances in psychological assessment* (Vol. 1). Palo Alto, Calif.: Science & Behavior Books, 1968.

McWhinnie, A. M. *Adopted children: How they grow up.* London: Routledge & Kegan Paul, 1967.

Mead, M. *Coming of age in Samoa.* New York: Dell, 1928, 1961.

Mead, M. Bisexuality: What's it all about? In S. Gordon & R. W. Libby (Eds.), *Sexuality today—and tomorrow.* North Scituate, Mass.: Duxbury, 1976.

Mearig, J. S., & Associates. (Eds.). *Working for children.* San Francisco: Jossey-Bass, 1978.

Meyers, L. The relationship between substitute child care, maternal employment and female marital satisfaction. In D. Peters (Ed.), *A summary of the Pennsylvania Day Care Study.* University Park: The Pennsylvania State University, 1973.

Milgram, S. *Obedience to authority.* New York: Harper & Row, 1974.

Miller, L., & Dyer, J. Four preschool programs: Their dimensions and effects. *Monographs of the Society for Research in Child Development*, 1975, *40*.

Minuchin, P., Biber, B., Shapiro, E., & Zimiles, H. *The psychological impact of school experience.* New York: Basic Books, 1969.

Mischel, W. *Personality and assessment.* New York: Wiley, 1968.

Mnookin, R. H. Foster care—in whose best interest? *Harvard Educational Review*, 1973, *43*, 599–610.

Mondale, W. F. Opening statement at Joint Senate–House Hearings on *Child and Family Services Act of 1975*, July 15, 1975.

Morgan, J. *Five thousand American families.* Ann Arbor, Mich.: Institute of Survey Research, 1974.

Morris, A. G., & Glick, H. The pediatric clinic playroom: A classroom for parents of preschoolers. *American Journal of Orthopsychiatry*, 1975, *45*, 256–257.

Morris, D. *The human zoo.* New York: Dell, 1970.

Morris, L. L., & Fitz-Gibbon, C. T. How to measure program implementation. In L. L. Morris (Ed.), *Program evaluation kit* (Vol. 4). Beverly Hills, Calif.: Sage, 1978.

Morrow, L. Wondering if children are really necessary. *Time*, March 5, 1979, p. 42.

Morse, W. C. Professionals in a changing society. In J. S. Mearig (Ed.), *Working for children.* San Francisco: Jossey-Bass, 1978.

Myrdal, A. *Towards equality.* Stockholm: Prisma, 1971.

Myrdal, A., & Klein, V. *Women's two roles: Home and work* (2nd ed.). London: Routledge & Kegan Paul, 1968.

Nance, J. *The gentle Tasaday.* New York: Harcourt, Brace, Jovanovich, 1975.

National Academy of Sciences. *Toward a national policy for child and families.* Washington, D. C.: U. S. Government Printing Office, 1976.

National Association for Retarded Citizens. *Residential Services: Position Statement No. 9.* Arlington, Texas: National Association for Retarded Citizens, 1968.

National Center on Child Abuse and Neglect. *1978 annual review of child abuse and neglect research* (OHDS 79–30168). Washington, D. C.: U. S. Department of Health, Education and Welfare, 1978.

National Commission on Neighborhoods. *Final report of the commission.* Washington, D. C.: U. S. Government Printing Office, 1979.

National Institute for Mental Health. *Planning for creative change in mental health services: A distillation of principles on research utilization* (Publication No. (HSM) 73–9148). Washington, D. C.: U. S. Department of Health, Education and Welfare, 1971.

Naumann, T. *Behavioral interaction analysis: A new approach in child study.* Ellensberg, Wash.: Central Washington State College, 1966.

Nedler, S. A bilingual early childhood program. In M. C. Day & R. K. Parker (Eds.), *The preschool in action: Exploring early childhood programs* (2nd ed.). Boston: Allyn & Bacon, 1977.

Neisworth, J. T., & Madle, R. A. Normalized day care: A philosophy and approach to exceptional and normal children. *Child Care Quarterly*, 1975, *4*, 163–171.

Neisworth, J. T., & Smith, R. M. Analysis and redefinition of "developmental disabilities." *Exceptional Children*, 1974, *40*, 345–347.

New York City Department of Social Services. *The parents' handbook: A guide for parents of children in foster care.* New York: Department of Social Services, 1977.

Nimnicht, G. P., Arango, M., & Cheever, J. The responsive educational program. In M. C. Day & R. K. Parker (Eds.), *The preschool in action: Exploring early childhood programs* (2nd ed.). Boston: Allyn & Bacon, 1977.

Nirje, B. The normalization principle and its management implications. In R. B. Kigel & W. Wolfensberger (Eds.), *Changing patterns in residential services for the mentally retarded.* Washington, D. C.: President's Committee on Mental Retardation, 1969.

Nixon, R. M. U. S. President message: Veto of economic opportunity amendments of 1971. *Weekly Compilation of President's Documents*, December 13, 1971, pp. 1634–1636.

North, R. C. *The portable Stanford: The world that could be.* Stanford, Calif.: Stanford Alumni Association, 1976.

Office of Assistant for Planning and Evaluation. *The appropriateness of the federal interagency day care requirements (FIDCR): Report on findings and recommendations.* Washington, D. C.: U. S. Government Printing Office, 1978.

Overton, W. F. *Klaus Riegel's theoretical contributions: Some thoughts on stability and change.* Paper presented at the Eighty-fifth Annual Convention of the American Psychological Association, San Francisco, California, August 1977.

Overton, W., & Reese, H. Models of development: Methodological implications. In J. H. Nesselroade & H. W. Reese (Eds.), *Life-span developmental psychology: Methodological issues.* New York: Academic Press, 1973.

Parke, R. D. Interactional design and experimental manipulation: The field lab interface. In R. B. Cairns (Ed.), *Social interaction: Methods, analysis, and illustration.* Hillsdale, N.J.: Lawrence Erlbaum Associates, 1978.

Parke, R., & Collmer, C. W. Child abuse: An interdisciplinary analysis. In E. M. Hetherington (Ed.), *Review of child development research* (Vol. 5). Chicago: University of Chicago Press, 1975.

Parker, R. Theory in early education curricula. In R. Colvin & E. Zaffiro (Eds.), *Preschool education: A handbook for the training of early childhood educators.* New York: Springer, 1974.

Parker, R. K. (Ed.). *The preschool in action.* Boston: Allyn & Bacon, 1972.

Paton, J. M. *The adopted break silence.* Philadelphia: Life History Study Center, 1954.

Patten, M. Q. *In search of impact: An analysis of the utilization of federal evaluation research.* Minneapolis: Center for Social Research, University of Minnesota, 1975.

Patterson, J. M. Analyzing early childhood education programs: Evaluation, *Educational Leadership,* 1971, *28,* 809–811.

Pavenstedt, E. *The drifters: Children of disorganized lower-class families.* Boston: Little Brown, 1967.

Pedersen, F. *Mother, father, infant as an interactive system.* Paper presented at the American Psychological Association Convention, Chicago, August 1975.

Peters, D. L. Early childhood education: An overview and evaluation. In H. Robinson & J. Horn (Eds.), *Psychological processes in early education.* New York: Academic Press, 1977.

Peters, D. L. Social science and social policy and the care of young children: Head Start and after. *Journal of Applied Developmental Psychology,* 1980, *1,* 7–27.

Peters, D. L., Cohen, A., & McNichol, M. The training and certification of early childhood personnel. *Child Care Quarterly,* 1974, *3,* 39–53.

Peters, D. L., & Dorman, L. Program planning and program goals. In R. W. Colvin & E. M. Zaffiro (Eds.), *Preschool education: A handbook for the training of early childhood educators.* New York: Springer, 1974.

Peters, D. L., Golbeck, S., & Busch-Nagel, N. A. Research on early childhood education: The aptitude by treatment interaction approach. Paper presented at the Annual Meeting of the National Association for the Education of Young Children, Chicago, November 1977.

Peters, D., & Marcus, R. Defining day care goals: A preliminary study. *Child Care Quarterly,* 1973, *2,* 270–276.

Phillips, M. H., Shyne, A. W., Sherman, E. A., & Haring, B. L. *Factors associated with placement decisions in child welfare.* New York: Child Welfare League of America, 1971.

Phillips, M. H., Shyne, A. W., Sherman, E. A., & Haring, B. L. *Permanent planning for children in foster care: A handbook for social workers.* Portland, Ore.: Regional Research Institute for Human Services, Portland State University, 1977.

Piaget, J. Piaget's theory. In P. H. Mussen (Ed.), *Carmichael's manual of child psychology* (Vol. 1). New York: Wiley, 1970.

Pifer, A. Perceptions of childhood and youth, president's report. In *Carnegie Council 1978 annual report.* New York: Carnegie, 1978.

Polansky, N., Chalmers, M., Buttenwieser, L., & Williams, D. The isolation of the neglectful family. *American Journal of Orthopsychiatry,* 1979, *49,* 149–152.

Polier, J. W. In defense of children. *Child Welfare,* 1976, *55,* 75–82.

Popham, W. J. *Educational evaluation.* Englewood Cliffs, N.J.: Prentice-Hall, 1975.

Porter, B. R. The human element. *Forum,* 1979, Spring-Summer, 14–15.

Pottinger, P. S. Efforts expand to check professional misconduct. *Pro Forum,* 1978, *1,* 3.

Powell, D. R. The interpersonal relationship between parents and caretakers in day care settings. *American Journal of Orthopsychiatry,* 1976, *48,* 680–689.

Prescott, E. *A pilot study of day care centers and their clientele.* Washington, D.C.: U.S. Dept. of Education and Welfare, Children's Bureau, 1965.

Prescott, E. A. A comparison of three types of day care and nursery school/home care. Paper presented at the meeting of the Society for Research in Child Development, Philadelphia, March 1973.

Proceedings of the Conference on the Care of Dependent Children. Washington, D.C.: U.S. Government Printing Office, January 25–26, 1909.

Provence, E., Naylor, A., & Patterson, J. *The challenge of day care.* New Haven, Conn.: Yale University Press, 1977.

Provus, M. Evaluation of ongoing programs in the public school systems. In R. W. Tyler (Ed.), *Educational evaluation: New forms, new means. Sixtyeighth yearbook of the National Society for the Study of Education, Part II.* Chicago: University of Chicago Press, 1969.

Rabin, A. I. The sexes: Ideology and reality in the Israeli kibbutz. In G. M. Seward & L. C. Williamson (Eds.), *Sex roles in a changing society.* New York: Random House, 1970.

Radbill, S. A history of child abuse and infanticide. In R. Helfer & C. H. Kempe (Eds.), *The battered child.* Chicago: University of Chicago Press, 1974.

Radinsky, E., & Associates. Recruiting and serving foster parents. *Child Welfare,* 1963, 42.

Rambusch, N. *Learning how to learn: An American approach to Montessori.* Baltimore: Helicon Press, 1962.

Raven, J. C. *Raven's coloured progressive matrices.* New York: Psychological Corp., 1956, 1962.

Raven, J. C. *Guide to using the coloured progressive matrices.* London: H. K. Lewis, 1965.

Reese, H., & Overton, W. Models of development and theories of development. In L. Goulet & P. Baltes (Eds.), *Life-span developmental psychology: Research and theory.* New York: Academic Press, 1970.

Rein, M., & White, S. H. Can policy research help policy? *The Public Interest,* 1977, *12,* 119–136.

Remini, R. V. (Ed.). *The age of Jackson.* Los Angeles: University of Southern California Press, 1972.

Resnick, L. B., Wang, M. C., & Rosner, T. Adaptive education for young children: The Primary Education Project. In M. C. Day & R. K. Parker (Eds.), *The preschool in action: Exploring early childhood programs* (2nd ed.). Boston: Allyn & Bacon, 1977.

Rettig, K. S. Relation of social systems to intergenerational changes in moral attitudes. *Journal of Personality and Social Psychology,* 1966, *4,* 400–414.

Rhine, W. R. Strategies for evaluating follow through. In R. M. Rippey (Ed.), *Studies in transactional evaluation.* Berkeley, Calif.: Cutcheon, 1973.

Rhodes, W. C. Normality and abnormality in perspective. In J. S. Mearig (Ed.), *Working for children.* San Francisco: Jossey-Bass, 1978.

Robinson, H. B., Robinson, N. M., Wolins, M., Bronfenbrenner, U., & Richmond, J. B. *Early child care in the United States.* London: Gordon & Breach, 1973.

Robinson, N. M., & Robinson, H. B. *The mentally retarded child: A psychological approach* (2nd ed.). New York: McGraw-Hill, 1976.

Robinson, N. M., Robinson, H. B., Darling, N., & Holm. G. *A world of children: Day care and preschool institutions.* Monterey, Calif.: Brooks/Cole, 1979.

Rock, M. Gorilla mothers need some help from their friends. *Smithsonian,* 1978, *9,* 58–63.

Rodgers, R. H. *Family interaction and transaction: The developmental approach.* Engelwood Cliffs, N.J.: Prentice-Hall, 1973.

Rodham, H. Children under the law. In A. Skolnick (Ed.), *Rethinking childhood: Perspectives on development and society.* Boston: Little Brown, 1976.

Rohe, W., & Patterson, A. The effects of varied levels of resources and density on behavior in a day care center. In D. H. Arson (Ed.), *Man-environment interactions.* New York: Education Development, Research Association, 1974.

Roopnarine, H., & Lamb, M. The effects of day care on attachment and exploratory behavior in a strange situation. *Merrill-Palmer Quarterly,* 1979, *24,*(2).

Roosevelt, T. Special message to congress, February 15, 1909. *Proceedings of the White House Conference on the Care of Dependent Children* 1909, 6–7.

Rosenberg, B. G., & Sutton-Smith, B. Sibling age spacing effects upon cognition. *Developmental Psychology,* 1969, *1,* 661–668.

Rosenblum, B. *Foster homes for adolescents.* Hamilton, Ontario: Children's Aid Society of Hamilton-Wentworth, 1977.

Ross, H. L., & Sawhill, I. V. *Time of transition; The growth of families headed by women.* Washington, D.C.: Urban Institute, 1975.

Rossi, A. S. A biosocial perspective on parenting. In A. S. Rossi, J. Kagan, & T. Hareven (Eds.), *The family.* New York: Norton, 1977.

Rossi, P. H. Issues in evaluation of human services delivery. *Evaluation Quarterly,* 1978, *2,* 573–599.

Rossi, P. H., Freeman, H. E., & Wright, S. R. *Evaluation: A systematic approach.* Beverly Hills, Calif.: Sage, 1979.

Rossi, P. H., & Williams, W. (Eds.), *Evaluating social programs.* New York: Springer, 1972.

Rubenstein, H., & Howes, C. Caregiving and infant behavior in day care and in homes. *Developmental Psychology,* 1979, *15,* 1–24.

Rubenstein, J. L., Pedersen, F. A., & Yarrow, L. J. What happens when mother is away: A comparison of mothers and substitute caregivers. *Developmental Psychology,* 1977, *13,* 529–530.

Ruderman, F. A. *Child care and the working mother: A study of arrangements made for daytime care of children.* New York: Child Welfare League of America, 1968.

Rutter, M. Protective factors in children's responses to stress and disadvantage. In M. W. Kent & J. E. Rolf (Eds.), *Primary prevention of pathology.* Vol. 3: *Social competence in children.* Hanover, N. H.: University Press of New England, 1979.

Rutter, M., Quinton, D., & Yule, B. *Family pathology and disorder in children.* London: Wiley, 1977.

Ryan, S. (Ed.). *A report on longitudinal evaluations of preschool programs,* Vol. 1: *Longitudinal evaluations* (Publication No. 76-30024). Washington, D.C.: U.S. Department of Health, Education, and Welfare, 1974.

Sanger, M. *Margaret Sanger: An autobiography.* New York: Norton, 1938.

Sarafino, E. An estimate of nationwide incidence of sexual offenses against children. *Child Welfare,* 1979, *58,* 127–134.

Sarason, S. B., & Doris, J. *Psychological problems in mental deficiency* (2nd ed.). New York: Harper & Row, 1969.

Sauber, J., & Jenkins, S. *Paths to child placement.* New York: Community Council of Greater New York, 1966.

Sawhill, I. V. Economic perspectives on the family. In A. Rossi, J. Kagan, & T. Hareven (Eds.), *The family.* New York: Norton, 1977.

Schechter, M. Observation on adopted children. *AMA Archives of General Psychiatry,* 1960, *3,* 13–21.

Schlesinger, A. M., Jr. *The age of Jackson.* Boston, Mass.: Little Brown, 1945. (Originally published, 1909.)

Schneider, C., Hoffmeister, J., & Helfer, R. A predictive screening questionnaire for potential problems in mother-child interaction. In R. Helfer, & C. H. Kempe (Eds.), *Child abuse and neglect: The family and the community.* Cambridge, Mass.: Ballinger, 1976.

Schoggen, M., & Schoggen, P. *Environmental forces in home lives of three-year-old children in three population subgroups.* (DARCEE Papers and Reports, Vol. 5, 2). Nashville, Tenn.: George Peabody College for Teachers, 1971.

Schorr, A. L. *Explanations of social policy.* New York: Basic Books, 1968.

Schrag, P., & Divoky, D. *The myth of the hyperactive child.* New York: Pantheon, 1975.

Schultz, T. W. *Economics of the family: Marriage, children, and human capital.* Chicago: University of Chicago Press, 1974.

Schumacher, E. F. *Small Is beautiful.* New York: Harper & Row, 1973.

Sciarra, D. J., & Dorsey, A. G. *Developing and administering a child care center.* Boston: Houghton Mifflin, 1979.

Scott, D. B. *A report on characteristics of registrants for adoption, children placed, and services rendered by adoption agencies.* New York: Travelers Aid International Social Services, 1976.

Scriven, M. The methodology of evaluation. In R. Stake (Ed.), *Perspectives of curriculum evaluation* (American Education Research Association monograph series on curriculum evaluation No. 1). Chicago: Rand McNally, 1967.

Senn, M. J. E. *Speaking out for America's children.* New Haven, Conn.: Yale University Press, 1977.

Shapiro, E., & Biber, B. The education of young children: A developmental interaction approach. *Teachers College Record,* 1972, *74,* 55–79.

Shore, M. F. Review of the literature. *American Journal of Orthopsychiatry,* 1977, *47,* 359–360.

Shore, M. F. Legislation, advocacy, and the rights of children and youth. *American Psychologist,* 1979, *34,* 1017–1019.

Shyne, A., & Schroeder, A. W. *National study of social services to children and their families.* Rockville, Md.: Westat, 1978.

Sigel, I. Developmental theory and preschool education: Issues, problems, and implications. In I. J. Gordon (Ed.), *Early childhood education.* Chicago: University of Chicago Press, 1972.

Silver, L. Frequency of adoption in children with neurological learning disability syndrome. *Journal of Learning Disabilities,* 1970, *3,* 306–310.

Simon, R. A., & Alstein, H. *Transracial adoption.* New York: Wiley, 1977.

Simon, A., & Boyer, E. G. (Eds.). *Mirrors for behavior II: An anthology of observation instruments.* Philadelphia: Research for Better Schools, 1970.

Skeels, H. M. Adult status of children with contrasting early life experiences: A follow-up study. *Monographs of the Society for Research in Child Development,* 1966, *31,*(3).

Slater, E. P., & Harris, W. Therapy at home. *Practice Digest,* 1978, *1,* 20–21.

Sloan, W., & Birch, J. W. A rationale for degrees of retardation. *American Journal of Mental Deficiency,* 1955, *60,* 258–264.

Smith, R. M., & Neisworth, J. T. *The exceptional child: A functional approach.* New York: McGraw-Hill, 1975.

Soar, R., & Soar, R. An empirical analysis of selected follow-through programs. In I. Gordon (Ed.), *Early childhood education.* Chicago: National Society for the Study of Education, 1972.

Social Research Group. *Interagency research information system: A user's manual.* Washington, D. C.: Social Research Group, George Washington University, 1979.

Sorokin, P. A. Social differentiation. In D. L. Sills (Ed.), *International encyclopedia of the social sciences* (Vol. 14). New York: Macmillan, 1968.

Sorosky, A. D., Baran, A., & Pannor, R. *The adoption triangle—The effects of the sealed record on adoptees, birth parents and adoptive parents.* New York: Doubleday, 1978.

Spitz, R. A. Hospitalism: An inquiry into the genesis of psychiatric conditions in early childhood. *Psychoanalytic Study of the Child,* 1945, *2,* 53–74.

Stake, R. E. The countenance of educational evaluation. *Teachers College Record,* 1967, *68,* 523–540.

Stake, R. E. Objectives, priorities, and other judgment data. *Review of Educational Research,* 1970, *40,* 181–212.

Stake, R. E. *Evaluating educational programs.* Organization for Economic Cooperational Development, 1976.

Stallings, J. Implementation and child effects of teaching practices in follow-through classrooms. *Monographs of the Society for Research in Child Development,* 1975, *40.*

Standing, E. M. *The Montessori revolution in education.* New York: Schocken Books, 1966.

Stanford Research Institute (SRI). *Implementation of planned variation in Head Start: Preliminary evaluations of planned variation in Head Start according to follow-through approaches (1969-1970).* Menlo Park, Calif.: Stanford Research Institute, 1971.

Stanford Research Institute (SRI). *Interim evaluation of the national follow-through program 1969-1971: A technical report.* Menlo Park, Calif.: Stanford Research Institute, 1973.

Stark, R., & McEvoy, J. Middle-class violence. *Psychology Today,* 1970, *4,* 52–65.

Stein, T. J. Early intervention in foster care. *Public Welfare,* 1976, *34,* 39–44.

Stein, T. J., & Gambrill, E. *Decision making in foster care—A training manual.* Berkeley, Calif.: University Extension Publications, 1976.

Steinberg, L. Research in the ecology of adolescent development: A longitudinal study of the impact of physical maturation on changes in the family system in early adolescence. Paper presented at the Conference on Research Perspectives in the Ecology of Human Development, Cornell University, Ithaca, New York, August 1977.

Steinberg, L., & Green, C. *Three types of day care: Causes, concerns, and consequences.* Unpublished manuscript, University of California, Irvine, 1978.

Steinberg, L. D., & Green, C. How parents may mediate the effect of day care. Paper presented at the biennial meeting of the Society for Research in Child Development, San Francisco, California, March 1979.

Steiner, G. Y. *The children's cause.* Washington, D.C.: Brookings Institution, 1976.

Steinfels, M. O. *Who's minding the children? The history and politics of day care in America.* New York: Simon & Schuster, 1973.

Stephens, J. M. *The process of schooling: A psychological examination.* New York: Holt, Rinehart, & Winston, 1967.

Straus, M. Stress and child abuse. In R. Hefler & H. Kempe (Eds.), *The battered child.* Chicago: University of Chicago Press, 1980.

Straus, M., Gelles, R., & Steinmetz, S. *Behind closed doors.* New York: Doubleday, 1979.

Streib, V. *Juvenile justice in America.* Port Washington, N.Y.: Kennikat Press, 1978.

Streissguth, A. P., & Bee, H. L. Mother-child interaction and cognitive development in children. In W. Hartup (Ed.), *The young child: Review of research* (Vol. 2). Minneapolis, Institute of Child Development, University of Minnesota, 1972.

Suchman, E. *Evaluative research: Principles and practice in public service and social action programs.* New York: Russell Sage Foundation, 1967.

Sunley, R. Family advocacy: From case to cause. In C. E. Munson (Ed.), *Social work with families.* New York: Free Press, 1980.

Swire, M. R., & Kavaler, F. The health status of foster children. *Child Welfare,* 1977, *56,* 635–650.

Task Panel Reports (Vol. 3). Submitted to the President's Commission on Mental Health. Washington, D. C.: U. S. Government Printing Office, 1978.

Taylor, P. A., & McGuire, T. O. A theoretical evaluation model. *Manitoka Journal of Educational Research,* 1966, *2,* 12–17.

Teitelbaum, L. E., & Harris, L. J. Some historical perspectives on governmental regulation of children and parents. In L. E. Teitelbaum & A. R. Gough (Eds.), *Beyond control.* Cambridge, Mass.: Ballinger, 1977.

Thomas, A., & Chess, S. *Temperament and development.* New York: Brunner/Mazel, 1977.

Tietjen, A. Formal and informal support systems: A cross-cultural perspective. In J. Garbarino & S. H. Stocking (Eds.), *Protecting children from abuse and neglect.* San Francisco: Jossey-Bass, 1980.

Tinker et al. v. *Des Moines Independent Community School District et al.* 393 U.S. 503, 1969.

Touliatos, J., & Lindholm, B. W. Development of a scale measuring potential for foster parenthood. *Psychological Reports,* 1977, *40,* 1190.

Travers, J., & Ruopp, R. *National day care study: Preliminary findings and their implications.* Cambridge, Mass.: Abt Associates, 1978.

Truax, C. B., & Carkhuff, R. R. *Towards effective counseling and psychotherapy: Training and practice.* Chicago: Aldine, 1967.

Trujillo, R. The program and community participation. In R. W. Colvin & E. M. Zaffiro (Eds.), *Preschool education: A handbook for the training of early childhood educators.* New York: Springer, 1974.

Tulkin, S. R. Mother-infant interaction in the first year of life: An inquiry into the influences of social class. In W. Hartup (Ed.), *The young child: Review of Research* (Vol. 2). Minneapolis: University of Minnesota Press, 1972.

Tulkin, S. R., & Kagan, J. Mother-infant interaction: Social class differences in the first year of life. Paper presented to the American Psychological Association, Miami, Florida, September 1970.

Twentieth Century Fund Task Force Report on Sentencing Policy Toward Young Offenders. *Confronting youth crime.* New York: Holmes & Meier, 1978.

United Nations. Day care services for children. *International Social Service Review, January 1956, 1.*

U. N. General Assembly. The declaration of the rights of the child. (Resolution 1386 [XIV]). In *Official records of the General Assembly, Fourteenth Session,* Supplement 16, 1970. New York: United Nations, 1959.

U. S. Advisory Council on Social Security. *Final Report.* December 10, 1938, Senate Doc. 4, 76 Congress, 1 Session, 1939, pp. 17–19.

U. S. Bureau for the Education of the Handicapped. *Short-term analysis issues in education of handicapped children.* Washington, D. C.: Bureau for the Education of the Handicapped, 1971.

U. S. Congress. *Senate Report of the Advisory Council on Child Welfare Services.* Document No. 92, 86 Congress, 2 Session, 1960, pp. 3–6.

U. S. Congress. *Adoption and foster care 1975. Hearings before the subcommittee on children and youth of the committee on labor and public welfare.* U. S. Senate, April, July 1975. Washington, D. C.: U. S. Government Printing Office, 1975.

U. S. Department of Commerce, Bureau of the Census. *Historical Statistics of the United States, Colonial Times to 1970.* Washington, D. C., U. S. Department of Health, Education, and Welfare, 1970.

U. S. Department of Health, Education, and Welfare. *The appropriateness of the federal interagency day care requirements: Report of findings and recommendations.* Washington, D. C.: U. S. Government Printing Office, 1978.

U. S. Department of Health, Education, and Welfare, Office of Child Development. *National child consumer study, II.* Washington, D. C.: U. S. Government Printing Office, 1975.

U. S. Department of Health, Education, and Welfare, Administration for Children, Youth, and Families, Office of Human Development Services. *Day-care centers in the United States: A national profile 1976–1977.* Washington, D. C.: U. S. Government Printing Office, 1979.

U. S. Department of Health, Education, and Welfare, Division of Developmental Disabilities. *Guidelines for services and programs for developmentally disabled persons.* Washington, D. C.: U. S. Department of Health, Education, and Welfare, May 1972.

U. S. Department of Health and Human Services. *The Status of Children, Youth, and Families 1979* (DHHS Publication No. (OHDS) 80-30274). Washington, D. C.: Office of Human Development

Services Administration for Children, Youth and Families Research Demonstration and Evaluation Division, U.S. Department of Health and Human Services, 1980.

U.S. Senate Committee on Finance. *Child care data and materials.* Washington, D.C.: U.S. Government Printing Office, 1974.

U.S. White House Conference on Children. *Report to the President—1970.* Washington, D.C.: U.S. Government Printing Office, 1970.

vanWaters, M. The juvenile court from the child's viewpoint. In J. Addams (Ed.), *The child, the clinic, and the court.* Washington, D.C.: Juvenile Justice System, Library of Congress, 1971. (Originally published, 1925.)

Verma, S., & Peters, D. Day care practices and habits. *alberta Journal of Educational Research,* 1975, *21,* 46–55.

Viano, E. C. Attitudes toward child abuse among American professionals. Paper presented at the biennial meeting of the International Society for Research on Aggression, Toronto, June 1974.

Wachs, T. D. The optimal stimulation hypothesis and human development: Does anyone have a match? In I. Uzgiriz & F. Weizmann (Eds.), *The structuring of experience.* New York: Plenum, 1977.

Wade, C. The family day-care program in Milwaukee. *Child Welfare,* 1970, *49,* 336–341.

Wald, M. Legal policies affecting children: A lawyer's request for aid. *Child Development,* 1976, *47,* 1–5.

Wallia, C. S. *Toward century 21.* New York: Basic Books, 1970.

Walters, R., & Parke, R. Social motivation, dependency, and susceptibility to social influence. In L. Berkowitz (Ed.), *Advances in experimental social psychology.* New York: Academic Press, 1964.

Webb, E. J., Campbell, D. T., Schwartz, D., & Sechrist, L. *Unobtrusive measures: Nonreactive research in the social sciences.* Chicago: Rand McNally, 1966.

Weber, C. U., Foster, P. W., & Weikart, D. P. *An economic analysis of the Ypsilanti Perry Preschool Project* (Monograph No. 5). Ypsilanti, Mich.: High/Scope Educational Research Foundation, 1978.

Weikart, D. Relationship of curriculum, teaching, and learning in pre-school education. In J. Stanley (Ed.), *Preschool programs for the disadvantaged.* Baltimore: Johns Hopkins Press, 1972.

Weikart, D. P., Bond, J. T., & McNeil, J. T. *The Ypsilanti Perry Preschool Project: Preschool years and longitudinal results through fourth grade* (Monograph No. 3). Ypsilanti, Mich.: High Scope/Educational Research Foundation, 1978.

Weikart, D. P., Epstein, A., Schweinhart, L., & Bond, J. T. *The Ypsilanti preschool curriculum demonstration project: Preschool years and longitudinal results* (Monograph No. 4). Ypsilanti, Mich.: High/Scope Educational Research Foundation, 1978.

Weikart, D. P., & Schweinhart, L. J. Perry preschool effects in adolescence. High Scope Educational Research Foundation. Paper presented at the Society for Research in Child Development, San Francisco, March 1979.

Weiss, C. H. Utilization of evaluation: Toward comparative study. In C. H. Weiss (Ed.), *Evaluating action programs.* Boston: Allyn & Bacon, 1972.

Weiss, C. H. Between the cup and the lip. *Evaluation,* 1973, *10,* 49–55.

West, D. J., & Farrington, D. P. *The delinquent way of life.* London; Heinemann, 1973.

Westhoff, C. R., & Parke, R., Jr. (Eds.). Commission on population and growth and the American future. Washington, D.C.: U.S. Government Printing Office, 1972.

Westinghouse Report. *The Impact of Head Start.* Springfield, Mass.: Westinghouse Learning Corporation, 1969.

White, B.L., Kaban, B. T., Attanucci, H., & Shapiro, B. B. *Influences on the development of the young child* (Vol. 2). Englewood Cliffs, N.J.: Prentice-Hall, 1978.

White, S. H., Day, M. C., Freeman, P. K., Hantman, S. A., & Messenger, K. P. *Federal programs for young children: Review and recommendations.* Washington D.C.: U.S. Government Printing Office, 1973.

White House Conference on Children. *Profiles on children.* Washington, D.C.: U.S. Government Printing Office, 1970.

Wholey, J. S. Evaluability assessment. In L. Rutman (Ed.), *Evaluation research methods: A basic guide.* Beverly Hills, Calif.: Sage, 1977.

Williams, G. J., & Gordon, S. (Eds.). *Clinical child psychology: Current practices and future perspectives.* New York: Behavioral Publications, 1974.

Williams, W., & Elmore, R. F. (Eds.). *Social program implementation.* New York: Academic Press, 1976.

Winston, E. A national policy on the family. *Public Welfare,* 1969, *27,* 54–58.

Wisconsin v. *Yoder.* 406 U.S. 206, 1972.

Wolfensberger, W. Will there always be an institution? The impact of new service models: Residential alternatives to institutions. *Mental Retardation,* 1971, *9,* 31–38.

Wolfensberger, W. *The principle of normalization in human services.* Toronto: National Institute on Mental Retardation, 1972.

Woodward, K. L., & Malamud, P. The parent gap. *Newsweek,* September 22, 1975, pp. 48–56.

Woolsey, S. H. Pied piper politics and the child-care debate. In A. Rossi, J. Kagan, & T. Hareven (Eds.), *The family.* New York: Norton, 1977.

Worthen, B. R., & Sanders, J. R. *Educational evaluation: Theory and practice.* Worthington, Ohio: Jones, 1973.

Wray, J. The federation of independent schools. Unpublished pamphlet, Federation of Independent Community Schools, 2637 N. 11th St., Milwaukee, Wisconsin, 1971.

Wright, A. *Islandia.* New York: Holt, Rinehart, & Winston, 1942.

Wright, H. F. *Children's behavior in communities differing in size.* (Parts I, II, III, and Supplement; Report to Project Grant MH 01098, NIMH). Department of Psychology, University of Kansas, 1969.

Yeomans, A. Day care—An alternative to placement away from home. *Child Welfare,* 1953, *32,* 12–24.

Young, L. *Wednesday's children.* New York: McGraw-Hill, 1964.

Zigler, E. Project Head Start: Success or failure? *Learning,* 1973, *1,* 43–47.

Zigler, E. The unmet needs of America's children. *Children Today,* May/June 1976, 39–42.

Zigler, E., & Muenchow, S. Mainstreaming: The proof is in the implementation. *American Psychologist,* in press.

Zigler, E., & Seitz, V. Status of research on children. In *The Status of Children, Youth, and Families 1979.* Washington, D.C.: Office of Human Development Services, U.S. Department of Health and Human Services, 1980.

Zigler, E., & Trickett, P. K. The role of national social policy in promoting social competence in children. In M. W. Kent & J. E. Rolf (Eds.), *Primary prevention of pathology.* Vol. 3: *Social competence in children.* Hanover, N.H.: University Press of New England, 1979.

Zober, E. Postplacement service for adoptive families. *Child Welfare,* 1961, *40,* 32–44.

Zunich, M. A study of relationships between child rearing attitudes and maternal behavior. *Journal of Experimental Education,* 1962, *29-30,* 231–241.

Name Index

Subject Index